Building Data Mining Applications for CRM

Alex Berson

Stephen Smith

Kurt Thearling

McGraw-Hill
New York • San Francisco • Washington, D.C.
Auckland • Bogotá • Caracas • Lisbon • London
Madrid • Mexico City • Milan • Montreal • New Delhi
San Juan • Singapore • Sydney • Tokyo • Toronto

Library of Congress Cataloging-in-Publication Data

Berson, Alex.
    Building data mining applications for CRM / Alex Berson, Stephen Smith,
    and Kurt Thearling.
        p.   cm.
    ISBN 0-07-134444-6
    1. Data mining. 2. Decision support systems. I. Smith, Stephen,
1953– II. Thearling, Kurt. III. Title.
QA76.9.D343B47   1999
658.4'038—dc21   99-39159
                                                                 CIP

McGraw-Hill

A Division of The McGraw·Hill Companies

3 4 5 6 7 8 9 0 DOC/DOC 0 4 3 2 1 0

ISBN 0-07-134444-6

The sponsoring editor for this book was Simon Yates and the production supervisor was
Clare Stanley. It was set in New Century Schoolbook by D&G Limited, LLC.

Printed and bound by R.R. Donnelley & Sons Company.

Throughout this book, trademarked names are used. Rather than put a trademark symbol
after every occurrence of a trademarked name, we use names in an editorial fashion only,
and to the benefit of the trademark owner, with no intention of infringement of the trademark. Where such designations appear in this book, they have been printed with initial
caps.

 This book is printed on recycled, acid-free paper containing a minimum
of 50 percent recycled de-inked fiber.

BUILDING DATA MINING
APPLICATIONS FOR CRM

To Irina, Vlad, and Michelle
   —Alex

To Noel
   —Steve

To Grace
   —Kurt

CONTENTS

Part 2   FOUNDATION—THE TECHNOLOGIES AND TOOLS

Chapter 4   DataWarehousing Components   55

Chapter 5   Data Mining   89

Contents

Contents

PREFACE

"You have no choice but to operate in a world shaped by globalisation and the information revolution. There are two options: adapt or die."

—Andy Grove, Chairman, Intel

The last few years have seen a growing recognition of information as a key business tool. Those who successfully gather, analyze, understand, and act upon the information are among the winners in this new "information age". Therefore, it is only reasonable to expect the rate of producing and consuming the information to grow. We can define information as "that which resolves uncertainty". We can further say that the decision-making is the progressive resolution of uncertainty, and is a key to a purposeful behavior by any mechanism (or organism). In general, the current business market dynamics make it abundantly clear for any company that information is the key to its very survival.

This fact is magnified many-fold by the emergence and widespread adoption of the Web and its revolutionary effect on all aspect of our existence, including the way we live, learn, interact with each other and conduct the business.

One of the more interesting business aspects of this profound change brought in by the Web is the realization that the winners in the future competitive game are the players that are agile, efficient, flexible, focused on their core competencies, and are masters of the relationship game. Indeed, the Web has changed the traditional economics of the business. The sky-high market valuations of the new "Web businesses" reflect the recognition that moving at the "Web speed," being first to market, and developing and enhancing relationships with the customers and business partners are the attributes that differentiate winners from losers in the new E-Business economy.

But what is an E-Business? There are many definitions, and rather than get into the definition debate, let's define E-Business as business designed to use Internet-based information to enable new relationships between businesses and customers.

Thus defined, E-business brings into play an organization's resources and partners in new and innovative ways to create clear strategic advantage. The potential of E-Business goes far beyond new technologies to impact and engage all aspects of a business including strategy, process, technology, and organization in order to extend the business beyond its conventional boundaries.

A successful E-business enterprise can create new significant value propositions including the ability to open a new business within a week, a new market overnight, new products in an hour, new services all the time. This ability results in a clear market leadership that is achieved by using innovative information technologies designed to build customer loyalty, help reach new markets, create new products and services, optimize business processes, manage risks, and enhance its human capital.

And clearly, technology and technology-induced change is at the core of the E-Business adoption. Developments in computing, communications, and content have provided businesses with the power needed to change the rules of competitive engagement in an environment where past performance is no guarantee of future success.

What organizations traditionally consider "customer loyalty" may be no more than inertia. Indeed, an Internet search engine can wipe out thirty years of branding in thirty seconds. Companies have to squeeze costs out of their business to survive as a brand. Brand survival will depend on organizational ability to partner. To put it simply, the more you know about customers and business partners the more you can compete on service to deepen your brand identity.

Thus, a key to a new E-Business enterprise is customer relationships. Therefore, this book is not just about the need, the value, and the technological means of acquiring and using the information in the information age. This book is focused on analyzing the E-Business inspired approaches to an effective customer relationship management (CRM). This goal is achieved by looking at the foundation technologies of data warehousing and data mining, and the applications and tools of the customer relationship management.

From that perspective, this book is intended to become the handbook and the guide for anybody who's interested in, planning or working on database marketing, data mining, Customer Relationship Management, and related issues. This audience is quite large, and includes both the technology and business people. Among them are business and technology strategists, information technology managers, business analysts, sales and marketing managers, product planners, business intelligence application developers, data warehouse managers and administrators, information security officers, and customer service center specialists. Customer relationship management business and technical issues are discussed on the background of the data warehousing architecture and technology, Web information delivery, and data mining techniques. The book ends with a brief look into the current state of the data mining and CRM solution market and a future potential of these technologies and applications.

Who Should Read This Book

This book has been written as a result of authors' experiences in participating in several large scale CRM projects and in developing and data warehousing and data mining solutions for various industry segments.

In discussing the technologies and applications of data mining enabled CRM, the authors met with many business and IT managers, system integrators, system administrators, database and data communications specialists, and system programmers, all of which can be potential readers of this book.

This book can be used as a guide for system integrators, designers of data warehouse and data mart systems, and those who are planning to implement and support data mining and CRM applications.

Prerequisite

The authors assume readers have little or no previous knowledge about data warehousing, OLAP, data mining and CRM. This book is targeted to two classes of readership – business professionals including sales and marketing managers, product planners, and financial experts, and technology professionals. Both groups of readers can understand this book – no previous data warehousing experience is necessary. Readers with any degree of knowledge of information technology can benefit from this book.

Style Used

The book has been structured as a self-teaching guide, with the introduction to the business problems related the effective customer relationship management and data mining; a technology backgrounder for those readers looking for details on data warehousing and data mining; a discussion on data mining and CRM applications including customer acquisition, sales force automation, customer service, campaign management, customer profitability, cross-sales, customer retention and market segmentation; and an overview of the data mining and CRM tools market.

The book concludes with a brief look at prevailing trends and directions in this highly dynamic area of business and technology.

The book includes a fair amount of diagrams, figures, examples and illustrations in an attempt to present a lot of rather complicated material in as simple form as possible. Data warehousing, data mining and CRM are complex, involved and often misunderstood subjects, so that whenever possible, theoretical issues are explained on practical examples. For example, the authors made a serious effort to explain complex issues related to data mining using both simple examples and theoretical discussions.

For those readers interested in the theory, the book provides sufficient theoretical overview of artificial intelligence and predictive modeling.

This book is about a very dynamic subject. All material included in the book is current at the time the book is written. The authors realize that as E-Business in general and the Customer Relationship Management and data mining continue to evolve, and as vendors continue to improve and expand on their product quality and functionality, the changes would be necessary. The authors intend to revise the book if a significant development in the data mining and the CRM arena makes it necessary to add, delete or change parts of the text.

What Is Included

Part 1 begins with the introduction to the domain of business problems addressed by the Customer Relationship Management (Chapters 1 and 3). This part introduces the reader to the broad class of technologies that enable CRM, including data warehousing and data mining (Chapter 2). This part is aimed at the reader that is looking to understand the applications of CRM and relationship between CRM, data warehousing, and data mining.

Part 2 offer a technology backgrounder and contains chapters devoted to the overview of the data warehousing architecture and components (Chapter 4), Web-enabled data warehousing, and even touches on some emerging standards including XML. For a reader interested in data mining techniques this part provides chapters 5 through 7 that deal with this subject.

Part 3 is focused on the business value and application functions of data mining enabled customer relationship management enhanced by data mining. It contains chapters that discuss customer profitability (Chapter 9), customer acquisition (Chapter 10), cross-selling applications (Chapter 11), customer retention (Chapter 12), and market/customer segmentation (Chapter 13).

Part 4 of the book deals with the keys to a successful implementation of data mining and CRM solutions. It includes Chapter 14 (Building the Business Case), Chapter 15 (Steps to Deploying Data Mining), Chapter 16 (Collecting Data), Chapter 17 (Customer Scoring Techniques), Chapter 18 (Optimizing the CRM Process), and Chapter 19 (Data Mining and CRM Tools Market).

The book concludes with Chapter 20 that discusses the impact of E-Business on the market landscape, the trends and directions for the data mining as a whole, and applications of data mining that are focused on CRM.

The appendices include the glossary of terms and an extensive bibliography.

ACKNOWLEDGMENTS

First, I am grateful to Steve Smith and Kurt Thearling for their knowledge, persistence, attention to details, and dedication, without which this book would not have happened. Very special thanks to my many friends and colleges at PricewaterhouseCoopers for providing creative and challenging atmosphere. Working with people like Bernie Plagman, Ed Sheehy, Chuck Shelton, Richard Cohen, Lee Knight, Larry Gosselin, Paul Maiste, Matt Cohn, Adam Steinberg, Shanker Ramamurthy, Glen Finch, Walter Hamscher and many others gave me an opportunity to learn and work in a very stimulating and challenging environment on the leading edge of computer technology.

I also have to thank my numerous friends at ADT, Enterprise Associates, EEI, FCB, Cohera, Informix, IBM, Merrill Lynch, enCommerce, CitiGroup, and Candle Corporation, specifically Peter Meekin, Guy Pujol, Larry Johnson, Joe Hollander, George Anderson, Larry Caminiti, Anatoly Kissen and Steve Wolfe.

I am very grateful to Dr. Michael Stonebraker for the inspiration, vision and invaluable insight. Very special thanks to Alberto Yepez for his engaging optimism and support.

I would like to thank all those who have helped me with clarifications, criticism and valuable information during the writing of this book, were patient enough to read the entire manuscript and made many useful suggestions. And of course, this book would have never been finished without invaluable assistance and thoroughness of McGraw-Hill's Simon Yates and Jennifer Perillo and copyediting skills of Beth Brown.

Finally, the key reason for this book's existence is my family. My very special thanks to my wife Irina, my son Vlad, my daughter Michelle and the rest of my family for giving me time to complete the book, understanding its importance, and never-ending optimism, support and love. I am especially grateful to my son Vlad for his help in explaining more intricate aspects of designing the Web-based information management, acquisition and delivery.

Alex Berson

This is now the second book that I have had the privilege of writing with Alex Berson and with the publishers of McGraw-Hill. It provides a blueprint of how to apply to business the technology that we described in our first book *Data Warehousing Data Mining and OLAP*. It was once again a pleasure to work with Alex whose high level of professionalism and hard work have made this book a success. Much of the inspiration for business applications in CRM and elsewhere have come from our new co-author and my long time associate Kurt Thearling. Kurt provided new insights and good writing from his deep understanding of customer relationship management and the use of technologies within it.

For my part I would like to acknowledge the influence and insights that I have gained from my friends and colleagues. Especially Paul Buta, Rick Myers and Steve Huson of Optas who have together turned some good ideas into a solid business; and to my business associates Curt Wilbur and Nethra Sambamoorthi who have successfully created a state of the art customer management system for their company. And also to Robert Mansell who shared with us his thesis detailing a CRM project in the European wireless phone industry.

Thanks to Simon Yates, Jennifer Perillo and Beth Brown at McGraw-Hill for their hard work in organizing and publishing this book.

Most importantly, thanks to my wife Noel and our children Samantha, Nathaniel and Emily for giving me the encouragement, the time (and the silence) to complete this work.

Stephen Smith

The genesis of my involvement with this book began sometime in the early 1990s, while Steve and I were working together at a very interesting company called Thinking Machines Corporation. At the time, Thinking Machines made some of the biggest and fastest supercomputers in the world and our job was to figure out cool and interesting ways to use all that computational power. One of the things we did was develop complicated data mining algorithms that could harness the power of a supercomputer. In the years since I worked with supercomputers, I have learned that it takes much more than cool technology to solve real-world business problems. Hopefully this book will help bridge that gap.

I would like to thank my friends and colleagues from Thinking Machines, Pilot Software, and Exchange Applications for their insight and support over the years. Much of what I know about data mining and CRM can be traced to my working with Steve Smith, Alex Berson, Dave Waltz, Anand Bodapati, Jim Bailey, Brij Masand, Mario Bourgoin, Joe Yarmus, Emily Stone, Gary Drescher, Kris Carlson, Marc Levitt, Ed Zyszkowski, Peter Meekin, and Mike McGonagle. Finally, I would like to thank my family, especially my wife and best friend, Grace, for being there whenever I needed someone to talk to or lean on. That's what really matters.

Kurt Thearling

The Impact of Data Mining on CRM

Your customers are not your customers. You are merely their caretaker until one of your competitors can provide and communicate a better offer. In this day of technology and businesses moving at the speed of the internet it is difficult to tell when this might happen. Will your industry be the next to have the privilege of seeing the rise of the next paradigm shifting business like Amazon.com or E*TRADE? You just never know. The best you can do is to prepare. Preparation means taking care of your customers better than your competition can. This means using the best tools at your disposal.

The chapters in this first part of the book introduce the basic concepts of the tools you will need to take care of your customers and the impact they will have on your business. The first chapter provides an overview of the business benefits that accrue to those who use the tools of Customer Relationship Management (CRM) and Data Mining. The second and third chapter provide a primer to the base technologies and methodologies of Data Mining and CRM that make it possible to successfully build and maintain systems that keep your customers satisfied if not delighted and, for as long as possible, doing business with you and not your competition.

CHAPTER 1

Customer
Relationships

Introduction

The way in which companies interact with their customers has changed dramatically over the past few years. A customer's continuing business is no longer guaranteed. As a result, companies have found that they need to understand their customers better, and to quickly respond to their wants and needs. In addition, the time frame in which these responses need to be made has been shrinking. It is no longer possible to wait until the signs of customer dissatisfaction are obvious before action must be taken. To succeed, companies must be proactive and anticipate what a customer desires.

It is now a cliche that in the days of the corner market, shopkeepers had no trouble understanding their customers and responding quickly to their needs. The shopkeepers would simply keep track of all of their customers in their heads, and would know what to do when a customer walked into the store. But today's shopkeepers face a much more complex situation. More customers, more products, more competitors, and less time to react means that understanding your customers is now much harder to do.

A number of forces are working together to increase the complexity of customer relationships:

- *Compressed marketing cycle times.* The attention span of a customer has decreased and loyalty is a thing of the past. A successful company needs to reinforce the value it provides to its customers on a continuous basis. In addition, the time between a new desire and when you must meet that desire is also shrinking. If you don't react quickly enough, the customer will find someone who will.

- *Increased marketing costs.* Everything costs more. Printing, postage, special offers (and if you don't provide the special offer, your competitors will).

- *Streams of new product offerings.* Customers want things that meet their exact needs, not things that sort-of fit. This means that the number of products and the number of ways they are offered have risen significantly.

■ *Niche competitors.*   Your best customers also look good to your competitors. These competitors will focus on small, profitable segments of your market and try to keep the best for themselves.

Successful companies need to react to each and every one of these demands in a timely fashion. The market will not wait for your response, and customers that you have today could vanish tomorrow. Interacting with your customers is also not as simple as it has been in the past. Customers and prospective customers want to interact on their terms, meaning that you need to look at multiple criteria when evaluating how to proceed. You will need to automate:

■ The Right Offer

■ To the Right Person

■ At the Right Time

■ Through the Right Channel

The right offer means managing multiple interactions with your customers, prioritizing what the offers will be while making sure that irrelevant offers are minimized. The right person means that not all customers are cut from the same cloth. Your interactions with them need to move toward highly segmented marketing campaigns that target individual wants and needs. The right time is a result of the fact that interactions with customers now happen on a continuous basis. This is significantly different from the past, when quarterly mailings were cutting-edge marketing. Finally, the right channel means that you can interact with your customers in a variety of ways (direct mail, email, telemarketing, etc.). You need to make sure that you are choosing the most effective medium for each particular interaction.

The purpose of this book is to provide you with a thorough understanding of how a technology like data mining can help solve vexing issues in your interactions with your customers. We describe situations in which a better understanding of your customers can provide tangible benefits and a measurable return on investment.

It is important to realize, though, that data mining is just a part of the overall process. Data mining needs to work with other technologies (for example, data warehousing and marketing automation), as well as with established business practices. If you take nothing else from this book, we hope that you will appreciate that data mining needs to work as part of a larger business process (and not the other way around!).

What Is Data Mining?

Data mining, by its simplest definition, automates the detection of relevant patterns in a database. For example, a pattern might indicate that married males with children are twice as likely to drive a particular sports car than married males with no children. If you are a marketing manager for an auto manufacturer, this somewhat surprising pattern might be quite valuable.

However, data mining is not magic. For many years, statisticians have manually "mined" databases, looking for statistically significant patterns.

Data mining uses well-established statistical and machine learning techniques to build models that predict customer behavior. Today, technology automates the mining process, integrates it with commercial data warehouses, and presents it in a relevant way for business users.

The leading data mining products are now more than just modeling engines employing powerful algorithms. Instead, they address the broader business and technical issues, such as their integration into today's complex information technology environments.

In the past, the hyperbole surrounding data mining suggested that it would eliminate the need for statistical analysts to build predictive models. However, the value that an analyst provides cannot be automated out of existence. Analysts will still be needed to assess model results and validate the plausibility of the model predictions. Because data mining software lacks the human experience and intuition to recognize the difference between a relevant and an irrelevant correlation, statistical analysts will remain in high demand.

An Example

Imagine that you are a marketing manager for a regional telephone company. You are responsible for managing the relationships with the company's cellular telephone customers. One of your current concerns is customer attention (sometimes known as "churn") which has been eating severely into your margins. You understand that the cost of keeping customers around is significantly less than the cost of bringing them back after they leave, so you need to figure out a cost-effective way of doing this.

The traditional approach to solving this problem is to pick out your good customers (that is, the ones who spend a lot of money with your company) and try to persuade them to sign up for another year of service. This persuasion might involve some sort of gift (possibly a new phone) or maybe a discount calling plan. The value of the gift might be based on the amount that a customer spends, with big spenders receiving the best offers.

This solution can be very wasteful. There are undoubtedly many "good" customers who would be willing to stick around without receiving an expensive gift. The customers to concentrate on are the ones that will be leaving. Don't worry about the ones who will stay.

This solution to the churn problem has been turned around from the way in which it should be perceived. Instead of providing the customer with something that is proportional to their value to your company, you should instead be providing the customer with something proportional to your value to them. Give your customers what they need. There are differences between your customers, and you need to understand those differences in order to optimize your relationships. One big spending customer might value the relationship because of your high reliability, and thus wouldn't need a gift in order to continue with it. On the other hand, a customer who takes advantage of all of the latest features and special services might require a new phone or other gift in order to stick around for another year. Or they might simply want a better rate for evening calls because their employer provides the phone and they have to pay for calls outside of business hours. The key is determining which type of customer you are dealing with.

It is also important to consider timing in this process. You can't wait until a week before a customer's contract and then pitch them an offer in order to prevent them from churning. By then, they have likely decided what they are going to do and you are unlikely to affect their decision at such a late date. On the other hand, you don't want to start the process immediately upon signing a customer up. It might be months before they have an understanding of your company's value to them, so any efforts now would also be wasted. The key is finding the correct middle ground, which could very well come from your understanding of your market and the customers in that market. Or, as we will discuss later, you might be using data mining to automatically find the optimal point.

Relevance to a Business Process

For data mining to impact a business, it needs to have relevance to the underlying business process. Data mining is part of a much larger series of steps that takes place between a company and its customers. The way in which data mining impacts a business depends on the business process, not the data mining process. Take product marketing as an example. A marketing manager's job is to understand their market. With this understanding comes the ability to interact with customers in this market, using a number of channels. This involves a number of areas, including direct marketing, print advertising, telemarketing, and radio/television advertising, among others.

The issue that must be addressed is that the results of data mining are different from other data-driven business processes. In most standard interactions with customer data, nearly all of the results presented to the user are things that they knew existed in the database already. A report showing the breakdown of sales by product line and region is straightforward for the user to understand because they intuitively know that this kind of information already exists in the database. If the company sells different products in different regions of the county, there is no problem translating a display of this information into a relevant understanding of the business process.

Data mining, on the other hand, extracts information from a database that the user did not know existed. Relationships between variables and customer behaviors that are non-intuitive are the jewels that data mining hopes to find. And because the user does not know beforehand what the data mining process has discovered, it is a much bigger leap to take the output of the system and translate it into a solution to a business problem.

This is where interaction and context comes in. Marketing users need to understand the results of data mining before they can put them into actions. Because data mining usually involves extracting "hidden" patterns of customer behavior, the understanding process can get a bit complicated. The key is to put the user in a context in which they feel comfortable, and then let them poke and prod until they understand what they didn't see before.

How does someone actually use the output of data mining? The simplest way is to leave the output in the form of a black box. If they take the black box and score a database, they can get a list of customers to target (send them a catalog, increase their credit limit, etc.). There's not much for the user to do other than sit back and watch the envelopes go out. This can be a very effective approach. Mailing costs can often be reduced by an order of magnitude without significantly reducing the response rate.

Then there's the more difficult way to use the results of data mining: getting the user to actually understand what is going on so that they can take action directly. For example, if the user is responsible for ordering a print advertising campaign, understanding customer demographics is critical. A data mining analysis might determine that customers in New York City are now focused in the 30-to-35-year-old age range, whereas previous analyses showed that these customers were primarily aged 22 to 27. This change means that the print campaign might move from the *Village Voice* to the *New Yorker*. There's no automated way to do this. It's all in the marketing manager's head. Unless the output of the data mining system can be understood qualitatively, it won't be of much use.

Both of these cases are inextricably linked. The user needs to view the output of the data mining in a context they understand. If they can understand what has been discovered, they will trust it and put it into use. There are two parts to this problem: 1) presenting the output of the data mining process in a meaningful way, and 2) allowing the user to interact with the output so that simple questions can be answered. Creative solutions to the first part have recently been incorporated into a number of commercial data mining products. Response rates and (probably most importantly) financial indicators (for example, profit, cost, and return on investment) give the user a sense of context that can quickly ground the results in reality.

Data Mining and Customer Relationship Management

Customer relationship management (CRM) is a process that manages the interactions between a company and its customers. The primary users of CRM software applications are database marketers who are looking to automate the process of interacting with customers.

To be successful, database marketers must first identify market segments containing customers or prospects with high-profit potential. They then build and execute campaigns that favorably impact the behavior of these individuals.

The first task, identifying market segments, requires significant data about prospective customers and their buying behaviors. In theory, the more data the better. In practice, however, massive data stores often impede marketers, who struggle to sift through the minutiae to find the nuggets of valuable information.

Data mining applications automate the process of searching the mountains of data to find patterns that are good predictors of purchasing behaviors.

After mining the data, marketers must feed the results into campaign management software that, as the name implies, manages the campaign directed at the defined market segments.

In the past, the link between data mining and campaign management software was mostly manual. In the worst cases, it involved "sneaker net," creating a physical file on tape or disk, which someone then carried to another computer and loaded into the marketing database.

This separation of the data mining and campaign management software introduces considerable inefficiency and opens the door for human errors. Tightly integrating the two disciplines presents an opportunity for companies to gain competitive advantage.

How Data Mining Helps Database Marketing

Data mining helps marketing users to target marketing campaigns more accurately; and also to align campaigns more closely with the needs, wants, and attitudes of customers and prospects.

If the necessary information exists in a database, the data mining process can model virtually any customer activity. The key is to find patterns relevant to current business problems.

Typical questions that data mining addresses include the following:

- Which customers are most likely to drop their cell phone service?

- What is the probability that a customer will purchase at least $100 worth of merchandise from a particular mail-order catalog?

- Which prospects are most likely to respond to a particular offer?

Answers to these questions can help retain customers and increase campaign response rates, which, in turn, increase buying, cross-selling, and return on investment (ROI).

Scoring

Data mining builds models by using inputs from a database to predict customer behavior. This behavior might be attrition at the end of a magazine subscription, cross-product purchasing, willingness to use an ATM card in place of a more expensive teller transaction, and so on.

The prediction provided by a model is usually called a score. A score (typically a numerical value) is assigned to each record in the database and indicates the likelihood that the customer whose record has been scored will exhibit a particular behavior.

For example, if a model predicts customer attrition, a high score indicates that a customer is likely to leave, whereas a low score indicates the opposite. After scoring a set of customers, these numerical values are used to select the most appropriate prospects for a targeted marketing campaign.

The Role of Campaign Management Software

Database marketing software enables companies to deliver timely, pertinent, and coordinated messages and value propositions (offers or gifts perceived as valuable) to customers and prospects.

Today's campaign management software goes considerably further. It manages and monitors customer communications across multiple touch-points, such as direct mail, telemarketing, customer service, point of sale, interactive web, branch office, and so on.

Campaign management automates and integrates the planning, execution, assessment, and refinement of possibly tens to hundreds of highly segmented campaigns that run monthly, weekly, daily, or intermittently. The software can also run campaigns with multiple "communication points," triggered by time or customer behavior such as the opening of a new account.

Increasing Customer Lifetime Value

Consider, for example, customers of a bank who use the institution only for a checking account. An analysis reveals that after depositing large annual income bonuses, some customers wait for their funds to clear before moving the money quickly into their stock-brokerage or mutual fund accounts outside the bank. This represents a loss of business for the bank.

To persuade these customers to keep their money in the bank, marketing managers can use campaign management software to immediately identify large deposits and trigger a response. The system might automatically schedule a direct mail or telemarketing promotion as soon as a customer's balance exceeds a predetermined amount. Based on the size of the deposit, the triggered promotion can then provide an appropriate incentive that encourages customers to invest their money in the bank's other products.

Finally, by tracking responses and following rules for attributing customer behavior, the campaign management software can help measure the profitability and ROI of all ongoing campaigns.

Combining Data Mining and Campaign Management

The closer data mining and campaign management work together, the better the business results. Today, campaign management software uses the scores generated by the data mining model to sharpen the focus of targeted customers or prospects, thereby increasing response rates and campaign effectiveness. Ideally, marketers who build campaigns should be able to apply any model logged in the campaign management system to a defined target segment.

Evaluating the Benefits of a Data Mining Model

Figure 1-1, which shows a "gains chart," suggests some benefits available through data mining. The diagonal line illustrates the number of responses expected from a randomly selected target audience. Under this scenario, the number of responses grows linearly with the target size.

The top curve represents the expected response if you allow the model scores to determine the target audience. The target is now

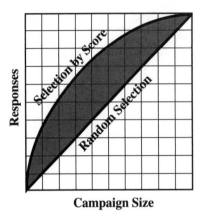

Campaign Size

likely to include more positive responders than in a random selection of the same size. The shaded area between the curve and the line indicates the quality of the model. The steeper the curve, the better the model.

Other representations of the model often incorporate expected costs and expected revenues to provide the most important measure of model quality: profitability. A profit optimal ability graph such as Figure 1-2 can help determine the number of prospects to include in a campaign. In this example, it is easy to see that contacting all customers will result in a net loss. However, selecting a threshold score of approximately 0.8 will maximize profitability.

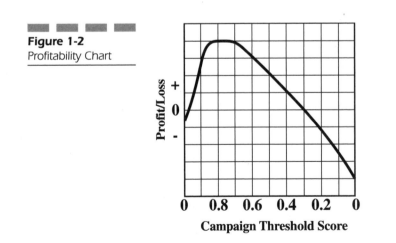

Campaign Threshold Score

CHAPTER 2

Data Mining and Data Warehousing— A Connected View

Introduction

During the decade of the 1990s, organizations began to recognize the strategic use of data as an entirely different discipline from operational use. Operational database systems have been traditionally designed to meet mission-critical requirements for online transaction processing and batch processing. These systems represented (often successful) attempts to automate the established business processes by leveraging the power of computers to obtain significant improvements in efficiency and speed.

Today, however, automation alone is not enough. The business competition of the 21st century is beyond the speed to market—it's the competition between business models and the ability to acquire, accumulate, and effectively use the collective knowledge of the organizations. Indeed, efficiency is no longer the only key to business success, it is flexibility and responsiveness that differentiate competitors in the new Web-enabled, e-business economy. Many analysts predict that those organizations that have harnessed the power of information will have a massive competitive advantage over their rivals. The key to this will be an effective data-management strategy of data warehousing and interactive data analysis capabilities that culminates with data mining.

Thus, this chapter will provide a high-level overview of the technologies of data warehousing and data mining, explain the rationale by which these two disciplines are connected, and illustrate the benefit of the holistic (connected) view with the example of the Customer Relationship Management (CRM) architecture framework.

Data Mining and Data Warehousing — the Connection

Data mining describes a collection of techniques that aim to find useful but undiscovered patterns in collected data. The goal of data mining is to create models for decision-making that predict future behavior based on analyses of past activity. Data mining supports knowledge discovery, defined by William Frawley and Gregory Piatetsky-Shapiro (MIT Press, 1991) as " . . . *the nontrivial extraction of implicit, previously unknown, and potentially useful information from data . . . .*"

This definition holds the key to the substantial interest in data warehousing and data mining. Many leading organizations now realize that their huge transactional databases contain information about customer purchasing habits that are valuable, both to themselves as they decide what services to provide and also to their clients.

A good example is the financial services industry. Typical financial institutions, such as banks and brokerage firms, make most of their profit from the top 5% of their customers. There is a growing realization that in order to succeed, the companies must obtain an ever-greater share of these top customers' business. Specifically, a profitable retail customer of a bank has multiple accounts and a home mortgage, has a car loan and an active investment portfolio, maintains a high overall balance, and is most likely in his/her most profitable earning years. Clearly, the bank needs a mechanism to allow it to retain these desirable customers for as long as possible and thus gain more of their business. The current view of this mechanism is to integrate the bulk of the existing customer repositories into a customer data warehouse, and provide the tools that allow management and customers to analyze large volumes of data quickly and easily. The key component of the analytical suite is a capability to mine these huge data repositories. Thus, there are ways to find new profitable customers, understand their needs and behaviors, and provide them with a targeted individualized set of products and services that result in better customer acquisition and retention—to name just a few benefits.

A recent example of how such information can be used to create a new service is provided by First Data Corporation—one of the largest third-party conventional and Internet credit card purchasers in the world.

First Data created a new service on behalf of its issuing and acquiring banks called USA Value Exchange, or U$AVE. U$AVE helps credit card issuers differentiate their products, build cardholder loyalty, and leverage the value of their customer relationships and data. U$AVE accomplishes this by delivering targeted discount and rebate offers from merchants to cardholders in their monthly statements.

Although offering rebates in credit card statements is not new, U$AVE is different because the set of offers is uniquely chosen for each customer. It is based on criteria set by the merchants and card issuers, as well as analyses of the transaction histories stored in First Data's data stores.

This example is typical of trends in the industry today. As Internet-enabled channels apply huge pressures on the prices and time-to-market, organizations have to decide on where to focus their energies and budgets. As electronic commerce over the Internet becomes a dominant form of commerce, the ability to provide more innovative and better quality services to the customers will become the major competitive advantage.

Why link data mining with data warehousing? A conventional point of view is that data mining is the technology that has its roots in computational sciences and mathematics, and does not require nor is benefited from data warehousing.

This is not entirely accurate. One of the keys to successful data mining is the capability to get access to accurate, complete, and integrated data. This is also very true of data warehousing. Not only is a data warehouse a means of and a focal point for data integration, but all data warehouse solutions start with and depend on the quality and effectiveness of their data sourcing component (known in the data warehousing world as Extract, Transform, and Load—or ETL—tools).

Therefore, the authors strongly believe (and this is being confirmed by all major industry analysts) that the data mining applications that can leverage the data preparation and integration capabilities of data warehousing are better positioned to achieve the sustainable competitive advantage.

Data Warehousing Overview

Data warehousing is a blend of technologies aimed at the effective integration of operational databases into an environment that enables the strategic use of data. These technologies include relational and multidimensional database management systems, client/server architecture, metadata modeling and repositories, graphical user interfaces, and much more.

Data Warehousing ROI

In the 1996 study by the International Data Corporation (IDC) on the financial impact of data warehousing, the focus has been on what the economists label the *productivity paradox*. This refers to the fact that up until the early 1990s, the benefits of technology were running well behind the pace of investment. The IDC report states that the IT investments have not delivered the expected benefits. Indeed, with the IT investment portfolio measured at about $464 billion (US) spent on technology around the world in 1994 alone, senior managers are justifiably asking for more evidence of IT benefits than ever before.

One of the reasons for this poor return on investment (ROI) comes from the fact that traditionally computing technology was focused on automating routine clerical tasks, improving the efficiency of existing processes, and collecting data. Unfortunately, even though large amounts of data have been collected, until recently, the value of this data was difficult to understand and use.

With the advent of data warehousing, companies can use information already collected as raw data to get a large return on investment, to obtain and sustain a significant competitive advantage. According to IDC, some of the reasons for seeing large financial returns in data warehousing implementations include the following:

- The capability to focus on business processes and perform a complete financial analysis of these processes, thus enabling organizations to make decisions based on the understanding of the entire system rather than using rough estimates based on incomplete data

- The capability to rationalize and automate the process of building an integrated enterprise-wide information store rather than developing many individual decision-support systems and the corresponding infrastructure

- The hardware, software, and storage costs related to the development, deployment, and maintenance of large informational data stores continue to decline
- The benefits of data warehousing can be easily extended to strategic decision making, which can yield very large and tangible benefits
- The capability to simultaneously understand and manage both the macro and micro perspectives of the organization can save organizations countless hours of manual work and can help avoid making costly mistakes that can be a result of assumptions made from incomplete or incorrect data

The IDC study concluded that an average three-year return on investment in data warehousing reached 401%, with more than 90% of the surveyed companies reporting a 40+% ROI, half of the companies reporting over 160% ROI, and one quarter showing returns greater than 600%!

Although the detailed analysis of the IDC report is beyond the scope of this book, we will use its findings to demonstrate how data warehousing and data mining can be and should be used to achieve these enviable results.

Operational and Informational Data Stores

Corporations have a variety of online transaction-processing systems (e.g., financial, order entry, work scheduling, and point-of-sale systems) that create operational data. Operational data focuses on transactional functions such as bankcard withdrawals and deposits. This data is part of the corporate infrastructure; it is detailed, nonredundant, and updateable; and it reflects current values. It answers such questions as "How many gadgets were sold to a customer, number 123876, on September 19th?"

Informational data, on the other hand, is organized around subjects such as customer, vendor, and product. It focuses on providing answers to problems posed by decisionmakers, such as "What three products resulted in the most frequent calls to the hotline over the past quarter?" Informational data is often summarized, is redundant to support varying data views, and is nonupdateable. In an operational system, a single data record can change constantly, whereas decision support requires that the record be stored as a series of snapshots of instances of that record over time.

Informational data is obtained from operational data sources (including any or all applications, databases, and computer systems within the enterprise). Because operational data is fragmented and inconsistent (for example, names and addresses for customers might be handled differently on each system), it must be "cleaned up" to conform to consistent formats, naming conventions, and access methods in order for it to be useful in decision support.

Data warehousing is designed to provide an architecture that will make corporate data readily accessible and usable to knowledge workers and decisionmakers. This differs from the operational systems that do the following:

- Organize by application
- Support daily business processing on a detailed transactional level
- Are update-intensive
- Use current data
- Are optimized for high performance
- Access few records per transaction, often direct access by primary key
- Support a large number of relatively short transactions
- Support a large number of concurrent users

Although the majority of informational and operational databases use the same underlying relational DBMS technology, the following characteristics of information data illustrate its difference from operational data:

- *Data access.* Tends to be ad hoc versus predefined, structured access
- *Data model* (schema). Reflects end-user analysis needs, whereas operational data model is normalized to support ACID transactional properties

- *Time base*.   Recent, aggregated, derived and historical data, whereas operational data tends to be current data or a snapshot of recent data

- *Data changes*.   Informational data changes are mostly periodic, scheduled batch updates, whereas operational data is subject to continuous high-frequency changes

- *Unit of work*.   Informational data is queried; whereas operational data is subject to concurrent update, insert, delete

- *Records range accessed per transaction*.   Millions for informational data versus tens for operational

- *Number of concurrent users*.   Typically, hundreds for informational versus thousands for operational

- *Transaction volume*.   Relatively low for informational data versus high for operational

- *Types of users*.   Analytical, managerial versus clerical, operational users; frequently, a user of the operational data is another system

- *Number of indexes*.   Often many complex, compound versus few, simple

These differences between the informational and operational databases are summarized in the following table.

Operational Data Store.   An interesting variation on the theme is an idea of rationalizing and integrating operational systems for the purpose of performing the decision support and analysis on the operational, transactional data. In other words, an Operational Data Store (ODS) is an architectural concept to support day-to-day operational decision support and contains current value data propagated from operational applications. This causes the data maintained in the ODS to be subjected to frequent changes as the corresponding data in the operational system changes. ODS provides an alternative to operational decision support system (DSS) applications that access data directly from the OLTP systems, thus eliminating the performance impact that such DSS activities can have on the OLTP systems.

Table 2-1

Operational versus
Informational
Databases

	Operational Data	Informational Data
Data Content	Current Values	Summarized archived, derived
Data Organization	By application	By Subject
Data Stability	Dynamic	Static until refreshed
Data Structure	Optimized for transactions	Optimized for complex queries
Access Frequency	High	Medium to low
Access Type	Read/Update/Delete Field-by-field	Read/Aggregate Added to
Usage	Predictable Repetitive	Ad hoc, unstructured Heuristic
Response Time	Sub-second to 2–3 seconds	Several seconds to minutes

We can categorize ODS systems based on the frequency of updates, as follows:

- Real time or near real time
- Periodic
- Overnight

Although ODS attributes are quite different from that of a data warehouse, ironically, the last two categories make the ODS quite similar to a data warehouse. That's why many of the application requirements of the ODS can be accomplished through well-defined access directly to the operational data or by enhancing the extraction process used to populate the data warehouse. However, some significant challenges of the ODS still remain. Among them are the following:

- Location of the appropriate sources of data
- Transformation of the source data to satisfy the ODS data model requirements
- Complexity of near-real time propagation of changes from the operational systems to the ODS (including tasks to recognize, obtain, synchronize, and move changes from a multitude of disparate systems)
- A database management system (DBMS) that combines effective query processing with transactional processing capabilities that ensure the ACID transaction properties (atomicity, consistency, isolation, and durability)
- A database design that is optimized to support the most critical DSS activities and at the same time reducing the number of indexes to minimize the impact on update performance

In a typical data warehouse systems, information passes through levels of transformation, from source to ODS, and finally to the data warehouse. Thus, we can now compare operational databases, operational data stores, and data warehouses. This comparison is presented in the following table.

ODS and Data Flow.   As data is placed into the ODS, it is still operational data in a non-integrated state. Operational data classically reflects data needed to assess and display the current status of data, (i.e., the value of data at the moment of access). This current value data is operational in nature (data is updateable) and transaction-specific, and this is reflected in the table structures.

Current value data is absolutely necessary for the running of operational systems, but current value data is not very useful for the analysis of information over a spectrum of time. Instead, atomic data, in which values of data over time are stored, is more useful for analysis. Atomic data, once correctly transformed and aggregated, is difficult to change. The data should be transformed and integrated at the atomic level, that is, integrated across the enterprise. This means that data is aggregated by subject area (i.e., Party, Trade, Transaction, Organizational Unit, Time, Location, Instrument, Customer, Employee, Role, etc.). The end result of these aggregations and transformations is the capability to provide shared data access for all CRM

Table 2-2

Comparison of Operational Data-bases, Operational Data Stores, and Data Warehouses

Measure	Operational Databases	Operational Datastores	Data Warehouse
Data Content	Current Values	Current and Near Values	Archival, Summarized Data, Calculated Data
Data Organization	Application by Application	Subject Area— data integration	Subject Area valid across the enterprise
Nature of Data	Dynamic (Changes Often)	Dynamic (Changes Often)	Static until refreshed
Data Structure and Format	Complex: suitable for operational computation	Complex to Simple	Simple: suitable for business analysis
Access Probability	High	High to Moderate	Moderate to Low
Data Update	Updated on a field by field basis	No update	Accessed and manipulated: No direct update
Data Access	Several Records per transaction	Several records per transaction	Many records per transaction
Usage	Highly structured, repetitive processing, transaction processing	Highly structured, repetitive processing, transaction processing and Ad-Hoc	Analytical processing : DSS with broad range of data to discern trends
Response Time Requirements	Sub-second to 2–3 seconds	Sub-second to 2–3 seconds	Several seconds to minutes, sometimes hours
Performance Requirements	High	Moderate to High	Moderate

campaigns, inventory movement, freight balancing, and similar applications where a rapid analysis is required to manage the business, and where a central ODS will facilitate this analysis. Additionally, ODS can be used for shared knowledge discovery services—the patterns of transaction data can be analyzed and summarized for their business intelligence contents using ODS as a primary data store.

In addition, the ODS can also serve as a replacement for change logs used to refresh other DSS files in the enterprise.

Definition and Characteristics of a Data Warehouse

A data warehouse can be viewed as an information system with the following attributes:

- It is a database designed for analytical tasks, using data from multiple applications
- It supports a relatively small number of users with relatively long interactions
- Its usage is read-intensive
- Its content is periodically updated (mostly additions)
- It contains current and historical data to provide a historical perspective of information
- It contains a few large tables
- Each query frequently results in a large result set and involves frequent full table scan and multi-table joins

A formal definition of the data warehouse is offered by W.H. Inmon:

"A data warehouse is a subject-oriented, integrated, time-variant, nonvolatile collection of data in support of management decisions."

In other words, a data warehouse combines the following:

- One or more tools to extract fields from any kind of data structure (flat, hierarchical, relational, or object; open or proprietary), including external data
- The synthesis of the data into a nonvolatile, integrated, subject-oriented database with a metadata "catalog"

There are a number of other terms related to the data warehouse. Following are some informal definitions of these terms:

- *Current detail data.*   Data that is acquired directly from the operational databases, and often represents an entire enterprise. The current detail data is organized along subject lines (i.e., customer profile data, customer activity data, demographics data, sales data, etc.).

- *Old detail data.*   Represents aged current detail data or the history of the subject areas; this data is what makes trend analysis possible.

- *Data mart.*   An implementation of the data warehouse, where its data scope is somewhat limited compared to the enterprise-wide data warehouse. A data mart may contain lightly summarized departmental data and can be customized to suit the needs of a particular department that owns the data. In a large enterprise, data marts tend to be a way to build a data warehouse in a sequential, phased approach. A collection of data marts composes an enterprise-wide data warehouse; conversely, a data warehouse may be construed as a collection of subset data marts. More on data marts can be found in Part II of this book.

- *Summarized data.*   Data that is aggregated along the lines required for executive-level reporting, trend analysis, and enterprise-wide decision making; summarized data volumes are much smaller than current and old detail data.

- *Drill-down.*   The ability of a knowledge worker to perform business analysis in a top-down fashion, traversing the summarization levels from highly summarized data to the underlying current or old detail. For example, if highly summarized geographical sales data indicate a reduction in sales volumes in North America, an analyst can drill down into the state, county, city, and even the address of the sales offices with the worst sales records.

- *Metadata.*   One of the most important aspects of data warehousing. Metadata is data about data. It contains the location and description of warehouse system components; the names, definition, structure, and content of the data warehouse and end-user views; the identification of authoritative data sources (systems of record); the integration and transformation rules used to populate the data warehouse; a history of warehouse updates and refreshments; the metrics used to analyze warehouse performance vis-à-vis end-user usage patterns; security authorizations; and so on.

Although users' needs related to a data warehouse will differ from company to company, similarities will exist. The following classification defines and describes some data warehouse attributes:

- A data warehouse provides a mechanism for separating operational and informational processing, with information being the domain of the warehouse. Because the warehouse is populated by data created by the operational environment, the flow of information is usually one way—from the operation data stores to the data warehouse.

- There is an holistic perspective that eliminates the vertical, line-of-business orientation of the operational data and provides an integrated perspective across the enterprise. The data warehouse is designed to help resolve inconsistencies in data formats, semantics, and usage across multiple operational systems.

- Part of a warehouse's function will include processing the data from its raw form in the operational databases. Data warehouse procedures include aggregating, reconciling, and summarizing data to make it more relevant and useful for users.

- The data content of the warehouse is a subset of all data in an organization. Even though the warehouse contains data originating from the operational environment, the contents of the warehouse are unique. Within the informational landscape, however, the warehouse should be considered as a universal set of all data emanating from inside and outside the company.

- Collecting data throughout the enterprise can result in an overwhelming amount of information. An effective means to navigate through the data maze can make a big difference as to whether the warehouse is used.

- Frequently, data from outside the company contributes to the decision-making process. Incorporating external data and mapping it to the appropriate applications are important data warehouse functions and should be transparent to the user.

■ Automating the data extraction and the required frequency of updates needs to be the warehouse's responsibility. Often, subsets of informational data need to be replicated for remote sites. Because data consolidation needs to precede replication, the warehouse becomes a logical place for the consolidation to occur. Monitoring the data-replication process to ensure that remote sites are synchronized with events at the central site also falls under the purview of the warehouse solution.

Although these attributes are normally associated with a data warehouse, they may not be immediately required by an organization's data warehouse implementation. But planning ahead for future needs will result in a data warehouse solution that is flexible.

Data Warehouse Architecture

The data warehouse architecture is based on a relational database management system server that functions as the central repository for informational data. In the data warehouse architecture, operational data and processing is completely separate from data warehouse processing (see Figure 2-1).

Figure 2-1
Data Warehouse
Environment

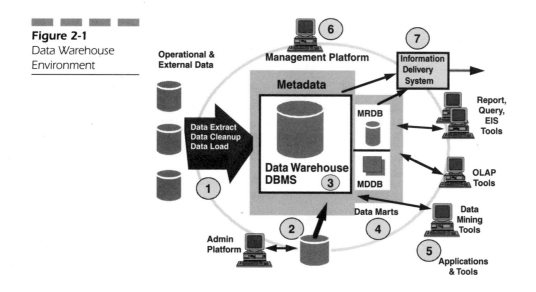

The source data for the warehouse are the operational applications. As the data enters the data warehouse, it is transformed into an integrated structure and format. The transformation process may involve conversion, summarization, filtering, and condensation of data. Because data within the data warehouse contains a large historical component (sometimes from 5 to 10 years), the data warehouse must be capable of holding and managing large volumes of data, as well as different data structures for the same database over time.

This book is focusing on the data mining technology and applications as they relate to data warehousing. In this context, ODS is considered to be an important component of the overall data warehousing environment, especially in relationship to data mining and similar analytical activities. The conceptual ODS/Data Warehouse Architecture is shown in Figure 2-2.

As was discussed previously, ODS can be used not only for decision support activities against the operational data, but also as a staging area for the data acquisition into the data warehouse (see Figure 2-2, item 8). The operational data store can sustain the same frequency

Figure 2-2
Data Warehouse and
Operational Data
Stores

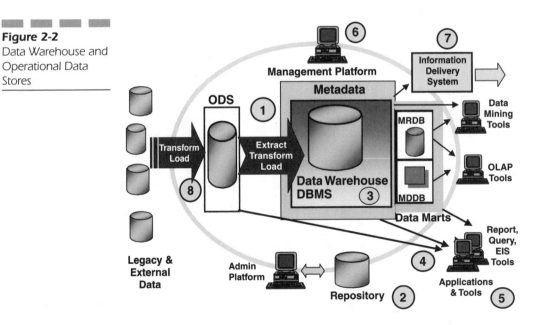

of updates as the underlying operational (legacy) data, thus providing a consistent view of operational data for decision support and analysis.

In relationship with a data warehouse, ODS may be used as a data staging area for data warehouse data sourcing. Conversely, the ODS does not have to act as the data staging area for the warehouse, especially if the data warehouse needs to acquire data from external sources that may not be found in the ODS. In this case, the data warehouse can be sourced separately from the ODS, or additional data sources can be included into the data warehouse data extraction component.

The data warehousing architecture shown in Figure 2-2 clearly identifies eight data warehouse components:

1. Data sourcing, cleanup, transformation, and migration tools
2. Metadata repository
3. Data Warehouse database technology
4. Data marts
5. Data query, reporting, analysis, and mining tools
6. Data warehouse administration and management
7. Information delivery system
8. Operational Data Store (ODS)

A detailed discussion of all these components is beyond the scope of this book.

Data Warehouse Access and Client/Server Architecture. From the end-user perspective, the data warehouse represents a source of data, access to which is provided by the end user query, reporting, analysis, or data mining tools. In other words, the data warehouse can be viewed as an information server to its clients—end users using front-end tools. Let's consider two client/server models that apply to data warehouse access.

Two-tiered data warehouse architecture is based on the first generation of client/server architecture and demonstrates the same characteristics.

Specifically, it is a "fat" client model, whose client system functions include user interface, query specification, data analysis, report formatting, aggregation, and data access. The data warehouse server performs data logic, data services, and file services; and maintains metadata (see Figure 2-3).

The two-tiered architecture lacks the scaleability and flexibility of the multi-tiered model. Multi-tiered data warehouse architecture reflects the multi-tiered client/server model (see Figure 2-4).

This architecture solves the scaleability and flexibility issues of the two-tiered data warehouse. Application servers perform data filtering, aggregation, and data access; support metadata; and provide multidimensional views.

NOTE: *Alternatively, application servers can be data mart servers, with all the benefits of a dependent data mart environment already integrated into a single scaleable architecture. A client system is left with GUI, query specification, data analysis, report formatting, and data access.*

Figure 2-3
Two-tiered Data
Warehouse
Architecture

Clients

Warehouse Server

• **GUI/ Presentation logic**
• **Query Specification**
• **Data Analysis**
• **Report Formatting**
• **Summarizing**
• **Data Access**

MetaData

Warehouse Data

• **Data Logic**
• **Data Services**
• **Metadata**
• **FileServices**

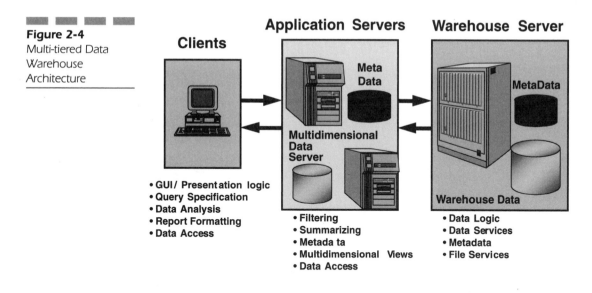

Figure 2-4
Multi-tiered Data
Warehouse
Architecture

Data Mining

The business problems solved by data warehousing and complementary technologies all have one common trend—they provide the
organizations with a sustainable competitive advantage frequently
provided by data mining. Let's define data mining space, introduce
some classification principles, and look at it from two different view-
points: applications of data mining and approaches to data mining.

Data Mining Defined

We gave a formal definition of data mining in the beginning of this
chapter. Here, we'll paraphrase that formal definition and define
data mining as the process of discovering *meaningful new* correlations, patterns, and trends by digging into (mining) large amounts of
data stored in warehouses. The major attraction of data mining is its
capability to build *predictive* rather than *retrospective* models (see
Table 2-3).

Data mining is not specific to any industry. It requires intelligent
technologies and the willingness to explore the possibility of hidden

Table 2-3

Predictive versus
Retrospective
Models

Traditonal DSS/EIS tools are Retrospective:	Data Mining tools are Predictive
"Print out last month's expenses by cost center"	"Predict and Explain next month's demand"
"List the biggest spenders from the last mailing"	"Define concentrated micro-market to reduce future mailing costs and improve success rates"
"Using this model, tell me how well it describes last year's cancellations of our contracts"	"Explain why some customers defect to our competitors" "Find some new patterns of customer behavior we are not aware of yet"

knowledge that resides in the data. Most organizations engage in data mining to do the following:

- *Discover knowledge.*   The goal of knowledge discovery is to determine explicit hidden relationships, patterns, or correlations from data stored in an enterprise's database.

- *Visualize data.*   Analysts must make sense out of a huge amount of information stored in corporate databases. Prior to any analysis, the goal is to "humanize" the mass of data they must deal with and find a clever way to display the data.

- *Correct data.*   While consolidating massive databases, many enterprises find that the data is not complete, and invariably contains erroneous and contradictory information. Data mining techniques can help identify and correct problems in the most consistent way possible.

Data Mining Application Domains

Consider the business application domains of decision support. It is a general category of applications that enables organizations to make informed and rational decisions about all aspects of their business, from the CRM point of view, the data mining applications include but not limited to the following:

- *Customer retention.* Sophisticated customer-retention programs begin with modeling those customers who have defected to identify patterns that led to their defection. These models are then applied to the current customers to identify likely defectors so that preventive actions can be initiated.

- *Sales and Customer Service.* In today's highly competitive environment, superior customer service creates the sales leaders. When information is properly aggregated and delivered to front-line sales and service professionals, customer service is greatly enhanced. If customer information is available, rule-based software can be employed to automatically recommend products. The programs like market-basket analysis (analysis of transactional databases to find sets of items that appear frequently together in a single purchase) have already shown phenomenal gains in cross-selling ratios, floor and shelf layout and product placement improvements, and better layout of catalog and Web pages.

- *Marketing.* Marketing depends heavily on accurate information to execute retention campaigns, lifetime value analysis, trending, targeted promotions, etc. Indeed, only by having a complete customer profile can promotions be targeted, and targeting dramatically increase response rates and thus decreases campaign costs. Direct mail costs are directly proportional to the completeness and accuracy of customer data.

- *Risk Assessment and Fraud Detection.* An accessible customer base significantly reduces the risk of entering into undo risk. For example, a mail order retailer can identify payment patterns from different customers at the same address, identifying potentially fraudulent practices by an individual using different names. An insurance company can identify its complete relationship with a client who may have different kinds of policies totaling more than an acceptable level of exposure. A bank can identify fiscally related companies that may be in financial jeopardy before extending a loan to them.

Data Mining Categories and Research Focus

Data mining techniques deal with discovery and learning, and as such can fall into three major learning modes: supervised, unsupervised, and reinforcement learning.

- *Supervised learning* includes the most widely used techniques. It is equivalent to "programming by example." Supervised techniques involve a training phase during which historic training data whose characteristics map to known outcomes are fed to the data mining algorithm. This process trains the algorithm to recognize key variables and values that will later become the basis for making predictions when scanning new data.

- *Unsupervised learning* does not involve a training phase; it instead depends on the use of algorithms that detect all patterns, such as associations and sequences, which occur above specified significance criteria in input data. This approach leads to the generation of many rules that characterize the discovered associations, clusters, and segments. These rules are then analyzed to determine those of significant interest.

- *Reinforcement learning*, although used less frequently than the other methods today, has applications in optimization over time and adaptive control. Reinforcement learning is the most like real life. It is very much like on-the-job training, where an employee is given a set of tasks requiring decisions. At some point in time, the employee is given a appraisal that determines the employee's performance, and forces the employee to evaluate his or her decisions in light of the performance results. Because the reinforcement learning process does not provide immediate corrective actions, it can be used to solve some very difficult time-dependent problems.

In addition to the learning modes, there are other ways by which data mining techniques can be categorized. The categories of data mining technique can be based on the following:

- Representation of models and results (i.e., decision trees, rules, associations, deviations, correlations)

- The type of data the technique operates on (i.e., continuous, discreet, time series, nominal)
- Application type (economic models, biology, genetics, Web log mining)
- Pattern attributes (accuracy, precision, interpretability, newness, expressiveness)

Even more interesting is to look at data mining techniques through the categories of the business problems that are best addressed by data warehousing and data mining. In this approach, we may first categorize data mining as the following:

- *Retrospective analysis*, which focuses on the issues of past and present events. For example, an organization may have to decide that it requires an in-depth analysis of the performance of the sales organization for the last two years across different geographical regions, demographics, and type of products.
- *Predictive analysis*, which focuses on predicting certain events or behaviors, based on historical information. For example, an organization may want to build a predictive model that describes the attrition rates of their customers to the competition, and also defines steps that would reduce the attrition with a certain degree of confidence.

These two classes of business problems can be further classified by considering the following application types and techniques:

- *Classification.* This technique is used to classify database records into a number of predefined classes based on certain criteria. For example, a credit card company may classify customer records as a good, medium, or poor risk. A classification system may then generate a rule stating that "If a customer earns more than $40,000, is between 45 to 55 in age, and lives within a particular ZIP code, he or she is a good credit risk."
- *Clustering / Segmentation.* This technique is used to segment a database into subsets, or clusters, based on a set of attributes. For example, in the process of understanding its customer base, an organization may attempt to segment the known population

to discover clusters of potential customers based on attributes never before used for this kind of analysis (for example, the type of schools they attended, the number of vacations per year, and so on). Clusters can be created either statistically or by using artificial-intelligence methods. Clusters can be analyzed automatically by a program or by using visualization techniques.

- *Associations.*   These techniques identify affinities among the collection, as reflected in the examined records. These affinities are often expressed as rules. For example: "60% of all the records that contain items A and B also contain C and D." The percentage of occurrences (in this case, 60) is the confidence factor of the association. Association technique is often applied to market basket analysis, where it uses point-of-sales transaction data to identify product affinities.

- *Sequencing.*   This technique helps identify patterns over time, thus allowing, for example, an analysis of customer purchases during separate visits. It could be found, for instance, that if a customer buys engine oil and filter during one visit, he'll buy gasoline additive the next time. This type of analysis is particularly important for catalog companies. It's also applicable in financial applications to analyze sequences of events that affect the prices of financial instruments.

Common goals of all these data mining applications and techniques include the detection, interpretation, and prediction of qualitative and/or quantitative patterns in data. To achieve these goals, data mining solutions employ a wide variety of techniques of machine learning, artificial intelligence, statistics, and database query processing. These techniques are also based on mathematical approaches such as multi-valued logic, approximation theory, and dynamic systems.

Although the majority of the data mining techniques are discussed in more detail in Chapters 5 and 6, let's take a closer look at the approaches that underlie the most contemporary research in data mining:

- The *induction* approach is based on the principle of proceeding from the specific to the general (a reversal of the deduction process), and has its roots in machine learning and artificial intelligence (AI). It is usually implemented as a search through the space of possible scenarios or hypotheses, and employs some special criteria to arrive at a good generalization.

- The *database querying* approach has its roots in the database management systems. It is based on the fact that because most corporate data stores are implemented as a form of a data warehouse built on top of a relational database, then the process of data mining can be viewed as a form of a database query processing (albeit quite sophisticated). Research in this area is focused on two tacks:

  - Enhancements of the semantic expressions of query languages such as SQL (structured query language) and OQL (object query language) to allow a data mining question (e.g., find all customers that have a propensity to buy more of a given product) to be defined within the constraints of the language grammar

  - Enhancements of the underlying data model; this approach is dealing with the issue of whether the relational data model that is a good vehicle for data abstraction is also a good model for data mining

- The *compression* approach is based on the computational learning theory and the feasibility of models based on the Minimum Description Length principle. Several commercial data mining systems use this approach to determine the effectiveness of uncovered patterns. The essence of the approach is as follows:

  - Several data mining techniques can be applied to the same data set to potentially yield similar results.

  - Rather than use several techniques and perform an exhaustive analysis of all patterns, the idea is to compress the entire answer space to a smaller but stronger set of discovered patterns that are easier to describe; thus the approach is called compression.

- The approach of *approximation* and *searching* may appear counterintuitive because it starts with the exact model and intentionally introduces approximations in the assumption that some hidden structures and patterns can be uncovered. This approach applies to text searching and text mining as well (see Chapter 25). For instance, a technique called Latent Semantic Indexing (patented by Bellcore), uses linear algebraic matrix transformations and approximations to identify hidden patterns in word usage, thus enabling searches beyond simple keyword matching. This and similar approaches can improve the efficiency of search algorithms by contracting the space of possible patterns.

In short, data mining, although it has its roots in several established areas of science and technology, is still an emerging science and is a subject of continuous research.

Throughout the book, we'll show how the business problems defined previously can be addressed by properly implementing and using a data warehouse and companion technologies such as OLAP and data mining. We'll also discuss various CRM technologies and solutions that are designed to enable organizations to transform from a mass marketing model to provide interactive and continuous one-to-one marketing.

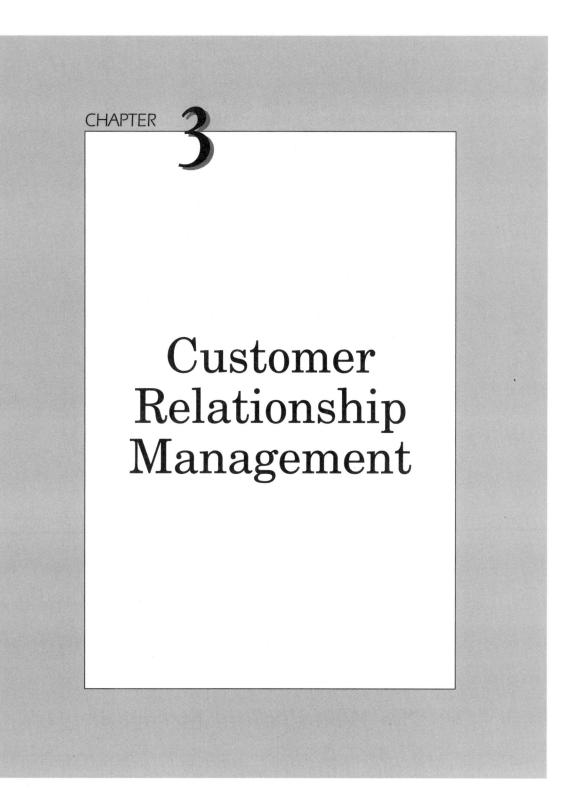

CHAPTER 3

Customer Relationship Management

Introduction

- Companies must spend far more money to get a new customer than to retain an existing customer.

- It is far more expensive to win back a customer after they have left than it is to keep them satisfied in the first place.

- It is far easier to sell a new product to an existing customer than it is to a new customer.

- Some customers are vastly more profitable than other customers. Some customers are unprofitable, and some customers are unprofitable and will never be profitable.

This is the reality of business today. The good news is that the profitability of each customer can be measured and effected. This is possible because of the development of new technology that now provides a unique opportunity that many companies are rushing to exploit. These companies are seeking to move from single sales models to continuing selling relationships with their customers. They are seeking to understand how to build and maintain a loyal customer relationship, and to discover the most profitable way to build that relationship.

Only a small portion of a customer's positive feelings and loyalty are generated by your products. The rest comes from the intangibles: service, store experience, etc. Companies need to know their customers' preferences—not only for products, but also for style, service, and image. They need to manage the relationship with each and every customer, and make each as profitable as possible. Those companies that are successful will find increased revenue at lower cost of sales and marketing, and decreased cost from lost customers and ineffective sales and marketing. The methodology that makes this possible is called Customer Relationship Management, or CRM.

The Most Profitable Customer

Most business sectors are consolidating, as bigger operations gain share and drive small independents out of business. The challenge and opportunity are clear: companies must continue to gain the economies of scale from efficient operations, while delivering frequent and customized interaction with customers at the same time. To achieve these customized interactions, Customer Relationship Management Systems seek to provide timely answers to questions such as the following:

- Which customers are most profitable to me? Why?
- What promotions are most effective? For which customers?
- What kind of customers will be interested in my new product?
- Which customers are at risk to defect to my competitor?
- How do I identify prospects with the greatest profit potential?

Customer information is rapidly becoming a company's most important asset to answer these questions. However, to answer these questions in broad generalities is not enough. Each customer must be analyzed and potentially treated uniquely. This need for customized interaction is driven by the fact that most organizations find that the differential value of their customers is quite skewed. The importance of understanding and leveraging customer knowledge is clear: Identifying and expanding your relationships with profitable customers is vital. Customer relationship management provides the framework for analyzing customer profitability and improving marketing effectiveness.

Customer Relationship Management

Many organizations have collected and stored a wealth of data about their customers, suppliers, and business partners. However, the inability to discover valuable information hidden in the data prevents these organizations from transforming this data into knowledge. The business desire is, therefore, to extract valid, previously unknown, and comprehensible information from large databases and use it for profit.

To fulfill these goals, organizations need to follow these steps:

- Capture and integrate both the internal and external (purchased) data into a comprehensive view that encompasses the whole organization.
- "Mine" the integrated data for information.
- Organize and present the information and knowledge in ways that expedite complex decision-making.

To do all these things, organizations need to integrate various components of decision sciences applications (often called *decision engines*) to organize data in ways that facilitate analysis. One of the fastest growing area of the applications of decision sciences technologies and data mining—Customer Relationship Management (CRM).

In order to stay competitive, companies develop strategies to become customer-focused, customer-driven, and customer-centric. All these terms define the companies' desire to build lasting customer relationships. CRM is viewed as a solution that makes these efforts valuable to the company and the customer alike, so that consumers don't view these efforts as trivial or useless.

The objective of CRM is the optimization of profitability. It begins with the premise that not all customers are created equal. It is only the companies that really understand if, what, and how customers want to interact that are likely to achieve customer loyalty and the associated profitability improvements.

CRM allows companies to better discriminate and more efficiently allocate resources to their most-desirable customers. The caveat, however, is that as CRM matures, many companies will compete for the same set of attractive consumers. Because most consumers tend to have only a handful of meaningful relationships, some companies will lose even their existing customers. Thus, the need and the capability to develop, maintain and continuously execute effective customer relationship programs are paramount.

Through enterprise-wide CRM efforts, companies attempt to better coordinate customer contact points, so that the enterprise can more efficiently manage its marketing resources and establish more meaningful relationships with its customers. Effective customer relationships require an understanding of what this relationship entails, an ability to provide personalized services, a means for building mutual value and respect, and a commitment to the relationship itself—in short, the same things that create a strong personal relationship.

From the architecture point of view, therefore, the entire CRM framework can be classified into three key components:

- *Operational CRM.* The automation of horizontally integrated business processes, including customer touch-points, channels, and front-back office integration

- *Analytical CRM.* The analysis of data created by the Operational CRM

- *Collaborative CRM.* Applications of collaborative services including e-mail, personalized publishing, e-communities, and similar vehicles designed to facilitate interactions between customers and organizations

Let's look at the holistic view of the CRM architecture (see Figure 3-1). In this architecture, you can see a number of customer touch points and delivery channels that produce and consume information. This information needs to be integrated and analyzed in order to obtain a complete and accurate picture of the customers

Figure 3-1
CRM architecture

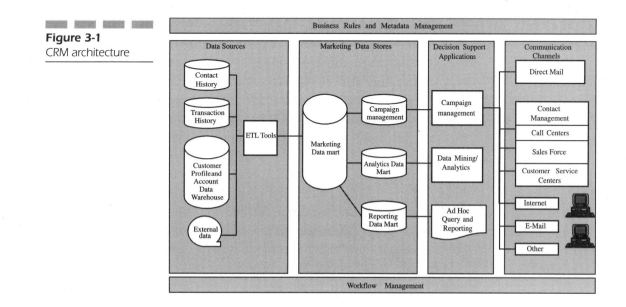

—their preferences, needs, complaints, and attributes that can make them life-long members of the organizational "network" of products and services. As a result, all major components of the data warehousing environment are being deployed to perform a number of critical functions related to the integration and analysis. Among these components are not just data warehouses and data marts, but also data mining, reporting, OLAP engines, and the metadata management repository.

The Customer Centered Database

All of this would be much easier if there were a single database of information available about each customer. The reality is that building a picture of your customer is more like a mosaic, in which small glimpses of what the customer really looks like come from many different directions. Only when these different views are all put together does an image appear that truly reflects the characteristics and behaviors of that customer.

Each of these incomplete images comes from a different source—usually one in which your company has had some contact with the customer. For instance, when the sales force landed the customer they may have had a certain image of what that customer looked like. When the customer called in with a problem to the customer service line, he or she reflected some view of themselves to your company (satisfied or dissatisfied). Each of these points of contact, where you have the opportunity to interact and "touch" your customers or they touch your company, are called "touchpoints". They provide some of the best information about your customer. The problem is that there are many of them. The customer information exists, but it is fragmented, and each piece by itself is incomplete.

In the mid-1980s some banks sought to solve this problem by building databases called Marketing Customer Information Files (MCIFs). As the name implies, they were a lot more like files than databases, but they did serve the same function as what would later be called a data warehouse. There were many providers who created systems such as Marketing Profiles, Customer Insight, OKRA, and Harte-Hanks. Because these data systems were not much more sophisticated than large flat files (without a relational database structure), they were difficult to maintain and update. Also, these systems were more handcrafted than they were production-oriented. Nonetheless, these systems provided a well-rounded view of all of the marketing activity that was associated with each customer for the first time. This meant that customers could be contacted through direct mail campaigns with an understanding of what recent promotion they had been sent and whether they had already purchased the product that was being promoted.

Managing Campaigns

These MCIF systems were relatively fragile, but they did provide the first views into what a world would look like that had a central repository of customer-centered information. They laid the groundwork for the more sophisticated and robust campaign management systems that grew into the Customer Relationship Management systems of today.

Campaign management systems are, as their name implies, systems that help marketing professionals manage and execute campaigns. Such systems are the forerunners of CRM systems, in that they require as complete a view of the customer as possible (hence a central customer information data store). and they must manage interactions between the company and the customer. Figure 3-2 shows a sample screen of how promotions are assigned to customer segments for the campaign management function of a CRM system. Their genesis, however, was typically only from one touchpoint (direct mail). It focused on mostly the nuts and bolts: making sure that the consumer got the right promotion, and that the name and address were correctly assigned and labeled the envelope or postcard.

These were important problems that were addressed by some of the early systems from Exchange Applications and others. These systems, however, needed to quickly grow from just being able to reliably execute each campaign to the point where they could also provide the following:

- Marketing insights from data mining about what new promotions to create

- Accommodation of many new touchpoints besides direct mail (for example, the Web, direct TV, hard copy advertising, customer service, and even the sales force)

- Focus on profitability (not only on which customer was most profitable, but also on what was the most profitable promotion that could be sent.e.g. send the $0.25 postcard rather than the $25 rebate if both would have the same effect)

- Optimization of the sequence of promotion delivery

- Tools for constructing experiments that allow the marketing professional to test out the effectiveness of new promotions and new segmentation techniques

- Accommodation by the system of predictive modeling (from data mining), which provides insights into future customer behavior and future customer profitability

This transition from just defining and deploying a direct mail campaign to supporting all customer touchpoints (as well as providing marketing research insights, budget and customer profitability planning, and measurement of the campaign after its launch) marked the features that were added to the initial campaign management systems. This moved them toward more complete CRM systems, focusing on customer profitability across all touchpoints.

The Evolution of Marketing

The optimization of marketing processes represents the confluence of new marketing strategies with recent developments in information technology. Rather than a revolution, these changes can be seen as evolving over time (as shown in Table 3-1).

Table 3-1

The evolution of marketing processes

Marketing Age	Techniques	Technology
The Dark Ages	Artistry and Alchemy	None
The Renaissance	Craftsmanship	Focus groups, telephone interviews
The Industrial revolution	Mass Marketing	Computers store mailing lists
The Information Age	Database Marketing	Flat File MCIFs
The Age of Optimization	Customer Relationship Management	Data Warehousing, Data Mining, Analysis Tools (OLAP)

Closed Loop Marketing

The desire for CRM systems is that they provide "closed loop marketing": They not only execute marketing campaigns, but they also "close the loop" and measure the results of the campaigns. Once marketing's effectiveness can be measured, it can be improved the next time around. Experiments can be conducted to understand better what is working, what is not working, and why. The results of these experiments and the measurements of marketing success (at a level of customer profitability) is the information that drives the data mining systems to become increasingly better at targeting and predicting the future behavior of customers.

Closed loop marketing consists of three basic steps that lead to an upward spiral of continuing marketing improvement:

- *Measure.*   Measure the results of the marketing effort, based on customer profitability. Use Web-based tools to access the customer data warehouse and perform enterprise-level ROI analysis.
- *Predict.*   Use data mining technology to predict consumer behavior and learn from past experiments. Use the results of the data mining system to focus and refine future campaigns.
- *Act.*   Use campaign management systems to be sure that the campaigns are executed in an understandable and measurable way, and that the results and actions are captured in the customer data warehouse or data mart.

The CRM Architecture

At a high level, the architecture for a CRM system is like the structure of a building. There is the bedrock or foundation on which it rests, the cornerstone by which the trueness of corners and straightness of walls is measured, And the architectural blueprint for the way the building should hold together. Finally, the capstone—the final piece that completes the building. Following this analogy:

- The customer touchpoints are the bedrock.
- Data warehousing is the foundation.
- Customer profitability is the cornerstone.
- Data mining is the architectural blueprint.
- Web applications are the capstone.

These technologies are all used together to build a complete CRM system that can execute closed loop marketing to display continuous improvement over time.

Next Generation CRM

The next generation of CRM systems will continue to expand in functionality and in scope across the enterprise. They will begin to merge with the other main customer touchpoints that are already being automated through sales force automation and through enterprise resource planning. This is an inevitable trend. Consider the pharmaceutical industry, in which the direct sales force has long dominated the sales and marketing efforts. Today, however, direct-to-consumer marketing in the pharmaceutical industry has become a reality with more than $100 million per year being spent on single products, independent of sales force initiatives. The Holy Grail, however, is that sales and marketing work together in a coordinated effort so that each supports the efforts of the other.

The combination of CRM with ERP is also important. Resource allocation for everything—from having sufficient product stock, to satisfying customer demand, to having sufficient inventory of marketing direct mail promotions, to executing a campaign—will eventually be important constraints to incorporate into any CRM system that is trying to optimize customer profitability.

The forces opposing this fusing of information and technology come from two sources: the first internal and the second external. Internally, the greater good of having an enterprise-wide CRM system may suffer due to the political fragmentation of various groups within the organization. One of the most difficult parts of building a powerful CRM system is the difficulty of getting customer information from different customer touchpoints within the same company. Often, individual groups do not want to cooperate or share information because they see it as being detrimental to the profitability of their own cost center, even though it may be highly profitable for the organization overall.

The second force that opposes enterprise-wide CRM systems (and CRM in general) is the desire for customer privacy. Consumers prefer privacy; CRM systems require consumer information in order to function well. As we will show, the debate is far from over in terms of how much privacy a consumer can expect and how much sharing of consumer information can be performed, either within or between organizations.

Foundation —The Technologies and Tools

As was stated in Chapter 2, the data warehouse is the foundation of and the means for data integration that leads to a strategic data usage. Data mining is a collection of techniques and algorithms that, when applied to the cleaned and rationalized data stored in a data warehouse, leads to an effective customer relationship management. It is not the same as a decision support system. Rather, a data warehouse is a platform with integrated data of improved quality to support many decision support and analytical applications and processes within an enterprise.

This part of the book looks at several technologies and tools that represent a technical foundation for the robust enterprise-scale data mining-enabled customer relationship management (CRM).

Data warehousing components, data mining techniques, and the revolutionary impact of the Web on the business and technologies of customer management are all part of this foundation.

A reader who does not wish to get familiar with the technology foundation of the data mining-enabled CRM may skip this part in its entirety or skip some selected chapters.

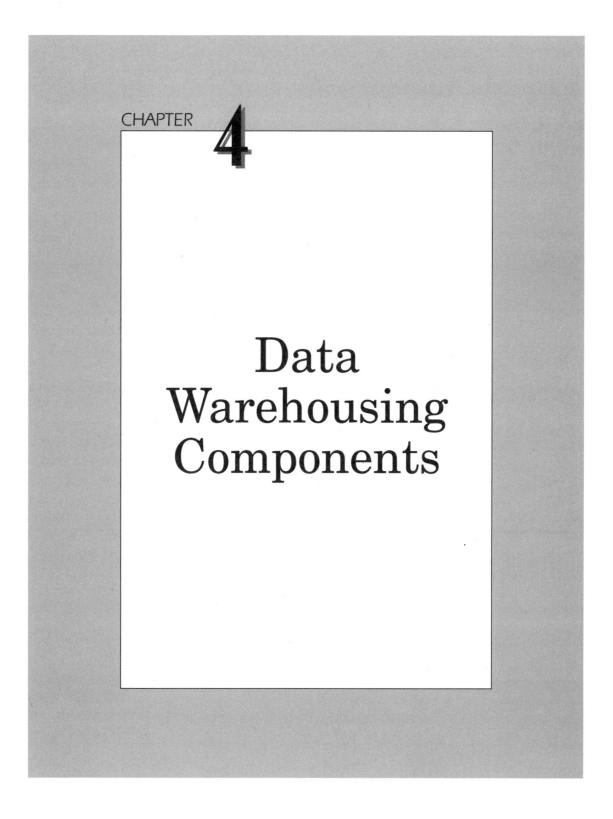

CHAPTER 4

Data Warehousing Components

Introduction

Customer relationship management is the core activity of e-business. The current emphasis on CRM is a result of the shift in the way business is done today. Customer loyalty, brand loyalty, Web-enabled ease of switching from one provider to another, and lower costs for market entry make it imperative for an e-business to get to know its customer base at a far more detailed level than in the past. The business that has the enduring working relationship with the customer is the business that will win the competition war.

The technology area associated most often with CRM is personalization. Personalization entails tailoring the presentation of a Web site to individuals or classes of customers based on profile information, demographics, or prior transactions. The goal is to market and sell one-to-one, and to enhance the user experience so the customer returns to the merchant's Web site. The personalization is predicated on the organization's capability to collect, clean up, integrate, and effectively use all available information about the customer. This information includes transaction and credit history, propensity to buy/sell products, demographic and social information, personal and professional preferences, financial planning, life events, and so on. The foundation for the collection, integration, and analysis of all customer data can be traced to the technologies of data warehousing and data mining. These technologies include relational and multidimensional database management systems, client/server architecture, metadata modeling and repositories, graphical user interfaces, and much more.

Overall Architecture

The data warehouse architecture is based on a relational database management system server that functions as the central repository for informational data. In the data warehouse architecture, operational data and processing is completely separate from data warehouse processing. This central information repository is surrounded by a number of key components, designed to make the entire environment functional, manageable, and accessible by both the operational systems that source data into the warehouse and by end user query and analysis tools (see Figure 4-1).

Typically, the source data for the warehouse comes from the operational applications or from an operational data store, or ODS (discussed briefly in Chapter 2). As the data enters the data warehouse, it is transformed into an integrated structure and format. The transformation process may involve conversion, summarization, filtering, and condensation of data. Because data within the data warehouse contains a large historical component (sometimes from five to 10 years), the data warehouse must be capable of holding and managing large volumes of data as well as different data structures for the same database over time.

Figure 4-1
Data warehouse
architecture

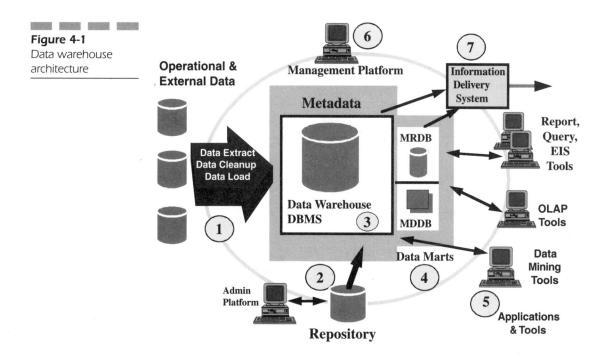

The following section takes a close look at the seven major data warehousing components identified in Figure 4-1.

Data Warehouse Database

The central data warehouse database is a cornerstone of data warehousing environment. Marked as item (3) on the architecture diagram, this database is almost always implemented on the relational database management system (RDBMS) technology. However, a warehouse implementation based on traditional RDBMS technology is often constrained by the fact that traditional RDBMS implementations are optimized for transactional database processing. Certain data warehouse attributes such as very large database size; ad hoc query processing; and the need for flexible user view creation including aggregates, multi-table joins, and drill-downs, have become drivers for different technological approaches to the data warehouse database. These approaches include the following:

- Parallel relational database designs that require a parallel computing platform, for example, symmetric multiprocessor (SMP), massively parallel processors (MPPs), and/or clusters of uni- or multiprocessors (the discussion on this technology is outside the scope of this book).

- An innovative approach to speed up a traditional RDBMS by using new index structures to bypass relational table scans.

- Multidimensional databases (MDDBs) that are based on proprietary database technology or implemented using already familiar RDBMS. Multidimensional databases are designed to overcome any limitations placed on the warehouse by the nature of the relational data model. This approach is tightly coupled with the online analytical processing (OLAP) tools that act as clients to the multidimensional data stores. These tools architecturally belong to a group of data warehousing components jointly categorized as the data query, reporting, analysis, and mining tools.

Sourcing, Acquisition, Cleanup and Transformation Tools

A significant portion of the data warehouse implementation effort is spent extracting data from operational systems and putting it in a format suitable for informational applications that will run off the data warehouse.

The data sourcing, cleanup, transformation, and migration tools (identified as item (1) on the architecture diagram) perform all of the conversions, summarizations, key changes, structural changes, and condensations needed to transform disparate data into information that can be used by the decision support tool. It produces the programs and control statements, including the COBOL programs, MVS job control language (JCL), UNIX scripts, and SQL data definition language (DDL) needed to move data into the data warehouse from multiple operational systems. It also maintains the metadata. The functionality includes the following:

- Removing unwanted data from operational databases
- Converting to common data names and definitions
- Calculating summaries and derived data
- Establishing defaults for missing data
- Accommodating source data definition changes

The data sourcing, cleanup, extract, transformation and migration tools have to deal with some significant issues, as follows:

- *Database heterogeneity.* DBMSs are very different in data models, data access language, data navigation, operations, concurrency, integrity, recovery, and so on.
- *Data heterogeneity.* This is the difference in the way data is defined and used in different models—homonyms, synonyms, unit incompatibility (U.S. vs. metric), different attributes for the same entity, different ways of modeling the same fact.

These tools can save a considerable amount of time and effort. However, significant shortcomings do exist. For example, many available tools are generally useful for simpler data extracts. Frequently, customized extract routines need to be developed for the more complicated data-extraction procedures. The vendors prominent in this arena include Ardent/Prism Solutions, Evolutionary Technologies, Inc. (ETI), Vality, Informatica, Praxis, and Carleton.

Metadata

Metadata is data about data that describes the data warehouse. It is used for building, maintaining, managing, and using the data warehouse. Metadata can be classified into the following:

- Technical metadata that contains information about warehouse data for use by warehouse designers and administrators when carrying out warehouse development and management tasks. Technical metadata documents include the following:
  - Information about data sources
  - Transformation descriptions—the mapping method from operational databases into the warehouse, and algorithms used to convert/enhance/transform data
  - Warehouse object and data structure definitions for data targets
  - The rules used to perform data cleanup and data enhancement
  - Data-mapping operations when capturing data from source systems and applying it to the target warehouse database
  - Access authorization, backup history, archive history, information delivery history, data acquisition history, data access, and so on
- Business metadata contains information that gives users an easy-to-understand perspective of the information stored in the data warehouse. Business metadata documents information about the following:
  - Subject areas and information object type, including queries, reports, images, video and/or audio clips
  - Internet home pages

- Other information to support all data warehousing components. For example, the information related to the information delivery system should include subscription information; scheduling information; details of delivery destinations; and the business query objects such as pre-defined queries, reports, and analyses.

■ Data warehouse operational information such as data history (snapshots, versions), ownership, extract audit trail, usage data

Equally as important, metadata provides interactive access to users to help understand content and find data. One of the issues dealing with metadata relates to the fact that many data extraction tools' capabilities to gather metadata remain fairly immature. Therefore, often there is a need to create a metadata interface for users, which may involve some duplication of effort.

Metadata management is provided via a metadata repository and accompanying software (see item (2) Figure 4-1). Metadata repository management software can be used to map the source data to the target database, generate code for data transformations, integrate and transform the data, and control moving data to the warehouse. This software, which typically runs on a workstation, enables users to specify how the data should be transformed, such as by data mapping, conversion, and summarization.

As users' interaction with the data warehouse increases, their approach to reviewing the results of their requests for information can be expected to evolve from relatively manual analysis for trends and exceptions to agent-driven initiation of the analysis based on user-defined thresholds. The definition of these thresholds, configuration parameters for the software agents using them, and the information directory indicating where the appropriate sources for the required information can be found, are all stored in the metadata repository as well.

One of the important functional components of the metadata repository is the information directory. The content of the information directory is the metadata that helps technical and business users to exploit the power of data warehousing. This directory helps integrate, maintain, and view the contents of the data warehousing system.

From the technical requirements' point of view, the information directory and the entire metadata repository will have the following attributes:

- Should be a gateway to the data warehouse environment, and thus should be accessible from any platform via transparent and seamless connections

- At a minimum, the information directory components should be accessible by any Web browser, and should run on all major platforms, including MS Windows 95/98 , Windows NT, and UNIX

- The data structures of the metadata repository should be supported on all major relational and/or object-oriented database platforms

- Should support an easy distribution and replication of its content for high performance and availability

- Should be searchable by business-oriented key words

- Should be able to define the content of both structured and unstructured data

- Should act as a launch platform for end user data access and analysis tools

- Should support the sharing of information objects such as queries, reports, data collections, subscriptions, and so on between users

- Should support a variety of scheduling options for requests against the data warehouse, including on-demand, one-time, repetitive, event-driven, and conditional delivery (in conjunction with the Information Delivery system)

- Should support the distribution of the query results to one or more destinations in any of the user-specified formats (in conjunction with the Information Delivery system)

- Should support and provide interfaces to other applications such as e-mail, spreadsheets, and schedulers

- Should support end user monitoring of the status of the data warehouse environment (in conjunction with the Administration and Management components.)

These requirements define a very sophisticated repository of metadata information. In reality, however, existing products often come up short when implementing all of these requirements. Additionally, most of the other data warehousing components employ their own set of metadata definitions, often with a narrow scope defined specifically to enable this particular component. Therefore, a critical requirement for a robust, full-featured metadata repository is the capability to integrate various metadata stores provided by multiple data warehouse tools and components.

Because the capability to do the extracts periodically, and to refresh and update the synthesized data via copy management tools is very important for the well-being of a data warehouse, the maintenance of the information directory becomes one of the key critical issues in data warehousing.

The relative immaturity of metadata repositories is also reflected in the state of terminology. For example, some data warehousing vendors name the metadata repository as a dictionary or encyclopedia. And, very few of the current metadata repository architectures clearly identify its internal components, such as the information directory.

Examples of metadata repositories include Microsoft Repository, R&O's Rochade, Prism Solution's Directory Manager, and "CA/Platinum Technologies" Information Repository.

Access Tools

The principal purpose of data warehousing is to provide information to business users for strategic decision making. These users interact with the data warehouse using front-end tools (item(s) on Figure 4-1). Many of these tools require an information specialist, a domain expert, who can analyze the information and can interact with the data warehousing environment in order to reach meaningful conclusions. This is especially true for data mining tools when defining the problem, configuring the tool, and analyzing the results. Both dynamic and preplanned analyses are enabled in a high-performance environment because joins, summations, and periodic reports are preplanned, and results are usually moved to servers as close to end users as possible for immediate access.

Although ad hoc requests, regular reports, and custom applications are the primary delivery vehicles for the analysis done in most data warehouses, many development efforts in the data warehousing arena are focusing on exceptional reporting, also known as *alerts*. The alert lets a user know when a certain event has occurred. For example, if the data warehouse is designed to assess the risk of currency trading, an alert can get activated when certain currency rates drop below a predefined threshold. When an alert is well synchronized with the key objectives of the business, it can provide warehouse users with a tremendous advantage.

Accessing and Visualizing Information

Data warehouses are causing a surge in popularity of data-visualization techniques. The reason for this renewed interest is clear—it is the limitation of the maximum bandwidth with which human beings can absorb information. No matter how large the database and no matter how fast the computer, in the end, the information must flow through the tightest of bottlenecks—the speed at which the human brain can absorb and process new information.

The volumes of data are overwhelming and the human visual systems and brain are not equipped to work with the data in this form. Using data visualization can allow much faster processing of the data and, in many cases, the capability to see patterns in the data that would not be possible in any other way.

If you think of your data warehouse as a mountain of data ready to be mined, try to imagine getting a grasp of a real mountain— Mount Everest, for example—by viewing it as a listing of elevation and position coordinates across the mountain for every square foot of its several thousand square miles of area. It would be easy to say what the exact elevation for the mountain was at any given latitude and longitude, but it would be very difficult to develop even the most basic intuitions about the overall shape of the mountain: Was it high? Did it have multiple peaks? A simple photograph or, better yet, a low-resolution, three-dimensional computer model could contain far fewer bits of information, but could convey these critical facts about the mountain. If you can think of the terabytes of data in your data warehouse as contributing to a mountain, you can see how visualization of your data can be critically helpful for quickly conveying the general structure of your data mountain.

Data visualization seeks to combat the data understanding problem by utilizing the newfound computer power to make it easier for the human being to absorb information. These systems allow the end user to take high-level views of the data, and then build and confirm intuitions based on these views.

Data visualization is not a separate class of tools. Instead, it is a method of presenting the output of all of the previously mentioned tools so that the entire problem and/or the solution is clearly visible to domain experts and even casual observers. (For example, the result of a relational or multidimensional query, or the result of a data mining discovery.)

Data visualization goes far beyond simple bar and pie charts. It is a collection of complex techniques that currently represent an area of intense research and development, focusing on determining how to best display complex relationships and patterns on a two-dimensional (flat) computer monitor. Similar to medical imaging research, current data-visualization techniques experiment with various colors, shapes, 3D imaging, sound, and virtual reality to help users really see and feel the problem and its solutions.

Data Visualization Principles. In general, much of data visualization has to do with finding a mapping between multidimensional spaces that exist in the database or the predictive model and the two-dimensional space that exists on the computer screen.

There is some latitude in the way dimensionality can be expressed on a computer screen. For instance, three dimensions are mapped onto the screen, and even four dimensions can readily be expressed through the use of color. Fundamentally, however, the information is passing through a two-dimensional device, and when the problem is defined in more than three dimensions, it becomes increasingly difficult to represent it effectively. For instance, it has been argued that even though three-dimensional graphs are commonplace in desktop applications, it is still fundamentally difficult to "see" what is going on in the three-dimensional graph, unless the graph is animated and the user can flip it and turn it to see around obscuring features.

Thus, information "animation" has been born. Techniques such as dynamic rotation and fly-through have been enabled so that the user can interact with the simulated three-dimensional view as if they were holding the object in their hands or navigating over the data terrain on foot or by plane.

Even the use of color is problematic—given the number of color-blind people using computers today. And for data mining, this could be critical if someone is red/green color blind, and color-coded stop-and-go tags are added to the visualization.

Historically, data visualization has come from three areas (and not surprisingly from folks being overwhelmed by data):

■ Simulations of natural phenomena on the computer

■ Statistics

■ Data collected from natural systems

In the first category are the simulations that have been performed on supercomputers, ranging from simulating the smog buildup over Los Angeles to the simulation of the propagation of faults at the atomic level that could result in the structural failure of an airplane wing. These systems create their own data by simulating natural processes.

In statistics, data often comes not from a physical system or its simulation, but from much higher-dimensional spaces generated by human data collection—such as hundreds of the test results that define information about a cancer patient. In general, statisticians like to see data compressed into distributions that show the high-level view of the expected value and the variance, or a two-dimensional scatter plot that can show the relationship between two predictors.

Data collected from natural systems include the visualization of a MRI or CAT scan data. The data was collected from a process that actually occurred in nature, so it should be relatively easy to visualize. Because of the detailed nature of the data, however, even more can be done than could be seen in nature. The data can be used to re-create the three-dimensional structures, but can also be used to show internal structures, based on density, which could not otherwise be seen. Such visualizations will have a knob that controls the density of the object to be visualized and can, for example, be set to filter out all structures except for bone, muscle, or skin from a person's MRI.

Effective data visualization provides the user with the following:

- Capability to compare data
- Capability to control scale (look from a high level or drill down to detail)
- Capability to map the visualization back to the detail data that created it
- Capability to filter data to look only at subsets of it or sub-regions of it at a given time

As a result, data visualization is used in a number of places within data mining:

- As a first-pass look at the "data mountain," which provides the user with some idea of where to begin mining
- As a way to display the data mining results and predictive model so it is understandable to the end user
- As a way of providing confirmation that the data mining was performed the correct way (for example, to confirm intuitions and common sense at a very high level)
- As a way to perform data mining directly through exploratory analysis, allowing the end user to look for and find patterns so efficiently that it can be done in real time without using automated data mining techniques

Examples of powerful data visualization techniques can be found in Chapter 20, in which we discuss future trends in data mining, text mining, and semantic computing.

Tool Taxonomy

The end user tools area spans a number of components. For example, all end user tools use metadata definitions to obtain access to data stored in the warehouse, and some of these tools (OLAP tools, for example) may employ additional/intermediary data stores (multidimensional database, for example). These additional data stores play a dual role—they may act as specialized data stores for a given end user tool, or just be a subset of the data warehouse covering a specific subject area (a data mart, for example).

For the purpose of this discussion, let's divide these tools into five main groups:

- Data query and reporting tools
- Application development tools
- Executive Information System (EIS) tools
- Online analytical processing tools
- Data mining tools

These tools are discussed in the following sections.

Query and Reporting Tools

This category can be further divided into two groups: reporting tools and managed query tools.

Reporting tools   These tools can be divided into two groups: production reporting tools and desktop report writers, as follows:

- Production reporting tools let companies generate regular operational reports or support high-volume batch jobs, such as calculating and printing paychecks.
- Report writers, on the other hand, are inexpensive desktop tools designed for end users.

Managed query tools   These tools shield end users from the complexities of SQL and database structures by inserting a meta-layer between users and the database. Meta-layer is the software that provides subject-oriented views of a database and supports point-and-click creation of SQL. These tools are designed for ease-of-use, point-and-click, visual navigation that either accepts SQL or generates SQL statements to query relational data stored in the warehouse. Some of these tools format the retrieved data into easy-to-read reports, whereas others concentrate on the onscreen presentation. These tools are the preferred choice of the users of business applications such as segment identification, demographic analysis, territory management, and customer mailing lists. As the complexity of the questions grows, these tools may rapidly become inefficient.

Applications

Often, the analytical needs of the data warehouse user community exceed the built-in capabilities of query and reporting tools. Or, the tools require such a complex set of queries and sophisticated data models that the business users may find themselves overwhelmed by the need to become SQL and/or data modeling experts. This situation will almost certainly defeat the ease-of-use attraction of the query and reporting tools. In this case, organizations will often rely on a true and proven approach of in-house application development, using graphical data access environments designed primarily for client/server environments. Some of these application development platforms integrate well with popular OLAP tools, and can access all major database systems, including Oracle, Sybase, and Informix. Examples of these application development environments include PowerBuilder from PowerSoft, Visual Basic from Microsoft, Forte from Forte Software, and Business Objects from Busi-ness Objects.

OLAP Tools

Online analytical processing (OLAP) tools are based on the concepts of multidimensional databases. They allow a sophisticated user to analyze the data using elaborate, multidimensional, complex views. Typical business applications for these tools include product performance and profitability, effectiveness of a sales program or a marketing campaign, sales forecasting, and capacity planning. These tools assume that the data is organized in a multidimensional model that is supported by a special multidimensional database (MDDB) or by a relational database designed to enable multidimensional properties (multirelational database, or MRDB).

The OLAP tools can be classified as multidimensional, or MOLAP tools (those that operate on multidimensional data stores); relational, or ROLAP tools (those that access data directly from a relational database); and hybrid, or HOLAP tools (those that can combine the capabilities of the previous tool groups). Some of the more popular OLAP tools include Essbase from Arbor/Hyperion, Oracle Express, Cognos PowerPlay, Microstrategy DSS Server, Microsoft Decision Support Service, Prodea from Platinum Technologies, MetaCube from Informix, and Brio Technologies.

Data Mining Tools

A critical success factor for any business today is its capability to use information effectively. This strategic use of data can result from opportunities presented by discovering hidden, previously undetected and frequently extremely valuable facts about consumers, retailers and suppliers; business trends and direction; and significant factors. Knowing this information, an organization can formulate effective business, marketing, and sales strategies; precisely target promotional activity; discover and penetrate new markets; and successfully compete in the marketplace from a position of informed strength. A relatively new and promising technology aimed at achieving this strategic advantage is known as *data mining*.

We have defined data mining as the process of discovering meaningful new correlations, patterns, and trends by digging into (mining) large amounts of data stored in warehouses, using artificial intelligence, statistical and mathematical techniques. Data mining can reach beyond the capabilities of the OLAP, especially because the major attraction of data mining is its capability to build *predictive* rather than *retrospective* models.

Data mining is not specific to any industry—it requires intelligent technologies and the willingness to explore the possibility of hidden knowledge that resides in the data. Industries that are already taking advantage of data mining include retail, financial, medical, manufacturing, environmental, utilities, security, transportation, chemical, insurance, and aerospace. The early success stories are coming primarily from the retail, financial, and medical sectors.

Organizations that use data mining techniques report gaining insights into their respective businesses by revealing implicit relationships, patterns, surprisingly significant facts, trends, exceptions, and anomalies previously unavailable through the human analysts. These experiences show that, although data mining is still an emerging discipline, it has a huge potential to gain significant benefits in the marketplace. Most organizations engage in data mining to do the following:

- *Discovering knowledge*   The goal of knowledge discovery is to determine explicit hidden relationships, patterns, or correlations from data stored in an enterprise's database. Specifically, data mining can be used to perform the following:

  - *Segmentation*   (for example, to group customer records for custom-tailored marketing)

  - *Classification*   (assignment of input data to a predefined class, discovery and understanding of trends, and text document classification)

  - *Association*   (discovery of cross-sales opportunities)

  - *Preferencing*   (determining preference of customer's majority)

- *Visualizing data*   Analysts must make sense out of a huge amount of information stored in corporate databases. Prior to any analysis, the goal is to "humanize" the mass of data they must deal with and find a clever way to display the data.

- *Correct data*   While consolidating massive databases, many enterprises find that the data is not complete, and discover that it invariably contains erroneous and contradictory information. Data mining techniques can help identify and correct problems in the most consistent way possible. The number of applications within this category is somewhat limited due to the difficult nature of the correction process. Replacing missing values, or correcting what are perceived to be "wild" values, requires judgment calls that are difficult to provide automatically.

The strategic value of data mining is time-sensitive, especially in the retail, marketing and finance sectors of the industry. Indeed, organizations that exploit the data first will gain a strategic advantage in serving and attracting customers. Consequently, the benefits derived from the data mining process provide early adopters of the technology with a sustainable competitive advantage.

Using data mining to build predictive models in decision making has several benefits. A model should explain why a particular decision was made. Adjusting a model based on feedback from future decisions will lead to experience accumulation and true organizational learning. Finally, a predictive model can be used to automate a decision step in a larger process. For example, using a model to instantly predict whether a consumer will default on his credit card payments will allow automatic adjustment of credit limits, rather than depending on expensive staff that make inconsistent decisions.

Data mining tools and their applications, including their role in the Customer Relationship Management, are the main subjects of this book.

Data Marts

The concept of the data mart is causing a lot of excitement and attracting much attention in the data warehouse industry. In general, data marts are being presented as an inexpensive alternative to a data warehouse, taking significantly less time and money to build. However, the term *data mart* means different things to different people.

A rigorous definition of data mart states that it is a data store that is a subsidiary of a data warehouse of integrated data. The data mart is directed at a partition of data (often called a *subject area*) that is created for the use of a dedicated group of users. A data mart might, in fact, be a set of denormalized, summarized, or aggregated data.

Sometimes, such a set could be placed on the data warehouse database rather than a physically separate store of data. In most instances, however, the data mart is a physically separate store of data; and it is normally resident on a separate database server, often on the local area network serving a dedicated user group. Sometimes, the data mart simply comprises relational OLAP (online analytical processing) technology, which creates highly denormalized star schema relational designs, or hypercubes, of data for analysis by groups of users with a common interest in a limited portion of the database. In other cases, the data warehouse architecture may incorporate data mining tools that extract sets of data for a particular type of analysis. All these types of data marts, called *dependent data marts* because the data content is sourced from the data warehouse, have a high value. No matter how many are deployed and no matter now many different enabling technologies are used, the different users are all accessing the information views derived from the same single integrated version of the data.

Unfortunately, the misleading statements about the simplicity and low cost of data marts sometimes result in organizations or vendors incorrectly positioning them as an alternative to the data warehouse. This viewpoint defines *independent data marts* that, in fact, represent fragmented point solutions to a range of business problems in the enterprise. This type of implementation should be rarely deployed in the context of an overall technology or applications architecture. Indeed, it is missing the ingredient that is at the heart of the data warehousing concept—that of data integration. Each independent data mart makes its own assumptions about how to consolidate the data, and the data across several data marts may not be consistent.

Moreover, the concept of an independent data mart is dangerous—as soon as the first data mart is created, other organizations, groups, and subject areas within the enterprise embark on the task of building their own data marts. As a result, you create an environment in which multiple operational systems feed multiple non-integrated data marts that are often overlapping in data content, job scheduling, connectivity, and management. In other words, you have transformed a complex *many-to-one* problem of building a data warehouse from operational and external data sources to a *many-to-many* sourcing and management nightmare.

Another consideration against independent data marts is related to the potential scaleability problem: the first simple and inexpensive

data mart was most probably designed without any serious consideration about the scaleability (for example, you wouldn't consider an
expensive parallel-computing platform for an "inexpensive" and
"small" data mart). But, because usage begets usage, the initial small
data mart needs to grow (in data sizes and in the number of concurrent
users) without any capability to do so in a scaleable fashion.

We would like to make clear that the point-solution independent
data mart is not necessarily a bad thing, and it is often a necessary
and valid solution to a pressing business problem, thus achieving the
goal of rapid delivery of enhanced decision support functionality to
end users. The business drivers underlying such developments
include the following:

- Extremely urgent user requirements
- The absence of a budget for a full data warehouse strategy
- The absence of a sponsor for an enterprise-wide decision support
  strategy.
- The decentralization of business units
- The attraction of easy-to-use tools and a mind-sized project

To address the data integration issues associated with data marts,
the recommended approach proposed by Ralph Kimball is as follows:
For any two data marts in an enterprise, the common dimensions
must conform to the *equality and rollup* rule. This rule says that
these dimensions are either the same or one is a strict rollup of
another.

Thus, in a retail store chain, if the purchase orders database is one
data mart and the sales database is another data mart, the two data
marts will form a coherent part of an overall enterprise data warehouse if their common dimensions (for example, time and products)
conform. The time dimensions from both data marts might be at the
individual day level, or, conversely, one time dimension is at the day
level but the other is at the week level. Because days roll into weeks,
the two time dimensions are conformed. The time dimensions would
not be conformed if one time dimension were weeks and the other time
dimension were fiscal quarters. The resulting data marts could not
usefully coexist in the same application.

In summary, data marts present two problems: the problem of scaleability in situations where an initial small data mart grows quickly in multiple dimensions, and the problem of data integration. Therefore, when designing data marts, the organization should pay close attention to system scaleability, data consistency, and manageability issues. The key to a successful data mart strategy is the development of an overall scaleable data warehouse architecture, and the key step in that architecture is identifying and implementing the common dimensions.

Data Warehouse Administration and Management

Data warehouses tend to be as much as four times as large as related operational databases, reaching terabytes in size, depending on how much history needs to be saved. They are not synchronized in real time to the associated operational data, but are updated as often as once a day if the application requires it.

In addition to the main architectural components already described, almost all data warehouse products include gateways to transparently access multiple enterprise data sources without having to rewrite applications to interpret and utilize the data. Furthermore, in a heterogeneous data warehouse environment, the various databases reside on disparate systems, thus requiring internetworking tools. Although there are no special data warehousing internetworking technologies, and a typical data warehouse implementation relies on the same communications software as messaging and transaction processing systems, the need to manage this infrastructure component is obvious.

To summarize, managing data warehouses (item 6 of Figure 4-1) includes the following:

■ Security and priority management

■ Monitoring updates from multiple sources

■ Data quality checks

■ Managing and updating metadata

- Auditing and reporting data warehouse usage and status (for managing the response time and resource utilization, and providing chargeback information)
- Purging data
- Replicating, subsetting, distributing data
- Backup and recovery
- Data warehouse storage management (for example, capacity planning; hierarchical storage management, or HSM; purging of aged data)

Impact of the Web

Even a surface analysis of the information technology industry indicates that the two most pervasive themes in computing have been the Internet/WWW and data warehousing. From a marketing perspective, a marriage of these two giant technologies is a natural and unavoidable event. The reason for these trends is simple: the compelling advantages in using the Web for access are magnified even further in a data warehouse.

The magnification of the scaleability and accessibility brought by the Web has been facilitated by the maturity in scaleable database technology, rapidly improving network bandwidth and transmission rates, the availability of robust OLAP and data mining tools, digital telephony, and efficient and cost-effective storage devices, to name just a few.

We already stated that the value of the information in data warehouses is extraordinary. If you look at the revenue potential of a purchased data, you'll see multimillion dollar revenue streams selling this data via static magnetic media or using online access. (For example, A.C. Nielsen of Schaumburg, Ill. provides data on more than one million consumer products to consumer package goods manufacturers, retailers and brokers.) The interesting fact is that the industry has so far extracted approximately one percent of the value from these warehouses. This is mostly because of the technical, logistical, security, and management difficulties of deploying data warehouses to large numbers of users across organizational boundaries, while relying on conventional client/server technology.

Fortunately, the challenges of deploying decision support applications are being addressed by Internet technology. The intranet movement has resulted in a drastic decrease in the capital intensity and the project expense of creating and deploying applications on the Web. Today, corporations can set up a RDBMS server, DSS server and Web server in a single location; build a decision support application using standard tools; and then immediately deploy to hundreds or even thousands of users anywhere on the corporate intranet.

Application maintenance, code upgrades, and security privileges are now administered centrally. New users can be brought online quickly and with minimal effort; and support of the client software, operating system and network components can be outsourced much more easily.

Another argument for the Internet/intranet deployment of data warehouses is the realization that the customer does not necessarily need to own and maintain the data warehouse in order to obtain useful insight from it. There are whole classes of decision-support reports that can be obtained using the data collected by transaction providers or syndicators. In order to obtain this insight in an economical and practical fashion, the data must be centrally captured and maintained by the service originator, and then distributed back to customer firms in the form of a commercial DSS offering. We can see these widely deployed data warehouses as the killer applications of the Web.

As an example, consider deploying a single relational online analytical processing (OLAP) application, such as the Sabre computer reservation system, to thousands of client firms via the Web. As a result, consumers can now perform travel planning and purchase tickets over the Web (http://www.travelocity.com/). The goal of this deployment is to automate travel budgeting, booking, and data analysis to help corporations control travel expenses and better manage quality. Consider how many corporations would like to take advantage of this opportunity and at the same time cut the inefficiencies from their travel processes.

The implications are awesome. This single application would likely have 100 to 500 times as many users as the typical modern data warehouse. The value-in-use of this system would be proportional to the number of users, and far exceeds many data warehousing efforts performed to date. A conservative estimate would place the recoverable waste in a $20 million company's travel budget at $20,000 annually, which implies billions of dollars in potential savings for a system broadly deployed. Providers of a data warehouse application like this would benefit either from selling the DSS service or by using it to obtain greater market share for its transaction services.

There are thousands of data warehousing applications, including banking, purchasing, travel, insurance, supply chain, credit card, market research, credit, investment analysis, telecommunications, federal, defense, municipal, and more that are worth selling via the Web; and a ready and willing customer base of millions. The result is a consumer market for decision support, with billions of dollars of revenue for those companies capable of making the transition and providing solutions for the new medium.

Approaches to Using the Web

Web access to a data warehouse should be an open solution, allowing the use of any Web browser or Web server. Obviously, the look and feel of the client presentation can be enhanced with Java applets to build more powerful applications and utilize JavaScript language. Any Web authoring tool can be used for the page design. Additionally, Web browsers incorporate many attributes that are especially useful in analytical applications as standard features. These attributes include local caching of pages, which drastically improves the response time for repetitive analyses; viewing of partial results as the page is loaded, which is particularly useful for speed-of-thought analysis; and asynchronous processing, data compression, and data encryption features that may not be included in client-server OLAP, query, or reporting tools. See Figure 4-2.

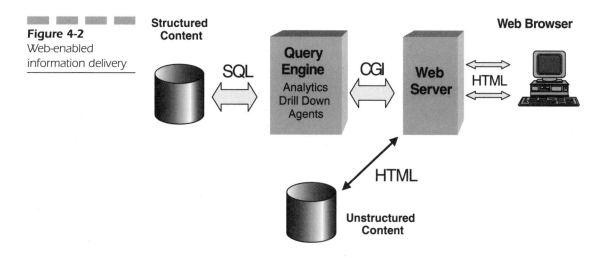

Figure 4-2
Web-enabled
information delivery

In short, Web access can be an extremely cost-effective way to provide widespread connection, achieving remarkable economies of scale.

Design Options and Issues

Issues Web access offers some clear advantages over existing architectures, but there are some very clear issues and concerns. To deal with these issues successfully, one has to understand the general usage patterns of Web users. These issues include the following:

- *Security.* The availability of sensitive company information to almost everybody on the Web is a serious concern. Of course, encryption schemes and secure servers have reduced the exposure, but still the most secure solution is to use intranets and hide the valuable information behind robust firewalls.

- *Performance.* This issue is the result of a potentially significant increase in the user base. Designing for scaleability should help, but sometimes an underlying technology presents a formidable obstacle. One specific technology in question relates to the way corporate databases talk to the Web. The CGI (Common Gateway Interface) protocol for message passing to and from Web servers is inefficient (single-threaded), and requires writing code in C, which is a step backward in a drive toward 4GL tools for higher developer productivity. There are alternatives to gateways and CGI, including Java scripts and servlets that help solve this particular problem.

- *Statelessness.*   The interaction between a Web browser and a Web server is stateless, meaning that the familiar client/server notion of a connection to a data source just doesn't exist in the Web. The Web server acts as a message-passing server, responding to messages it receives, and in turn, contacting other resources on the network or replying to the Web browser. If each query to a database through a Web browser required a connection and login to the database, the accumulated overhead would have a severe negative impact on the database server and consequently on the user. This particular problem has a number of solutions. One is to employ the Web gateways using the CGI API: when the user generates a query, product-specific tags are inserted into HTML and passed to the Web server. These are then passed to the Web gateway, which generates the request in the API of the data server. The process is reversed on the way back to the user, passing the returned data to the Web gateway, which converts it to HTML and sends it to the Web server. By maintaining the connection to the data sources from the server and keeping track of each client messaging in from the Web browsers, the data or the analytic (OLAP) engines control the whole interaction. This gets around the stateless problem of the Web.

- *Functionality.*   This issue is more evident on the example of the OLAP drill-down—a common manipulation technique that creates a series of analyses, each containing more detail about all or part of the previous analysis. This is often displayed as a series of overlapped windows in step fashion, lending a handy visual metaphor to the process. This memory of previous analyses is often referred to as a context of the interaction.

Reproducing this in a Web browser requires some elaborate designs. For example, the Web gateways for these products will have to produce much more complex pages that look like overlapped windows. This may have performance implications as well.

- *Presentation.* Data visualization is one of the key elements of analytical processing. The standard method for displaying graphics with Web browsers now is to broadcast the images from the server, which can be prohibitively slow. In order to draw charts dynamically at the client, based on a small burst of data from the server, additional capabilities need to be built into the products—usually involving charting applets developed in Java or Microsoft's ActiveX.

To optimize a data warehouse for the Web, designers have to deal with security, performance, persistence (the stateless nature of HTTP), and complexities of the multi-tiered architecture. Some of these issues are not new, and have been successfully addressed in distributed client/server architectures. Therefore, we can offer the following suggestions:

- Design your data warehouse very carefully. Try to avoid the usual pitfalls, and focus on scaleability and integration. This includes an understanding and efficient exploitation of multi-threading (for example, remember that CGI is not multi-threaded).

- Minimize the number and size of data transmissions per access. Consider not using or reducing the number of frames (each frame is probably a separate transmission). Take advantage of generating dynamic pages and transmitting changes only.

- Use more server-based processing, including stored procedures and server-side functions.

- Ensure that the server is extensible, highly available, and that its workload is balanced. It is especially important in the Web environment, in which thin clients prevail (use technologies such as Java applets and servlets).

The technologies supporting the Internet and the Web continue to advance very rapidly. Therefore, when evaluating data warehousing products for Web access, you can safely assume that the features you see in the current release should not be the deciding factor. In order to stay competitive, the vendors will continue to improve their products' Web capabilities.

XML

XML, which stands for eXtensible Markup Language, is the descendent of the Standard Generalized Markup Language (SGML), which is the parent of the current generation of markup languages. SGML is a very complex language that came out of the publishing and natural-language-processing communities. Originally, it had support from a number of tool vendors, including ArborText and OmniMark. In 1986, SGML was accepted as an ISO standard (ISO 8879) and found its place at large corporations, where it was used to encode and structure technical documents.

With the emergence of the Internet and HTML came the realization that the rich functionality of SGML was difficult to deliver to the Internet due to its complexity and the wealth of options. At the same time, if SGML was too "heavyweight" for the Internet, HTML was "lightweight," but not suitable for defining data structures. Furthermore, HTML cannot be extended with new tags, so it does not support user-defined typing. As a result, the new approach, which focused more on data structures and less on presentation, was born.

In the summer of 1996, Jon Bosak of Sun Microsystems formed the XML Working Group under the auspices of World Wide Web Consortium (W3C). According to the formal design goals of the XML Working Group, XML should be the following:

- Easy to use over the Internet
- Compatible with SGML
- Capable to be processed by easy-to-write programs
- Legible and reasonably clear to users

In addition to the XML standard, several auxiliary standards are needed to complete the functionality of XML. For example, XSL, XLink, and XPointer are among the proposed standards that provide XML support for style sheets, hyperlinks, and other features.

XML Basic Syntax XML is a markup language like HTML, which requires special markers called *tags* to be added to text documents to give some added meaning to the document. However, the ultimate goal of XML is to convert a text stream into a data object that can have a highly complex internal structure.

The power of XML lies in its capability to define how to encode structured data into a text stream in a standard way. Because the encoding is standard, everyone can read the structure and understand the message. XML can turn a text byte stream into a structured data object that is ready for use in applications.

Moreover, XML is extensible because it allows users to define their own data and document types. It supports a hierarchy of tags that provide the structure of a document or a data object. The XML-defined object may look like an object model or like a parse tree, and is easy to read by humans and computers. An XML document forms a coherent set of tagged elements that are properly nested and constructed. In short, XML can be used to easily represent relational and object data models, and it is easy to parse.

Even more interesting, XML allows for verification of the validity of the document (structure, missing data, and incorrect type of data). This capability is provided by declaring the exact structure of the document. This is done using a document type declaration (DTD).

The DTD contains a number of object attributes, some of which can function like primary and foreign keys in a data model. That allows for key-like document searching.

To summarize, XML provides enough syntax and mechanisms to declare the structure and contents of most data objects.

XML Products and Tools Although many commercial XML products are still relatively immature, they can already benefit an enterprise by decreasing the cost of the project by using XML-based technologies to manipulate application configuration files. Using XML can reduce custom logic and increase application reliability and consistency. Many message brokers (for example, TSI International Software's Mercator and Active Software's ActiveWorks) can manipulate XML data natively, which reduces custom logic. So, if an organization decides to adopt XML, it needs to understand the XML tools landscape. The list of the tool categories that are required to successfully develop XML applications includes the following:

- *XML parsers.* A number of XML parsers are available on the market, including parsers from Sun, DataChannel, IBM (XML Parser for Java, C++), Microsoft (XML Parser for Java, C++), and Oracle (XML Parser for Java).

- *XML repositories.* Examples of XML repositories are Object Design's eXcelon and Software, DataChannel's Xstor, and X-Machine (Tamino).

- *XML application servers.* The examples of XML application servers include Arkona's Universal Update Server, Bluestone Software's XML-Server, Innovision's Financial Server, Microsoft's BizTalk Server, OnDisplay's CenterStage, Oracle's Oracle8i, Sybase's Financial Server, and webMethods' B2B Integration Server.

- *XML authoring tools.* Although XML documents can be built by using just a text editor, specialized editors are necessary for building large numbers of data and document objects and DTDs. Major software vendors are rapidly moving toward extending their product offerings to support XML. For example, Microsoft Office 2000 is positioned to support the publishing of XML documents.

- *XML databases.* As the amount of XML-encoded data increases, it becomes advantageous to store the data in a native XML database. Many traditional database vendors are in the process of enabling native XML support in their products. Moreover, emerging standards, such as XQL for querying XML documents, will probably result in the appearance of the specialized XML data stores.

- *XML-enabled browsers.* The majority of popular browsers support receiving data in XML and presentation instructions in XML Style Sheet Language, or XSL. Examples include Microsoft's Internet Explorer v.5.0 and Netscape Communications' Navigator v.5.0.

- Middleware

  - *Message-oriented middleware.* (MOM): XML appears to be a natural fit for a message-oriented middleware technology designed to link and integrate distributed loosely coupled enterprise systems. Thus, many MOM vendors are in the process of adding XML support to their products. Examples of MOM products include Active Software's ActiveWorks, IBM's MQIntegrator, New Era of Network's NEONet, Tibco's Active Enterprise, TSI International Software's Mercator, and Vitria Technology's BusinessWare.

- *Remote procedure calls (RPC).* This group of middleware tools focuses on supporting RPC requests between Web servers, enabling direct execution of RPCs and transactions over the Internet. An example of this class of tools is WIDL from webMethods.

- *Business object libraries.* In the absence of completed and accepted relevant standard definitions, the current suites of business object libraries have been mostly developed by individual companies such as CommerceOne/Veo Systems' CBL (Common Business Library), Ariba cXML (commercial XML), and Microsoft BizTalk.

- *XML/EDI engines.* The adoption of standard business objects for XML is the prerequisite for XML to become a viable alternative to EDI. Among the pioneers in this space is Sterling Commerce that developed a data transformation engine to support XML. Similar activities are happening in the financial services markets. For example, J.P. Morgan & Co. and PricewaterhouseCoopers LLP recently announced the release of FpML (financial products markup language). This is a new protocol for Internet-based electronic dealing and information sharing of financial derivatives, initially handling interest rate and foreign exchange products. Another example is that the data interchange protocol called FIX is being expanded to enable XML (FIXML). A similar effort is underway to expand another financial data exchange protocol, called SWIFT, to become XML-enabled.

- *XML data integration.* XML-based data is typically expressed in a *syntax* that is based on the XML specifications. Other applications can parse XML data, but in order for the application to *understand* this data, the data itself has to convey the meaning (*semantics*). Sophisticated semantic XML specifications are still being developed. Indeed, major database vendors (IBM, Oracle, and Sybase) and enterprise resource planning vendors (Oracle, PeopleSoft and SAP) are delivering XML interfaces so that data can be exchanged in XML. Those interfaces facilitate direct access to data from XML-enabled application servers, clients, and other technologies.

XML Middleware   Among the potentially valuable opportunities offered by XML is its capability to provide certain middleware functionality with relative ease, as follows:

- XML specification is relatively short and easier to understand and implement than other standards.
- Data formatted by using the base XML is positioned to take advantage of possible semantic interoperability when XML semantic specifications are finalized.
- XML is inherently Web-oriented, and is designed specifically for (but not limited to) Web-based resources, including HTML documents and HTTP-based communications.
- XML is driving the development of new XML-based application functionality (for example, Resource Description Framework and WebBroker) that is inherently designed to enable Web-based application integration.

In short, XML is ideally positioned to become a middleware solution for Web-enabled application integration projects.

As we stated earlier, there are two major classes of XML middleware: RPC-based and messaging-based. The latter doesn't change the basic messaging paradigm, and is being adopted by many messaging middleware vendors.

The former, on the other hand, is somewhat unique in that it enables a direct execution of applications and transactions over the HTTP on the Web. As an example, consider webMethods' WIDL. It is an XML-based middleware that encodes an RPC request as an XML document. WebMethods' WIDL server can exchange WIDL requests with another WIDL server over HTTP (see Figure 4-3).

This approach provides a native wide area network middleware that can pass requests across Internet firewalls. This solution is significantly different from the LAN-based middleware solutions, which

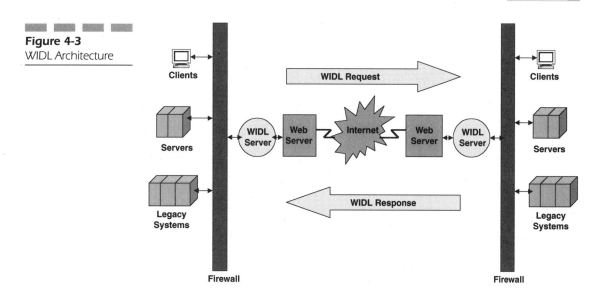

Figure 4-3
WIDL Architecture

have to overcome the challenges of running on the Internet without resorting to HTTP tunneling or other such techniques.

XML-Enabled Opportunities   The richness of capabilities and a promise of reduced project costs offered by XML means that adopting an XML approach may have a significant impact on the IT architecture in general, and on the data warehousing and CRM architecture in particular.

XML can provide enterprises with long-term, incremental application-integration project cost savings. It can also provide increased opportunities for improvements in application data interoperability. These include universal data format; a serialization of data objects into text streams; the production of documents that can be passed easily over a variety of network protocols; and a rich set of complementary standards to support browser presentation, hyperlinks, and querying.

A number of application categories are currently being built by using XML. Among them are the applications dealing with document management, e-commerce, data interchange, and many others. As far as the main topic of this book is concerned, XML is emerging as a key vehicle for the following:

- Data and metadata interchange for data sourcing (Extract, Transform, Load [ETL] applications)
- Data acquisition from the customer touchpoints across the variety of channels within the CRM framework
- Data integration for data warehousing and OLAP applications

A brief list of the some of more common application areas includes the following:

- *Information interchange.*   Metadata and content exchange between software tools. This approach is being actively explored in the data warehouse, CRM, and OLAP markets.

- *Document repository.*   Similar to traditional SGML usage, an XML document repository can store documents in XML; and deliver in a variety of presentation formats, including HTML, searchable catalogs, and print catalogs.

- *Business-to-business exchanges.*   As more business object formats are standardized in XML, businesses can share information and/or transactions across the Web more easily. Procurement systems are taking the lead in adopting this type of business-to-business data interchange (for example, Web sites that provide shared product catalogs from multiple suppliers to multiple buyers).

Communication between Web applications is far easier to build over HTTP than over other protocols/middleware, such as IIOP/CORBA and COM+. Thus, the most exciting new architectural approach may be the capability to use XML-based middleware, and the exchange of XML business objects to integrate business processes across corporate firewalls. XML promises to bring IT architecture to a new level and an opportunity to exploit this technology in future environments.

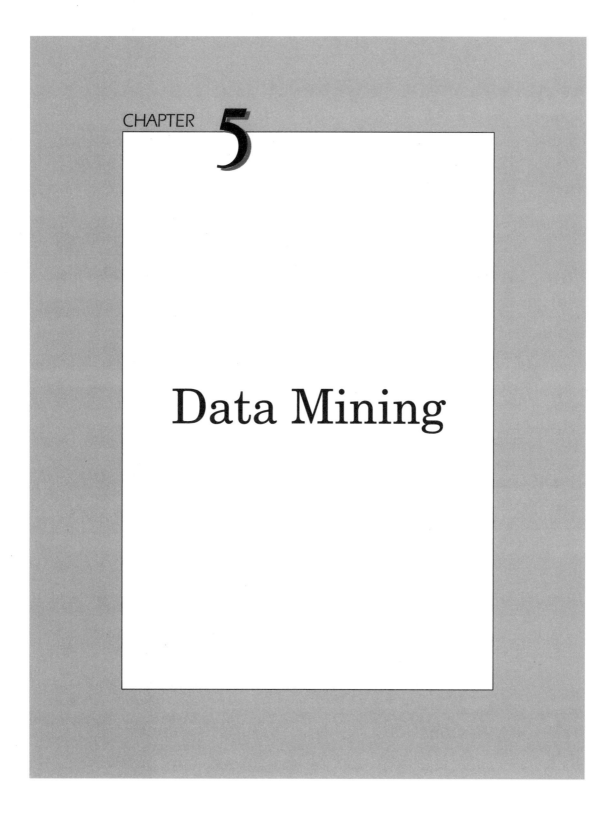

CHAPTER 5

Data Mining

What Is Data Mining?

In this chapter, we will give you an introduction to what data mining is and what it is not. This can be a somewhat difficult task because the term "data mining" is being redefined today by the popular press to mean something much broader than its original definition. In today's computer industry, the term has caught on—at least in part because it seems so understandable to the average businessperson or even IT professional. Much as "data warehousing" as a term made good intuitive sense to most people ("Hey, let's have a common area where we can store and distribute all of our enterprise-wide data— just like a warehouse is the common place for storing and distributing real inventory"), data mining also seems to make good sense ("Now that I've built this mountain of data in my data warehouse, I now need a way to systematically go through it and understand it. I know that a lot of my data is not useful or interesting to me at this time, but I need some tools to use to mine through the data in order to find the valuable pieces of information"). Despite mixing the metaphors of a warehouse and a mountain, the analogies appeal to information workers because they represent two of the hardest problems they have:

■ Where do I go to get my data and how do I store it?

■ Now that I've stored it, what do I do with it?

The Mining Analogy

Data Mining gains its name, and to some degree its popularity, by playing off of a meaning that the data that you have stored is much like a "mountain" and that buried within the mountain (just as buried within your data) are certain "gems" of great value. The problem is that there are also lots of non-valuable rocks and rubble in the mountain that need to be mined through and discarded in order to get to that which is valuable. The trick is that both for mountains of rock and mountains of data you need some power tools to unearth the value of the data. For rock, this means earthmovers and dynamite; for data, this means powerful computers and data mining software.

What Data Mining Isn't

Statistics

The basic algorithms or "recipes" that guide data mining tools through the data to uncover the gems are often derived either directly from statistics or from the same basic techniques that are used in statistics. In general, though, statistical tools take longer to run, are less robust on messy real world data, and must often be wielded by a master craftsman. Data mining tools are often more forgiving and, if packaged correctly with the right user interface, will allow the end user to wield the tool with a minimum of training (although the end user will still need to understand both the data and the business problem well).

OLAP

Online Analytical Processing is the name given to the database and user interface tools that allow end users to quickly navigate within their data. Keep in mind that any navigating that can be done is done because the data has be re-formed and recompiled in a way that makes it possible to access. The data itself really hasn't changed. If we stretch the mining analogy a bit, we could say that OLAP provides a tool for looking quickly anywhere within the mountain. What it doesn't do is tell you what is valuable and what isn't, and it still requires you to find the important and valuable places within the mountain. Which, if the mountain is large, can be quite a time-consuming task in and of itself, even if the OLAP tools are very powerful for getting you where you want to go quite quickly.

Data Warehousing

Data mining is different from data warehousing in that one of the most painful and difficult prerequisites to finding the gems in your mountain is to have the mining rights to the mountain itself! Outside of the mining analogy, this means that it is important to have a place where all of the data is collected and organized as much as possible. It must be cleansed as much as possible as well, so that there are no errors in the data. Otherwise, what you are looking at might be fool's gold, not real gold.

Data Mining Has Come of Age

Have you heard about data mining? Pick up the latest issue of your favorite industry or business magazine, and you may well find an article talking about "data mining." What is data mining? And why are so many people talking about it in both the computer industry and in direct marketing?

The answer is simple: *data mining helps end users extract useful business information from large databases.* What makes this definition interesting is the word "large." If the database were small, you wouldn't need any new technology to discover useful information. If, for instance, you lived in the early 1800s and you were the owner of a general store, you wouldn't need to employ data mining (or direct marketing) because you would probably have only a few hundred customers. You would know each of them by name, who they were, and what they bought. When you have only a few hundred customers, you really don't need much of a computer to mine the data. The best database analysis and predictive models could be done in the shopkeeper's head.

Today, however, the "shopkeeper" of the new millennium has hundreds of thousands to millions of customers. For the first time in history, the data on these customers is being accumulated at one location, where consistent access and consistent storage is being guaranteed—the data warehouse. The metaphors between "data warehouses" and "data mining" can be confusing. The idea that ties them together is that the large data collection in your data warehouse is the "data mountain" presented to data mining tools. Data warehousing allows you to build that mountain. Data mining allows you to sift that mountain down to the essential information that is useful to your business.

What is so new about extracting information from data to make your businesses run better? You've been doing that for years? Right? In fact, what you see, as various new data mining products begin to enter the marketplace, is that many of them perform the same types of activities that were performed by the other database products. Once the data warehouse exists, you have to have ways to look at it and navigate it. If the database is of any reasonable size (typically, they are made up of hundreds of millions to billions of records), you can no longer easily access it via a spreadsheet, and to do so you need to move into the realm of the tools created for database professionals. These tools allow you to access your database via a language called SQL (Structured Query Language). SQL is the lingua franca of those other brave souls, climbing the data mountain. The problem is that SQL, though standard, is different from the language that most people in marketing speak. Sort of like having to communicate your business problem by using only a computer language. You can say what you need to say, but it will be difficult to get the point across and the result may be so complex that it may have many'errors.

The allure of data mining is that it promises to fix the problem of miscommunication between you and your data, and allows you to ask complex questions of your data, such as "What has been going on?" or "What is going to happen next and how can I profit?" The answer to the first question can be provided by the data warehouse and multidimensional database technology that allow the user to easily navigate and visualize the data. The answer to the second question can be provided by data mining tools built on some of the latest computer algorithms: Decision Trees (CART, CHAID, AID), Neural Networks, Nearest Neighbor, and Rule Induction.

The Motivation for Data Mining Is Tremendous

As an example of the impact that data mining can have on a business, consider the following direct marketing problem. John, a typical cellular phone user, has just decided not to renew his contract with you, his current cellular provider. Why? Because he was just made an offer by the competing provider for a free phone. Because that Motorola phone that he got from you last year was really starting to look like old technology and the competition had the same rate plan that you have, John opted for their offer. This is good news for John and good news for John's new cellular provider, but really bad news for John's old provider (you), who invested in John to the tune of $700 to land him as a customer less than one year ago. The sad thing is that if you had only known that John was at risk of leaving, you surely would have invested the extra $100 to upgrade John's phone (John does $350 worth of calling per month). Now that John has signed the contract with the competition, it is too late. The really aggravating thing is that you could have known that John was at risk. If you had used data mining on your customer account database, you could have built a predictive model that would have shown that John and others like him are at grave risk of attrition. With this predictive model, you could have launched a successful and profitable direct marketing campaign to save your valuable customers.

Today, the cellular phone industry looks very much the way the credit card industry looked only a few years ago. The cellular industry is growing at around 50% per year, and everyone is scrambling for market share. At the same time, margins are dropping as the industry becomes more and more competitive, and as the market begins to saturate. What happens when everyone who wants a cellular phone already has one? What happens when the market saturates and everyone starts playing a zero-sum game of trading customers? This is the state of the credit card industry today, and it may foreshadow some of what is to come in the next five years for the cellular industry. Specifically, some of the methods and techniques for preventing and reversing customer attrition that are in use today in the credit industry may well make sense for the cellular industry. One of these techniques, data mining, has been employed within the credit industry with very positive results.

The following should sound somewhat familiar to the path the cellular industry has been taking recently: In 1981, there were 116 million credit cards issued in the United States; within ten years, there were more than 263 million. In the next ten years, however, there was not another doubling of this number because there are only 250 million people in the United States and they can only carry so many credit cards with them in their wallets and purses. It is, in fact, the belief of industry analysts that the credit card market has already stopped growing and has been saturated since 1988.

Such a saturated marketplace means that whatever gains are made by one company come only at the expense of another—a zero-sum game. Those customers lost to competitors are called "attriters," and credit card companies can typically lose 1 to 10 percent of their customers to their competition each year. In the long run, the winners are those who eke out fractional improvements in understanding and reacting to their customers' needs. The key attribute of these winning companies is their capability to retain their good customers at minimum cost. Data mining tools that make use of existing customer transactional and demographic data are a necessity for the credit industry, and will likely become so for the cellular industry as well. Those companies in the cellular industry that can prepare for this shift to a saturated market will be in the best possible position when it actually occurs.

Learning from Your Past Mistakes

"Those who cannot remember the past are condemned to repeat it"
— G. Santayana

How does data mining work? It isn't magic. Instead, it works the same way as a human being does. It uses historical information (experience) to learn from the past. However, in order for the data mining technology to pull the "gold" out of your database, you do have to tell it what the gold looks like (what business problem you would like to solve). It then uses the description of that "gold" to look for similar examples in the database, and uses these pieces of information from the past to develop a predictive model of what will happen in the future.

For instance, let's say that you have a direct marketing program, and you want to make an offer to only that subset of your customers who would be interested in such an offer. Contacting only those customers who would be interested optimizes your profit by maximizing your revenue while minimizing your costs. It also is good news for your prospects and current customers because they are not bothered with offers that don't make sense for them. Examples include mailing out offers for balance transfer to credit card customers, or targeting interested customer segments with niche catalogs for a catalog house selling craft supplies.

The trick to building a successful predictive model is to have some data in your database that describes what has happened in the past. If you have already sent out a small test mailing, you now have some information about what types of customers responded and which ones didn't. Data mining tools are designed to learn from these past successes and failures (just as you would), and then be able to predict what is going to happen next. One of the key differences between you and a data mining tool is that the data mining tool can automatically go through the entire database and find even the smallest pattern that may help in a better prediction. These tools also check for the statistical significance of the pattern and report it back to the user. For instance, suppose that your data mining tool found that 100% of the people in the database from one particular ZIP code with high credit limits responded to your offer, but that there were only three people with these characteristics. The data mining tool would report this information, with a warning that it was very likely to be an idiosyncrasy of the database rather than a usable predictive pattern.

Data Mining? Don't Need It — I've Got Statistics

An obvious question at this point is to ask how data mining differs from statistics. After all, people have been using statistics for better targeting of their marketing efforts for many years now.

Statistics has the same general uses and results as data mining. Regression is often used in statistics to create models that are predictive of customer behavior, and these models are built from large stores of historical data. The main difference between data mining and statistics is that data mining is meant to be used by the business end user—not the statistician. Data mining effectively automates the statistical process, thereby relieving some of the burden from the end user. This results in a tool that is easier to use. For instance, it may have occurred to you to ask "If most of statistics is a matter of making a guess and then checking it out, why don't we just let the computers make those guesses and then test them automatically?"

For this reason, data mining tools are often coupled with other tools that make it easier to apply data-analysis techniques and understand the results. These tools then no longer need to be wielded solely by the data analyst, but used instead by the business user. This may sound like a dangerous idea—giving powerful predictive technologies to an end user who may or may not have taken a statistics course on his way to completing his MBA. The capability to keep business users from harm while allowing them to access much of the power of predictive and descriptive data analysis is why data mining is a technology to watch.

Measuring Data Mining Effectiveness — Accuracy, Speed, Cost

For someone who might like to use a data mining tool, there are many choices. To make the right one, they need to evaluate it in comparison to existing statistical techniques and also compare among the large number of new data mining products that are currently on the market. Data mining technology is actually quite similar to statistics in the way it builds a predictive model from data. Often, the accuracy of that prediction depends more on the correct deployment of the technology and the quality of the data than it does on the technology itself. The choice of data mining should be driven by the advantages that it brings to the bottom line of the entire business process—not just the statistical predictive accuracy.

Let's look a little more closely at the complete calculation of profit or return on investment from a targeted marketing offer, and contrast it to the way that these targeted marketing offers are now being performed.

In the following example, we are mailing out offers to customers. If they respond, we make money; if they don't respond, we lose money proportional to the cost of the mailing (and sometimes proportional to the cost of the offer). Let's assume that the size of the targeted customers is fixed (this is often the case because of fixed marketing budgets), and call it the "target size." Then:

- Profit = Revenue–Fixed Costs–Variable Cost × Target Size

- Revenue = Responders × Response Value

- Fixed Costs = Marketing Design + Production + Infrastructure + Mistakes

The impact of predictive accuracy can be seen in the revenue calculation by noting that in many cases:

Responders = Target Size × Prediction Accuracy

For a given size customer or prospect target population, the higher the predictive accuracy of the technique being used, the greater the number of responders that will be captured in that targeted set. It is often argued that data mining techniques such as neural networks will increase the predictive accuracy beyond what can be attained via standard statistical techniques. The reality is, however, that many of the techniques do quite well and their relative success is more often due to data quality and data quantity, and the skills of the person wielding the tool. There can also be some variation in optimal accuracy among the models from problem to problem in different domains.

The other way that data mining techniques are often measured is by speed. The reasoning is that the faster the tool runs, the larger is the data set to which it can be applied. The larger the database is, the better the accuracy of the predictive model will be. Thus, many data mining tools are implemented on parallel computers in order to increase the speed of their execution. This improved speed can be substantial (factors of a thousand or more speedup).

To truly determine which technologies are best, it is helpful to look at the big picture, which includes a much larger business process than just data analysis. The full process includes data collection, data analysis (data mining), predictive model visualization, and the launching of a marketing program against a customer set. Too often, data analysis tools are measured only by their predictive accuracy (where it is difficult to distinguish a winner) and their speed. But these systems do not work in isolation. They are part of this much larger picture, and the tools that provide adequate predictive accuracy and also fit seamlessly into this bigger picture will be the most effective for your business.

The average marketing department that uses predictive data mining or any kind of data analysis goes through the following business process:

1. First, the marketing user, having a good understanding of the business, gets an idea for a new marketing program or maybe a question about the performance of a current marketing program. From this idea or question they need to build a predictive model in order to launch their marketing program.

2. The marketing department makes a request to its analytics department. The analytics department interviews the marketing user in order to understand the business problem. When this is done, the analytics department makes a request to the IT department for a data extract from which to build the model.

3. Several days or weeks are spent by the analyst in crafting a model from this extract (getting the extract from the IT department may require days or weeks to achieve by itself). When the model is complete, it is presented to the marketing department.

4. If the marketing department likes the model (if it makes business sense as well as statistical sense) the program will be launched. This often means recoding the predictive model from a statistical format to one that can be executed on the data warehouse where the customer data resides.

Total turnaround time from idea to execution is a minimum of several days, and can be up to several months. This can be a problem in fast-changing markets. A bigger problem than this lengthy processing time is that, with all this transfer of data between the marketing, analytics, and IT departments, there are many possible places where major errors can occur in the translation and movement of that data. This could result in the wrong model being built and the wrong marketing program being launched.

In the banking industry, a large mistake was recently made when the analytics department of a large bank requested a "random" sample of customers from the data warehouse. They wanted to build a model to predict which customers would be interested in a new retirement account product. A "randomly" ordered list of customer accounts was returned to the analytics department, from which they took the first 100,000 records to build the model and the second 100,000 records to test the model. The model worked quite well on the test data, so a targeted mailing was launched. When the returns came in, the customer response to the promotion was significantly below what was predicted by the model.

When the analytics department staff finally uncovered the problem, they found that the IT department had sorted the customers by account balance in order to achieve a "random" list. This was not a random list at all—in fact, the result was probably worse than if the original "non-randomized" data had been used. The problem was that all the good customers were at the front of the list, and these were the customers who were used to build the model. Unfortunately, the model was then applied to the general customer population, which had significantly different behavior than this good customer subpopulation.

Embedding Data Mining into Your Business Process

Major errors, like the one in the banking industry, occur more often than not as the data is moved, translated, and recoded from one department to another, and from one piece of hardware and database to another. (Often, data goes from a mainframe or large server running a relational data warehouse, to a UNIX workstation running a specialized database for data analysis, to a small extract file that the marketing professional interacts with via Microsoft Excel, Access, or a multidimensional database tool.) Avoiding these major errors can be a much more important part of determining predictive accuracy than the subtle differences in accuracy between different technologies.

The cost of this distributed business process is also quite high. There are multiple types of databases, operating systems, and computers to maintain and train your staff on. There are also costs that are specific to the model itself, such as having to recode the model back on the mainframe, and then spending a significant amount of time retesting the model to make sure that no mistakes were made. It would be much less expensive, much faster, and much less error-prone to have this entire marketing business process more directly under the control of the marketing professional and running seamlessly within the existing data warehouse. In order to achieve this the data analysis must be:

- Embedded into the data warehouse
- Understandable and usable by the marketing professional

These two criteria can be fulfilled by several of the new data mining technologies more adeptly than existing statistical techniques can. It is the capability of data mining technologies, such as decision trees, to embed into data warehouses and to provide understandable results to the business end user that provide the greatest improvements in accuracy, speed, and cost. This is the big difference between data mining and classical statistics.

This "embedded data mining" concept seeks to reduce the errors and costs of the current data analysis system while, for the first time, allowing the marketing professional to truly see what is going on in their database. Data mining needs to be embedded into the data warehouse without the requirement of a data extract. Similarly, the predictive model should be placed back into the data warehouse without the requirement of recoding and retesting it. It can then be applied to any database in the warehouse and used by others as well. It is, in the parlance of data warehousing, "metadata," or data about the data. Additional metadata can be used to create the focused "data mart," which is a high-speed view into the data warehouse that is specifically tailored to make it easy for a businessperson to access and navigate in an otherwise complex data warehouse. These data marts are typically implemented via multidimensional database technology.

The More Things Change, the More They Remain the Same

There is nothing new under the sun. — Ecclesiastes

Except in the computer industry. — Anon

It may seem that all the articles about data mining and all the new products are just heralding the rediscovery of a great new age of statistics or (because statistics has been in use for decades) just more of the same. But despite the overlap in usage and even technology, data mining is bringing something new to the party—namely, an easy way for business and marketing professionals to access the power of statistics. This is not a small feat.

The real opportunity provided by data mining is that it represents an empowerment of the end user in much the same way that the spreadsheet first empowered the business user almost two decades ago. Before the spreadsheet appeared, the business user could run financial analyses. But to do so, they would have to call their finance department, who in turn would call the data processing department, and then between the two they would try to figure out what the business user wanted to model. The business user would have a usable financial analysis within days or weeks.

Contrast this scenario to what we see today. Business and marketing professionals regularly build and run small financial models themselves without ever calling the data processing or finance organizations. They build these models immediately and interactively by working directly with their modeling tools. Their turnaround time has gone from days and weeks to seconds and minutes, and a whole new way of interacting with their financial data has been born. They are able to gain understanding and intuitions from their data that just were not possible when that data and those models were being built for them by others. They are now in control of the way their real business problems are communicated to the database.

This basic promise of the spreadsheet proved to be a powerful force in creating a new, functional tool for the business end user. This is also the promise of data mining. To achieve it, however, data mining must be deployed as an embedded technology within the data warehouse. When this is done, there are improvements in accuracy, speed, and cost.

Discovery versus Prediction

Gold in Them Thar Hills

The image that usually comes to mind when people hear the term "data mining" is that there exists a "mountain" of data and some nugget of gold in the mountain that would otherwise be too costly or too difficult to find without some powerful mining tools. The other metaphor is like looking for a needle in a haystack. In any case, finding either the nugget or the needle is only one piece of what data mining can do for you. Data mining can also take that mountain of data and tell you what your mountain is going to look like next month (not just where the gold is today, but where the gold might be tomorrow). Thus, data mining also includes prediction as one of its benefits.

If we took the data mining analogy a step further, this second part of data mining would correspond to understanding the tectonics of mountains—how they are changing and moving—not just what they look like today. We will call these two important features of data mining "discovery" when we are looking for an existing useful nugget in our databases, and "prediction" when we are seeking to use what we have found to predict what is going to happen next.

Discovery—Finding Something That You Weren't Looking for

One of the obvious things about real mining is that when you come across a diamond or a vein of gold, you know that you have found it. You can recognize the important properties of diamonds or gold because they have been discovered before and you know what they look like and feel like. You know that you can always take them into the lab to do detailed tests to make sure that they are genuine (you have not stumbled upon some iron pyrite, or fool's gold). In the case of large databases, sometimes users ask the impossible: "Tell me something I didn't know but would like to know." How do you describe the characteristics of this nugget of gold when even the end user doesn't know exactly what it is that they want?

Here's an example from the telephone industry. In the database, how does the data mining tool know that losing nearly complete revenue from a class of customers over the summer who later return is an important "nugget" of information? How does it know the following nugget of information is important: "Customers who buy large numbers of your product tend to be the highest-revenue customers." This is much less interesting because this is an obvious association between the number of purchases and total revenue.

Distinguishing between these two nuggets will be important for any data mining system to accomplish. Certain algorithms can be employed, however, to help to pull the gold out of the dross, and distinguish between the gold and the pyrite. We will talk more about this in the section on discovery and rule induction, but the main idea of how these systems work is by making three measurements:

How strong is the association? How unexpected is it? How ubiqui-tous is it?

These are all good requirements for sifting out the gold from your data. The first rule requires that the pattern in the data be a strong pattern (for example, that it occurs 90% of the time). The second measure ensures that the pattern is interesting to the user and not obvious. The fulfillment of the third ensures that the pattern occurs often enough that it is useful. (For example, a pattern that occurs for only one customer in your database of 10 million customers will be interesting but unlikely to be valuable.)

Prediction

Now, contrast discovery to prediction. With prediction, you as the end user have a very specific event or attribute that you want to find a pat-tern in association with. For instance, suppose you want to predict cus-tomer attrition. One of the most important parts of predicting customer attrition is having historical information in your database about which customers have attrited in the past. There may be many interesting patterns in your database—say, between the age of your customers and their buying habits—that you might like to discover, but in this case, you know very well that attrition is costing you a lot of money. So for now, you will be very well pleased to discover the fac-tors contributing to attrition within your database and to predict which of your customers are at risk of attriting in the near future. After you do this, you may also be interested in discovery.

Overfitting

Originally, the term "data mining" was used in the statistical com-munity with a negative connotation. Namely, if you "mined through your data" long enough, eventually you'd find something that looked like a useful pattern. This was also called "fishing"—if you fish long enough, you will eventually catch something. The difficulty with mining and fishing in this sense is that you end up catching something just because you were trying so hard—not because there really were useful reproducible patterns in your database.

State of the Industry

The current offerings in data mining software products emphasize different important aspects of the algorithms and their usage. The different emphases are driven because of differences in the targeted user and the types of problems being solved. There are four main categories of products:

- Targeted Solutions
- Business Tools
- Business Analyst Tools
- Research Analyst Tools

Targeted Solutions

The products in this category have taken the power of data mining and applied it to a particular problem or industry. An example of this type of product is the HNC Falcon system, which is a neural network-based solution that is targeted specifically at the credit card fraud and risk-assessment problem. Other targeted examples are the Churn Prophet product from Lightbridge, Inc., which has been created specifically for detecting customer "churn" (non-renewal of contract) in the cellular phone industry.

These systems, because they have been tailored to a particular industry or problem, can automate or eliminate much of the complexity inherent in the data mining algorithms. For instance, in the case of cellular phone customer churn, the emphasis of the product is in producing understandable and actionable results. Particular types of random sampling can be determined a priori as being most useful across the industry. Or, the ROI (return on investment) models can be simplified to match the marketing interventions that are in the cellular phone company's arsenal—which usually consist of giving something away in order to preserve the customer relationship (the newest technology cellular phone in return for a year extension on the contract).

Business Tools

The products in this category have been targeted for the business end user to present the power of data mining in a way that is easy enough to use. These tools make data mining understandable enough so that the business user can get some value from the tool and avoid any mistakes from misusing the product. These products should be likened to a child's sandbox, where there are many useful things to play with, but as long as the child stays inside the sandbox, the child is relatively safe.

These types of tools usually provide sophisticated, interactive ROI analysis on the predictive models. but also automate some of the parts of the algorithm that can get the user into trouble if misused. For instance, random sampling of the database and validation of the model are often automated in these tools because many mistakes have been made by overly aggressive marketing managers in creating predictive models that are based on particular bad "random" samples—and then maybe even validated, on the database from which the model was created.

Business Analyst Tools

There is also a class of tools provided for users of tools for business applications where the user wielding the tool has some sense of how data mining works and what some of the different variations accomplish. Typically, these tools will have simplified the data mining process to a great degree, probably automating things such as sampling, connecting to the database, and validation. They will also expose to the expert business user a whole host of knobs and controls that affect how the data mining algorithm works. For instance, in a decision tree algorithm, these tools would expose the choice of metric for making the splits (either Gini or entropy, and so on). They would also probably allow the user to force splits in the decision tree if the user wanted to the split to take place rather than having the algorithm always make the decision.

These tools also present the results in a form that is closer to the data mining algorithm rather than the business end user. For instance, the structure of the neural network or the decision tree would be exposed and available to the user. Higher-level business views of the results such as segmentation analysis, the construction of descriptive rules or ROI and profit analysis would also be available. In general, these tools will allow the user much greater latitude in how the data mining functions but will, in general, still protect the user from any egregious error. For instance, these tools would either strongly warn the user or prevent the user from using a model that was not statistically valid and had been overfitted to the data.

Research Analyst Tools

The last class of commercial offerings is targeted at the data mining researcher or statistical analyst who desires the utmost control over the algorithm, as well as the greatest latitude in choosing an algorithm. These offerings often include huge libraries of statistical, graphing, and visualization software and will be offered as the cutting edge in technology. These tools will generally be the first to include any new techniques coming out of the research labs or from academia.

From the business user's perspective, these tools should be wielded with extreme caution because they assume that the user has detailed knowledge about how the algorithms work. Consequently, the users can easily create models that are significantly below the optimal or are statistically invalid.

Data Mining Methodology

The methodology used today in data mining, when it is well thought out and well executed, consists of just a few very important concepts. The first of these is the concept of finding a pattern in the data. In many cases, this just means any collection of data that occurs a surprising number of times. Usually "surprising" is better defined, but in general it means any sequence or pattern of data that occurs more often than one would expect it to if it were a random event. The second important concept is that of sampling or not having to use all of the data in order to make significant conclusions about what might be happening with other parts of the data.

Another very important concept associated with data mining is that of validating the predictive models that arise out of data mining algorithms. Specifically, if you have found a pattern somewhere in your data, you must be sure that any model that you build that predicts that the pattern will occur elsewhere must be validated in some way. Finally, if you've found a pattern, and made sure that it is reproducible somewhere else, then it all comes down to finding the pattern or model that is the best. The four parts of data mining technology (patterns, sampling, validation and choosing the model) are discussed in the following sections.

What Is a Pattern? What Is a Model?

To get a basic insight into what patterns and models are, consider the simple problem of trying to determine the next number in the following sequence: 121212 . . . ? If you had to make a guess, you'd probably guess the number 2 because there are many patterns of a 1 followed by a 2 that have occurred in the data. Because the pattern "12" is found often enough, you have some confidence in the predictive model that says, "if 1, then 2 will follow."

This is an example of a pattern, a model, and some training examples. In this case, detecting the pattern is relatively simple. In other cases, however, detecting the pattern could be much more difficult. Consider, for instance, if you had fewer examples (121 . . . ?), or if the sequence were much longer (1212123121212 . . . ?).

Both of these examples show how models can be created by detecting the patterns in some historical data, and then making calculated guesses about how likely those patterns are to be repeatable. A predictive model then has something in common with the small plastic airplane models you may have glued together as a child. In each case, you built a model that is quite a bit smaller than the real thing (either the real airplane or the entire database), but it represents some important characteristic of the larger thing that is being modeled. In the case of the model airplane, it is unable to fly, but it nonetheless captures the shape and look of the real thing. In the case of the database model, it captures a pattern in the database that describes an important aspect of the database. It certainly does not describe the entire database, however. (For instance, the database may be hundreds of gigabytes in size, but the model may only be a few kilobytes in size.)

For real-world business applications, a model can be anything from a mathematical equation, to a set of rules that describes customer segments, to the computer representation of a complex neural network architecture, which translates to several sets of mathematical equations. Some of these more-complex models are effectively computer programs that take in data about the current situation and output other data that is used as a prediction for some unknown. The user can then take action on that predicted information. This process can be viewed at a very high level as a black box or oracle that produces answers to relevant questions, as shown in Figure 5-1. Here, a model is used to make a prediction about a record that represents some new state of the world. The model is a limited reflection of the entire historical database from which it was built.

Alhough there are many ways to define patterns and models, here is what they mean in the context of data warehousing and data mining:

- *Model.*   A description of the original historical database from which it was built that can be successfully applied to new data in order to make predictions about missing values or to make statements about expected values.

- *Pattern.*   An event or combination of events in a database that occurs more often than expected. Typically, this means that its

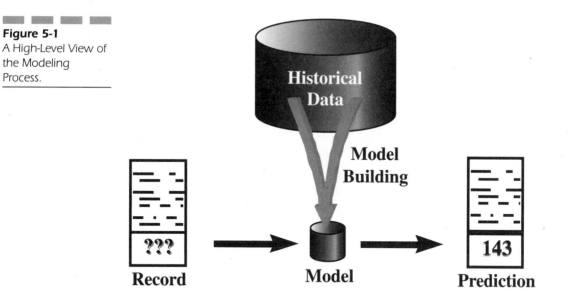

Figure 5-1
A High-Level View of
the Modeling
Process.

actual occurrence is significantly different than what would be expected by random chance.

This definition of a model is fairly general-purpose, but also centered on databases and data warehousing. This is not to say that a plastic replica of an airplane is not also a perfectly good model. Our definition is just more tuned into the type of model that we will be talking about in this book. It might also seem that the definition of a pattern given above is fairly weak, but it does a good job of sifting through the essentials of a pattern. For instance, it is not enough for a pattern to repeat, but the number of repetitions must be significant. In general, no pattern is of any interest if it cannot be successfully applied in new situations.

One final question then might be the following: What is the difference between a pattern and a model? There may not be a crisp dividing line between the two (in the number sequence example, the pattern "123" was also the model). In general, however, patterns are driven by the data and generally reflect the data itself, whereas a model generally reflects a purpose and may not be driven by the data necessarily. For instance, one can build a model of the physical world using the equations of Newtonian physics that do a great job of explaining the data of the world (how fast something falls or how far it flies), but the equations are not really patterns in any sense. On the other hand, most of the models talked about in this book will in fact be driven by data.

In this case, the biggest distinction between a model and a pattern (besides the fact that models are created for some purpose) is that patterns are usually less complex and there are usually many of them. One model of customer behavior may be very complex and contain hundreds of patterns that have been gleaned from the database.

Visualizing a Pattern

The example that has been used so far of finding the patterns in a sequence of numbers could be visualized on a graph. Because human beings are pretty good at picking out visual patterns, people will often try to map their data to a graph in order to "see" it. Sometimes, they are able to visually see patterns that might not otherwise have been noticed. For instance, the simple example of numbers (1212123121212 . . .) that we have been using so far could be mapped to a graph as shown in Figure 5-2.

If there are more complicated patterns to be detected, such as the sequence of numbers shown in Table 5-1, it can be much more difficult to detect any patterns. However, when the data is graphed, even with ten times as many data points it seems to form a pretty simple and understandable pattern, as is shown in Figure 5-3.

Even though the data is complicated, these patterns are still easy to detect visually because the value to be predicted next varies smoothly with the position on the x-axis. A much more complicated situation would arise on a graph where the next value was dependent on not only the position along the x-axis, but also along some other axis that wasn't being graphed. In most real-world prediction problems, the value to be predicted is dependent on many more factors than just one. As we'll see in later chapters, there are very powerful techniques for building these complex models and some new visualization techniques that make it possible to see higher-dimensional data.

Figure 5-2
A Graphical
Representation of a
Number Sequence.

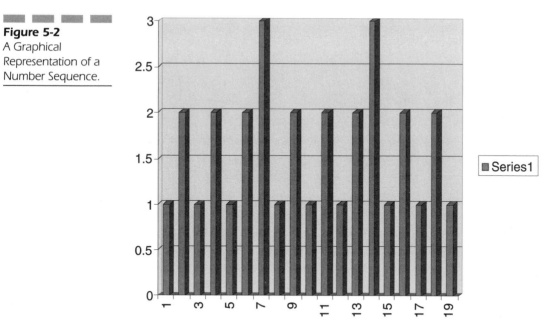

Table 5-1

A More Complex
Pattern of Numbers

0.0998334166468282E-02	0.198669330795061
0.198669330795061	0.389418342308651
0.29552020666134	0.564642473395035
0.389418342308651	0.717356090899523
0.479425538604203	0.841470984807897
0.564642473395035	0.932039085967226
0.644217687237691	0.98544972998846
0.717356090899523	0.999573603041505
0.783326909627483	0.973847630878195
0.841470984807897	0.909297426825682

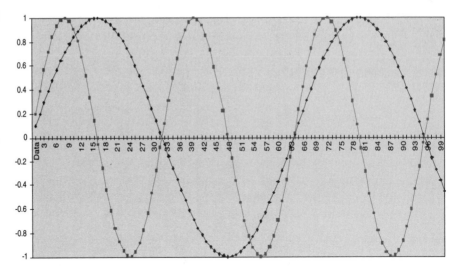

Figure 5-3
A graphical representation of a complex number sequence appears much more understandable than the raw data.

A Note on Terminology

So far, we have talked quite a bit about data in terms of the data warehouse—which, more often than not, means talking about the data in terms of how it is stored—rows, columns, tables, relations, keys, and so on. When we talk about predictive modeling, however, the main consideration is what data is being predicted, how it will be used to make those predictions, and how many historical examples exist. Consequently, the focus and terminology for predictive modeling is on the data structures that relate to this important modeling information, although the physical storage of this data is as important for performance and data management reasons as it is for the RDBMS. The number one concern for modeling systems is predictive accuracy. The terminology is thus slightly different to reflect this difference:

- *Database.* The collection of data that has been collected, on which data analysis will be performed, and from which predictive models and exploratory models will be created. This is often called the historical database to refer to data that has been collected over time. In machine learning and data mining, there is often a differentiation between the training database and the test database. Both of these databases are constructed from the historical database and constitute non-overlapping subsets of the historical database. As their names imply, one is used for training (building the model) and the other is used for testing the model.

- *Record.* The atomic-level data structure that holds the data pertinent to individuals in the database. A record corresponds to a row of a table in a denormalized database. Each record is made up of values for each field that it contains, including the predictor fields and the prediction field. Many databases have a record for each customer or account. In general, a record represents some state of the world about which a prediction can be made.

- *Field.* The data structure that represents an attribute of a record. Fields correspond to columns in a relational database, and to dimensions and measures in a multi-dimensional database. Fields are also called attributes, features, variables, and dimensions.

- *Predictor.* A field that can be used in building a predictive model. Some function of the predictor values of a record produces the prediction value for that record. In general, predictors are what fields are called when they are being used for prediction or data exploration.

- *Prediction.* The field that will have a value created for it by the predictive model. It is also the field that is passed to the data mining technique in order for the model to be built. In general, the prediction field is similar to any other field, except in the way it is handled by the predictive model building process.

- *Value.* Each field has a value (for example, the field "age" for the record representing a customer has the value 34).

In different areas of research, each of these concepts gets a slightly different name. Although there are sometimes subtle differences in meaning, these names are often used interchangeably, depending on who you are talking to. Table 5-2 shows how these concepts can be translated between different disciplines. Although data mining has not settled on a particularly well-defined naming convention, the naming that is used in this book is displayed in that column.

Table 5-2

Translation of
Several Predictive
Modeling Concepts

Data Mining	Relational Databases	Online Analytical Processing	Statistics	Artificial Intelligence
Database	Table, Database	Multidimensional Database, Cube	Dataset, Sample	Dataset, Training Set
Record	Row	NA	Record, Datum	Example, Record
Field	Column	Variable, Dimension, Measure	Variable	Field, Feature, Dimension
Predictor	Column	Variable, Dimension, Measure	Independent Variable	Field, Feature, Dimension
Prediction	Column	Variable, Dimension, Measure	Dependent Variable	Classification, Target

A Note on Knowledge and Wisdom

Along with the concepts of prediction and the automated building of models goes the idea that perhaps some of these systems are doing more than just data processing or computation. Some people believe and will tell you that data mining, and particularly artificial intelligence, have moved into the realms of intelligence and knowledge creation. For instance, another name used interchangeably for data mining is knowledge discovery. Some have even gone so far as to create elaborate hierarchies of intelligence to show how these new technologies can transform data to information, information to knowledge, and knowledge to wisdom. These sorts of claims are interesting to think about, but they belong more in the realm of a philosophical discussion rather than in the practicalities of building and mining a data warehouse.

Data is a fairly well-defined concept; information, though many people don't use the term in its strict technical sense, also has a very precise definition. Knowledge, intelligence, and wisdom are much more difficult to define; and very difficult to recognize, even if they do exist. For this reason, we will stick to these very well-defined though less-glamorous descriptions of what these systems are capable of. In general, you should be wary of vendors or scientists selling these types of modeling systems as being more than what they are. They are very powerful in their own right, without needing to create human-like qualities about them.

Sampling

One of the things that we notice about patterns and models is that a model is, by definition, only a small part of the greater space in which something is going on. For instance, the patterns in the data that we have been looking at could probably be recognized without having to see every single example for every possible combination of variables (dimensions).

For instance let's go back to the original case, where we are trying to predict the next number in the sequence "1212123121212 . . . ." Or, consider a more interesting real-world case, in which we may only have a few examples of fraud in our database of customers. In both examples, what is presented to us and from which we are supposed to build a model is only a small fraction of the total space that we could be looking at. We do not have in our database, no matter how large, an example of every possible customer and all of the variables that describe him or her. In fact, even if we have 100 million customer records in our database this will only be a fraction of the U.S. population—and an even smaller fraction of the total world population. Given that we don't have every example in our database, can we still build a reliable model? The answer is yes. The model will never be as good as it would be if you had all the possible examples, but it will be a lot better than having no model at all.

There are, of course, other times when you don't have all the possible data points that you might want to have. Sometimes, you just don't have enough data; other times, you may not want to use all of the data that you have because it may be difficult to process or store all of it as you are looking for patterns in trying to build a model. In this case, you can perform sampling.

Sometimes, people will denigrate sampling techniques because they believe that you won't get the right answer from the "right" model unless you use "all" of the data. The problem is that you rarely, if ever, have the opportunity to use all of the data. For instance, if you were classifying fraud cases, you might have some information about people, such as their income and their credit limit. In general, you know that people who have low incomes and high credit limits are more likely to commit fraud, and that those who have high incomes and low credit limits are as well. You know that in your credit card company there are credit limits from $100 to $10,000 in $100 increments—which translates to 100 different possible credit limits that people can have. For the customers' income, you could likewise come up with 100 different values, from no salary to professional athletes and CEOs making up to $10 million each year. You picked 100 different salaries and 100 different credit limits—which translates to 10,000 different types of customers, based on just income and credit limit. Even in a database of over one million customers (a reasonable-sized credit card company), it would be unlikely that you would find every possible combination of income and credit limit represented by at least one database record. Or, consider the case where you represent personal income in $1 increments—now there are $10,000,000 \times 100$, or 1 billion possible types of customers in your database that might or might not be representative of fraud.

If you consider that this is just the number of examples that you have with two variables and how much larger the "space" of examples could be if you added more and more variables. This would likely mean that your space would be so large that you would never be able to fill in all of the empty slots with viable examples of customers. And, of course, this is exactly the problem that you run into in real world situations. Thus, sampling is something that we are doing all of the time, whether we want to do it or not. The question then is "If sampling is unavoidable in all but the most pristine academic settings, then maybe we should instead embrace it and make use of it."

Random Sampling

One of the ways to make use of sampling is to use it to effectively make your database smaller to find the predictive patterns. For instance, if you had a database of one billion examples of people who had committed credit card fraud, you would be hard-pressed to wade through all of that data—either by hand or even with a computer in any reasonable amount of time. But, if on the other hand, you were given 10 randomly chosen examples from this huge database, you might quickly begin to see a pattern.

By randomly sampling the database, an impossible problem becomes feasible and a possible model is offered up almost immediately. Such a model can then be refined and confirmed by further sampling of the data with larger numbers of samples. As will be shown in the following section, it can be critical that this sampling be done by some random process in order to avoid any possible bias that would create a less than optimal model.

Validating the Model

Validating any model that comes out of a data mining tool is going to be the most important thing that you can do. If you are responsible for introducing data mining at your company, the success of your project (and, in fact, your employment) may well depend on how well you can perform validation of the data mining models. Part of the reason for this is that the results of data mining are often used for strategic issues throughout the company. Effectively, the results that come out of the data mining systems steer the corporate ship— in the most important way possible—by telling you how to treat your customers. If the wrong message is coming in from the data mining system, it can affect the course of the entire ship. Watch out for icebergs!

That was the warning. The reality is that data mining can be used effectively without making mistakes. Some care must be taken to make sure that not only is the process that builds the predictive models correct, but also that the process that applies those models and even the process that processes the data to feed the data mining system are well validated.

In its simplest form, the validation required for data mining is that after you build the model on some historical data, you apply the model to similar historical data from which the model was not built.

Because the data is historical, you already know the outcome so that the accuracy of the predictive model can be measured.

Model building is always a matter of picking out a pattern in one place and applying it somewhere else. Validation is just the process of trying out that application where you already know the answer, and comparing the output from the data mining system with the output that you know to be correct. If there is a large difference, you should consider that the model you just built might also not work when you apply it for real.

Picking the Best Model

One of the most important things that needs to be done when you are building a predictive model is to make sure that you have picked up the essential patterns in the data that will hold true the next time you apply your model. For instance, when you vault your data, as described previously, you may well want to vault data from last month and train on data from two months ago. Then, the model that you built would be tried out on new data "from the future." The performance of this data should give you a great deal of confidence that your model will work next month as well.

Have you ever taken a test in college, say in physics, where you memorized a couple of specific examples of how to work out problems —the same ones that the professor wrote out on the board during class? Then, during the test the professor gave problems that were just different enough that you were unable to solve them? This is known as cookbook physics, in which you memorize the equations and a few particular applications, but never really understand the whole problem or how the pieces fit together. You knew how to solve the problem in a particular area, but were unable to extract the general information or knowledge about the problem and how it should be solved if the situation changed slightly. The same thing can happen to predictive models. Consider a predictive model built with an artificial neural network.

Here, the neural network "learns" by being repeatedly presented with examples of the predictors and the prediction (or, in statistical parlance, the independent and dependent variables). As the network is presented with more and more examples, it subtly modifies the connection strengths between the different pieces of data coming in and the required answer coming out. By doing this, the network begins to make fewer and fewer mistakes. In some cases, the network will result in no mistakes made for the particular prediction after the training data has been run by it enough times. Interestingly, though, the performance on the validation data shows a different behavior. The error rate on the validation data reaches a minimum at one point of learning, and then begins to increase after that—even while the error rate on the training data continues to decrease.

This effect, called "overfitting," corresponds to that physics student who tries to memorize exactly the right thing to do on a handful of physics problems, rather than trying to understand the general rules for predicting physical systems. The neural network at first is extracting general rules for prediction. Over time, however, as the same examples are repeatedly presented to it, the network effectively begins to memorize the answers to the particular examples that it has in the training set. This works well for decreasing the error rate on the training set, as the network comes closer and closer to fully memorizing the data. It also means that the network has begun to extract patterns that are not predictive of the problem being solved, but are only predictive given some of the idiosyncrasies of the particular database. For instance, you could find the analogous rule that all people named Jonathan David Smith are poor credit risks embedded in the neural network. It may be the case that both people named Jonathan David Smith in the training database were bad credit risks, but it is unlikely that someone's full name is predictive of creditworthiness.

The Types of Data Mining Applications

Data mining has been applied to a wide variety of data-based problems: From predicting the likelihood of toxic waste contamination in inland waterways to tracking down suspicious cash transactions in the southeastern United States that may be associated with money laundering. It has been used to classify census returns and to help people find the appropriate articles in the *Wall Street Journal*. If there is data, people will want to ask questions about it. For just about all of those questions, there is a data mining technique that can help.

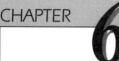

Classical Techniques: Statistics, Neighborhoods, and Clustering

The Classics

This chapter and the one that follows will describe, at a high level, the different types of data mining techniques and how they work. But, as they say, a little knowledge is a dangerous thing. You will be dangerous after having read this chapter. Just don't be overconfident—the devil is in the details. For the detailed descriptions of how the techniques work, the reader is referred to the text, *Data Warehousing, Data Mining and OLAP*, also written by the authors.

In these two chapters, six broad classes of data mining techniques are covered, although there are many other techniques and many variations of the techniques described. One of the techniques from this group of six is almost always used in real-world deployments of data mining for CRM systems.

These two chapters have been divided, based on when the data mining technique was developed and when it became technically mature enough to be used for business, especially for optimizing customer relationship management systems. Thus, this chapter contains descriptions of techniques that have classically been used for decades. The next chapter represents techniques that have been widely used for CRM only since the early 1980s.

This chapter should help the user to understand the rough differences in the techniques, and have at least enough information to be dangerous and well-armed enough to not be baffled by the vendors of different data mining tools.

The main techniques that we will discuss here are the ones that are used 99.9% of the time on existing business problems. There are certainly many other ones, as well as proprietary techniques from particular vendors—but, in general, the industry is converging on the techniques that work consistently and are understandable and explainable.

Statistics

By strict definition, statistics or statistical techniques are not data mining. They were being used long before the term "data mining" was coined to apply to business applications. However, statistical techniques are driven by the data and are used to discover patterns and build predictive models. And, from the user's perspective, you will be faced with a conscious choice when solving a data mining problem—whether you wish to attack it with statistical methods or other data mining techniques. For this reason, it is important to have some idea of how statistical techniques work and how they can be applied.

What Is Different between Statistics and Data Mining?

I flew the Boston to Newark shuttle recently and sat next to a professor from one of the Boston area universities. He was going to discuss the drosophila's (fruit fly's) genetic makeup with a pharmaceutical company in New Jersey. He had compiled the world's largest database on the genetic makeup of the fruit fly and made it available to other researchers on the Internet through Java applications accessing a larger relational database.

He explained to me that they were not only now storing the information on the flies, but also were doing data mining. He added as an aside, "which seems to be very important these days, whatever that is." I mentioned that I had written a book on the subject, and he was interested in knowing what the difference was between data mining and statistics. There is no easy answer.

The techniques used in data mining are successful for precisely the same reasons that statistical techniques are successful (for example, clean data, a well-defined target to predict, and good validation to avoid overfitting). And, for the most part, the techniques are used in the same places for the same types of problems (prediction, classification, and discovery). In fact, some of the techniques that are classically defined as data mining, such as CART and CHAID, arose from statisticians.

So what is the difference? Why aren't we as excited about statistics as we are about data mining? There are several reasons. The first is that the classical data mining techniques, such as CART, neural networks, and nearest neighbor techniques, tend to be more robust for messier real-world data and also more robust for use by less-expert users. But that is not the only reason. The other reason is that the time is right. Because of the use of computers for closed loop business data storage and generation, there now exist large quantities of data that are available to users. If there were no data, there would be no interest in mining it. Likewise, the fact that computer hardware has dramatically upped the ante by several orders of magnitude in storing and processing the data makes some of the most powerful data mining techniques feasible today.

The bottom line though, from an academic standpoint at least, is that there is little practical difference between a statistical technique and a classical data mining technique. Hence, we have included a description of some of the most useful techniques in this chapter.

What Is Statistics?

Statistics is a branch of mathematics concerning the collection and the description of data. Usually, statistics is considered to be one of those scary topics in college, right up there with chemistry and physics. However, statistics is probably a much friendlier branch of mathematics because it really can be used every day. Statistics was, in fact, born from very humble beginnings of real-world problems from business, biology, and gambling!

Knowing statistics in everyday life will help the average businessperson make better decisions by allowing them to figure out risk and uncertainty when all the facts either aren't known or can't be collected. Even with all the data stored in the largest of data warehouses, business decisions still just become more informed guesses. The more and better the data and the understanding of the statistics, the better is the decision that can be made.

Statistics had been around for a long time, easily a century and arguably many centuries, when the ideas of probability began to gel. It could even be argued that the data collected by the ancient Egyptians, Babylonians, and Greeks were all statistics long before the field was officially recognized. Today, data mining has been defined independently of statistics, although mining data for patterns and predictions is really what statistics is all about. Some of the techniques that are classified under data mining, such as CHAID and CART, really grew out of the statistical profession more than anywhere else; and the basic ideas of probability, independence and causality, and overfitting are the foundation on which both data mining and statistics are built.

Data, Counting, and Probability

One thing that is always true about statistics is that there is always data involved, and there is usually enough data so that the average person cannot keep track of all the data in their heads. This is certainly truer today than it was when the basic ideas of probability and statistics were being formulated and refined, early in this century. Today, people have to deal with terabytes of data, and have to make sense of it and glean the important patterns from it. Statistics can help greatly in this process by helping to answer several important questions about the data:

- What patterns are there in my database?
- What is the chance that an event will occur?
- Which patterns are significant?
- What is a high-level summary of the data that gives me some idea of what is contained in my database?

Certainly, statistics can do more than answer these questions, but for most people today, these are the questions that statistics can help answer. Consider, for example, that a large part of statistics is concerned with summarizing data; more often than not, this summarization has to do with counting. One of the great values of statistics is in presenting a high-level view of the database that provides some useful information without requiring every record to be understood in detail. This aspect of statistics is the part that people run into every day when they read the daily newspaper and see, for example, a pie chart reporting the number of U.S. citizens with different eye colors, or the average number of annual doctor visits for people of different ages. Statistics at this level is used in the reporting of important information, from which people may be able to make useful decisions. There are many different parts of statistics but the idea of collecting data and counting it is often at the base of even these more sophisticated techniques. The first step then in understanding statistics is to understand how the data is collected into a higher-level form—one of the most notable ways of doing this is with the histogram.

Histograms

One of the best ways to summarize data is to provide a histogram of the data. In the simple example database shown in Table 6-1, we can create a histogram of eye color by counting the number of occurrences of different eye colors in our database. For this sample database of 10 records, this is fairly easy to do, and the results are only slightly more interesting than the database itself. However, for a database of many more records, this is a very useful way of getting a high-level understanding of the database.

Table 6-1

An example database of customers with different predictor types

ID	Name	Prediction	Age	Balance	Income	Eyes	Gender
1	Amy	No	62	$0	Medium	Brown	F
2	Al	No	53	$1,800	Medium	Green	M
3	Betty	No	47	$16,543	High	Brown	F
4	Bob	Yes	32	$45	Medium	Green	M
5	Carla	Yes	21	$2,300	High	Blue	F
6	Carl	No	27	$5,400	High	Brown	M
7	Donna	Yes	50	$165	Low	Blue	F
8	Don	Yes	46	$0	High	Blue	M
9	Edna	Yes	27	$500	Low	Blue	F
10	Ed	No	68	$1,200	Low	Blue	M

The histogram shown in Figure 6-1 depicts a simple predictor (eye color), which will have only a few different values, no matter whether there are 100 customer records in the database or 100 million. There are, however, other predictors that have many more distinct values and can create a much more complex histogram. Consider, for instance, the histogram of ages of the customers in the population. In this case, the histogram can be more complex but can also be enlightening. Consider if you found that the histogram of your customer data looked as it does in Figure 6-2.

By looking at this second histogram, the viewer is in many ways looking at all of the data in the database for a particular predictor or data column. By looking at this histogram, it is also possible to build an intuition about other important factors, such as the average age of the population, and the maximum and minimum age. All of these are important. These values are called summary statistics. Some of the most frequently used summary statistics include the following:

- *Max.* The maximum value for a given predictor.
- *Min.* The minimum value for a given predictor.
- *Mean.* The average value for a given predictor.

Figure 6-1

This histogram shows the number of customers with various eye colors. This summary can quickly show important information about the database such as that blue eyes occur most frequently.

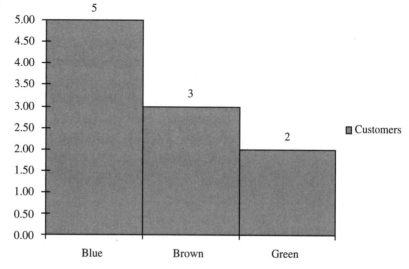

Figure 6-2
This histogram
shows the number
of customers of
different ages and
quickly tells the
viewer that the
majority of customers
are over the age
of 50.

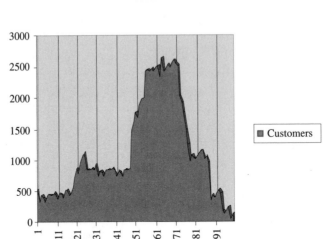

Customers

- *Median.* The value for a given predictor that divides the database as nearly as possible into two databases of equal numbers of records.
- *Mode.* The most common value for the predictor.
- *Variance.* The measure of how spread out the values are from the average value.

When there are many values for a given predictor, the histogram begins to look smoother and smoother (compare the difference between the two histograms in the previous figures). Sometimes, the shape of the distribution of data can be calculated by an equation rather than just represented by the histogram. This is what is called a data distribution. Like a histogram, a data distribution can be described by a variety of statistics. In classical statistics, the belief is that there is some true underlying shape to the data distribution that would be formed if all possible data were collected. The shape of the data distribution can be calculated for some simple examples. The statistician's job, then, is to take the limited data that may have been collected; and, from that, make the best guess about what the true, or at least most likely, underlying data distribution might be.

Many data distributions are well described by just two numbers: the mean and the variance. Although the mean is something most people are familiar with, the variance can be problematic. The easiest way to think about it is that it measures the average distance of each predictor value from the mean value over all the records in the database. If the variance is high, it implies that the values are all over the place and very different. If the variance is low, most of the data values are fairly close to the mean. To be precise, the actual definition of the variance uses the square of the distance rather than the actual distance from the mean, and the average is taken by dividing the squared sum by one less than the total number of records. In terms of prediction, a user could make a guess at the value of a predictor, without knowing anything else, just by knowing the mean; and could also gain some basic sense of how variable the guess might be, based on the variance.

Statistics for Prediction

In this book, the term "prediction" is used for a variety of types of analyses that may elsewhere be more precisely called "regression." We have done so in order to simplify some of the concepts, and to emphasize the common and most important aspects of predictive modeling. Nonetheless, regression is a powerful and commonly used tool in statistics and is discussed here.

Linear Regression

In statistics, prediction is usually synonymous with regression of some form. There are a variety of different types of regression in statistics, but the basic idea is that a model is created that maps values from predictors, so that the fewest errors occur when making a prediction. The simplest form of regression is simple linear regression that contains only one predictor and a prediction. The relationship between the two can be mapped on a two-dimensional space and the records plotted for the prediction values along the Y-axis and the predictor values along the X-axis. The simple linear regression model then could be viewed as the line that minimizes the error rate between the actual prediction value and the point on the line (the prediction from the model). Graphically, this would look as shown in Figure 6-3. The simplest form of regression seeks to build a predictive model that is a line that maps between each predictor value to a prediction value. Of the many possible lines that could be drawn through the data, the one that minimizes the distance between the line and the data points is the one that is chosen for the predictive model.

On average, if you guess the value on the line, it should represent an acceptable compromise among all the data giving conflicting answers at that point. Likewise, if there is no data available for a particular input value, the line will provide the best guess at a reasonable answer based on similar data.

The predictive model is the line shown in Figure 6-3. The line will take a given value for a predictor and map it into a given value for a prediction. The actual equation would look something like Prediction $= a + b \times$ Predictor. This is just the equation for a line $Y = a + bX$.

Figure 6-3
Linear regression is similar to the task of finding the line that minimizes the total distance to a set of data.

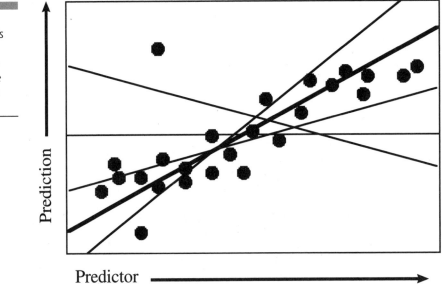

As an example for a bank, the predicted average consumer bank balance might equal $1,000 + 0.01 × customer's annual income. The trick, as always with predictive modeling, is to find the model that best minimizes the error. The most common way to calculate the error is the square of the difference between the predicted value and the actual value. Calculated this way, points that are very far from the line will have a great effect on moving the choice of line toward themselves in order to reduce the error. The values of a and b in the regression equation that minimize this error can be calculated directly from the data relatively quickly.

What If the Pattern In My Data Doesn't Look Like a Straight Line?

Regression can become more complicated than the simple linear regression we've introduced so far. It can get more complicated, in a variety of different ways, in order to better model particular database problems. There are, however, several main modifications that can be made:

- More predictors than just one can be used.
- Transformations can be applied to the predictors.
- Predictors can be multiplied together and used as terms in the equation.
- Modifications can be made to accommodate response predictions that just have yes/no or 0/1 values.

Adding more predictors to the linear equation can produce more complicated lines that take more information into account and hence make a better prediction. This is called multiple linear regression and might have an equation like the following if 5 predictors were used (X1, X2, X3, X4, X5):

$$Y = a + b1(X1) + b2(X2) + b3(X3) + b4(X4) + b5(X5)$$

This equation still describes a line, but it is now a line in a six-dimensional space rather than the two-dimensional space.

By transforming the predictors by squaring, cubing, or taking their square root, it is possible to use the same general regression methodology and now create much more complex models that are no longer simple shapes such as lines. This is called non-linear regression. A model of just one predictor might look like this:

$$Y = a + b1(X1) + b2(X12)$$

In many real-world cases, analysts will perform a wide variety of transformations on their data just to try them out. If they do not contribute to a useful model, their coefficients in the equation will tend toward zero and can be removed. The other transformation of predictor values that is often performed is multiplying them together. For instance, a new predictor created by dividing hourly wage by the minimum wage might be a much more effective predictor than hourly wage by itself.

When trying to predict a customer response that is just yes or no (for example, they bought the product or they didn't, or they defaulted or they didn't), the standard form of a line doesn't work. Because there are only two possible values to be predicted, it is relatively easy to fit a line through them. However, that model would be the same, no matter which predictors were being used or what particular data was being used. Typically in these situations, a transformation of the prediction values is made in order to provide a better predictive model. This type of regression is called logistic regression; because so many business problems are response problems, logistic regression is one of the most widely used statistical techniques for creating predictive models.

Nearest Neighbor

Clustering and the nearest neighbor prediction technique are among the oldest techniques used in data mining. Most people have an intuition that they understand what clustering is—namely, that like records are grouped or clustered together. Nearest neighbor is a prediction technique that is quite similar to clustering—in order to predict what a prediction value is in one record, look for records with similar predictor values in the historical database and use the prediction value from the record that is "nearest" to the unclassified record.

A Simple Example of Clustering

A simple example of clustering would be the clustering that most people perform when they do the laundry—grouping the permanent press, dry cleaning, whites, and brightly colored clothes is important because they have similar characteristics. And it turns out that they have important attributes in common about the way they behave (and can be ruined) in the wash. To "cluster" your laundry, most of your decisions are relatively straight-forward. There are, of course, difficult decisions to be made about which cluster your white shirt with red stripes belongs to (because it is mostly white, but has some color and is permanent press). When clustering is used in business, the clusters are often much more dynamic—even changing weekly to monthly—and many more of the decisions concerning which cluster a record falls into can be difficult.

A Simple Example of Nearest Neighbor

A simple example of the nearest neighbor prediction algorithm is when you look at the people in your neighborhood (in this case, those people that are geographically near to you). You may notice that, in general, you all have somewhat similar incomes. Thus, if your neighbor has an income greater than $100,000, chances are good that you also have a high income. Certainly, the chances that you have a high income are greater when all of your neighbors have incomes over $100,000 than if all of your neighbors have incomes of $20,000. Within your neighborhood, there may still be a wide variety of incomes possible among even your closest neighbors. If you had to predict someone's income based on only knowing their neighbors, however, your best chance of being right would be to predict the incomes of the neighbors who live closest to the unknown person.

The nearest neighbor prediction algorithm works in very much the same way except that nearness in a database may consist of a variety of factors, not just where the person lives. It may, for instance, be far more important to know which school someone attended and what degree they attained when predicting income. The better definition of "near" might in fact be other people that you graduated from college with rather than the people that you live next to.

Nearest neighbor techniques are among the easiest to use and understand because they work in a way similar to the way that people think—by detecting closely matching examples. They also perform quite well in terms of automation because many of the algorithms are robust with respect to dirty data and missing data. Finally, they are particularly adept at performing complex ROI calculations because the predictions are made at a local level, where business simulations could be performed in order to optimize ROI. Because they enjoy similar levels of accuracy compared to other techniques, the measures of accuracy such as lift are as good as from any other.

How to Use Nearest Neighbor for Prediction

One of the essential elements underlying the concept of clustering is that one particular object (whether it is a car, a food item, or a customer) can be closer to another object than can some third object. It is interesting that most people have an innate sense of ordering based on a variety of different objects. Most people would agree that an apple is closer to an orange than it is to a tomato, and that a Toyota Corolla is closer to a Honda Civic than to a Porsche. This sense of ordering on many different objects helps us place them in time and space, and to make sense of the world. It is what allows us to build clusters—both in databases on computers as well as in our daily lives. This definition of nearness that seems to be ubiquitous also allows us to make predictions.

The nearest neighbor prediction algorithm simply stated is as follows:

Objects that are "near" each other will also have similar prediction values. Thus, if you know the prediction value of one of the objects, you can predict it for its nearest neighbors.

Where Is the Nearest Neighbor Technique Used In Business?

One of the classic areas that nearest neighbor has been used for prediction has been in text retrieval. The problem to be solved in text retrieval is one in which the end user defines a document (for example, a Wall Street Journal article, technical conference paper, etc.) that is interesting to them, and they solicit the system to "find more documents like this one." They effectively define a target of "this is the interesting document" or "this is not interesting." The prediction problem is that only a very few of the documents in the database actually have values for this prediction field (namely, only the documents that the reader has had a chance to look at so far). The nearest neighbor technique is used to find other documents that share important characteristics with those documents that have been marked as interesting.

Using Nearest Neighbor for Stock Market Data

As with almost all prediction algorithms, nearest neighbor can be used in a variety of places. Its successful use is mostly dependent on the preformatting of the data, so that nearness can be calculated and where individual records can be defined. In the text retrieval example, this was not too difficult—the objects were documents. This is not always as easy as it is for text retrieval. Consider what it might be like in a time series problem—predicting the stock market, for example. In this case, the input data is just a long series of stock prices over time without any particular record that could be considered to be an object. The value to be predicted is just the next value of the stock price.

The way that this problem is solved for both nearest neighbor techniques and for some other types of prediction algorithms is to create training records. You can take, for instance, 10 consecutive stock prices and use the first nine as predictor values and the tenth as the prediction value. Doing things this way, if you had 100 data points in your time series, you could create 10 different training records.

You could create even more training records than 10 by creating a new record starting at every data point. For instance, you could take the first 10 data points and create a record. Then, you could take the 10 consecutive data points starting at the second data point, followed by the 10 consecutive data points starting at the third data point. Even though some of the data points would overlap from one record to the next, the prediction value would always be different. In our example of 100 initial data points, 90 different training records could be created this way, as opposed to the 10 training records created via the other method.

Why Voting Is Better—K Nearest Neighbors

One of the improvements that is usually made to the basic nearest neighbor algorithm is to take a vote from the K nearest neighbors rather than just relying on the sole nearest neighbor to the unclassified record. In Figure 6-4, you can see that unclassified example C has a nearest neighbor that is a defaulter, yet it is surrounded almost exclusively by records that are good credit risks. In this case, the nearest neighbor to record C is probably an outlier—which may be incorrect data or some non-repeatable idiosyncrasy. In either case

Figure 6-4
The nearest neighbors are shown graphically for three unclassified records: A, B, and C.

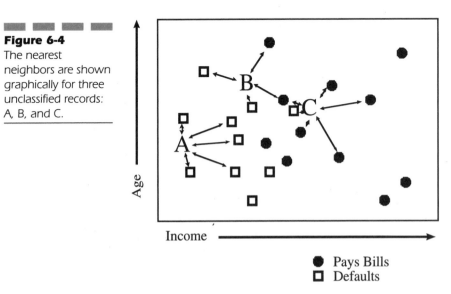

it is more than likely that C is a non-defaulter, yet would be predicted to be a defaulter if the sole nearest neighbor were used for the prediction.

In cases like these, a vote of the 9 or 15 nearest neighbors would provide a better prediction accuracy for the system than would just the single nearest neighbor. Usually, this is accomplished by simply taking the majority or plurality of predictions from the K nearest neighbors if the prediction column is a binary or categorical, or taking the average value of the prediction column from the K nearest neighbors.

How Can the Nearest Neighbor Tell You How Confident It Is with the Prediction?

Another important aspect of any system that is used to make predictions is that the user be provided with not only the prediction, but also some sense of the confidence in that prediction (for example, the prediction is defaulter with the chance of being correct 60% of the time). The nearest neighbor algorithm provides this confidence information in a number of ways.

The distance to the nearest neighbor provides a level of confidence. If the neighbor is very close or an exact match, then there is much higher confidence in the prediction than if the nearest record is a great distance from the unclassified record.

The degree of homogeneity among the predictions within the K nearest neighbors can also be used. If all the nearest neighbors make the same prediction, there is much higher confidence in the prediction than if half the records made one prediction and the other half made another prediction.

Clustering

Clustering is the method by which like records are grouped together. Usually, this is done to give the end user a high-level view of what is going on in the database. Clustering is sometimes used to mean segmentation, which most marketing people will tell you is useful for coming up with a birds-eye view of the business.

Clustering for Clarity

Two of these clustering systems are the PRIZM system from Claritas Corporation and MicroVision from Equifax Corporation. These companies have grouped the population by demographic information into segments that they believe are useful for direct marketing and sales. To build these groupings, they use information such as income, age, occupation, housing, and race collected in the U.S. census. Then, they assign memorable nicknames to the clusters. Some examples are shown in Table 6-2.

This clustering information is then used by the end user to tag the customers in their database. Once this is done, the business user can get a quick high-level view of what is happening within the cluster. Once the business user has worked with these codes for some time,

Table 6-2

Some commercially available cluster tags

Name	Income	Age	Education	Vendor
Blue Blood Estates	Wealthy	35–54	College	Claritas Prizm
Shotguns and Pickups	Middle	35–64	High School	Claritas Prizm
Southside City	Poor	Mix	Grade School	Claritas Prizm
Living Off the Land	Middle-Poor	School Age Families	Low	Equifax MicroVision
University USA	Very low	Young—Mix	Medium to High	Equifax MicroVision
Sunset Years	Medium	Seniors	Medium	Equifax MicroVision

they also begin to build intuitions about how these different customers clusters will react to the marketing offers particular to their business. For instance, some of these clusters may relate to their business and some of them may not. But given that their competition may well be using these same clusters to structure their business and marketing offers, it is important to be aware of how your customer base behaves in regard to these clusters.

Finding the Ones That Don't Fit In— Clustering for Outliers

Sometimes, clustering is performed not so much to keep records together as to make it easier to see when one record sticks out from the rest.

Here's an example. Most wine distributors that sell inexpensive wine in Missouri and that ship a certain volume of product produce a certain level of profit. There is a cluster of stores that can be formed with these characteristics. One store stands out, however, as producing significantly lower profit. On closer examination, it turns out that the distributor was delivering products to but not collecting payment from one of their customers.

A sale on men's suits is being held in all branches of a department store for Southern California. All stores with these characteristics have seen at least a 100% jump in revenue since the start of the sale, except one. It turns out that this store had, unlike the others, advertised via radio rather than television.

How Is Clustering Like the Nearest Neighbor Technique?

The nearest neighbor algorithm is basically a refinement of clustering, in the sense that they both use distance in some feature space to create either structure in the data or predictions. The nearest neighbor algorithm is a refinement because part of the algorithm usually is a way of automatically determining the weighting of the importance of the predictors and how the distance will be measured within

142

Part 2:   Foundation—The Technologies and Tools

the feature space. Clustering is one special case of this, in which the importance of each predictor is considered to be equivalent.

How to Put Clustering and Nearest Neighbor to Work for Prediction

To see clustering and nearest neighbor prediction in use, let's go back to our example database and look at it in two ways. First, let's try to create our own clusters. If they are useful, we can use them internally to help to simplify and clarify large quantities of data (and maybe if we do a very good job selling these new codes to other business users). Second, let's try to create predictions based on the nearest neighbor.

First, take a look at the data. How would you cluster the data in Table 6-3?

If these were your friends rather than your customers (hopefully they could be both), and they were single, you might cluster them

Table 6-3

A simple example database

ID	Name	Prediction	Age	Balance	Income	Eyes	Gender
1	Amy	No	62	$0	Medium	Brown	F
2	Al	No	53	$1,800	Medium	Green	M
3	Betty	No	47	$16,543	High	Brown	F
4	Bob	Yes	32	$45	Medium	Green	M
5	Carla	Yes	21	$2,300	High	Blue	F
6	Carl	No	27	$5,400	High	Brown	M
7	Donna	Yes	50	$165	Low	Blue	F
8	Don	Yes	46	$0	High	Blue	M
9	Edna	Yes	27	$500	Low	Blue	F
10	Ed	No	68	$1,200	Low	Blue	M

based on their compatibility with each other. Create your own mini-dating service. If you were a pragmatic person, you might create three clusters because you think that marital happiness is mostly dependent on financial compatibility, as shown in Table 6-4.

Is There Another Correct Way to Cluster?

If, on the other hand, you are more of a romantic, you might note some incompatibilities between 46-year old Don and 21-year old Carla (even though they both make very good incomes). You might instead consider age and some physical characteristics to be most important in creating clusters of friends. Another way you could cluster your friends would be based on their ages and on the color of their eyes (shown in Table 6-5). Here, three clusters are created, in which each person in the cluster is about the same age, and some attempt has been made to keep people of like eye color together in the same cluster.

There is no best way to cluster.

Table 6.4	ID	Name	Prediction	Age	Balance	Income	Eyes	Gender
A simple clustering of the example database	3	Betty	No	47	$16,543	High	Brown	F
	5	Carla	Yes	21	$2,300	High	Blue	F
	6	Carl	No	27	$5,400	High	Brown	M
	8	Don	Yes	46	$0	High	Blue	M
	1	Amy	No	62	$0	Medium	Brown	F
	2	Al	No	53	$1,800	Medium	Green	M
	4	Bob	Yes	32	$45	Medium	Green	M
	7	Donna	Yes	50	$165	Low	Blue	F
	9	Edna	Yes	27	$500	Low	Blue	F
	10	Ed	No	68	$1,200	Low	Blue	M

Table 6-5

A more romantic clustering of the example database to optimize for your dating service

ID	Name	Prediction	Age	Balance	Income	Eyes	Gender
5	Carla	Yes	21	$2,300	High	Blue	F
9	Edna	Yes	27	$500	Low	Blue	F
6	Carl	No	27	$5,400	High	Brown	M
4	Bob	Yes	32	$45	Medium	Green	M
8	Don	Yes	46	$0	High	Blue	M
7	Donna	Yes	50	$165	Low	Blue	F
10	Ed	No	68	$1,200	Low	Blue	M
3	Betty	No	47	$16,543	High	Brown	F
2	Al	No	53	$1,800	Medium	Green	M
1	Amy	No	62	$0	Medium	Brown	F

This example, though simple, points up some important questions about clustering. For instance, is it possible to say whether the first clustering that was performed previously (by financial status) was better or worse than the second clustering (by age and eye color)? Probably not, because the clusterings were constructed for no particular purpose except to note similarities between some of the records, and that the view of the database could be somewhat simplified by using clusters. But even the differences that were created by the two different clusters were driven by slightly different motivations (financial versus romantic). In general, the reasons for clustering are just this ill-defined because clusters are used more often than not for exploration and summarization, as much as they are used for prediction.

How Are Tradeoffs Made When Determining Which Records Fall into Which Clusters?

Notice that for the first clustering example there was a pretty simple rule by which the records could be broken up into clusters—

namely by income. In the second clustering example, there were less-clear dividing lines because two predictors were used to form the clusters (age and eye color). Thus, the first cluster is dominated by younger people with somewhat mixed eye colors, whereas the latter two clusters have a mix of older people whose eye colors have been used to separate them out (the second cluster is entirely blue-eyed people). In this case, these tradeoffs were made arbitrarily, but when clustering much larger numbers of records, these tradeoffs are explicitly defined by the clustering algorithm.

Clustering Is the Happy Medium between Homogeneous Clusters and the Fewest Number of Clusters.

In the best possible case, clusters would be built in which all records within the cluster had identical values for the particular predictors that were being clustered on. This would be the optimum in creating a high-level view because knowing the predictor values for any member of the cluster would mean knowing the values for every member of the cluster, no matter how large the cluster was. Creating homogeneous clusters in which all values for the predictors are the same is difficult to do when there are many predictors and/or the predictors have many different values (high cardinality).

It is possible to guarantee that homogeneous clusters are created by breaking apart any cluster that is unhomogeneous into smaller clusters that are homogeneous. In the extreme, though, this usually means creating clusters with only one record in them, which usually defeats the original purpose of the clustering. For instance, in our 10-record database, 10 perfectly homogeneous clusters could be formed with one record each, but not much progress would have been made in making the original database more understandable.

The second important constraint on clustering is then that a reasonable number of clusters are formed. Reasonable is again defined by the user, but it is difficult to quantify beyond that except to say that just one cluster is unacceptable (too much generalization), and that many clusters and original records is also unacceptable. Many clustering algorithms either let the user choose the number of clusters that they want to see created from the database, or they provide the user a knob by which they can create fewer or greater numbers of clusters interactively after the clustering has been performed.

What Is the Difference between Clustering and the Nearest Neighbor Prediction?

The main distinction between clustering and the nearest neighbor technique is that clustering is what is called an unsupervised learning technique, and nearest neighbor is generally used for prediction or a supervised learning technique. Unsupervised learning techniques are unsupervised in the sense that when they are run, there is not a particular reason for the creation of the models the way there is for supervised learning techniques that are trying to perform prediction. In prediction, the patterns that are found in the database and presented in the model are always the most important patterns in the database for performing some particular prediction. In clustering, there is no particular sense of why certain records are near each other or why they all fall into the same cluster. Some of the differences between clustering and nearest neighbor prediction can be summarized in Table 6-6.

Table 6-6

Some of the differences between the nearest neighbor data mining technique and clustering

Nearest Neighbor	Clustering
Used for prediction as well as consolidation	Used mostly for consolidating data into a high-level view and general grouping of records into like behaviors
Space is defined by the problem to be solved (supervised learning).	Space is defined as default n-dimensional space, or is defined by the user, or is a predefined space driven by past experience (unsupervised learning).
Generally, only uses distance metrics to determine nearness	Can use other metrics besides distance to determine nearness of two records—for example linking two points together

What Is an *n*-Dimensional Space? Do I Really Need to Know This?

When people talk about clustering or nearest neighbor prediction, they will often talk about a "space" of *n* dimensions. What they mean is that in order to define what is near and what is far away, it is helpful to have a space defined where distance can be calculated. Generally, these spaces behave just like the three-dimensional space that we are familiar with, in which distance between objects is defined by Euclidean distance (just like figuring out the length of a side in a triangle).

What goes for three dimensions works pretty well for more dimensions as well. This is a good thing because most real-world problems consist of many more than three dimensions. In fact, each predictor (or database column) that is used can be considered to be a new dimension. In the previous example, the five predictors (age, income, balance, eyes, and gender) can all be construed to be dimensions in an *n*-dimensional space where *n*, in this case, equals 5. It is sometimes easier to think about these and other data mining algorithms in terms of *n*-dimensional spaces because it allows for some intuitions to be used about how the algorithm is working.

Moving from three dimensions to five dimensions is not too large a jump, but there are also spaces in real-world problems that are far more complex. In the credit card industry, credit card issuers typically have more than one thousand predictors that could be used to create an *n*-dimensional space. For text retrieval (for example, finding useful *Wall Street Journal* articles from a large database or finding useful Web sites on the Internet), the predictors (and hence the dimensions) are typically words or phrases that are found in the document records. In just one year of the *Wall Street Journal*, there are more than 50,000 different words used—which translates to a 50,000-dimensional space, in which nearness between records must be calculated.

How Is the Space for Clustering and Nearest Neighbor Defined?

For clustering, the n-dimensional space is usually defined by assigning one predictor to each dimension. For the nearest neighbor, algorithm predictors are also mapped to dimensions, but then those dimensions are literally stretched or compressed, based on how important the particular predictor is in making the prediction. The stretching of a dimension effectively makes that dimension (and hence predictor) more important than the others in calculating the distance.

For instance, if you are a mountain climber and someone told you that you were two miles from your destination, the distance is the same whether it's one mile north and one mile up the face of the mountain or two miles north on level ground. Clearly, the former route is much different from the latter, however. The distance traveled straight upward is the most important if figuring out how long it will really take to get to the destination, so you would probably like to consider this dimension to be more important than the others. In fact, as a mountain climber, you could weight the importance of the vertical dimension in calculating some new distance by reasoning that every mile upward is equivalent to 10 miles on level ground.

If you used this rule of thumb to weight the importance of one dimension over the other, it would be clear that in one case you were much further away from your destination (11 miles) than in the second (2 miles). In the next section, we'll show how the nearest neighbor algorithm uses distance measure that similarly weights the important dimensions more heavily when calculating a distance measure.

Hierarchical and Non-Hierarchical Clustering

There are two main types of clustering techniques: those that create a hierarchy of clusters and those that do not. The hierarchical clustering techniques create a hierarchy of clusters, from small to big. The main reason for this is that, as was already stated, clustering is an unsupervised learning technique, and as such, there is no absolutely correct answer. For this reason and depending on the particular application of the clustering, fewer or greater numbers of clusters may be desired. With a hierarchy of clusters defined, it is possible to choose the number of clusters that are desired. At the extreme, it is possible to have as many clusters as there are records in the database. In this case, the records within the cluster are optimally similar to each other (because there is only one) and are certainly different from the other clusters. Of course, such a clustering technique misses the point because the idea of clustering is to find useful patters in the database that summarize it and make it easier to understand. Any clustering algorithm that ends up with as many clusters as there are records has not helped the user understand the data any better. Thus, one of the main points about clustering is that there be many fewer clusters than there are original records. Exactly how many clusters should be formed is a matter of interpretation. The advantage of hierarchical clustering methods is that they allow the end user to choose from either many clusters or only a few.

The hierarchy of clusters is usually viewed as a tree, where the smallest clusters merge together to create the next-highest level of clusters and those at that level merge together to create the next-highest level of clusters. Figure 6-5 shows how several clusters might form a hierarchy. When a hierarchy of clusters like this is created, the user can determine what the right number of clusters is to adequately summarize the data while still providing useful information. (At the other extreme, a single cluster containing all the records is a great summarization, but does not contain enough specific information to be useful.)

This hierarchy of clusters is created through the algorithm that builds the clusters. There are two main types of hierarchical clustering algorithms:

- *Agglomerative.* Agglomerative clustering techniques start with as many clusters as there are records where each cluster contains just one record. The clusters that are nearest each

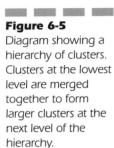

Figure 6-5
Diagram showing a hierarchy of clusters. Clusters at the lowest level are merged together to form larger clusters at the next level of the hierarchy.

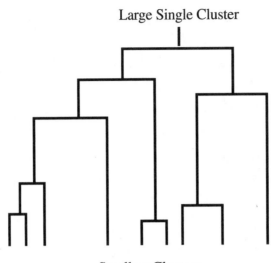

Large Single Cluster

Smallest Clusters

other are merged together to form the next largest cluster. This merging is continued until a hierarchy of clusters is built with just a single cluster containing all the records at the top of the hierarchy.

■ *Divisive.*   Divisive clustering techniques take the opposite approach from agglomerative techniques. These techniques start with all the records in one cluster, and then try to split that cluster into smaller pieces and then in turn to try to split those smaller pieces.

Of the two, the agglomerative techniques are most commonly used for clustering and have more algorithms developed for them. We'll talk about these in more detail in the next section. The non-hierarchical techniques in general are faster to create from the historical database, but require that the user make some decision about the number of clusters desired or the minimum nearness required for two records to be within the same cluster. These non-hierarchical techniques often are run multiple times, starting off with some arbitrary or even random clustering and then iteratively improving the clustering by shuffling some records around. Or, these techniques sometimes create clusters that are created with only one pass through the database, adding records to existing clusters when they exist and creating new clusters when no existing cluster is a good candidate for the given record. Because the definition of which clusters are formed can depend on these initial choices of which starting clusters should be chosen or even how many clusters, these techniques can be less repeatable than the hierarchical techniques. They can sometimes create either too many or too few clusters because the number of clusters is predetermined by the user, not determined solely by the patterns inherent in the database.

Non-Hierarchical Clustering

There are two main non-hierarchical clustering techniques. Both of them are very fast to compute on the database, but have some drawbacks. The first are the single pass methods. They derive their name from the fact that the database must be passed through only once to create the clusters (that is, each record is read from the database only once). The other techniques are called reallocation methods. They get their name from the movement or reallocation of records from one cluster to another, in order to create better clusters. The reallocation techniques do use multiple passes through the database, but are relatively fast in comparison with the hierarchical techniques.

Some techniques allow the user to request the number of clusters that they would like to be pulled out of the data. Predefining the number of clusters rather than having them driven by the data might seem to be a bad idea because there might be some very distinct and observable clustering of the data into a certain number of clusters that the user might not be aware of.

For instance, the user may wish to see their data broken up into 10 clusters but the data itself partitions very cleanly into 13 clusters. These non-hierarchical techniques will try to shoehorn these extra three clusters into the existing 10 rather than creating 13, which best fit the data. The saving grace for these methods, however, is that, as we have seen, there is no one right answer for how to cluster, so it is rare that by arbitrarily predefining the number of clusters you would end up with the wrong answer. One of the advantages of these techniques is that often the user does have some predefined level of summarization that they are interested in (for example, "25 clusters is too confusing, but 10 will help to give me an insight into my data"). The fact that greater or fewer numbers of clusters would better match the data is actually of secondary importance.

Hierarchical Clustering

Hierarchical clustering has the advantage over non-hierarchical techniques in that the clusters are defined solely by the data (not by the users predetermining the number of clusters), and that the number of clusters can be increased or decreased by simple moving up and down the hierarchy.

The hierarchy is created by starting either at the top (one cluster that includes all records) and subdividing (divisive clustering), or by starting at the bottom with as many clusters as there are records and merging (agglomerative clustering). Usually, the merging and subdividing are done two clusters at a time.

The main distinction between the techniques is their capability to favor long, scraggly clusters that are linked together record by record; or to favor the detection of the more classical, compact, or spherical cluster that was shown at the beginning of this chapter. It may seem strange to want to form these long, snaking, chain-like clusters, but in some cases they are the patters that the user would like to have detected in the database. These are the times when the underlying space looks quite different from the spherical clusters, and the clusters that should be formed are not based on the distance from the center of the cluster, but instead are based on the records being linked together. Consider the example shown in Figure 6-6 or Figure 6-7. In these cases, there are two clusters that are not very spherical in shape, but could be detected by the single-link technique.

When looking at the layout of the data in Figure 6-6, there appears to be two relatively flat clusters running parallel to each along the income axis. Neither the complete link nor Ward's method would, however, return these two clusters to the user. These techniques rely on creating a center for each cluster and picking these

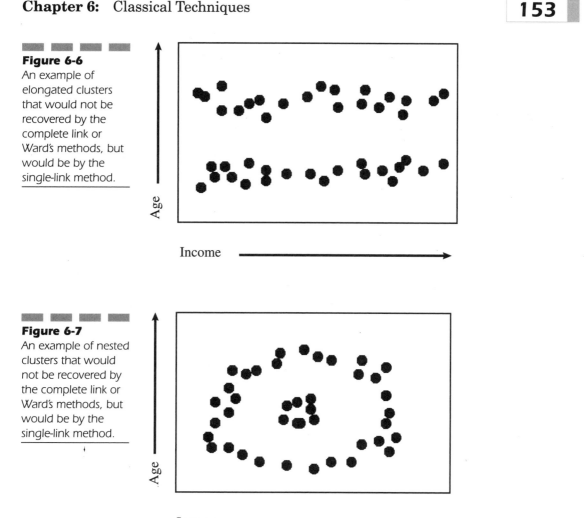

Figure 6-6
An example of elongated clusters that would not be recovered by the complete link or Ward's methods, but would be by the single-link method.

Figure 6-7
An example of nested clusters that would not be recovered by the complete link or Ward's methods, but would be by the single-link method.

centers, so that they average distance of each record from this center is minimized. Points that are very distant from these centers would necessarily fall into a different cluster.

What makes these clusters visible in this simple two-dimensional space is the fact that each point in a cluster is tightly linked to some other point in the cluster. For the two clusters, we see that the maximum distance between the nearest two points within a cluster is less than the minimum distance of the nearest two points in different clusters. For any point in this space, the nearest point to it is always going to be another point in the same cluster. Now, the center of gravity of a cluster could be quite distant from a given point, but every point is linked to every other point by a series of small distances.

Choosing the Classics

There is no particular rule to tell you when to choose one particular technique over another one. Sometimes, those decisions are made relatively arbitrarily, based on the availability of data mining analysts who are most experienced in one technique over another. Even choosing classical techniques over some of the newer techniques is more dependent on the availability of good tools and good analysts. Whichever techniques are chosen, whether classical or next generation, all of the techniques presented here have been available and tried for more than two decades. So even the next generation is a solid bet for implementation.

CHAPTER 7

Next Generation Techniques: Trees, Networks and Rules

The Next Generation

The data mining techniques in this chapter represent the most-often-used techniques that have been developed over the last two decades of research. They also represent the vast majority of the techniques that are being spoken about when data mining is mentioned in the popular press. These techniques can be used for either discovering new information within large databases or for building predictive models. Although the older decision tree techniques such as CHAID are currently widely used, the new techniques such as CART are gaining more acceptance.

Decision Trees

What Is a Decision Tree?

As its name implies, a decision tree is a predictive model that can be viewed as a tree. Specifically, each branch of the tree is a classification question, and the leaves of the tree are partitions of the dataset with their classification. For instance, to classify customers who churn (don't renew their phone contracts) in the cellular telephone industry, a decision tree might look something like that found in Figure 7-1.

You may notice some interesting things about the tree:

- It divides up the data on each branch point without losing any of the data (the number of total records in a given parent node is equal to the sum of the records contained in its two children).

- The number of churners and non-churners is conserved as you move up or down the tree.

- It is pretty easy to understand how the model is being built (in contrast to the models from neural networks or from standard statistics).

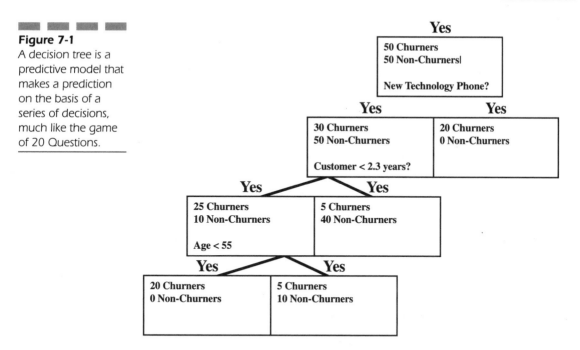

A decision tree is a predictive model that makes a prediction on the basis of a series of decisions, much like the game of 20 Questions.

- It is pretty easy to use this model if you actually have to target those customers who are likely to churn with a targeted marketing offer.
- You may also build some intuitions about your customer base (for example, "customers who have been with me for a couple of years and have up-to-date cellular phones are pretty loyal").

Viewing Decision Trees as Segmentation with a Purpose

From a business perspective, decision trees can be viewed as creating a segmentation of the original dataset (each segment would be one of the leaves of the tree). Segmentation of customers, products, and sales regions is something that marketing managers have been doing for many years. In the past, this segmentation has been performed in order to get a high-level view of a large amount of data—with no particular reason for creating the segmentation, except that the records within each segmentation were somewhat similar to each other.

In this case, the segmentation is done for a particular reason—namely, for the prediction of some important piece of information. The records that fall within each segment fall there because they have similarity with respect to the information being predicted—not only that they are similar—without the similarity being well-defined. These predictive segments that are derived from the decision tree also come with a description of the characteristics that define the predictive segment. Thus, although the decision trees and the algorithms that create them may be complex, the results can be presented in an easy-to-understand way that can be quite useful to the business user.

Applying Decision Trees to Business

Because of their tree structure and capability to easily generate rules, decision trees are the favored technique for building understandable models. Because of this clarity, they also allow for more complex profit and ROI models to be added easily in on top of the predictive model. For instance, suppose that a customer population is found with high predicted likelihood to attrite. A variety of cost models can be used to see whether an expensive marketing intervention should be used because the customers are highly valuable, or whether a less-expensive intervention should be used because the revenue from this sub-population of customers is marginal.

Because of their high level of automation and the ease of translating decision tree models into SQL for deployment in relational databases, the technology has also proven to be easy to integrate with existing IT processes. It requires little preprocessing and cleansing of the data, or extraction of a special-purpose file specifically for data mining.

Where Can Decision Trees Be Used?

Decision trees are data mining technology that has been around in a form very similar to the technology of today for almost twenty years, and early versions of the algorithms date back to the 1960s. Often, these techniques were originally developed for statisticians to automate the process of determining which fields in their databases were actually useful or correlated with the particular problem that they were trying to understand. Partially because of this history, decision tree algorithms tend to automate the entire process of hypothesis generation and then validation much more completely and in a much more integrated way than any other data mining techniques. They are also particularly adept at handling raw data with little or no pre-processing. Perhaps also because they were originally developed to mimic the way an analyst interactively performs data mining, they provide a simple-to-understand predictive model based on rules. For example, "90% of the time, credit card customers of less than three months who max out their credit limit are going to default on their credit card loan."

Because decision trees score so highly on so many of the critical features of data mining, they can be used in a wide variety of business problems for both exploration and for prediction. They have been used for problems ranging from credit card attrition prediction to time series prediction of the exchange rate of different international currencies. There are also some problems where decision trees will not do as well. Some very simple problems where the prediction is just a simple multiple of the predictor can be solved much more quickly and easily by linear regression. Usually, the models to be built and the interactions to be detected are much more complex in real-world problems, and this is where decision trees excel.

Using Decision Trees for Exploration

The decision tree technology can be used for exploration of the dataset and business problem. This is often done by looking at the predictors and values that are chosen for each split of the tree. Often, these predictors provide usable insights or propose questions that need to be answered. For instance, if you ran across the following in your database for cellular phone churn, you might seriously wonder about the way your telesales operators were making their calls, and maybe change the way that they are compensated:

IF customer lifetime < 1.1 years AND sales channel 5 telesales, THEN chance of churn is 65%

Using Decision Trees for Data Preprocessing

Another way that the decision tree technology is used is to pre-process data for other prediction algorithms. Because the algorithm is fairly robust with respect to a variety of predictor types (number, categorical), and because it can be run relatively quickly, decision trees can be used on the first pass of a data mining run to create a subset of possibly useful predictors. They can then be fed into neural networks, nearest neighbor and normal statistical routines—which can take a considerable amount of time to run if there are large numbers of possible predictors to be used in the model.

Decision Trees for Prediction

Although some forms of decision trees were initially developed as exploratory tools to refine and preprocess data for more standard statistical techniques such as logistic regression, they have also been used more and more often for prediction. This is interesting because many statisticians will still use decision trees for exploratory analysis, effectively building a predictive model as a by-product, but then ignore the predictive model in favor of techniques that they are most comfortable with. Sometimes, veteran analysts will do this, even excluding the predictive model when it is superior to that produced by other techniques. With a host of new products and skilled users now appearing, this tendency to use decision trees only for exploration seems to be changing.

The First Step Is Growing the Tree

The first step in the process is that of growing the tree. Specifically, the algorithm seeks to create a tree that works as perfectly as possible on all the data that is available. Most of the time, it is not possible to have the algorithm work perfectly. There is always noise in the database to some degree (there are variables that are not being collected that have an impact on the target you are trying to predict).

The name of the game in growing the tree is to find the best possible question to ask at each branch point of the tree. At the bottom of the tree, you will come up with nodes that you want to be all of one type or the other. Thus, the question "Are you over 40?" probably does not sufficiently distinguish between those who are churners and those who are not—let's say it is 40%/60%. On the other hand, there may be a series of questions that do quite a nice job of distinguishing those cellular phone customers who will churn and those who won't. Maybe the series of questions would be something like the following: "Have you been a customer for less than a year, do you have a telephone that is more than two years old, and were you originally landed as a customer via telesales rather than direct sales?" This series of questions defines a segment of the customer population in which 90% churn. These are then relevant questions to be asking in relation to predicting churn.

The Difference between a Good Question and a Bad Question

The difference between a good question and a bad question has to do with how much the question can organize the data—or in this case, change the likelihood of a churner appearing in the customer segment. If we start off with our population being half churners and half non-churners, then we would expect that a question that didn't organize the data to some degree into one segment that was more likely to churn than the other wouldn't be a very useful question to ask. On the other hand, if we asked a question that was very good at distinguishing between churners and non-churners—that split 100 customers into one segment of 50 churners and another segment of 50 non-churners—this would be considered to be a good question. In fact, it decreased the "disorder" of the original segment as much as possible.

The process in decision tree algorithms is very similar when trees are built. These algorithms look at all possible distinguishing questions that could possibly break up the original training dataset into segments that are nearly homogeneous with respect to the different classes being predicted. Some decision tree algorithms may use heuristics in order to pick the questions, or even pick them at random. CART picks the questions in a very unsophisticated way: It tries them all. After it has tried them all, CART picks the best one, uses it to split the data into two more organized segments, and then again asks all possible questions on each of those new segments individually.

When Does the Tree Stop Growing?

If the decision tree algorithm just continued growing, it could conceivably create more and more questions and branches in the tree, so that eventually there would be only one record in the segment. To let the tree grow to this size is computationally expensive, but also unnecessary. Most decision tree algorithms stop growing the tree when one of the following three criteria is met:

- The segment contains only one record. (There are no other questions that you can ask to further refine a segment of just one.)
- All the records in the segment have identical characteristics. (There is no reason to continue asking further questions because all the remaining records are the same.)
- The improvement is not substantial enough to warrant asking the question.

Why Would a Decision Tree Algorithm Stop Growing the Tree If There Wasn't Enough Data?

Consider the following example, shown in Table 7-1, of a segment that we might want to split further that has just two examples. It has been created out of a much larger customer database by selecting only those customers who are aged 27, have blue eyes, and earn salaries between $80,000 and $81,000.

This segment cannot be split further, except by using the predictor "name". All possible questions that could be asked about the two customers turn out to have the same value (age, eyes, salary) except for

	Name	Age	Eyes	Salary	Churned?
Table 7-1					
Decision Tree Algorithm Segment.	Steve	27	Blue	$80,000	Yes
	Alex	27	Blue	$80,000	No

the name. It would then be possible to ask a question such as the following: "Is the customer's name Steve?" and create the segments that would be very good at breaking apart those who churned from those who did not.

The problem is that we all have an intuition that the name of the customer is not going to be a very good indicator of whether that customer churns or not. It might work well for this particular two-record segment, but it is unlikely that it will work for other customer databases or even the same customer database at a different time. This particular example has to do with overfitting the model—in this case, fitting the model too closely to the idiosyncrasies of the training data. This can be fixed later on, but clearly stopping the building of the tree short of either one record segment or very small segments is a good idea.

Decision Trees Aren't Necessarily Finished after the Tree Is Grown

After the tree has been grown to a certain size (depending on the particular stopping criteria used in the algorithm), the CART algorithm has still more work to do. The algorithm then checks to see whether the model has been overfit to the data. It does this in several ways: using a cross-validation approach or a test set validation approach. Basically, it uses the same mind-numbingly simple approach it used to find the best questions in the first place—trying many different simpler versions of the tree on a held aside test set. The tree that does the best on the held-aside data is selected by the algorithm as the best model. The nice thing about CART is that this testing and selection is all an integral part of the algorithm, as opposed to the after-the-fact approach that other techniques use.

ID3 and an Enhancement—C4.5

In the late 1970s, J. Ross Quinlan introduced a decision tree algorithm named ID3. It was one of the first decision tree algorithms, yet built solidly on work that had been done on inference systems and concept learning systems from that decade, as well as from the preceding decade. Initially, ID3 was used for tasks such as learning good game-playing strategies for chess end games. Since then, ID3 has been applied to a wide variety of problems in both academia and industry; and has been modified, improved, and borrowed from many times over.

ID3 picks predictors and their splitting values, based on the gain in information that the split or splits provide. Gain represents the difference between the amount of information that is needed to correctly make a prediction before a split is made and after the split has been made. If the amount of information required is much lower after the split is made, then that split has decreased the disorder of the original single segment. Gain is defined as the difference between the entropy of the original segment and the accumulated entropies of the resulting split segments.

ID3 was later enhanced in the version called C4.5. C4.5 improves on ID3 in several important areas:

- predictors with missing values can still be used
- predictors with continuous values can be used
- pruning is introduced
- rule derivation

Many of these techniques (plus some others) appear in the CART algorithm, so we will go through this introduction in the CART algorithm.

CART—Growing a Forest and Picking the Best Tree

CART, which stands for Classification and Regression Trees, is a data exploration and prediction algorithm developed by Leo Breiman,

Jerome Friedman, Richard Olshen, and Charles Stone. It is nicely detailed in their 1984 book, *Classification and Regression Trees* (Breiman, Friedman, Olshen, and Stone, 1984). These researchers from Stanford University and the University of California at Berkeley showed how this new algorithm could be used on a variety of different problems from the detection of chlorine from the data contained in a mass spectrum.

Predictors are picked as they decrease the disorder of the data. In building the CART tree, each predictor is picked based on how well it teases apart the records with different predictions. For instance, one measure that is used to determine whether a given split point for a give predictor is better than another is the entropy metric. The measure originated from the work done by Claude Shannon and Warren Weaver on information theory in 1949. They were concerned with how information could be efficiently communicated over telephone lines. Interestingly, their results also prove useful in creating decision trees.

CART Automatically Validates the Tree

One of the great advantages of CART is that the algorithm has the validation of the model and the discovery of the optimally general model built deeply into the algorithm. CART accomplishes this by building a very complex tree and then pruning it back to the optimally general tree, based on the results of cross-validation or test set validation. The tree is pruned back, based on the performance of the various pruned versions of the tree on the test set data. The most complex tree rarely fares the best on the held aside data because it has been overfitted to the training data. By using cross-validation, the tree that is most likely to do well on new unseen data can be chosen.

CART Surrogates Handle Missing Data

The CART algorithm is relatively robust with respect to missing data. If the value is missing for a particular predictor in a particular record, that record will not be used to determine the optimal split when the tree is being built. In effect, CART utilizes as much information as it has on hand in order to make the decision for picking the best possible split.

When CART is being used to predict on new data, missing values can be handled via surrogates. Surrogates are split values and predictors that mimic the actual split in the tree, and can be used when the data for the preferred predictor is missing. For instance, although shoe size is not a perfect predictor of height, it could be used as a surrogate to try to mimic a split based on height when that information was missing from the particular record being predicted with the CART model.

CHAID

Another popular decision tree technology is CHAID, or Chi-Square Automatic Interaction Detector. CHAID is similar to CART in that it builds a decision tree, but it differs in the way that it chooses its splits. Instead of the entropy or Gini metrics for choosing optimal splits, the technique relies on the chi square test used in contingency tables to determine which categorical predictor is furthest from independence with the prediction values.

Because CHAID relies on the contingency tables to form its test of significance for each predictor, all predictors must either be categorical or be coerced into a categorical form via binning (for example, break up people's ages into 10 bins: 0–9, 10–19, 20–29, and so on). Although this binning can have deleterious consequences, the actual accuracy performances of CART and CHAID have been shown to be comparable in real-world direct marketing response models.

Neural Networks

What Is a Neural Network?

When data mining algorithms are talked about these days, people usually talk about either decision trees or neural networks. Of the two, neural networks have probably been of greater interest through the formative stages of data mining technology. As you will see, neural networks have disadvantages that can be limiting in their ease of use and ease of deployment, but they also have some significant advantages. Foremost among these advantages are their highly accurate predictive models that can be applied to a variety of different types of problems.

To be more precise with the term "neural network," you might better speak of an "artificial neural network." True neural networks are biological systems (a.k.a. brains) that detect patterns, make predictions, and learn. The artificial ones are computer programs implementing sophisticated pattern detection and machine learning algorithms on a computer to build predictive models from large historical databases. Artificial neural networks derive their name from their historical development, which started off with the premise that machines could be made to "think" if scientists found ways to mimic the structure and functioning of the human brain on the computer. Historically, neural networks grew out of the community of Artificial Intelligence rather than from the discipline of statistics. Despite the fact that scientists are still far from understanding the human brain, let alone mimicking it, neural networks that run on computers can do some of the things that people can do.

It is difficult to say exactly when the first "neural network" on a computer was built. During World War II, a seminal paper was published by McCulloch and Pitts. It first outlined the idea that simple processing units (such as the individual neurons in the human brain) could be connected together in large networks to create a system that could solve difficult problems and display behavior that was much more complex than the simple pieces that made it up. Since that time, much progress has been made in finding ways to apply artificial neural networks to real-world prediction problems and in improving the performance of the algorithm in general. In recent years, the greatest breakthroughs in neural networks have been in their application to more mundane real world problems. These include customer response prediction or fraud detection, rather than the loftier goals that were originally set out for the techniques: overall human learning, computer speech, and image understanding.

Don't Neural Networks Learn to Make Better Predictions?

Because of the origins of the techniques and because of some of their early successes, the techniques have enjoyed a great deal of interest. To understand how neural networks can detect patterns in a database, an analogy is often made that they "learn" to detect these patterns and make better predictions like human beings do. This view is encouraged by the way the historical training data is often supplied to the network—one record (example) at a time. Neural networks do "learn" in a very real sense, but under the hood the algorithms and techniques that are being deployed are not truly different from the techniques found in statistics or other data mining algorithms. It is, for instance, unfair to assume that neural networks could outperform other techniques because they "learn" and improve over time whereas the other techniques are static. The other techniques, in fact, "learn" from historical examples in exactly the same way, Often, however, the examples (historical records) to learn from are processed all at once in a more efficient manner than neural networks, which often modify their model one record at a time.

Are Neural Networks Easy to Use?

A common claim for neural networks is that they are automated so that the user does not need to know that much about how they work, about predictive modeling, or even about the database in order to use them. The implicit claim is also that most neural networks can be unleashed on your data straight out of the box without having to rearrange or modify the data very much to begin with.

Just the opposite is often true. There are many important design decisions that need to be made to effectively use a neural network, such as the following:

- How should the nodes in the network be connected?
- How many neuron-like processing units should be used?
- When should "training" be stopped in order to avoid overfitting?

There are also many important steps required for preprocessing the data that goes into a neural network. Most often, there is a requirement to normalize numeric data between 0.0 and 1.0, and categorical predictors may need to be broken up into virtual predictors that are 0 or 1 for each value of the original categorical predictor. And, as always, understanding what the data in your database means and having a clear definition of the business problem to be solved are essential for ensuring eventual success. The bottom line is that neural networks provide no shortcuts.

Applying Neural Networks to Business

Neural networks are very powerful predictive modeling techniques, but some of the power comes at the expense of ease-of-use and ease-of deployment. As you will see in this chapter, neural networks create very complex models that are almost always impossible to fully understand, even by experts. The model itself is represented by numeric values in a complex calculation that requires all of the predictor values to be in the form of a number. The output of the neural network is also numeric and needs to be translated if the actual prediction value is categorical. For example, predicting the demand for blue, white, or black jeans for a clothing manufacturer requires that the predictor values blue, black, and white for the predictor color be converted to numbers.

Because of the complexity of these techniques, much effort has been expended in trying to increase the clarity with which the model can be understood by the end user. These efforts are still in their infancy, but are of tremendous importance because most data mining techniques, including neural networks, are being deployed against real business problems where significant investments are made based on the predictions from the models. (For example, consider trusting the predictive model from a neural network that dictates which one million customers will receive a $1 mailing.)

These shortcomings in understanding the meaning of the neural network model have been successfully addressed in the following two ways:

- The neural network is packaged up into a complete solution such as fraud prediction. This allows the neural network to be carefully crafted for one particular application. After it has proved to be successful, it can be used over and over again, without requiring a deep understanding of how it works.

- The neural network is packaged up with expert consulting services. Here, the neural network is deployed by trusted experts who have a track record of success. Either the experts are able to explain the models or they are trusted that the models do work.

The first tactic has seemed to work quite well. When the technique is used for a well-defined problem, many of the difficulties in preprocessing the data can be automated (because the data structures have been seen before). Interpretation of the model is less of an issue because entire industries begin to use the technology successfully and a level of trust is created. There are several vendors who have deployed this strategy (for example, HNC's Falcon system for credit card fraud prediction and Advanced Software Applications' Model-MAX package for direct marketing).

Packaging up neural networks with expert consultants is also a viable strategy that avoids many of the pitfalls of using neural networks, but it can be quite expensive because it is human-intensive. One of the great promises of data mining is, after all, the automation of the predictive modeling process. These neural network-consulting teams are little different from the analytical departments many companies already have in-house. Because there is not a great difference in the overall predictive accuracy of neural networks over standard statistical techniques, the main difference becomes the replacement of the statistical expert with the neural network expert. With statistics or neural network experts, the value of putting easy-to-use tools into the hands of the business end user is still not achieved.

Where to Use Neural Networks

Neural networks are used in a wide variety of applications. They have been used in all facets of business, from detecting the fraudulent use of credit cards and credit risk prediction to increasing the hit rate of targeted mailings. They also have a long history of application in other areas: the military (for the automated driving of an unmanned vehicle at 30 miles per hour on paved roads) and biological simulations (such as learning the correct pronunciation of English words from written text).

Neural Networks for Clustering

Neural networks of various kinds can be used for clustering and prototype creation. The Kohonen network described in this chapter is probably the most common network used for clustering and segmentation of the database. Typically, the networks are used in an unsupervised learning mode to create the clusters. The clusters are created by forcing the system to compress the data by creating prototypes, or by algorithms that steer the system toward creating clusters that compete against each other for the records that they contain. This ensures that the clusters overlap as little as possible.

Neural Networks for Outlier Analysis

Sometimes, clustering is performed not so much to keep records together as to make it easier to see when one record sticks out from the rest. For instance, most wine distributors that sell inexpensive wine in Missouri and that ship a certain volume of product produce a certain level of profit. There is a cluster of stores that can be formed with these characteristics. One store stands out, however, as producing significantly lower profit. On closer examination, it turns out that the distributor was delivering product to but not collecting payment from one of their customers.

A sale on men's suits is being held in all branches of a department store in Southern California. All stores with these characteristics have seen at least a 100% jump in revenue since the start of the sale, except one. It turns out that this store had, unlike the others, advertised via radio rather than television.

Neural Networks for Feature Extraction

One of the important problems in all of data mining is that of determining which predictors are the most relevant and the most important in building models that are most accurate at prediction. These predictors may be used alone or in conjunction with other predictors to form "features." A simple example of a feature in problems that neural networks are working on is the feature of a vertical line in a computer image. The predictors or raw input data are just the colored pixels that make up the picture. Recognizing that the predictors (pixels) can be organized in such a way as to create lines, and then using the line as the input predictor can prove to dramatically improve the accuracy of the model and decrease the time necessary to create it.

Some features, such as lines in computer images, are things that humans are already pretty good at detecting. In other problem domains, it is more difficult to recognize the features. One novel way that neural networks have been used to detect features is with the idea that features are sort of a compression of the training database. For instance, you could describe an image to a friend by rattling off the color and intensity of each pixel on every point in the picture. You could also describe it at a higher level in terms of lines and circles; or describe it even at a higher level of features such as trees, mountains, and so on. In either case, your friend eventually gets all the information that they need to know what the picture looks like. Describing it in terms of high-level features requires much less communication of information than the "paint-by-numbers" approach of describing the color on each square millimeter of the image.

If we think of features in this way, as an efficient way to communicate our data, neural networks can be used to automatically extract them. The neural network shown in Figure 7-2 is used to extract features by requiring the network to learn to re-create the input data at the output nodes by using just five hidden nodes. Consider that if you were allowed 100 hidden nodes, re-creating the data for the network would be rather trivial. You would simply pass the input node value directly through the corresponding hidden node and on to the output node. Because there are fewer and fewer hidden nodes, however, that information has to be passed through the hidden layer in a more and more efficient manner.

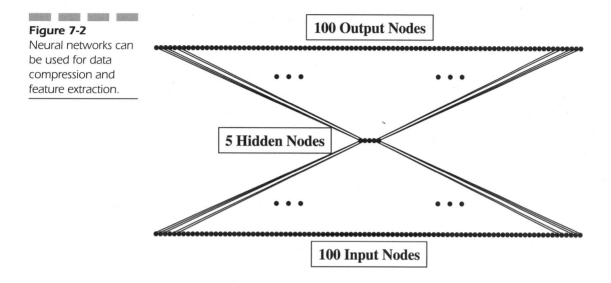

To accomplish this, the neural network tries to have the hidden nodes extract features from the input nodes that efficiently describe the record represented at the input layer. This forced "squeezing" of the data through the narrow hidden layer forces the neural network to extract only those predictors and combinations of predictors that are best at re-creating the input record. The link weights used to create the inputs to the hidden nodes are effectively creating features that are combinations of the input nodes' values.

What Does a Neural Net Look Like?

A neural network is loosely based on the way some people believe that the human brain is organized and how it learns. There are two main structures of consequence in the neural network:

- The node, which loosely corresponds to the neuron in the human brain

- The link, which loosely corresponds to the connections between neurons (axons, dendrites, and synapses) in the human brain

Figure 7-3 shows a drawing of a simple neural network. The round circles represent the nodes and the connecting lines represent the

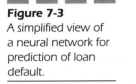

Figure 7-3
A simplified view of
a neural network for
prediction of loan
default.

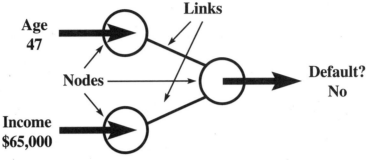

links. The neural network functions by accepting predictor values at the left, and then performs calculations on those values to produce new values in the node at the far right. The value at this node represents the prediction from the neural network model. In this case, the network takes in values for predictors for age and income, and predicts whether a person will default on a bank loan.

How Does a Neural Net Make a Prediction?

In order to make a prediction, the neural network accepts the values for the predictors on what are called the input nodes. These become the values for those nodes. Those values are then multiplied by values that are stored in the links (sometimes called links, and in some ways are similar to the weights that were applied to predictors in the nearest neighbor method). These values are then added together at the node at the far right (the output node,) a special thresholding function is applied, and the resulting number is the prediction. In this case, if the resulting number is 0, the record is considered to be a good credit risk (no default); if the number is 1, the record is considered to be a bad credit risk (likely default).

A simplified version of the calculations made in Figure 7-3 might look like what is shown in Figure 7-4. Here, the value age of 47 is normalized to fall between 0.0 and 1.0, it has the value of 0.47, and the income is normalized to the value 0.65. This simplified neural network makes the prediction of no default for a 47-year old making $65,000. The links are weighted at 0.7 and 0.1, and the resulting value, after multiplying the node values by the link weights, is 0.39.

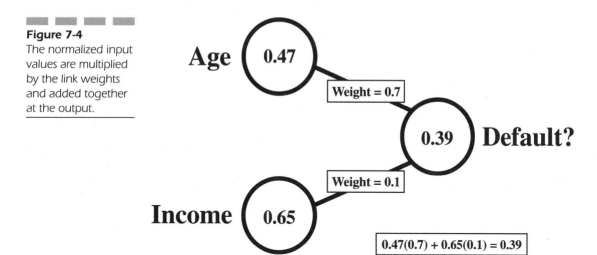

Figure 7-4
The normalized input
values are multiplied
by the link weights
and added together
at the output.

The network has been trained to learn that an output value of 1.0 indicates default and that 0.0 indicates non-default. The output value calculated here (0.39) is closer to 0.0 than to 1.0, so the record is assigned a non-default prediction.

How Is the Neural Net Model Created?

The neural network model is created by presenting it with many examples of the predictor values from records in the training set (in this example, age and income are used) and the prediction value from those same records. By comparing the correct answer obtained from the training record and the predicted answer from the neural network, it is possible to slowly change the behavior of the neural network by changing the values of the link weights. In some ways, this is like having a grade school teacher ask questions of her student (a.k.a. the neural network), and to verbally correct the student if the answer is wrong. The greater the error, the harsher the verbal correction. So large errors are given greater attention at correction than are small errors.

For the actual neural network, it is the weights of the links that actually control the prediction value for a given record. Thus, the particular model that is being found by the neural network is in fact fully determined by the weights and the architectural structure of the network. For this reason. it is the link weights that are modified each time an error is made.

How Complex Can the Neural Network Model Become?

The models shown in the previous figures were designed to be as simple as possible in order to make them understandable. In practice, no networks are as simple as these. Networks with many more links and many more nodes are possible. This was the case in the architecture of a neural network system called NETtalk, which learned how to pronounce written English words. Each node in this network was connected to every node in the level above it and below it, resulting in 18,629 link weights that needed to be learned in the network.

In this network, there is a row of nodes between the input nodes and the output nodes. These are called hidden nodes, or the hidden layer, because the values of these nodes are not visible to the end user the way that the output nodes are (that contain the prediction) and the input nodes (which just contain the predictor values). There are even more complex neural network architectures that have more than one hidden layer. In practice, however, one hidden layer seems to suffice.

Hidden Nodes Are Like Trusted Advisors to the Output Nodes

The meaning of the input nodes and the output nodes are usually pretty well understood—and are usually defined by the end user, based on the particular problem to be solved and the nature and structure of the database. The hidden nodes, however, do not have a predefined meaning and are determined by the neural network as it trains, which poses two problems:

- It is difficult to trust the prediction of the neural network if the meaning of these nodes is not well understood.

■ Because the prediction is made at the output layer, and the difference between the prediction and the actual value is calculated there, how is this error correction fed back through the hidden layers to modify the link weights that connect them?

The meaning of these hidden nodes is not necessarily well-understood, but sometimes they can be looked at after the fact to see when they are active and when they are not, and derive some meaning from them.

The Learning That Goes On in the Hidden Nodes

The learning procedure for the neural network has been defined to work for the weights in the links connecting the hidden layer. A good metaphor for the way this works is to think of a military operation in a war, in which there are many layers of command and a general is ultimately responsible for making the decisions on where to advance and where to retreat. The general probably has several lieutenant generals advising him, and each lieutenant general probably has several major generals advising him. This hierarchy continues downward to the colonels and privates at the bottom of the hierarchy.

This is not too dissimilar from the structure of a neural network with several hidden layers and one output node. You can think of the inputs coming from the hidden nodes as advice. The link weight corresponds to the trust that the general has in his advisors. Some trusted advisors have very high weights; some advisors may not be trusted, and have negative weights, in fact. The other part of the advice from the advisors has to do with how competent the particular advisor is for a given situation. Although the general may have a trusted advisor, if that advisor has no expertise in aerial invasion and the question at hand has to do with a situation involving the air force, this advisor may not have any strong opinion one way or another.

In this analogy, the link weight of a neural network to an output unit is like the trust or confidence that a commander has in his advisors, and the actual node value represents how strong an opinion the advisor has about this particular situation. To make a decision, the general considers how trustworthy and valuable the advice is, and how knowledgeable and confident each advisor is in making their suggestions. After taking all of this into account, the general makes the decision to advance or retreat.

In the same way, the output node will make a decision (a prediction) by taking into account all of the input from its advisors (the nodes connected to it). In the case of the neural network, this decision is reached by multiplying the link weight by the output value of the node and summing these values across all nodes. If the prediction is incorrect, the nodes that had the most influence on making the decision have their weights modified so that the wrong prediction is less likely to be made the next time.

This learning in the neural network is very similar to what happens when the wrong decision is made by the general. The confidence that the general has in all of those advisors that gave the wrong recommendation decreases—even more for those advisors who were very confident and vocal in their recommendation. On the other hand, any advisors who were making the correct recommendation but whose input was not taken as seriously would be taken more seriously the next time. Likewise, any advisor that was reprimanded for giving the wrong advice to the general would then go back to his advisors and determine which of them he had trusted more than he should have in making his recommendation, and which ones he should have listened more closely to.

Sharing the Blame and the Glory throughout the Organization

This feedback can continue in this way down throughout the organization—at each level giving increased emphasis to those advisors who had advised correctly and decreased emphasis to those who had advised incorrectly. In this way, the entire organization becomes better and better at supporting the general in making the correct decision more of the time.

A very similar method of training takes place in the neural network. It is called "back propagation," and it refers to the propagation of the error backward from the output nodes (where the error is easy to determine the difference between the actual prediction value from the training database and the prediction from the neural network). It then goes through the hidden layers and on to the input layers. At each level, the link weights between the layers are updated to decrease the chance of making the same mistake again.

Different Types of Neural Networks

There are literally hundreds of variations on the back propagation feedforward neural networks that were briefly described here. Most have to do with changing the architecture of the neural network to include recurrent connections, where the output from the output layer is connected back as input into the hidden layer. These recurrent nets are sometimes used for sequence prediction, where the previous outputs from the network need to be stored someplace and then fed back into the network to provide context for the current prediction. Recurrent networks have also been used for decreasing the amount of time that it takes to train the neural network.

Another twist on the neural net theme is to change the way that the network learns. Back propagation effectively uses a search technique called gradient descent to search for the best possible improvement in the link weights to reduce the error. There are, however, many other ways of doing a search in a high-dimensional space. These include Newton's methods and conjugate gradient, simulating the physics of cooling metals in a process called simulated annealing, or simulating the search process that goes on in biological evolution and using genetic algorithms to optimize the weights of the neural networks. It has even been suggested that creating a large number of neural networks with randomly weighted links and picking the one with the lowest error rate would be the best learning procedure.

Despite all of these choices, the back propagation learning procedure is the most commonly used. It is well understand, relatively simple, and seems to work in a large number of problem domains. There are, however, two other neural network architectures that are used relatively often. Kohonen feature maps are often used for unsupervised learning and clustering. Radial Basis Function networks are used for supervised learning, and in some ways represent a hybrid between nearest neighbor and neural network classification.

Kohonen Feature Maps

Kohonen feature maps were developed in the 1970s, and as such were created to simulate certain brain function. Today, they are used mostly to perform unsupervised learning and clustering.

Kohonen networks are feedforward neural networks generally with no hidden layer. The networks generally contain only an input layer and an output layer, but the nodes in the output layer compete among themselves to display the strongest activation to a given record. This is sometimes called "winner take all."

The networks originally came about when some of the puzzling yet simple behaviors of the real neurons were taken into effect. Namely, that physical locality of the neurons seems to play an important role in the behavior and learning of neurons.

When these networks were run, in order to simulate the real world visual system, the organization that was automatically being constructed on the data was also very useful for segmenting and clustering the training database. Each output node represented a cluster, and nearby clusters were near in the two-dimensional output layer. Each record in the database would fall into one and only one cluster (the most active output node), but the other clusters in which it might also fit would be shown and likely to be next to the best matching cluster.

How Much Like a Human Brain Is the Neural Network?

Since the inception of the idea of neural networks, the ultimate goal for these techniques has been to have them re-create human thought and learning. This has once again proved to be a difficult task—despite the power of these new techniques and the similarities of their architecture to that of the human brain. Many of the things that people take for granted are difficult for neural networks—like avoiding overfitting and working with real world data without a lot of preprocessing required. There have also been some exciting successes.

Combatting Overfitting—Getting a Model You Can Use Somewhere Else

As with all predictive modeling techniques, some care must be taken to avoid overfitting with a neural network. Neural networks can be quite good at overfitting training data with a predictive model that does not work well on new data. This is particularly problematic for neural networks because it is difficult to understand how the model is working. In the early days of neural networks, the predictive accuracy that was often mentioned first was the accuracy on the training set, and the vaulted or validation set database was reported as a footnote.

This is in part due to the fact that unlike decision trees or nearest neighbor techniques, which can quickly achieve 100% predictive accuracy on the training database, neural networks can be trained forever and still not be 100% accurate on the training set. Although this is an interesting fact, it is not terribly relevant because the accuracy on the training set is of little interest and can have little bearing on the validation database accuracy.

Perhaps because overfitting was more obvious for decision trees and nearest neighbor approaches, more effort was placed earlier on to add pruning and editing to these techniques. For neural networks, generalization of the predictive model is accomplished via rules of thumb, and sometimes in a more methodical way by using cross-validation, as is done with decision trees.

One way to control overfitting in neural networks is to limit the number of links. Because the number of links represents the complexity of the model that can be produced, and because more complex models have the capability to overfit while less-complex ones cannot, overfitting can be controlled by simply limiting the number of links in the neural network. Unfortunately, there are no good theoretical grounds for picking a certain number of links.

Test set validation can be used to avoid overfitting by building the neural network on one portion of the training database and using the other portion of the training database to detect what the predictive accuracy is on vaulted data. This accuracy will peak at some point in the training; as training proceeds, it will decrease while the accuracy on the training database will continue to increase. The link weights for the network can be saved when the accuracy on the held aside data peaks. The NeuralWare product and others provide an automated function that saves out the network when it is best performed on the test set and even continues to search after the minimum is reached.

Explaining the Network

One of the indictments against neural networks is that it is difficult to understand the model that they have built and how the raw data affects the output predictive answer. With nearest neighbor techniques, prototypical records are provided to "explain" why the prediction is made, and decision trees provide rules that can be translated into English to explain why a particular prediction was made for a particular record. The complex models of the neural network are captured solely by the link weights in the network, which represent a very complex mathematical equation.

There have been several attempts to alleviate these basic problems of the neural network. The simplest approach is to actually look at the neural network and try to create plausible explanations for the meanings of the hidden nodes. Some times, this can be done quite successfully. In the example given at the beginning of this chapter, the hidden nodes of the neural network seemed to have extracted important distinguishing features in predicting the relationship between people by extracting information such as country of origin, features that it would seem that a person would also extract and use for the prediction. But there were also many other hidden nodes, even in this particular example, which were hard to explain and didn't seem to have any particular purpose except to aid the neural network in making the correct prediction.

Rule Induction

Rule induction is one of the major forms of data mining and is perhaps the most common form of knowledge discovery in unsupervised learning systems. It is also perhaps the form of data mining that most closely resembles the process that most people think about when they think about data mining, namely "mining" for gold through a vast database. The gold in this case would be a rule that is interesting—that tells you something about your database that you didn't already know and probably weren't able to explicitly articulate (aside from saying "show me things that are interesting").

Rule induction on a database can be a massive undertaking where all possible patterns are systematically pulled out of the data, and then an accuracy and significance are added to them that tell the user how strong the pattern is and how likely it is to occur again. In general, these rules are relatively simple. For a market basket database of items scanned in a consumer market basket, you might find interesting correlations in your database, such as the following:

- If bagels are purchased, cream cheese is purchased 90% of the time, and this pattern occurs in 3% of all shopping baskets.

- If live plants are purchased from a hardware store, plant fertilizer is purchased 60% of the time, and these two items are bought together in 6% of the shopping baskets.

The rules that are pulled from the database are extracted and ordered to be presented to the user, based on the percentage of times that they are correct and how often they apply.

The bane of rule induction systems is also its strength—that it retrieves all possible interesting patterns in the database. This is a strength in the sense that it leaves no stone unturned, but it can also be viewed as a weakness because the user can easily become overwhelmed with such a large number of rules that it is difficult to look through all of them. You almost need a second pass of data mining to go through the list of interesting rules that have been generated by the rule induction system in the first place in order to find the most valuable gold nugget among them all. This overabundance of patterns can also be problematic for the simple task of prediction because when all possible patterns are culled from the database, there may be conflicting predictions made by equally interesting rules. Automating the process of culling the most interesting rules and of combing the recommendations of a variety of rules are well handled by many of the commercially available rule induction systems on the market today. This is also an area of active research.

Applying Rule Induction to Business

Rule induction systems are highly automated and are probably the best of the data mining techniques for exposing all possible predictive patterns in a database. They can be modified for use in prediction problems, but the algorithms for combining evidence from a variety of rules come more from rules of thumb and practical experience.

In comparing data mining techniques along an axis of explanation, neural networks would be at one extreme of the data mining algorithms and rule induction systems would be at the other end. Neural networks are extremely proficient at saying exactly what must be done in a prediction task (for example, who do I give credit to/who do I deny credit to) with little explanation. On the other hand, rule induction systems when used for prediction are like having a committee of trusted advisors, each with a slightly different opinion about to what to do but with a relatively well-grounded reasoning and a good explanation for why it should be done.

The business value of rule induction techniques reflects the highly automated way in which the rules are created. This makes it easy to use the system, but this approach can also suffer from an overabundance of interesting patterns, which can make it complicated in order to make a prediction that is directly tied to return on investment (ROI).

What Is a Rule?

In rule induction systems, the rule itself is of a simple form of "if this and this and this, and then this." For example, a rule that a supermarket might find in its data collected from scanners might be among the following:

- If pickles are purchased, then ketchup is purchased.
- If paper plates, then plastic forks.
- If dip, then potato chips.
- If salsa, then tortilla chips.

In order for the rules to be useful, there are two pieces of information that must be supplied as well as the actual rule:

- Accuracy—How often is the rule correct?
- Coverage—How often does the rule apply?

Just because the pattern in the database is expressed as a rule, that does not mean that it is true all the time. Thus, just as in other data mining algorithms it is important to recognize and make explicit the uncertainty in the rule. This is what the accuracy of the rule means. The coverage of the rule has to do with how much of the database the rule "covers" or applies to. Examples are shown in Table 7-2.

In some cases, accuracy is called the confidence of the rule and coverage is called the support. Accuracy and coverage appear to be the preferred ways of naming these two measurements.

Table 7-2	**Rule**	**Accuracy**	**Coverage**
Examples of Rule Accuracy and Coverage	If breakfast cereal purchased, then milk is purchased.	85%	20%
	If bread purchased, then Swiss cheese will be purchased.	15%	6%
	If 42 years old and purchased pretzels and dry roasted peanuts, then beer will be purchased.	95%	0.01%

The rules themselves consist of two halves. The left-hand side is called the antecedent and the right-hand side is called the consequent. The antecedent can consist of just one condition or multiple conditions, which must all be true in order for the consequent to be true at the given accuracy. Generally, the consequent is just a single condition (prediction of purchasing just one grocery store item), rather than multiple conditions.

What to Do with a Rule

When the rules are mined out of the database, the rules can be used either for understanding better the business problems that the data reflects or for performing actual predictions against some predefined prediction target. Because there is both a left side and a right side to a rule (antecedent and consequent,) they can be used in several ways in your business.

Target the Antecedent   In this case, all rules that have a certain value for the antecedent are gathered and displayed to the user. For instance, a grocery store may request all rules that have nails, bolts, or screws as the antecedent in order to try to understand whether discontinuing the sale of these low-margin items will have any effect on other higher margin. For instance, maybe people who buy nails also buy expensive hammers, but wouldn't do so at the store if the nails were not available.

Target the Consequent   In this case, all rules that have a certain value for the consequent can be used to understand what is associated with the consequent and perhaps what affects the consequent. For instance, it might be useful to know all of the interesting rules that have "coffee" in their consequent. These may well be the rules that affect the purchases of coffee and that a store owner may want to put close to the coffee in order to increase the sale of both items. Or, it might be the rule that the coffee manufacturer uses to determine in which magazine to place their next coupons.

Target Based on Accuracy   Sometimes, the most important thing for a user is the accuracy of the rules that are being generated. Highly accurate rules of 80% or 90% imply strong relationships that can be exploited, even if they have low coverage of the database and only occur a limited number of times. For instance, consider a rule that is likely to be correct, it only has 0.1% coverage, but 95% can be applied only one time out of one thousand. If this one time is highly profitable, it can be worthwhile. This, for instance, is how some of the most successful data mining applications work in the financial markets—looking for that limited amount of time when a very confident prediction can be made.

Target Based on Coverage   Sometimes, users want to know what the most ubiquitous rules are or want to know the rules that are most readily applicable. By looking at rules ranked by coverage, they can quickly get a high-level view of what is happening within their database most of the time.

Target Based on "Interestingness"   Rules are interesting when they have high coverage and high accuracy, and deviate from the norm. There have been many ways in which rules have been ranked by some measure of interestingness, so that the trade-off between coverage and accuracy can be made.

Because rule induction systems are so often used for pattern discovery and unsupervised learning, it is less easy to compare them. For example, it is very easy for just about any rule induction system to generate all possible rules. It is, however, much more difficult to devise a way to present those rules (which could easily be in the hundreds of thousands) in a way that is most useful to the end user. When interesting rules are found, they usually have been created to find relationships between many different predictor values in the database, not just one well-defined target of the prediction.

For this reason, it is often much more difficult to assign a measure of value to the rule, aside from its interestingness. For instance, it would be difficult to determine the monetary value of knowing the fact that if people buy breakfast sausage, they also buy eggs 60% of the time. For data mining systems that are more focused on prediction for things like customer attrition, targeted marketing response, or risk, it is much easier to measure the value of the system and compare it to other systems and other methods for solving the problem.

Caveat: Rules Do Not Imply Causality

It is important to recognize that even though the patterns produced from rule induction systems are delivered as if-then rules, they do not necessarily mean that the left-hand side of the rule (the "if" part) causes the right-hand side of the rule (the "then" part) to happen. Purchasing cheese does not cause the purchase of wine, even though the "if cheese, then wine" rule may be very strong.

This is particularly important to remember for rule induction systems because the results are presented as if-this, then-that as many causal relationships are presented.

Types of Databases Used for Rule Induction

Typically, rule induction is used on databases with either fields of high cardinality (many different values) or many columns of binary fields. The classical case of this is the supermarket basket data from store scanners that contains individual product names and quantities, and may contain tens of thousands of different items with different packaging that create hundreds of thousands of SKU (Stock Keeping Units) identifiers.

In these databases, sometimes the concept of a record is not easily defined within the database—consider the typical Star Schema for many data warehouses that store the supermarket transactions as separate entries in the fact table. Where the columns in the fact table are, there is some unique identifier of the shopping basket (so all items can be noted as being in the same shopping basket), the quantity, the time of purchase, and whether the item was purchased with a special promotion (sale or coupon). Thus, each item in the shopping basket has a different row in the fact table. This layout of the data is not typically the best for most data mining algorithms, which would prefer to have the data structured as one row per shopping basket, and each column to represent the presence or absence of a given item.

This can be an expensive way to store the data, however, because the typical grocery store contains 60,000 SKUs, or different items that could come across the checkout counter. This structure of the records can also create a very high-dimensional space (60,000 binary dimensions), which would be unwieldy for many classical data mining algorithms such as neural networks and decision trees. As you'll see, several tricks are played to make this computationally feasible for the data mining algorithm while not requiring a massive reorganization of the database.

Discovery   The claim to fame of these ruled induction systems is much more so for knowledge discovered in unsupervised learning systems than it is for prediction. These systems provide a very detailed view of the data, where significant patterns occur only a small portion of the time and can be found only when looking at the detail data. There is also a broad overview of the data, where some systems seek to deliver to the user an overall view of the patterns contained in the database. These systems thus display a nice combination of both micro and macro views:

- *Macro level.*   Patterns that cover many situations are provided that can be used very often and with great confidence, and can also be used to summarize the database.

- *Micro level.*   Strong rules that cover only a very few situations can still be retrieved by the system and proposed to the end user. These may be valuable if the situations that are covered are highly valuable (maybe they only apply to the most profitable customers). They are also valuable if they represent a small but growing subpopulation, which may indicate a market shift or the emergence of a new competitor (for example, customers are being lost only in one particular area of the country where a new competitor is emerging).

Prediction   After the rules are created and their interestingness is measured, there is also a call for performing prediction with the rules. Each rule by itself can perform prediction—the consequent is the target and the accuracy of the rule is the accuracy of the prediction. But because rule induction systems produce many rules for a given antecedent or consequent, there can be conflicting predictions with different accuracies. This is an opportunity for improving the overall performance of the systems by combining the rules. This can be done in a variety of ways by summing the accuracies as if they were weights or just by taking the prediction of the rule with the maximum accuracy.

Table 7-3 shows how a given consequent or antecedent can be part of many rules with different accuracies and coverages. From this example, consider the prediction problem of trying to predict whether milk was purchased based solely on the other items that were in the shopping basket. If the shopping basket contained only bread, then from the table we would guess that there was a 35% chance that milk was also purchased. If, however, bread and butter and eggs and cheese were purchased, what would be the prediction for milk then? 65% chance of milk because the relationship between butter and milk is the greatest at 65%? Or, would all of the other items in the basket increase even further the chance of milk being purchased to well beyond 65%? Determining how to combine evidence from multiple rules is a key part of the algorithms for using rules for prediction.

Table 7-3	**Antecedent**	**Consequent**	**Accuracy**	**Coverage**
Accuracy and Coverage in Rule Antecedents and Consequents.	bagels	cream cheese	80%	5%
	bagels	orange juice	40%	3%
	bagels	coffee	40%	2%
	bagels	eggs	25%	2%
	bread	milk	35%	30%
	butter	milk	65%	20%
	eggs	milk	35%	15%
	cheese	milk	40%	8%

The General Idea

The general idea of a rule classification system is that rules are created that show the relationship between events captured in your database. These rules can be simple with just one element in the antecedent, or they might be more complicated with many column value pairs in the antecedent—all joined together by a conjunction (item1 and item2 and item3 must all occur for the antecedent to be true).

The rules are used to find interesting patterns in the database, but they are also used at times for prediction. There are two main things that are important about understanding a rule:

- *Accuracy.* Accuracy refers to the probability that if the antecedent is true, the precedent will be true. High accuracy means that this is a rule that is highly dependable.
- *Coverage.* Coverage refers to the number of records in the database that the rule applies to. High coverage means that the rule can be used very often, and also that it is less likely to be a spurious artifact of the sampling technique or an idiosyncrasy of the database.

The Business Importance of Accuracy and Coverage

From a business perspective, accurate rules are important because they imply that there is useful predictive information in the database that can be exploited—namely, that there is something far from independent between the antecedent and the consequent. The lower the accuracy, the closer the rule comes to just random guessing. If the accuracy is significantly below what would be expected from random guessing, then the negation of the antecedent may well be useful (for instance, people who buy denture adhesive are much less likely to buy fresh corn on the cob than normal).

From a business perspective, coverage implies how often you can use a useful rule. For instance, you may have a rule that is 100% accurate but is only applicable in one out of every 100,000 shopping baskets. You can rearrange your shelf space to take advantage of this fact, but it will not make you much money because the event is not very likely to happen. Table 7-4. Displays the trade-off between coverage and accuracy.

Trading Off Accuracy and Coverage Is Like Betting at the Track

An analogy between coverage and accuracy, and making money is the following. Having a high accuracy rule with low coverage is like owning a racehorse that always won when he raced, but could only race once a year. In betting, you could probably still make a lot of money on such a horse. In rule induction for retail stores, it is unlikely that finding that one rule between mayonnaise, ice cream, and sardines that seems to always be true will have much of an impact on your bottom line.

How to Evaluate the Rule

One way to look at accuracy and coverage is to see how they relate to some simple statistics and how they can be represented graphically. From statistics, coverage is simply the *a priori* probability of

Table 7-4		Accuracy Low	Accuracy High
Rule Coverage versus Accuracy	Coverage High	Rule is rarely correct but can be used often.	Rule is often correct and can be used often.
	Coverage Low	Rule is rarely correct and can be only rarely used.	Rule is often correct but can be only rarely used.

the antecedent and the consequent occurring at the same time. The accuracy is just the probability of the consequent conditional on the precedent. So, for instance if we were looking at the following database of supermarket basket scanner data, we would need the following information in order to calculate the accuracy and coverage for a simple rule (let's say milk purchase implies eggs purchased):

■ T = 100 = Total number of shopping baskets in the database
■ E = 30 = Number of baskets with eggs in them
■ M = 40 = Number of baskets with milk in them
■ B = 20 = Number of baskets with both eggs and milk in them

Accuracy is, then, just the number of baskets with eggs and milk in them divided by the number of baskets with milk in them. In this case, it is 20/40 = 50%. The coverage would be the number of baskets with milk in them divided by the total number of baskets. This is 40/100 = 40%. This can be seen graphically in Figure 7-5.

The coverage of the rule "if milk, then eggs" is just the relative size of the circle corresponding to milk. The accuracy is the relative size of the overlap between the two to the circle representing milk purchased.

Figure 7-5
Graphically, the total number of shopping baskets can be represented in a space, and the number of baskets containing eggs or milk can be represented by the area of a circle.

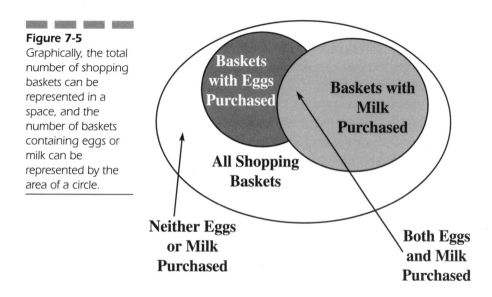

Baskets with Eggs Purchased

Baskets with Milk Purchased

All Shopping Baskets

Neither Eggs or Milk Purchased

Both Eggs and Milk Purchased

Notice that we haven't used the number of baskets with eggs in these calculations. One way that eggs could be used would be to calculate the expected number of baskets with eggs and milk in them, based on the independence of the events. This would give us some sense of how unlikely and how special the event is that 20% of the baskets have both eggs and milk in them. Remember from the statistics section that if two events are independent (have no effect on one another), the product of their individual probabilities of occurrence should equal the probability of the occurrence of them both together.

If the purchase of eggs and milk were independent of each other, one would expect that $0.3 \times 0.4 = 0.12$, or 12% of the time, we would see shopping baskets with both eggs and milk in them. The fact that this combination of products occurs 20% of the time is out of the ordinary if these events were independent. That is to say, there is a good chance that the purchase of one affects the other, and the degree to which this is the case could be calculated through statistical tests and hypothesis testing.

Defining "Interestingness"

One of the biggest problems with rule induction systems is the sometimes overwhelming number of rules that are produced, most of which have no practical value or interest. Some of the rules are so inaccurate that they cannot be used; some have so little coverage that, although they are interesting, they have little applicability; and, finally, many of the rules capture patterns and information that the user is already familiar with. To combat this problem, researchers have sought to measure the usefulness or interestingness of rules.

Certainly, any measure of interestingness would have something to do with accuracy and coverage. We might also expect it to have at least the following four basic behaviors:

- Interestingness = 0 if the accuracy of the rule is equal to the background accuracy (*a priori* probability of the consequent).

The example in Table 7-5 shows an example of this, where a rule for attrition is no better than just guessing the overall rate of attrition.

- Interestingness increases as accuracy increases (or decreases with decreasing accuracy) if the coverage is fixed.

- Interestingness increases or decreases with coverage if accuracy stays fixed.

- Interestingness decreases with coverage for a fixed number of correct responses (remember that accuracy equals the number of correct responses divided by the coverage).

There are a variety of measures of interestingness that are used that have these general characteristics. They are used for pruning back the total possible number of rules that might be generated and then presented to the user.

Other Measures of Usefulness

Another important measure is that of simplicity of the rule. This is important for the end user because complex rules, as powerful and

Table 7-5	Antecedent	Consequent	Accuracy	Coverage
Uninteresting rules	<no constraints>	then customer will attrite	10%	100%
	If customer balance > $3,000	then customer will attrite	10%	60%
	If customer eyes = blue	then customer will attrite	10%	30%
	If customer Social Security Number = 144 30 8217	then customer will attrite	100%	0.000001%

as interesting as they might be, may be difficult to understand or to confirm via intuition. Thus, the user has a desire to see simpler rules, and consequently this desire can be manifested directly in the rules that are chosen and supplied automatically to the user.

Finally, a measure of novelty is also required during the creation of the rules—so that rules that are redundant but strong are less favored to be searched than rules that may not be as strong, but cover important examples that are not covered by other strong rules. For instance, there may be few historical records to provide rules on a little-sold grocery item (for example, mint jelly) and they may have low accuracy. Because there are so few possible rules, however, they will be "novel" even if they are not interesting, and should be retained and presented to the user for that reason alone.

Rules versus Decision Trees

Decision trees also produce rules, but in a very different way than rule induction systems. The main difference between the rules that are produced by decision trees and rule induction systems is as follows:

Decision trees produce rules that are mutually exclusive and collectively exhaustive with respect to the training database. Rule induction systems produce rules that are not mutually exclusive and might be collectively exhaustive.

In plain English, this means that for any given record, there will be a rule to cover it and there will only be one rule for rules that come from decision trees. There may be many rules that match a given record from a rule induction system, and for many systems it is not guaranteed that a rule will exist for each and every possible record that might be encountered. (Although most systems do create very general default rules to capture these records.)

The reason for this difference is the way in which the two algorithms operate. Rule induction seeks to go from the bottom up and collect all possible patterns that are interesting, and then later use those patterns for some prediction target. Decision trees, on the other hand, work from a prediction target downward in what is known as a "greedy" search. They look for the best possible split on the next step (for example, greedily picking the best one without looking any further than the next step). Although the greedy algorithm can make choices at the higher levels of the tree which are less than optimal at the lower levels of the tree, it is very good at effectively squeezing out any correlations between predictors and the prediction. Rule induction systems, on the other hand, retain all possible patterns, even if they are redundant or do not aid in predictive accuracy.

For instance, consider that if there were two columns of data that were highly correlated (or in fact just simple transformations of each other) in a rule induction system, they would result in two rules. In a decision tree, one predictor would be chosen. Then, because the second one was redundant, it would not be chosen again. An example might be two predictors: annual charges and average monthly charges (average monthly charges being the annual charges divided by 12). If the amount charged was predictive, then the decision tree would choose one of the predictors and use it for a split point somewhere in the tree. The decision tree effectively "squeezed" the predictive value out of the predictor and then moved onto the next. A rule induction system, however, would create two rules, perhaps like the following:

- If annual charges > 12,000, then default = true 90% accuracy
- If average monthly charges > 1,000, then default = true 90% accuracy

In this case, we've shown an extreme case in which two predictors were exactly the same, but there can also be less-extreme cases. For instance, height might be used rather than shoe size in the decision tree, whereas in a rule induction system both would be presented as rules.

Neither one technique or the other is necessarily better, though having a variety of rules and predictors helps with the prediction when there are missing values. For instance, if the decision tree did choose height as a split point, and that predictor was not captured in the record (a null value) but shoe size was, the rule induction system would still have a matching rule to capture this record. Decision trees do have ways of overcoming this difficulty by keeping "surrogates" at each split point that work almost as well at splitting the data, as does the chosen predictor. In this case, shoe size might have been kept as a surrogate for height at this particular branch of the tree.

Another Commonality between Decision Trees and Rule Induction Systems

One other thing that decision trees and rule induction systems have in common is the fact that they both need to find ways to combine and simplify rules. In a decision tree, this can be as simple as recognizing that if a lower split on a predictor is more constrained than a split on the same predictor further up in the tree, both don't need to be provided to the user — only the more restrictive one. For instance, if the first split of the tree is age ,5 50 years and the lowest split for the given leaf is age ,5 30 years, only the latter constraint needs to be captured in the rule for that leaf.

Rules from rule induction systems are generally created by taking a simple high-level rule, and then adding new constraints to it until the coverage gets so small so it is not meaningful. This means that the rules actually have families or what is called "cones of specialization," where one more general rule can be the parent of many more specialized rules. These cones then can be presented to the user as high-level views of the families of rules, and can be viewed in a hierarchical manner to aid in understanding.

Which Technique and When?

Clearly, one of the hardest things to do when deciding to implement a data mining system is to determine which technique to use when. When are neural networks appropriate and when are decision trees appropriate? When is data mining appropriate at all, as opposed to just working with relational databases and reporting? When would just using OLAP and a multidimensional database be appropriate?

Some of the criteria that are important in determining the technique to be used are determined by trial-and-error. There are definite differences in the types of problems that are most conducive to each technique, but the reality of real world data and the dynamic way in which markets, customers, and the data that represents them is formed means that the data is constantly changing. These dynamics mean that it no longer makes sense to build the "perfect" model on the historical data because whatever was known in the past cannot adequately predict the future because the future is so unlike what has gone before.

In some ways, this situation is analogous to the business person who is waiting for all information to come in before they make their decision. They are trying out different scenarios, different formulae, and researching new sources of information. But this is a task that will never be accomplished — at least in part because the business, the economy, and even the world are changing in unpredictable and even chaotic ways that could never be adequately predicted. Better to take a robust model that perhaps is an under-performer compared to what some of the best data mining tools could provide with a great deal of analysis, and execute it today rather than wait until tomorrow when it may be too late.

Balancing Exploration and Exploitation

There is always the trade-off between exploration (learning more and gathering more facts) and exploitation (taking immediate advantage of everything that is currently known). This theme of exploration versus exploitation is echoed also at the level of collecting data in a targeted marketing system. From a limited population of prospects/customers to choose from, how many do you sacrifice to exploration (trying out new promotions or messages at random) versus optimizing what you already know?

There was, for instance, no reasonable way that Barnes and Noble bookstores could in 1995 look at past sales figures and foresee the impact that Amazon.com and others would have, based on the Internet sales model.

Compared to historic sales and marketing data, the event of the Internet could not be predicted based on the data alone. Instead, perhaps data mining could have been used to detect trends of decreased sales to certain customer subpopulations—such as to those involved in the high tech industry that were the first to begin to buy books online at Amazon.com.

So caveat emptor—use the data mining tools well, but strike while the iron is hot. The performance of predictive model provided by data mining tools have a limited half-life of decay. Unlike a good bottle of wine, they do not increase in value with age.

CHAPTER 8

When to Use
Data Mining

Introduction

An important question that should be answered before you commence any data mining project is whether data mining techniques are, in fact necessary. In determining this it is important to understand what level of sophistication of data mining is required. For instance, do you just need a few standardized printed reports or do you need interactive ROI analysis or OLAP analysis to see what your data looks like? Do you need or true data mining techniques that build predictive models to search through your database for useful patterns?

In this chapter, we discuss when to use which level of data mining —moving from your business problem to understanding the characteristics that make it suitable for one form or another of data mining.

Using the Right Technique

The bottom line in picking a data mining technology and then an actual product really depends on whether the product can deliver— value to the business. This always translates to profit, increased revenue, decreased cost, or return on investment. If the technique and tool do not provide one of these four in a measurable way, it is unlikely that anyone in your business will have time to mine their data. Data mining needs to be more than finding interesting patterns in large databases if it is to be successfully deployed in your business.

The Data Mining Process

To begin, let's look at the overall data mining process that has been proposed by those in the research community. They have argued that data mining (the actual generation of predictive models and patterns) is just one step along a much larger process of turning data into knowledge. The following steps have been proposed (note that this is a contrast with the simpler set of steps that have been proposed here to date).

Figure 8-1 shows the technology-centric view of the data mining process that focuses on optimizing the data preprocessing, but ignores many of the steps required for deploying a truly successful business application. This view of data mining shows how to move from raw data to useful patterns to knowledge. The better the data mining tool, the more automated and painless is the transition from one step to the next.

What All Data Mining Techniques Have In Common In order to make an intelligent selection of data mining tools and technologies, it is helpful to categorize where they differ. To more clearly discern this and because there is so much overlap, one of the best ways to see the valid distinctions between the algorithms is to see what is similar. For instance, each data mining algorithm has the following in common:

Figure 8-1
The technology-centric view of the data mining process

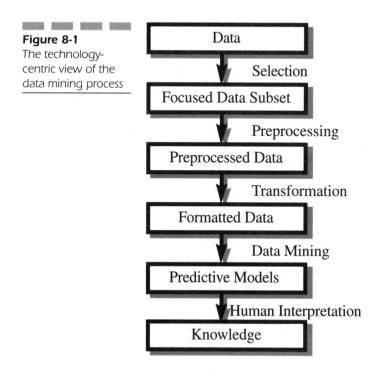

Data

Selection

Focused Data Subset

Preprocessing

Preprocessed Data

Transformation

Formatted Data

Data Mining

Predictive Models

Human Interpretation

Knowledge

- *Model structure.* The structure that defines the model. (Is it a tree, a neural network, or a neighbor?) This is the perceived model because the actual instantiation of the model might be SQL queries, in the case of decision trees and rule-based systems; or mathematical equations, in the case of statistical regression.

- *Search.* How does the algorithm amend and modify the model over time as more data is made available? For instance, neural networks search through link weight space via the back propagation algorithm, and the genetic algorithm searches through random permutation and genetic recombination.

- *Validation.* When does the algorithm terminate because it has created a valid model? For instance, CART decision trees use cross-validation to determine the optimal level of growth of the tree. Neural networks don't have a specific validation technique to determine termination, but cross-validation is often used outside of the neural network.

This description of the data mining algorithms should already be helpful because it makes more obvious how genetic algorithms are somewhat different from the other techniques mentioned as data mining algorithms. Genetic algorithms do not have any inherent model structure. Instead, they are merely the optimization strategy for whatever model structure is defined to be encoded into the genetic material. The chromosome itself is not the model structure, but the interpretation of the chromosome is. This distinction is made even in biology by calling the genetic material the genotype and what it grows (is translated) into as the phenotype. Because the genetic algorithm really is a search strategy without a model structure, genetic algorithms can be used in combination with any of the other data mining techniques. In Table 8-1, the data mining algorithms are categorized by these three features.

By organizing the algorithms by these three features, it is clear that some of the major differences reflect the use of validation. Some techniques do not have it built in at all, some validate directly against the data, and some use statistical significance tests to calculate the best model. Though helpful, this view glosses over some important

Table 8-1

Comparing the
data mining
algorithms

Algorithm	Structure	Search	Validation
CART	Binary Tree	Splits chosen by entropy or Gini metric	Cross Validation
CHAID	Multi-way Split Tree	Splits chosen by chi square test and Bonferroni adjustment	Validation performed at time of split selection
Neural Network	Forward propagation network with non linear thesholding	Back propagation of errors	Not Applicable
Genetic Algorithms	Not Applicable	Survival of the fittest on mutation and genetic crossover	Usually cross validation
Rule Induction	If-then rule	Add new constraint to rule and retain it if it matches the "interestingness" criterion based on accuracy and coverage	Chi Square test with statistical significance cutoff (P value set to low value to combat the multiple comparisons or "fishing" problem)
Nearest Neighbor	Distance of prototype in n-dimensional feature space	Usually there is no search	Cross validation used for reported accuracy rates but not for algorithm termination

features that can make all the difference. In fact, the model structure used can be critical to whether the problem can be solved at all in a reasonable amount of time.

How Decision Trees Are Like Nearest Neighbor

Consider also some of the similarities between the data mining algorithms. For instance, decision trees are doing a kind of nearest neighbor match. If, for instance, a decision tree were fully grown, there could be a branch point for every predictor/value pair for every record in the database. (For instance, at the first level, all values of a predictor would represent different branches; at the next level, all values for the next predictor would be used.) If such a tree were created and not pruned, then each leaf would effectively be executing an exact match between the record being classified and the training record that was used to build the tree.

If a slightly modified tree were built where some predictors were not used, this would correspond to the nearest neighbor algorithm where those missing predictors were given a weight of zero. The parallels are so close between the two algorithms that a decision tree-like structure is often used to speed up the detection of the nearest neighbors of a record that has no prediction value.

Remember also that there are multiple records in the leaf of the decision tree that may not all be of the same prediction value (non-homogeneous leaf). These records represent the K nearest neighbors of any record that is classified into that leaf. With the simplest K nearest neighbor algorithm, each neighbor gets to cast a vote as to the prediction of the unpredicted record. Typically, the predicted value is the majority vote in binary predictors, the plurality vote in multiple-valued categoricals, and the average in the case of continuous-ordered predictors. This is in fact exactly what the probability measure inside the leaf of the decision tree gives you for each of these types of predictions.

How Rule Induction Is Like Decision Trees

Rule induction is very similar to decision trees, except that the rules that are produced in rule induction do not partition the database into mutually exclusive subsets. No record from the training database will ever be classified by more than one rule in a decision tree algorithm, but a given training record may match any number of rules in a rule induction system—including no rules at all.

Decision trees create the most efficient and smallest possible set of rules that will create an optimal predictive model. If there is overlap between two predictors, the better of the two would be picked. In the rule induction system, however, both could well be represented, and the fact that one was slightly less accurate or had slightly lower coverage would be captured as data along with the rule.

A decision tree, because it is focused on a particular prediction problem, is not as efficient as a rule induction system at finding all possible "interesting" rules, but decision trees can be used in a slightly different way in order to accomplish this. They just need to be given each possible predictor/value combination as the target and see what rules arise. Again, the best links between predictor values and prediction values will be captured in the tree, and the others will be automatically discarded. Effectively using decision trees to find interesting combinations would be building a new tree for each prediction/value pair. This would be quite slow, but would automatically have done much of the filtering out of less-interesting rules that is a major post-processing step of rule induction systems.

Just as it is a bit of a stretch to use decision trees to perform rule induction, it is somewhat awkward to use rule systems as prediction systems. When rules systems are used for prediction, multiple rules may match a given unpredicted record—each perhaps having a different prediction, accuracy, and coverage. Usually, there are heuristic methods for combining the evidence of these multiple rules in order to arrive at a final prediction value. Normally, the combining of sources of evidence is not an issue for decision tree algorithms because each record would match only one rule (because the rules are mutually exclusive). This all changes with some of the newer techniques that are now being used for decision trees, in which multiple trees may be grown on different random samples of the training database. When multiple trees are used, a given record could fall into multiple leaves and hence have multiple rules that match it. The multiple trees algorithm for decision trees then combines evidence in ways that are quite similar to the rule induction systems, by averaging the predictions across the trees.

How to Do Link Analysis with a Neural Network

One of the oldest algorithms for training neural networks is Hebbian learning, which was created in an effort to simulate normal neuron firing patterns. Links between biological neurons appear to be strengthened when two neurons fire together often. Hebbian learning simulates this effect by increasing the link weight between two nodes in a neural network when they are both in an excited state at the same time. This learning algorithm could then also be used to find links between products in a shopping basket.

To accomplish this, one could construct a neural network with only an input layer and one node for each item in the shopping basket. The nodes would be fully connected with each other, so if there were n different possible items in a shopping cart, there would be n nodes and approximately $n^2/2$ links. If there were a large number of SKUs, the number of links could get quite large (for example, 100,000 SKUs is not unreasonable and would translate to a 100,000-node network with nearly five billion links). In general, it would be much more efficient to create the links between products via the more efficient association rules, which in this case would require only one read of the database from disk, whereas the neural network might require multiple passes through the database before the links weights converge.

Data Mining in the Business Process

If we look at the way many of the data mining products are deployed, we may see a very similar cycle. Data from the data warehouse is mined for important information about the customers, or some action to take against customers or competition (for example, making an offer of your new product at a reduced price to those customers who you predict will be price-sensitive). When that action is taken, there is generally some response (reaction) in the marketplace (either the customer buys the product, or doesn't). That reaction is data that then needs to be captured and entered into the data warehouse.

When data mining is used for non-exploratory reasons or whenever supervised learning techniques are used, this customer reaction provides a fairly well-defined target column within the database, which relates to the business process. The target must have the following attributes in order to be successful with data mining:

- *The target has value.* It has some relationship to bottom line business value (stopping loss through attrition or fraud, or increasing revenue through cross-selling). Predicting customer weight from their buying habits might have value, or it might not. To be a suitable target, it would need to have well-defined business value.

- *The target is actionable.* It is believed that there are actions that can be taken to influence the target. For instance, if retirement age is the main predictor of employee attrition, there is probably little you can do about how old your employees are. On the other hand, improving health care coverage is something that could be effective.

- *The effect of action can be captured.* If a good predictive model is created and an action is created, but the effect on the customer cannot be measured, there is little way to measure value. There is also no way to tell the exact impact of the action and to have that information fed back into the system so that the next model could be further improved.

The data path between the target, the action, and the customer reaction is captured in Figure 8-2. In order for data mining to work for predictive modeling and as part of the business process, the target to be predicted must be well-defined. It must have a presence in the historical database in order for it to be useful for the predictive model. In order for the predictive model to have business value, the target must be actionable, and the customer reaction to that action must be captured back into the data warehouse. A typical example of action and reaction would be the following scenario.

In a credit card balance transfer offer, the target is the customer response to the offer that had been previously sent out to a small random sample of the customer base. The results were captured in the database. In this case, the target has well-defined value (the credit card company should at least know how much needs to be transferred per account, at what interest rate, and how long it must stay as debt in order to be profitable). It is actionable (through the mailing of the offer), and the reaction of the customer is easily captured in the data warehouse because they either accept the offer or do not.

Avoiding Some Big Mistakes in Data Mining

The technology-centered view of the data mining process emphasizes getting the model right, with the assumption that the predictive product has been well-defined and that the data that has been captured to date is well understood. This is not always the case. We believe that this view of the process is helpful for the data processing itself, but is too limited to help in the actual evaluation of what data mining can do to enable business better.

The steps in this technology-centered process that appear to be just small steps toward getting to the hard work of data mining are often as hard and often much more time-consuming than the data mining itself. If they are not well-considered in the selection of the data mining tool and technology, they may well render the actual predictive model and patterns inconsequential because they will not be able to be used within the larger business context.

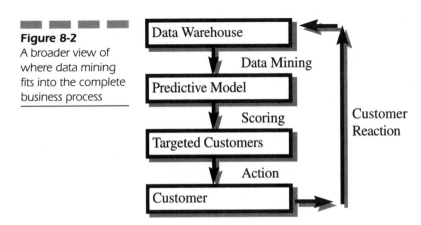

Figure 8-2
A broader view of where data mining fits into the complete business process

Understanding the Data

As an example, consider the analytics group at a bank, which requested from its information technology (IT) group an extract of 100,000 random bank customers, to whom they wanted to try out a cross-selling program of a new bank product. When the data was extracted from the data warehouse by IT and run through the data mining tools, a highly accurate targeted marketing model was found. However, when deployed, the model dramatically performed below expectations. In retracing its steps, the analytics group asked IT how the randomization for the 100,000 records was performed. The answer: the customers were sorted by account balance (in order to "randomize" them), and then the first 100,000 were delivered as the subset! Thus, there was a highly selective set of customers that were far from representative of the general customer population. From IT's perspective, this was a fair "random" subset. From the analysts' perspective, this was far from random.

This disconnect between the owners of the data and the owners of the data mining analysis causes significant errors to occur that can cause devastating losses. Disconnects between those who understand the business problem and those performing the analysis can be even worse. Consider a real-world case in the credit card industry, in which an outsourcing company that was building attrition models for a bank with a Visa card used a neural network to predict the attrition.

They likewise needed historical time series data from the original data source in order to train the neural network. Even though the analysts actually performed the extract, they inadvertently switched the meaning of time in the time series data. The result was that the neural net achieved very high rates in the lab, but when actually deployed in a targeted mailing, the response rate was half of what was expected. Because the time series information had been reversed, the neural network had been using current information in order to predict the past rather than using historical information to predict the future.

Despite the magnitude of the error, it was not detected until the program was deployed and the validation against real customers began. There were two factors contributing to the error occurring:

- The opacity of the neural network made it difficult to understand how the data was being processed. It was difficult to notice, for instance, that what should have been the oldest information seemed to be having the most impact on the model rather than the most recent, as would be expected.

- Although the same people who built the model also handled the data. the fact that the data had to be extracted, copied, and preprocessed allowed the inversion of the meaning of the time series information to occur. If the data had been kept in the data warehouse with a competent and up-to-date data dictionary and metadata store, the actual misunderstanding of the data could have been avoided.

Defining the Business Model   Another source of errors that can occur happens when the business problem is not fully understood by those responsible for the data handling or the analysis itself.

Consider, for instance, the statistical analyst posed with the problem of predicting customer attrition (churn) in the cellular phone industry. In this case, the predictive problem is communicated in a very simple and direct way, but the overall business problem is not communicated. Thus, the opportunity to deploy a marketing program to save the attriters by offering a free cellular phone as a giveaway is left open. If only the likelihood of churn is taken into account for the business problem, however, the program could be a big loss for the bottom line. Free cellular phones, at a cost of $100 each, would be given away to save customers who spend only $10 per month on their cellular service to begin with. If the owner of the business problem doesn't adequately communicate this requirement to the analyst, mistakes such as these can happen.

In another case in the insurance industry, the CEO of a major homeowners insurance company was concerned about the total payout that was going to be required after a hurricane devastated a certain county in Florida. The CEO's request to the IT department was to determine how many policies were issued for the county and to calculate the total downside if all the homeowners collected. The query was run and the figure posted to the CEO. When the claims came in, however, the total payout was almost twice what had been estimated.

The problem turned out to be that the IT department calculated the value based on how many policies were issued in the devastated county. This number was actually quite low because the main sales office was in an adjoining county. The actual number should have been calculated based on the home mailing address of the policy-holders, not the address of where the policies were issued.

The benefits of exposing the data mining tools to those familiar with the business can also bring in substantial upside when it is done correctly. When the business problem, revenue, and ROI are fully taken into consideration and reflected throughout the business information process, creative and highly profitable business solutions can be the outcome.

Consider, for instance, the following scenario:

- If the data mining tools were easy enough to use so that a product marketing manager (with an MBA, but no Ph.D. in statistics) could use them
- If the data mining process were tightly integrated with the existing data warehouse, so that end users could interact with the data
- If the resulting predictive modeling could be visualized in an intuitive way through OLAP technology

As a result, the business end user could perform this entire process in a tightly integrated way that would avoid many of the disconnects that currently occur.

In one situation, when the business end user felt comfortable using the data mining tools, he was able to recognize a targeted marketing opportunity available to him that he would otherwise not be aware of. Specifically, a prescription drug manufacturer was interested in knowing what effect the sales calls of his sales force was having on the prescription rates of a particular brand of antidepressant drug. When the data mining was performed, it was learned that for all of the doctors who prescribed large amounts of the drug, the sales force was having no effect except to keep the doctor at the desired level of prescribing.

These doctors were the customers that the pharmaceutical company was most interested in because although they represented only a small portion of the total number of doctors, they represented the bulk of the prescriptions. If the predictive modeling had been done in the typical way, the analysis would have ended there—with the result that there would be no way to increase prescriptions of the drug through sales interventions. In this case, however, the results were presented in a visual form in which the various subpopulations of doctors were broken up into segments of the total population. Each segment represented doctors at about the same level of prescriptions. Through this visualization, it was possible to see that although there was really very little to do for the problem as originally posed, there was still a business opportunity.

In this case, there were doctors who could be influenced by sales interventions and by free samples. These doctors turned out to be the low-volume doctors who wrote only a few prescriptions per month. This may have been true because they were overlooked by other competing sales forces, or perhaps because they relied more heavily on the salesperson for information than an expert in the field who might already be highly competent in that particular drug. They were more easily affected by the sales interventions.

From a business perspective, they represented an opportunity because the segment contained so many low-volume doctors that they represented a significant amount of total revenue. The only problem was that though they could be affected by the sales interventions, their volumes did not warrant the hundred dollars and more that was the cost of a salesperson's visit. There was, however, a way to exploit this segment—through low-cost direct mail. By allowing the marketing manager to directly interact with the predictive model and understand the answers, a wholly new marketing plan was developed to exploit this previously ignored customer niche.

Cases like these, in which money can be made and other cases in which money can be lost—not because of a lack of a good predictive modeling algorithm but because of the lack of clarity and exposure to larger business issues—makes us propose a more holistic view of the data mining process, as shown in Figure 8-3.

A business-centric view of the data mining process relies on the data mining product to automate much of the predictive modeling process. Here, the focus is on the business problem definition, ROI, and understanding of the data rather than the preprocessing and reformatting that are central to the technology-centric process.

The major difference between the technology-centric and business-centric data mining process is a matter of focus. The business-centric view assumes that "data mining" is fairly self-contained and automated once the business problem and data are understood. The overall allocation of resources might be quite different between the two approaches. With the business-centric view, a great deal of effort will be put in upfront in the definition of the business problem, the definition of the actual prediction, and the understanding of the data. Although much of the effort in the technology-centric view will be focused on the logistics of data processing and movement, and the human intensive cycle of trying out different data mining technologies.

The Case for Embedded Data Mining

As you look at different tools for data mining, decide whether your business needs are really so well understood and your data warehouse is so well constructed that you can concentrate on just the technology. You may need to look at the bigger picture of the business process and how data mining fits into it.

When evaluating data mining technology, the first thing to check is that the model is capable of creating accurate predictions for the types of problems that are common to your business. But be forewarned that accuracy by itself will not guarantee success. In fact, when well-implemented, data mining algorithms tend to provide similar results on real world business problems.

As shown in Figure 8-4, the normal way that data mining tools are judged is by the accuracy of the predictive model that they create. Because, the reasoning goes, you don't know which one will do best

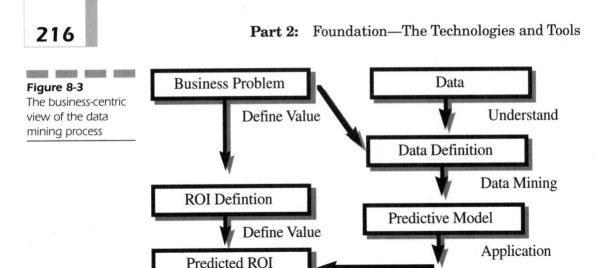

Figure 8-3
The business-centric view of the data mining process

on a given problem, the tool you use should provide a large number of different techniques that can be tried out on the problem, and the best result selected at the end. If these are the two axes by which data mining product should be judged, then there is already a clear winner: statistics.

Statistical methods for prediction and validation have been in use for decades. They produce comparable accuracy results to the newer data mining techniques, and because they have been in development for so long, most statistical tool packages such as SAS, SPSS, and SPlus have a wide variety of different algorithms to choose from. You may believe (as has been shown in several good head-to-head comparisons) that this type of technique can make only a small difference in the accuracy. If so, you are relegated to working with statistical toolsets or deciding to re-evaluate what the differences are with data mining technologies and how they should be measured. Our recommendation is that they should be measured along the lines of what matters to the business-centric process, not the technology-centric process.

As shown in Figure 8-5, the comparable accuracies of these techniques have been confirmed by a fair test of prediction accuracy held by the U.S. government. Although this test did not explicitly use decision trees or rule induction for this task, the task of character prediction from images is representative of the high-dimensional data mining problems that are encountered in the business world.

The Cost of a Distributed Business Process

One of the major sources of mistakes in building and deploying a data mining model is in the copying, transfer, and reformatting of data outside of the data store (data warehouse) where the original data dictionary and metadata are stored. This process can also be costly in terms of the amount of time taken to perform data mining to the degree in which a meaningful measure of ROI can be taken.

The example shown in Figure 8-6 and Table 8-2 is not atypical for companies in well-established industries with relatively static marketplaces and competition. These companies have had needs for predictive modeling and general data mining for some time, and have

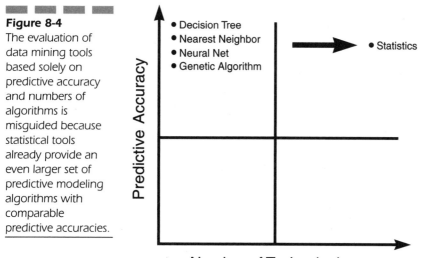

Figure 8-4
The evaluation of data mining tools based solely on predictive accuracy and numbers of algorithms is misguided because statistical tools already provide an even larger set of predictive modeling algorithms with comparable predictive accuracies.

created a department of analysts over time to work with the marketing and sales departments, as well as IT or the owner of the enterprise-level data. Typically, there are three main players in these systems: IT, the analysts, and the business end user (Table 8-3). Each of the players is usually separated from the others by the following:

- Physical distance (they may well be in different buildings or even different cities)

- Technology distance (each will have a different preferred platform for hardware and OS)

- Data distance (each will have a different preferred set of tools for data manipulation and storage)

- Skills distance (each will have a different set of skills in which they are expert, and prefer to use these skills rather than learn those of another player)

Because of this variety of distances, the time it can take from an end user coming up with a good idea and a model being built, tested,

Figure 8-5
Although there have not been many well-proctored, head-to-head comparisons of neural networks to nearest neighbor techniques, the U.S. Census and the National Institute of Standards and Technology held a competition for handwritten digit prediction from images. Twenty-nine groups participated. The top six performers on this task are shown here, all with very comparable performances.

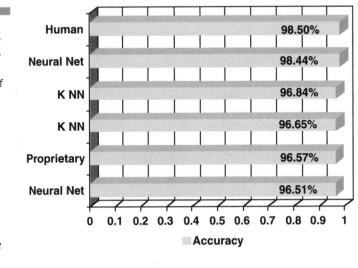

and deployed can easily be months. For these static industries, this may be acceptable. For many industries, three months is a huge open window of time in which the competition can respond or take the lead, and present a new campaign toward your customer base. The idea of target marketing a seasonal campaign is giving way to the idea of the "continuous campaign," where smaller targeted campaigns are constantly being launched, and their results are captured and added to the data warehouse in a process of continual improvement.

The Best Way to Measure a Data Mining Tool

As we've just seen, many current views toward data mining are penny-wise and pound-foolish. The systems are highly optimized for eking out the last fraction of a percent in accuracy, when, in fact, the market is moving so quickly that the likelihood that any predictive model could remain that accurate over time is very unlikely. (For this reason, even current debates over large data or small data and massive parallel processing hardware can become a moot point.) Or worrying about the accuracy of the system to boost the profit by a small

Figure 8-6

A typical data-driven business process (even after the data warehouse is completed) consists of multiple steps between multiple servers and data extracts, preprocessing, and conversions.

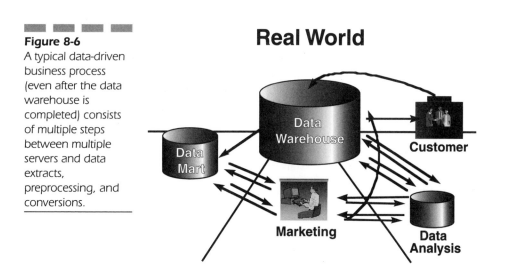

Table 8-2

There are many stages of activity between the time that a business end user comes up with a marketing program and the time that the program is deployed against the customer. The time can be substantial between the initial concept development and the actual deployment due to the number of different parties involved in the process.

Stage of Process	Activity	Time for Completion
Exploratory	Business user works with an OLAP data mart to build intuitions about the business and the data and propose possible marketing programs	Minutes to Hours
Definition	A statistical analyst works with the business user to try to understand the business process and determine what data to request for extraction	Days
Extraction	Statisticians request extract of the required data from the data warehouse into a format usable by statistical tools.	Weeks
Analysis	Statisticians use the extract database to build predictive models based on the understood business model.	Weeks
Confirmation	The predictive model recommended by the statisticians is returned to the business end user along with a guess at level of accuracy. Assumptions for the predictive model are reviewed by the business end user and the anticipated results evaluated.	Days
Recording	The statistical model built on the proprietary database is recoded to work on the original data warehouse data structures. The model must be completely retested in this new environment.	Weeks
Deployment	The new model is run against the detail customer information in the data warehouse and a marketing program is launched	Weeks
Collection	Customers react to the marketing program and the data is captured to enrich the warehouse	Weeks

Table 8-3

The stages of deployment for a marketing program often mean that a wide variety of different tools, database formats, operating systems, and hardware configurations must be used as the process moves between the business user, analytics, and IT. Every transition between systems is costly, both in terms of effort and time and in the possibility of mistakes being made.

Stage of Process	User	Database	Software	Hardware
Exploratory	Business end user	Multi-dimensional database extract	Windows or Web OLAP applications	PC connected to small NT or UNIX platform.
Definition	Statistician	NA	NA	NA
Extraction	IT staff or DBA	Data Warehouse or operational data store	SQL, COBOL	Mainframe or large multiprocessor hardware.
Analysis	Statistician	Proprietary database or flat file.	Sophisticated statistical analysis tools.	UNIX or NT server.
Confirmation	Business end user	Proprietary database or flat file.	Visualization applications from statistics tool.	PC
Recoding	IT staff, DBA, Statistician	Data warehouse or operational data store.	SQL, COBOL	Mainframe or large multiprocessor hardware.
Deployment	IT staff, DBA, Statistician	Data warehouse or operational data store	SQL, COBOL, campaign management and mailing applications.	Mainframe or large multiprocessor hardware.
Collection	IT staff, DBA, Statistician	Data warehouse or operational data store	SQL, COBOL	Mainframe or large multiprocessor hardware.

fraction when the database itself is corrupted because of data copying and transfers, or when the business model is ill-defined and the highly predictive model nonetheless leads in a misguided business direction.

Although predictive accuracy is what data mining is all about, there are really three key measures that must be made in order to fully evaluate a data mining tool. These three measures should be the golden rules for data mining tool development:

- *Accuracy.*   The data mining tool must produce a model that is as accurate as possible, but recognizing that small perceived improvements in accuracy between different techniques may be phantom effects caused by fluctuations in random sampling (even if you use the entire database for your model), or may be effects that are washed-out in the dynamics of the marketplace in which you deploy your models.

- *Explanation.*   The data mining tool needs to be able to "explain" how the model works to the end user in a clear way that builds intuition, and allows intuitions and common sense to be easily tested and confirmed. It should also allow for the explanation of the profit or ROI calculation in a clear manner.

- *Integration.*   The data mining tool must integrate with the current business process, and data and information flow in the company. Requiring copies of data to be made and massive preprocessing of the data create many points of process where errors can occur. With tight integration, many fewer possible points of error are created.

When these three requirements are well met, the data mining tools will produce highly profitable models that are likely to remain stable over long periods of time. Figure 8-7 shows how these two additional measures can be used once accuracy has been achieved.

The Case for Embedded Data Mining

With these new rules for effective data mining within the business process, several changes have to be made for data mining to achieve these goals. Copying the database, for instance, is often done because many algorithms require preformatting of the data by hand before the tools can be launched, and the flat file extracts are often made in order to increase the speed of the model building process. To avoid this, the data mining process needs to be embedded into the hardware, software, and DBMS where the data is being stored. This may mean writing the data mining algorithm in SQL for a relational database system, or writing stored procedures or special access functions for new data types. Independently of the way it is accomplished, the key will be to have a data mining system that does not require data extracts and minimizes any pre-processing of the columns of the database (whether instantiated or via views). And finally, a data mining system that is fully integrated will make as much use as possible of existing data dictionary information and other metadata, and conform the metadata that it produces to that which can be accommodated by the current data store.

To achieve quality explanation from the data mining system there are several routes that can be taken:

- Create powerful special-purpose visualization tools.
- Display the data mining results in visualization objects that are less powerful, but are familiar and reuse a user interface metaphor that the user is already familiar with and currently uses in solving the business problem targeted for data mining.

Figure 8-7
The measures for a data mining product should be first that it achieves acceptable levels of accuracy, but then that it be designed to fit seamlessly into your existing business process by providing an explanation of the results and integration with your existing IT data process.

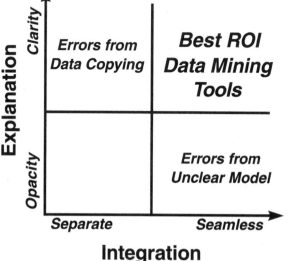

Both strategies are valid but clearly the second approach, if successful, makes it easiest on the end users. They don't have to learn about another tool, and they can compare and contrast the data mining results within a metaphor that they have already built intuitions about.

To fulfill both the integration and the explanation requirements for data mining requires that the data mining system embed into the existing data storage (data warehouse) infrastructure, and that the explanation facility embed into existing data navigation tools and applications that are familiar to the end user.

As an example of the way this could be done, Pilot Software's Discovery Server embedded the data mining engine directly into any RDBMS. It did this by executing a decision tree algorithm in SQL against any existing database, whether it was fully normalized, denormalized, or anywhere in between. No extract of the database was ever made, and the predictive model was stored in tables within the RDBMS as metadata. The model could then be applied to predict on new data entirely within the database system. In order to achieve a high degree of explanation for the predictive model, the decision tree was reformatted as a segmentation and embedded as a hierarchical dimension in a multidimensional database view. This provided business end users the common metaphor of segmentation to visualize the predictive model and the power of a full OLAP engine to navigate, drill down, drill up, etc., on the predictive model as well as any other dimension. This model is shown in Figure 8-8.

How to Measure Accuracy, Explanation, and Integration

Measuring Accuracy

When comparing data mining for prediction, the single most important measure by which the system is judged is the accuracy with which the system makes future predictions. For unsupervised learning systems such as clustering, or association rule mining, head-to-head measures are more difficult because the benefits of the result can depend on the particular circumstances in which the tool is used.

When prediction is performed in data mining, the most common ways of measuring the benefits from the system are the following:

■ *Accuracy.*   Accuracy is the percentage of total predictions that were correct. For a multiple-valued prediction or a binary prediction, this is easily calculated as being either right or wrong. For a continuous ordered prediction (such as predicting income), it could be accomplished by defining some threshold within which the prediction must come of the actual value in order for it to be considered correct (for example, predicting personal income within $10,000 is considered a correct prediction).

■ *Error rate.*   The error rate is the other side of accuracy—it simply measures the percentage of predictions that were wrong. Error rates are often preferred when the accuracy levels are very high and it is easier to see improvement when looking at the error rates. For instance, moving from 99.0% accuracy to 99.5% accuracy may seem less substantial an improvement than moving from a 50% accuracy to a 75% accuracy. In both cases, however, the error rate was cut in half (a dramatic improvement).

■ *Error rate at rejection.*   Often, when making a prediction, the data mining algorithm will both provide the prediction and the confidence that the prediction is correct (consider the K nearest neighbors algorithm when all K neighbors make the same prediction, as opposed to just a majority. The prediction might be the same in both cases, but in the unanimous case, the confidence in the prediction is much higher. By using the confidence, the predictions can be ordered and the least confident predictions rejected (that is, don't make a prediction). By using confidence, much higher accuracy rates can be achieved. For instance, the accuracy rate might be doubled if 80% of the predictions are rejected.

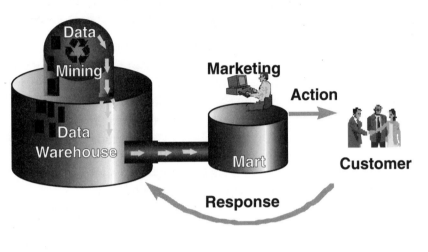

Embedded Data Mining For Business

- *Mean squared error.* For continuous, ordered predictions, the degree of mismatch between the prediction and the actual value can be captured by subtracting the two values and squaring the result. This "squared error" can then be averaged over all predictions to give an estimate of how much the prediction would be off by for a given prediction. The squaring is performed both to more severely weight very bad misses, and to make sure that all errors are positive and sum together when the average is taken. For example, if the prediction for one record was 20 and the prediction was 15, then the mean squared error would be 25 $= (15-20)^2$.

- *Lift.* Lift measures the degree to which the prediction model increased the density of responses for a given subset of the database over what would be achieved by no model (random selection). The performance improvement is usually measured for lift by stating the percentage of the population for which the prediction will be used and the lift for that subset. For instance, if the normal density of response in the population to a targeted mailing was 10%, but by focusing in on just the top one-quarter of the population predicted to respond by the predictive model the response is increased to 30%, then the lift would be 3 for the first quartile (quarter of the database, lift = 3 = 30%/10%). Because this method for measuring lift gives only a limited view of the improvement for one particular subset of the entire population, sometimes the area between the response curve for the predictive model and random marketing is used.

■ *Profit/ROI.* The truly best way to measure the benefits of a system is to calculate the maximum profit or return on investment (ROI) possible from the predictive model. If a profit or ROI model is available for the business problem, this calculation will dramatically simplify any guesses as to what size of subpopulation to use.

Measuring Explanation

After the accuracy of the data mining technique has been assessed, it will be important that the explanation facilities be built into the technique or product. Things to look for include the following:

■ *Automated rule generation.* Regardless of the technique, it is often possible to generate rules that explain the predictive model. Though the rules themselves cannot be guaranteed to be causal nor entirely capture the particular business problem of interest, they can nonetheless be useful for understanding the model.

■ *OLAP integration.* Check to see whether the results are embedded in an existing OLAP navigation environment. OLAP can often provide new ideas about how the data is to be used and to confirm intuitions about the model.

■ *Model validation.* The data mining system should aid in the automated validation of the model, whether by test set or cross-validation; and be able to allow the user to view both more complex and more general models, and their performances on vaulted data.

Measuring Integration

There are a variety of factors that go into the integration of the existing business and IT processes. These requirements are necessary for making it easy to integrate data mining into existing processes, with minimal disruption or requirements for new hardware, software, or data storage. The critical pieces to watch for fall into the following categories:

- *Proprietary data extracts.*   To achieve the best data mining performance, it will be important to find data mining tools that accommodate your data as it resides in your enterprise. Tools that require copying the data and transforming it into flat files or other formats run the risk of introducing errors and greatly increase the complexity of getting and keeping up-to-date data from the data warehouse.

- *Metadata.*   It will be tremendously beneficial if the predictive model is stored as metadata in the data warehouse, along with the actual scoring of records in the database by the predictive model. It will be beneficial to the data mining algorithms if they are able to access existing metadata structures.

- *Predictor preprocessing.*   Many current techniques require the end user to significantly modify the predictors in the database (converting values to between 0.0 and 1.0 for neural networks, for instance). Make sure that either the tool is able to do this automatically and still achieve acceptable levels of accuracy, or that easy-to-use tools are available for performing this data manipulation and feeding it into the data mining tool.

- *Predictor/prediction types.*   Be sure that the tool easily handles all common types of predictors in a seamless and understandable way, with respect to ordered versus categorical, with respect to high cardinality columns (for example, ZIP codes), and with respect to continuous values and binary values.

- *Dirty data.*   Sometimes, your data can mislead you. Sometimes, it does not have sufficient useful information in it, sometimes it is just plain wrong in a random way, and sometimes it is just plain wrong in a way that significantly affects the accuracy of the resulting predictive model. For the most part, data mining techniques handle the dirty data gracefully and do the best they can with whatever information is available. Cross-validation and test set validation of the database go a long way toward finding errors in the database and eliminating them. However, there are still cases in which data can be misleading in both the training data and the test data; thus, even cross-validation can let errors slip through. These are usually due to transformation errors, which can be mostly avoided if a proprietary data extract is not required.

■ *Missing values.* Another form of noise that you can find in the database are missing values. All tools should handle missing values, either by working around them (ignoring records that have missing values for critical predictors) or by trying to re-create them. (For example, by using the average value in place of the missing value or by predicting the missing value on the existing predictors without missing values.)

■ *Scaleability.* The tool should be able to handle both large and small databases by providing a robust and automated sampling routine, as well as by taking advantage of parallel processing hardware and RDBMS implementations.

What the Future Holds for Embedded Data Mining

Once the data mining process becomes easy enough to use and is seamlessly integrated into business processes and the general data and information flow around the enterprise, there will be new applications and synergies that will make data mining an even more critical requirement for any fully functioning data warehouse. Here are just a few:

■ Use data mining to improve the multidimensional database. One of the difficulties of OLAP and MDBs is that it can be difficult to determine which columns in the original data store should become dimensions in the multidimensional database. (Especially when the user may not be aware that they are actually important to their business perspective.) Data mining will be used here to create a predictive modeling dimension for the MDB or to provide a ranking of importance of the different columns of data, based on some business-specific prediction target.

- Use data mining to improve the data warehouse structure. One of the difficulties of moving from raw transaction level data to the data warehouse is in determining which data is relevant to the majority of business questions. Data mining will be used as a first-pass cut at what raw data is important from a business perspective, and should be added to the data warehouse.

- Multidimensional databases and summary data will enhance data mining performance. The more data, the better any data mining technique is. So, even though the most obscure and interesting patterns come at the detail level of data, the preprocessing of data into summary information, and even the use of metadata such as roll-up hierarchies in dimensions, can be important extra information that can be used to benefit data mining. Even directly mining a summary MDB without detail data will be fruitful and far more efficient than looking for patterns by hand in the MDB in the ad hoc way it is currently performed in OLAP systems.

PART

3

The
Business
Value

In the previous chapters we have provided a foundation of the technologies and how they work and when they can be used to provide robust architectures for customer relationship management. In this part of the book, these technologies will be applied to real business problems across a variety of industries.

Chapter 9 Customer Profitability - provides a blueprint for how to define and use customer profitability as the bedrock for your CRM processes.

Chapter 10 Customer Acquisition - shows how to use data mining to acquire new customers in the most profitable way possible.

Chapter 11 Customer Cross - details how this technology architecture can be used to increase the value of existing customers by selling more to them.

Chapter 12 Customer Retention - uses a case study from the telecommunications industry to show how to execute successful CRM systems to retain your profitable customers.

Chapter 13 Customer Segmentation - provides the business methodology of how to segment and manage your customers in a consistent and repeatable way across the enterprise.

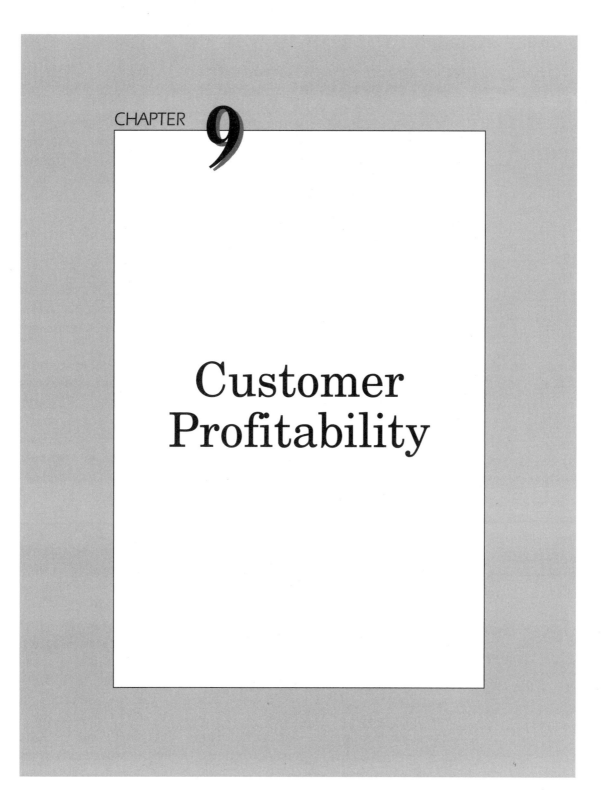

CHAPTER **9**

Customer
Profitability

Introduction

Customer profitability is the bedrock of data mining. Data mining earns its keep by helping you to understand and improve customer profitability. To improve customer profitability, however, takes more than just beginning to use or increasing the use of data mining. It must start with defining within the business exactly what is meant by "customer profitability". How does the organization define what a profitable customer is versus an unprofitable customer? Do you consider lifetime value of the customer? Should you consider the already invested costs of supporting different types of customers or assume that you can transition them all to the less expensive support channels? (For example, should customers who walk into the downtown bank branch be considered more expensive because to serve them requires an expensive physical infrastructure?)

The understanding of customer profitability is critical to the way that a company runs its business. As we shall see later in this chapter, customer profitability goes hand-in-hand with customer loyalty. It is also the measurement that allows you to aim data mining in the right direction. Without a measure of customer profitability, you can't optimize customer profitability. It sounds obvious, but the rule that is probably broken the most in building data mining applications is that data mining projects and applications are initiated without a thorough understanding of what the goal of the system is. And when it comes down to a business application, the goal is almost always about improved ROI. Improving ROI is almost always about making your relationship with your customer more profitable. It is the first and most fundamental step of data mining or any decision support system. It can also be very difficult to calculate.

The finance department in a bank may have one view of how to calculate profitability, marketing might have quite another view, and sales probably has a different view altogether. For instance, suppose that a banking customer frequents a downtown branch to do business. That branch is one of those solid-looking marble structures that may have been built 50 years ago at some expense, but now the property itself is worth a great deal of money. Specifically, the value of downtown real estate has skyrocketed. Should the infrastructure cost of those customers be near zero because the building has been paid off, or should it be relatively high when the current value of the building is considered?

Determining how to allocate fixed costs and amortizing dollars already invested is usually where the debates of cost to serve a customer come about. Despite this, it is clear that some customers are much more valuable than others and that some customers can become much more valuable than others. This touches on the subject of potential customer value and potential customer profitability: not only knowing where you are spending your money and where you are making profit, but also where you could be making profit and predicting where you might be leaving money on the table.

Why Calculate Customer Profitability?

Without knowing the value of your customers, it is hard to determine what the optimal marketing efforts would be—you don't know how much the customer is currently worth—so you might be wasting your money, or overinvesting, or you might not know what your customer might be worth, or how much business could be taken from some competitor who might currently be servicing your customer.

Without knowing the profitability of each customer, you are flying blind. If each customer were created equal and had the same value, then there would not be a problem. The whole game would be to first determine a way to serve a customer at profit, and then to attract and retain as many customers as possible.

The reality, however, is that there are vast differences in profitability among your customers, just as there are differences in the way that customers react to your marketing and sales efforts. Different customers may be positively or negatively affected by different marketing messages and promotions that have basically the same cost. In general, however, the more you spend on customers, the more likely they are to remain loyal and the more products they are likely to purchase.

For instance, suppose an airline gave double frequent-flyer miles to all of their customers, and allowed everyone to participate in special airline clubs. If all other things (price, service, etc.) were equal, then this airline would not want for customers. The reason that the airlines don't do this is, of course, the expense. In many ways, they have "purchased" their customers, and generally paid too high a price. Just as in any business endeavor, the price has to match the value gained from the purchased product or service. If you can think of a "customer" as something that can be purchased, then it becomes clear that some are worth a higher price than others. Knowing which ones are most valuable and how much you should "pay" for them is strongly aided by the use of data mining.

The Effect of Loyalty on Customer Profitability

Keeping a customer loyal can have profound effects on per-customer profitability. In the credit card industry, they lose an average of $80 on each customer in the first year. They make $40 per customer in the second year, but it is not until the fifth year that they make as much per customer as they lost in the first year—they make $87 per customer in the fifth year.

A customer who stays loyal is a customer who is still a customer years later when the relationship is the most profitable for the company. The loyal customer has no new costs of sales or marketing, and because a good relationship has been established between the customer and the company, the customer is willing to pay a premium for the excellent service that he is familiar with from the company.

Customer Loyalty and the Law of Compound Effect

Consider the simple example of two cellular phone companies: One loses customers at the industry average rate of 30% per year; the other has optimized its marketing to reduce the attrition to 20% per year. If both companies acquire new customers at a rate of 30% per year, then the first company is just treading water—after seven years, it is the same size that it was seven years previously. The second company, which has figured out to reduce customer churn to just 20%, has doubled in size over those same seven years.

The compounding effect of customer loyalty on customer profitability also increases because sales costs are lower and revenue generally has increased.

What Is Customer Relationship Management?

"Customer relationship management" is the term used for the business practice and associated tools and infrastructure allowing businesses that have more than a few customers to better serve and manage the interactions with those customers. If you have only a few customers, then managing those relationships is not too big a problem. You know each customer by name, and you and the customer's account manager probably know in some detail what their interest is and what their business is. You probably know what they like and dislike about your company and its products and services. If you have 10 million customers, you'd ideally like to have the same kind of relationship with them. It is not cost-effective to have multiple people from your company assigned to each customer, however. This is where you need help from the technologies and best practices of customer relationship management. Interestingly, in some circles, customer relationship management is also known as "customer profitability management." Both techniques have the same goal—making customers more profitable—and usually this is done by becoming more sophisticated in the personalized way that customers are treated by your sales, marketing, and customer support organizations.

The bottom line is that if you want to improve customer profitability, you almost always have to first improve the relationship that your company has with that customer. Often, the best way to improve profitability is to improve customer loyalty.

Optimizing Customer Profitability through Data Mining

Data mining can be used to predict customer profitability, under a variety of different marketing campaigns. One thing that you need to do is to predict profitability based on whether you have any marketing or sales at all. What happens to the profitability of your customer if you do nothing at all? Perhaps it is not as bad as you think. Chances are, however, that you do not know—because this would imply shutting down your sales and marketing force for some subset of your customer and prospect base. Politically, that can be a hard thing to get your sales and marketing groups to agree to. No matter how valuable an exercise it might be for calculating customer profitablity.

If, however, you can calculate customer profitability without sales and marketing intervention, you can create a baseline of customer profitability. This baseline is critical in order to understand what the effects of your sales and marketing efforts truly are. Though we have not gone into great depth on how data mining works, suffice it to say that data mining is not magic. It can only find and predict based on what has happened in the past—in essence it can find the patterns in your customer profiles that are predictive of high or low customer profitability, but it must have some target to shoot at. Having that target means that your organization must determine how it wants to calculate customer profitability. It might be as simple as revenue per customer minus costs of product, service, sales, and marketing; and any fixed costs are borne generally by all customers. Or it may be more sophisticated.

In general, though, if you as a business cannot decide on the definition of customer profitability, data mining is of limited benefit for the express purpose of increasing customer profitability. Data mining could still be used to uncover characteristics of customers or to predict new customers who might behave similarly under different situations—but these are limited in scope. Optimizing a marketing campaign to determine who is most likely to respond to a given offer with data mining can be a useful endeavor, but without some measure of customer profitability, it is not possible to know whether that optimization is actually profitable. Data mining will give you the best result, given the constraints, but unless you feed it the right target, it might not get you to the right place. It is a little bit like having a supersonic jet at your disposal to take you to wherever you want to go, but you don't have a compass to say where it is exactly you want to get to. You will get there with all due speed, but you may end up at the wrong place.

Predicting Future Profitability

Data mining can be used to predict anything. There may not always be enough information for it to produce a model that is useful, but more often than not, it can give you something that is better than nothing. It can be used to predict responses and profitability. For instance, if you are actively trying to acquire new customers for your new product and you have just finished a marketing blitz, your sales force may find itself overwhelmed with prospects. This is usually a nice problem to have, but because all customers come from prospects and not all customers are created equal, it is fair to say that not all prospects are created equal.

Some prospects close quickly, some slowly, some for large purchases, some for small. Some initiate their relationship with small purchases, but then quickly grow to very large-scale customers. Wouldn't it be nice if you had a way to prioritize your prospects based on the profitability of the customers they are likely to become?

If you knew what kind of customer your prospect would be when they grew up you could better know how to invest in them as a prospect. Are they worth a lot of your sales force's time? Are they worth the red carpet treatment or do they get sent the marketing packet, and that's it?

Clearly, many of these questions get answered directly by your sales force or perhaps your marketing department, but usually they are done somewhat blindly. Or, they are answered based on the company size of the prospect or the industry of the prospect, with little more than rules of thumb guiding the treatment of the prospect. Wouldn't it be helpful to provide your sales and marketing forces with strong indications of the value of the future customer? Data mining can provide this information by using the past experience of your sales people. The two missing ingredients that are required for data mining to do this, however, are the data that captures the characteristics of past prospects and the customers that they grew into, and a measure of the profitability of the customer. If you don't have a data set of past experience, there is nothing for the data mining system to learn from. If you don't have a measure of profitability, you don't have a target that data mining can aim at.

Predicting Customer Profitability Transitions

The other thing that data mining can do for you in terms of customer profitability is to model what the customer is likely to do in the future. For instance, how many of your "gold"-level—highly profitable—customers will transition to "bronze"-level this year? Or, on the positive side, how many of your "bronze"-level customers will become "gold"-level customers in the next twelve months? And then, you can ask the following questions: Is there anything I can do with my marketing, sales, or product that will keep the "gold" to "bronze" transition from happening? And, is there anything that I can do that will encourage more customers to transition from "bronze" to "gold," or to make that transition happen sooner rather than later? These simple transitions are depicted graphically in Figure 9-1.

Using Customer Profitability to Guide Marketing

Understanding current customer profitability based on current known customer information is hard, and often requires the collection of much important information as well as successful data mining. Beyond that, however, is the need to go to the next step to perform data mining to predict customer lifetime value, and ideally potential value and lifetime value.

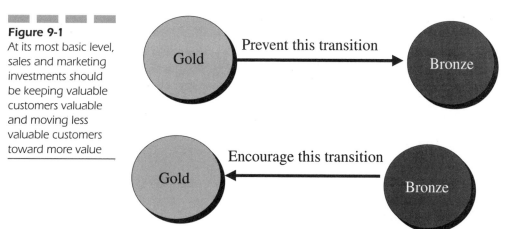

Figure 9-1
At its most basic level, sales and marketing investments should be keeping valuable customers valuable and moving less valuable customers toward more value

The difference between actual value and potential value is simply the difference between the value the customer will have to the company if things are maintained at the status quo versus the value the customer could have if he or she is well taken care of. Because estimating current customer value is such a difficult problem, you can well imagine that predicting future value as well as future potential value is even more difficult. It has been done, however, and the good news is, as always, that you don't need to be perfect in order the make a profit. You just need, at a minimum, to do better than you were doing before.

But just being able to make these predictions is not enough. You also need to know how to take action based on them and to coordinate the wide variety of actions that you may be taking to support your customer base. The name of the game, though, is pretty simple and has two rules for action, that if followed, will optimize the profitability of each customer:

- If the customer value and potential value are the same (the customer is as profitable as he can be), what is the minimum cost actions that can be taken that will keep that customer at that level of value?

- If the customer is at a current value but has a much higher potential value, what is the least expensive action that will transition her to the state of higher value that represents her potential?

In Table 9-1, we have drawn a simple example of such a customer value matrix of customer current value and potential value. This should be one of the first things that you do with data mining, and you should have it available in order to segment and control your consumer population. Keep in mind that this is the very first step in segmenting your customers, and it only gets more complicated from here. The reality is, however, that if you do even this first step, you will probably be far ahead of your competitors in understanding your customers.

Note that you may have many more customer segments than the six shown in this table, but you will usually have the main segments (those in which nothing needs to change—such as segments 1,2, and 6). Segment 1 has your best customers: They will remain your best customers throughout their lives and their current value matches their potential. Segment 2 is similar, except that they are likely to have low lifetime value, despite their high value today, probably because they are not loyal and are likely to switch to a competitor at some time in their customer life. Segment 6 represents your low-value customers that you will treat with some of your least expensive service. Segments 4 and 5 represent customers who, with the right care and service, can be transitioned to high-value customers, either near-term or long-term.

Table 9-1

A Customer Value Matrix, Showing Recommended Service Levels

Segment	Current Value	Lifetime Value (LTV)	Potential Value	Potential Lifetime Value (LTV)	Current Service Level	Best Service Level
1	High	High	High	High	Gold	Gold
2	High	Low	High	High	Gold	Gold
3	High	Low	High	Low	Gold	Bronze
4	Low	Low	Low	High	Bronze	Gold
5	Low	Low	High	High	Bronze	Gold
6	Low	Low	Low	Low	Bronze	Bronze

Why Revenue Isn't Enough

When we talk about customer value, we are generally speaking about profitability. We could also have been speaking about customer revenue. The problem with talking about customer revenue is that it is not always a good indication of who the people are that really matter. A customer that generates a lot of revenue, but requires a tremendous amount of care and feeding (at some high cost) may or may not be worth the effort. The revenues may be high but the profits may be low or even negative. Sometimes, investing in these types of customers is worthwhile as part of an overall strategy of growth. In the short amount of time that it takes today to build and then consolidate a market, however, it may or may not make sense to invest for very long in building certain customers. Even after you dominate the market, the market is so competitive that it is still difficult to turn those unprofitable customers into profitable ones. Sometimes, it makes more sense to just focus on the profitable customers from the very beginning.

Profit, however well measured, does not tell the whole story when measuring marketing effectiveness in order to optimize your marketing. Incremental customer profitability is the true measure that should be used to optimize your marketing.

Incremental Customer Profitability

Remembering that one of the main focuses of using data mining is to optimize profitability based on marketing and sales efforts, there is an important distinction between measuring the profitability of a customer that received an offer and measuring the increase in profitability BECAUSE they received the offer. The second measure is really the one that we are looking for. It is the one that gives us an indication of whether or not there is true value in our sales and marketing efforts. Perhaps there is not. For instance, it should not be considered a success if your marketing department comes up with a new program using data mining, and targets the gold customers with a special coupon program.

You should not let your marketing department off the hook so easily. They may have great response to the promotion, but they may not have actually done anything. Those customers were profitable before they received the promotion, and they are profitable after they received the promotion. Did the profit increase? Note that even if the revenue from those customers increased, it is not sufficient to claim victory. There was a cost involved with the coupon program and at least those costs have to be more than offset by the additional revenue.

It is the incremental profit that is caused by the promotion that you really want to measure. This can be hard to do, but it is the only true measure of whether you should be paying your ad agency and the salary of your product manager.

What Is Incremental Customer Profitability?

Incremental customer profitability can be defined as the profit that was made on a customer because of the increased revenue due to a promotion minus the cost of the promotion. Suppose that you had two identical twin customers who were purchasing at a certain level of your product and you promoted to one of them and didn't promote to the other. You could then measure the difference in revenue due to the promotion as the difference in revenue between these identical twins. The twin you didn't promote to represents what the customer would have done if left alone; the promoted-to twin represents the revenue that could be garnered with the application of the promotion.

In the real world, life is never so simple. The data to compare the benefits of a marketing promotion is never as easy to get your hands on. Certainly, finding subpopulations of your consumers who behave identically and are not influenced by outside factors is difficult. For instance, you could guess that consumers in the same income bracket might behave similarly, but they may or may not, depending on the particular product being marketed. One group might increase in sales due to the promotion; another group might increase in sales, regardless of the promotion. Yet another group might decrease in sales because of the promotion (we have included a case study from the wireless phone industry, where a beneficial marketing offer actually increased the rate at which customers churned—or didn't renew their cellular phone service).

Despite these caveats, there is also a great deal that can be done at a very high level. Specifically, incremental profitability can be estimated by simply promoting and not promoting to different consumer subpopulations at random (for instance, promoting to 100,000 randomly selected consumers and explicitly not promoting to 100,000 different randomly selected consumers). If the average revenue for the promoted group is $110 per year and for the non-promoted group is $100 per year, then it certainly appears that your promotion has had some positive impact on the per-consumer revenue. The $10 average difference between the two attributed to the promotion means that if the promotion itself cost less than $10 per consumer, then the promotion is a profitable one. If it cost more than $10, then even if you are significantly increasing the revenue per consumer, the endeavor is a money loser. It would be time to rethink your promotion, your targeting, or perhaps the way that you measure success. For example, you might not measure just incremental revenue in the near-term, but calculate improved lifetime value for consumers receiving the promotion—perhaps their lifetime value is greater than their current value).

Telling Your Sales Force to Stop Selling

So far, we've been talking about incremental profitability as if it were something that could be measured by promoting to one group and not promoting to another group. If this entails not mailing out 10,000 coupon packs out of a 10 million piece mailing, marketing and sales will probably not have too much problem letting you set up the experiment to measure the value of the promotion. This can be seen graphically in Figure 9-2.

Suppose, however, that the "promotion" that you want to measure is the effectiveness of sales calls on clients and you need to not call on 10% of your existing customers in order to perform a good measure of what the revenue would look like without the sales calls. You will have a hard time selling that idea to your sales force and asking them to not call on some of their clients for a few months "just to see what happens."

There is no easy way around political hurdles like these. Sometimes, they are solved in less than ideal ways, such as taking a very few consumers and using them as a control set. Other times, it may be a matter of using whatever data you might have on hand and doing the best you can with it. For instance, perhaps a sales region has been neglected, and no sales calls have been made in the region because the sales rep for the region quit and it took three months to find a replacement. You'd have a subpopulation in which the consumers had not been promoted, but it would be far from a random population. The performance of your product in that region may

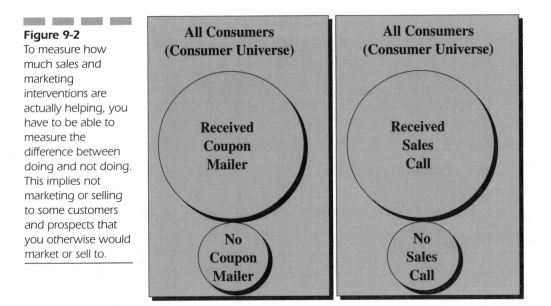

Figure 9-2
To measure how much sales and marketing interventions are actually helping, you have to be able to measure the difference between doing and not doing. This implies not marketing or selling to some customers and prospects that you otherwise would market or sell to.

have little bearing on the way your product has fared or will fare in other regions. For instance, the reason that the sales rep quit might have been because the sales region was notoriously unproductive, no matter how much promotion was done. Or, it might have been very productive no matter what was done, but the revenue per consumer could not be raised.

How Do I Get Organizational Buy-in?

Because of the business and political difficulties of telling your company to stop selling or promoting, it is often best to start small in building your case for the role of customer profitability. Find a small project (maybe a new product, or maybe a new medium for an old product, such as e-commerce selling and promoting) and set up the customer profitability equation on it. Show how the past campaigns have fared, show how profitable direct sales are per consumer, and be explicit about how you calculate profitability and costs. Then, publish it and show how overall profitability can be increased if this project's marketing and sales programs can be moved in the direction toward optimal marketing.

Then, expect arguments about how costs are calculated, long-term versus short-term revenues and customer investment, and not caring about already sunk costs—such as existing sales and marketing infrastructure. Then, we would suggest providing tools so that, given a basic model of incremental product consumption based on promotion costs, each individual can run his own scenarios based on how he or she would like to define costs and revenues.

You will certainly end up with a wide variety of different equations and determinations of incremental profitability, but at the end of the day, you will have raised the visibility of the fact that incremental profitability can be calculated, and that it is a meaningful and useful tool. If these scenario results can then be shared interactively so that a variety of managers within the company can share them and discuss them, they will go a lot further than just generating paper reports. Interactive tools over the Web are a great way to do this. One such tool is the Plan component of Optas Direct, shown in Figure 9-3.

Surrogates Are Often Worse Than Nothing at All

Sometimes, it is tempting to use a surrogate measure in place of customer profitability. For instance, you might at first consider all customers to be equal when it comes to revenue—thus, your whole optimization will be based on reducing costs. Or, you might use as a surrogate the response rate that you see from a particular customer to a particular offer. Or, you might determine whether they have turned in a survey or not. These events all indicate customer interest, but they may or may not reflect true customer revenue. In fact, it may be the opposite—there may be a correlation between fraud and coupon redemption—the higher redemption rates reflect

Figure 9-3
A Web-based interface for creating incremental profitability scenarios and sharing them across the enterprise. This is from the Plan component of Optas Direct's product.

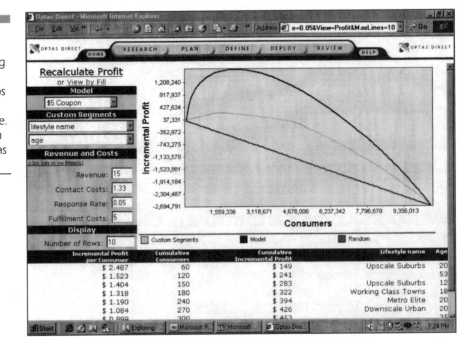

situations in which profits are dramatically negative—yet boosting the targeting of those people who respond may increase the response rate.

The Holy Grail

The chart in Figure 9-4 represents the Holy Grail of measuring promotion impact. It shows how one can view the value and impact from a campaign promotion on revenue per customer—clearly an important part of customer profitability, But to use only this revenue picture would be misleading, unless the cost per customer was identical across all customers—which is never the case.

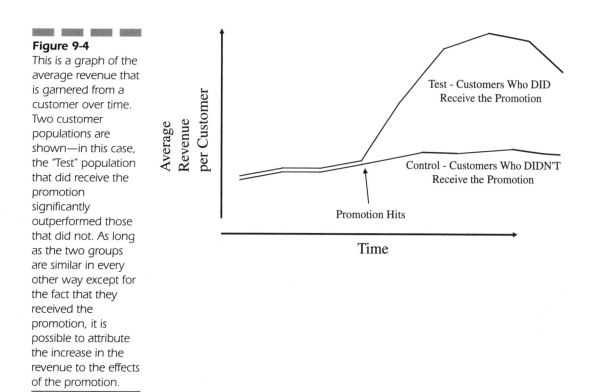

Figure 9-4
This is a graph of the average revenue that is garnered from a customer over time. Two customer populations are shown—in this case, the "Test" population that did receive the promotion significantly outperformed those that did not. As long as the two groups are similar in every other way except for the fact that they received the promotion, it is possible to attribute the increase in the revenue to the effects of the promotion.

How Do You Measure the Value of Data Mining?

Because data mining deals with larger amounts of data that you are looking for a pattern in, it generally also is used within industries and for problems where there is sufficient data to support accurate and useful results. Most often, these are problems where there are larger numbers of customers. Hence, data mining is often intertwined with industries and for applications where there are larger numbers of customers. Consequently, the per-customer profitability is a good measure of the value provided by the data mining application.

If data mining can be used to improve customer profitability, then its value can also be measured that way. And, if it is measured with customer profitability, then the investment in data mining can be easily evaluated as to its worth. As you shall see in later chapters, being able to evaluate the success of your data mining application in a believable and accurate way will be key—not only to your success but also to the further success of the data mining projects at your company.

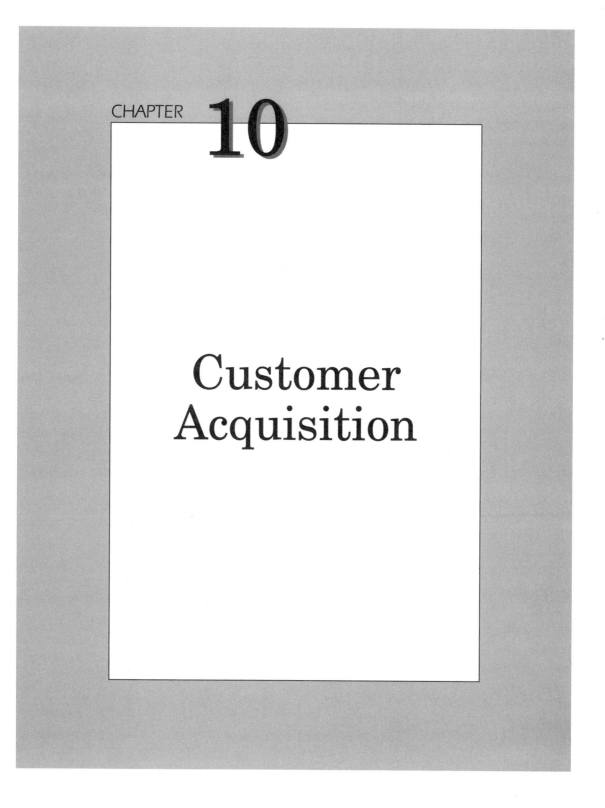

CHAPTER **10**

Customer
Acquisition

Introduction

For most businesses, the primary means of growth involves the acquisition of new customers. This could involve finding customers who previously were not aware of your product, were not candidates for purchasing your product (for example, baby diapers for new parents), or customers who in the past have bought from your competitors. Some of these customers might have been your customers previously, which could be an advantage (more data might be available about them) or a disadvantage (they might have switched as a result of poor service). In any case, data mining can often help segment these prospective customers and increase the response rates that an acquisition marketing campaign can achieve.

The traditional approach to customer acquisition involved a marketing manager developing a combination of mass marketing (magazine advertisements, billboards, etc.) and direct marketing (telemarketing, mail, etc.) campaigns based on their knowledge of the particular customer base that was being targeted. In the case of a marketing campaign trying to influence new parents to purchase a particular brand of diapers, the mass marketing advertisements might be focused in parenting magazines (naturally). The ads could also be placed in more mainstream publications whose readership demographics (age, marital status, gender, etc.) were similar to those of new parents.

In the case of traditional direct marketing, customer acquisition is relatively similar to mass marketing. A marketing manager selects the demographics that they are interested in (which could very well be the same characteristics used for mass market advertising), and then works with a data vendor (sometimes known as a service bureau) to obtain lists of customers who meet those characteristics. The service bureaus have large databases containing millions of prospective customers that can be segmented based on specific demographic criteria (age, gender, interest in particular subjects, etc.). To prepare for the "diapers" direct mail campaign, the marketing manager might request a list of prospects from a service bureau. This list could contain people, aged 18 to 30, who have recently purchased a baby stroller or crib (this information might be collected from people who have returned warranty cards for strollers or cribs). The service bureau will then provide the marketer with a computer file containing the names and addresses for these customers so that the diaper company can contact these customers with their marketing message.

It should be noted that because of the number of possible customer characteristics, the concept of similar demographics has traditionally been an art rather than a science. There usually are not hard-and-fast rules about whether two groups of customers share the same characteristics. In the end, much of the segmentation that took place in traditional direct marketing involved hunches on the part of the marketing professional. In the case of 18-30 year old purchasers of baby strollers, the hunch might be that people who purchase a stroller in this age group are probably making the purchase before the arrival of their first child (because strollers are saved and used for additional children). They also haven't yet decided which brand of diapers to use. Seasoned veterans of the marketing game know their customers well and are often quite successful in making these kinds of decisions.

How Data Mining and Statistical Modeling Change Things

Although a marketer with a wealth of experience can often choose relevant demographic selection criteria, the process becomes more difficult as the amount of data increases. The complexities of the patterns increase, both with the number of customers being considered and the increasing detail for each customer. The past few years have seen tremendous growth in consumer databases, so the job of segmenting prospective customers is becoming overwhelming.

Data mining can help this process, but it is by no means a solution to all of the problems associated with customer acquisition. The marketer will need to combine the potential customer list that data mining generates with offers that people are interested in. Deciding what is an interesting offer is where the art of marketing comes in.

Defining Some Key Acquisition Concepts

Before the process of customer acquisition begins, it is important to think about the goals of the marketing campaign. In most situations, the goal of an acquisition marketing campaign is to turn a group of potential customers into actual customers of your product or service. This is where things can get a bit fuzzy. There are usually many kinds of customers, and it can often take a significant amount of time before someone becomes a valuable customer. When the results of an acquisition campaign are evaluated, there are often different kinds of responses that need to be considered.

The responses that come in as a result of a marketing campaign are called "response behaviors." The use of the word "behavior" is important because the way in which different people respond to a particular marketing message can vary. How a customer behaves as a result of the campaign needs to take into consideration this varia-tion. A response behavior defines a distinct kind of customer action and categorizes the different possibilities so that they can be further analyzed and reported on.

Binary response behaviors are the simplest kind of response. With a binary response behavior, the customer response is either a yes or no. If someone is sent a catalog, did they buy something from the cat-alog or not? At the highest level, this is often the kind of response that is talked about. Binary response behaviors do not convey any subtle distinctions between customer actions, but these distinctions are not always necessary for effective marketing campaigns.

Beyond binary response behaviors are a type of categorical response behavior. As you would expect, a categorical response behav-ior allows for multiple behaviors to be defined. The rules that define the behaviors are arbitrary and are based on the kind of business you are involved in. Going back to the example of sending out catalogs, one response behavior might be defined to match if the customer pur-chased women's clothing from the catalog, whereas a different behav-ior might match when the customer purchased men's clothing. These behaviors can be refined a far as deemed necessary (for example, "purchased men's red polo shirt").

It should be noted that it is possible for different response behaviors to overlap. A behavior might be defined for customers that purchased over $100 worth of merchandising from the catalog. This could overlap with the "purchased men's clothing" behavior if the clothing that was purchased cost more than $100. Overlap can also be triggered if the customer purchases more than one item (both men's and women's shirts, for example) as a result of a single offer. Although the use of overlapping behaviors can tend to complicate analysis and reporting, the use of overlapping categorical response behaviors tends to be richer and therefore will provide a better understanding of your customers in the future.

There are usually several different kinds of positive response behaviors that can be associated with an acquisition marketing campaign. (This assumes that the goal of the campaign is to increase customer purchases, as opposed to an informational marketing campaign in which customers are simply told of your company's existence.) Some of the general categories of response behaviors (Figure 10-1) are:

- *Customer inquiry.* The customer asks for more information about your products or services. This is a good start. The customer is definitely interested in your products—it could signal the beginning of a long-term customer relationship. You might also want to track conversions, which are follow-ups to inquiries that result in the purchase of a product.

- *Purchase of the offered product or products.* This is the usual definition of success. You offered your products to someone, and

Figure 10-1

Example response analysis report broken down by behavior

VALEX Response Analyzer: Response Counts by Behavior						
Behavior	Measures	Day 12/12/98	12/19/98	12/26/98	1/2/99	TOTAL
Inquiry	Number of Responses	1,556	1,340	328	352	3,576
Purchase A	Number of Responses	210	599	128	167	1,104
Purchase B	Number of Responses	739	476	164	97	1,476
Purchase C	Number of Responses	639	647	113	105	1,504

they decided to buy one or more of them. Within this category of response behaviors, there can be many different kinds of responses. As mentioned earlier, both "purchased men's clothing" and "purchased women's clothing" fit within this category.

■ *Purchase of a product different that the ones offered.*   Despite the fact that the customer purchased one of your products, it wasn't the one you offered. You might have offered the deluxe product and they chose to purchase the standard model (or vice-versa). In some sense, this is very valuable response because you now have data on a customer/product combination that you would not otherwise have collected.

There are also typically two kinds of negative responses. The first is a non-response. This is not to be confused with a definite refusal of your offer. For example, if you contacted the customer via direct mail, there may be any number of reasons why there was no response (wrong address, offer misplaced, etc.). Other customer contact channels (outbound telemarketing, email, etc.) can also result in ambiguous non-responses. The fact there was no response does not necessarily mean that the offer was rejected. As a result, the way you interpret a non-response as part of additional data analysis will need to be thought out (more on this later).

A rejection (also known simply as a "no") by the prospective customer is the other kind of negative response. Depending on the offer and the contact channel, you can often determine exactly whether or not the customer is interested in the offer (for example, an offer made via outbound telemarketing might result in a definitive "no, I'm not interested" response). Although it probably does not seem useful, the definitive "no" response is often as valuable as the positive response when it comes to further analysis of customer interests.

It All Begins with the Data

One of the differences between customer acquisition and most other marketing applications of data mining revolves around the data that is used to build predictive models. The amount of information that you have about people that you do not yet have a relationship with is much more limited than the information you have about your existing customers. In some cases, the data might be limited to their address and/or phone number. The key to this process is finding a relationship between the information that you do have and the behaviors you want to model.

Most acquisition marketing campaigns begin with the prospect list. A prospect list is simply a list of customers that have been selected because they are likely to be interested in your products or services. There are numerous companies around the world that will sell lists of customers, often with a particular focus (for example, new parents, retired people, new car purchasers, etc.).

Sometimes, it is necessary to add additional information to a prospect list by overlaying data from other sources. For example, consider a prospect list containing only names and addresses. In terms of a potential data mining analysis, the information contained in the prospect list is very weak. There might be some patterns in the city, state, or ZIP code fields, but they would be limited in their predictive power. To augment the data, information about customers on the prospect list could be matched with external data. One simple overlay involves combining the customer's ZIP code with U.S. census data about average income, average age, and so on. This can be done manually or, as is often the case with overlays, your list provider can take care of this automatically.

More complicated overlays are also possible. Customers can be matched against purchase, response, and other detailed data that the data vendors collect and refine. This data comes from a variety of sources including retailers, state and local governments, and the customers themselves. If you are mailing out a car accessories catalog, it might be useful to overlay information (make, model, year) about any known cars that people on the prospect list might have registered with their department of motor vehicles.

Test Campaigns

Once you have a list of prospect customers, there is still some work that needs to be done before you can create predictive models for customer acquisition. Unless you have data available from previous acquisition campaigns, you will need to send out a test campaign in order to collect data for analysis. Besides the customers you have selected for your prospect list, it is important to include some other customers in the campaign, so that the data is as rich as possible for future analysis. For example, assume that your prospect list (that you purchased from a list broker) was composed of men over age 30 who recently purchased a new car. If you were to market to these prospective customers and then analyze the results, any patterns found by data mining would be limited to sub-segments of the group of men over 30 who bought a new car. What about women or people under age 30? By not including these people in your test campaign, it will be difficult to expand future campaigns to include segments of the population that are not in your initial prospect list. The solution is to include a small random selection of customers whose demographics differ from the initial prospect list. This random selection should constitute only a small percentage of the overall marketing campaign, but it will provide valuable information for data mining. You will need to work with your data vendor in order to add a random sample to the prospect list.

More sophisticated techniques than random selection do exist, such as those found in statistical experiment design. Deciding when and how to implement these approaches is beyond the scope of this book, but there are numerous resources in the statistical literature that can provide more information.

Although this circular process (customer interaction → data collection → data mining → customer interaction) exists in almost every application of data mining to marketing, there is more room for refinement in customer acquisition campaigns. Not only do the customers that are included in the campaigns change over time, but the data itself can also change. Additional overlay information can be included in the analysis when it becomes available. Also, the use random selection in the test campaigns allows for new segments of people to be added to your customer pool.

Evaluating Test Campaign Responses

Once you have started your test campaign, the job of collecting and categorizing the response behaviors begins. Immediately after the campaign offers go out, you need to track responses. The nature of the response process is such that responses tend to trickle in over time, which means that the campaign can go on forever. In most real-world situations, though, there is a threshold after which you no longer look for responses. At that time, any customers on the prospect list that have not responded are deemed non-responses. Before the threshold, customers who have not responded are in a state of limbo, somewhere between a response and a non-response.

Building Data Mining Models Using Response Behaviors

With the test campaign response data in hand, the actual mining of customer response behaviors can begin. The first part of this process requires you to choose which behaviors you are interested in predicting, and at what level of granularity. The level at which the predictive models work should reflect the kinds of offers that you can make, not the kinds of responses that you can track. It might be useful (for reporting purposes) to track catalog clothing purchases down to the level of color and size. If all catalogs are the same, however, it really doesn't matter what the specifics of a customer purchase for the data mining analysis. In this case (all catalogs are the same), binary response prediction is the way to go. If separate men's and women's catalogs are available, analyzing response behaviors at the gender level would be appropriate. In either case, it is a straightforward process to turn the lower-level categorical behaviors into a set of responses at the desired level of granularity. If there are overlapping response behaviors, the duplicates should be removed prior to mining.

In some circumstances, predicting individual response behaviors might be an appropriate course of action. With the movement toward one-to-one customer marketing, the idea of catalogs that are custom-produced for each customer is moving closer to reality. Existing channels such as the Internet or outbound telemarketing also allow you to be more specific in the ways you target the exact wants and needs of your prospective customers. A significant drawback of the modeling of individual response behaviors is that the analytical processing power required can grow dramatically because the data mining process needs to be carried out multiple times, once for each response behavior that you are interested in.

How you handle negative responses also needs to be thought out prior to the data analysis phase. As discussed previously, there are two kinds of negative responses: rejections and non-responses. Rejections, by their nature, correspond to specific records in the database that indicate the negative customer response. Non-responses, on the other hand, typically do not represent records in the database. Non-responses usually correspond to the absence of a response behavior record in the database for customers who received the offer.

There are two ways in which to handle non-responses. The most common way is to translate all non-responses into rejections, either explicitly (by creating rejection records for the non-responding customers) or implicitly (usually a function of the data mining software used). This approach will create a data set comprised of all customers who have received offers, with each customer's response being positive (inquiry or purchase) or negative (rejections and non-responses).

The second approach is to leave non-responses out of the analysis data set. This approach is not typically used because it throws away so much data, but it might make sense if the number of actual rejections is large (relative to the number of non-responses); experience has shown that non-responses do not necessarily correspond to a rejection of your product or services offering.

Once the data has been prepared, the actual data mining can be performed. The target variable that the data mining software will predict is the response behavior type at the level you have chosen (binary or categorical). Because some data mining applications cannot predict non-binary variables, some finessing of the data will be required if you are modeling categorical responses using non-categorical software. The inputs to the data mining system are the input variables and all of the demographic characteristics that you might have available, especially any overlay data that you combined with your prospect list.

In the end, a model (or models, if you are predicting multiple categorical response behaviors) will be produced that will predict the response behaviors that you are interested in. The models can then be used to score lists of prospect customers in order to select only those who are likely to respond to your offer. Depending on how the data vendors you work with operate, you might be able to provide them with the model, and have them send you only the best prospects. In the situation in which you are purchasing overlay data in order to aid in the selection of prospects, the output of the modeling process should be used to determine whether all of the overlay data is necessary. If a model does not use some of the overlay variables, you might want to save some money and leave out these unused variables the next time you purchase a prospect list.

CHAPTER 11

Cross-selling

Introduction

The relationship between a company and its customers is a constantly moving process. Once you have a relationship with a customer, there are a number of ways to optimize the two-way nature of the relationship:

- Maximize the length of the relationship
- Maximize the number of interactions during the relationship
- Maximize the profit associated with each interaction

If you look at some of the recent mega-mergers in the financial services industry, one of the driving forces behind the scenes was the expected capability to sell products and services to the entire customer base. Consider the Citicorp/Travelers Group merger. Travelers Group is hoping to increase sales of insurance products, whereas Citicorp is looking to increase sales of financial services. By merging their customer bases, each organization sees opportunities to sell its wares to the other's existing customers. In addition, they are hoping that customers are looking to do one-stop shopping for financial service and insurance products, thus increasing sales opportunities.

The goal is to create a win-win situation, in which both the company and the customer benefit. The customer benefits by receiving a service that better matches their needs, and the company benefits by increasing sales.

This is cross-selling. Cross-selling is the process by which you offer your existing customers new products and services. Customers who purchase baby diapers might also be interested in hearing about your other baby products. That example is relatively easy to comprehend. The real value comes when more subtle patterns are found. Data mining allows this to happen.

One form of cross-selling, sometimes called "up selling," takes place when the new offer is related to existing purchases by the customer. For example, an up-sell opportunity might exist for a telephone company to market a premium long-distance service to existing long distance customers who currently have the standard service.

How Cross-selling Works

Using data mining for cross-selling begins with data about purchasing behaviors for your existing customers. Most forms of cross-selling are not much different from the analysis required for single product customer acquisition. Each of the different possible cross-selling offers is evaluated as if it were a single product offering. The key is to then optimize the product offerings across all customers, so that the offer (or offers) that a customer receives provides the greatest benefit for both buyer and seller.

Consider the following example. Assume that you are a marketing manager for a mid-size bank. You have the following products available for your customers:

- Value checking account
- Plus checking account
- Standard credit card
- Gold credit card
- Platinum credit card
- Primary mortgage
- Secondary mortgage

Of these products, you are responsible for marketing the mortgage products to your customers. Your goal is to find out which customers might be interested in a mortgage offering at least 60 days before they would apply for the loan. It is important that any predictions are made with sufficient lead time (in this case, two months), so that any interactions with the customer take place before they are committed to a relationship with your competition.

You have already done some thinking about your customers and their motivations in this area and came up with several scenarios, which you presented to your boss when pitching this new campaign:

- *Customers preparing to buy a new home.* These customers might be building up cash reserves in their checking and/or savings account in order to put together a down payment.

- *Customers preparing to refinance an existing home.* These customers might be paying off credit card debt (thus making them more acceptable from a risk point of view), and hold a mortgage whose interest rate is higher than the current interest rate.

- *Customers preparing to add a second mortgage.* These customers might have increasing credit card debt, an on-time payment history for both their credit cards and existing mortgage (which means that they are a good risk), and enough equity in their house to cover the outstanding credit card balance.

Steps in the Process

Before you can begin to look for cross-selling opportunities using data mining, you need to determine what kinds of offers you are interested in making available to your customers. In this example, there are three possible offers (new first mortgage, refinance of first mortgage, or second mortgage). Only one of these will be made to a customer (assuming that any offer is made at all). Once the offers are determined, the next step is to collect the data to support the analysis. In recent years, this has often meant the access to a data warehouse that holds all of your customer information, but any kind of historical data repository should allow you to begin the process of analyzing customer data to look for cross-selling opportunities. The model that will be created as a result of the data mining process will predict the probability that a customer will sign up for a mortgage with your company. By ranking the customers by their predicted probability, you will be able to identify the best prospects for your mortgage products.

The historical data contains all information that you have about your customers and their mortgage purchases, including demographic and account-level information (age, income, marital status, and ZIP code), as well as transactional information (recent balances, number of purchases, and types of purchases). Your experience might also tell you to include external macroeconomic information from the time of the mortgage that could be relevant to the decision-making process (for example, the average mortgage rate at that time, housing starts, consumer confidence, etc.). In the end, you will end up with a collection of several hundred (or thousand) pieces of information about each customer, at various points of time in their relationship with you.

It should be noted that some information might not be available, either because you don't know it (marital status), it doesn't make sense (the outstanding first mortgage balance for someone who doesn't already have a mortgage with your company), or the data is missing (whether they are new customers). Depending on the data mining technique that is used to analyze the data set, these incomplete records might or might not be included in the eventual analysis. When customers are excluded from the analysis, they should not be ignored completely because they might be used in a different analysis with a different time frame or prediction target.

The first step in preparing the data is to determine which of the customers included in the historical data set has previously completed mortgage financing through your company. Because the goal is to identify customers two months before they would close on a mortgage, you will need to create a sixty-day window of data for every customer/month combination. This means that each customer will potentially contribute multiple pieces of data to the historical data set. In months that they did not sign up for a mortgage, the data (along with information about the two previous months) will indicate a negative response (no mortgage product purchase). In the month(s) when a customer did sign up for a mortgage, the data will indicate a positive response.

Figure 11-1 shows how the windowing of data for each customer is handled. Some data mining systems can handle the windowing of the data automatically; others will require users to manually create multiple records for each customer, corresponding to each two-month window of data.

Because there are three different mortgage products being analyzed, the historical data set will need to include positive response information about each potential offer.

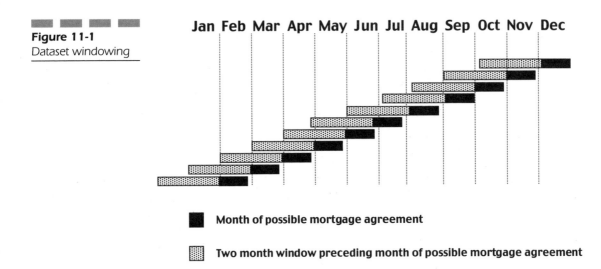

Figure 11-1
Dataset windowing

■ Month of possible mortgage agreement

▦ Two month window preceding month of possible mortgage agreement

The Analysis Begins

The actual data mining process contains three distinct steps when doing cross-sell analysis:

- Modeling of individual behaviors
- Scoring data with predictive models
- Optimization of the scoring matrices

Modeling is the process whereby data mining algorithms analyze the data, creating mathematical functions (the models) that can be used to predict customer behavior (in this case, two months before that behavior will be exhibited). For cross-selling, there will be one model for each cross-selling offer. Once the cross-selling models have been generated, each can be applied to new customer data in order to make predictions about those customers. The scores are simply the outputs of the models, and they might correspond to the predicted probability that a customer will purchase a specific mortgage product two months in the future. Because we have three different cross-sell offers, there will be three different scores for each customer. This ends up producing a matrix of scores, with one row for each customer and one column for each cross-sell score. The final step of the process is the optimization of the scoring matrix—selecting which of the multiple offers will be made to each customer.

Modeling

The process of modeling can be broken down into subprocesses, each of which involves creating models for each of the different cross-sell offers. At this point, the analysis for each offer is independent of the other cross-sell offers. There might be some overlap in the customers you use to carry out the analyses, but the actual model-building processes would be independent. For example, one customer might buy a house with a mortgage and then later add on a second mortgage.

Once the models have been created, they can be used repeatedly until they are no longer needed. This might happen if the models lose their effectiveness or the behaviors that they predict might no longer be of interest. In any event, the steps that follow modeling (scoring and optimization) can be carried out over time using a single set of models.

Scoring

Once you have generated the three cross-selling models, it is time to apply them to new customer data to determine which mortgage offers to send to which people. Deciding which customer to score with a particular model might require some thought because there are usually some sort of filtering criteria used to pre-select customers for consideration of a particular order. For example, you might score only those customers who don't have a house with the refinance model. This might mean that you would score a customer with the "New Mortgage Model," even though they might have already signed a mortgage with another company, although you don't know it. You might also use a set of risk criteria in order to remove from the scoring process those customers who are considered to have a high risk of nonpayment.

In the end, you will generate a matrix like Table 11-1. For each customer, you will have three different scores. In some cases, the customer/score entry is NULL due to the fact that you did not score that customer with that model because it did not make sense to do so (for example, you don't score customers living in an apartment with the second mortgage model).

Optimization

Once you have a cross-sell matrix like Table 11-1, you can then begin the process by which you determine which offer to make to which customer. Optimization of the scoring matrix selects the best of the possible offers for each customer. There are four possible levels of optimization of this process, ranging from simple to complex:

- Naïve
- Average economic
- Individual economic
- Constraint optimized

Let's start with naïve optimization. In a naïve optimization, all you do is select the highest scoring offer for each customer. If the scores are predictions of the probability of responding to a particular offer, the naïve optimization will maximize the possible number of responses to the marketing campaign. Naïve optimization chooses the offer that a customer is most likely to respond to, regardless of any financial implications of such a response (a less likely but more lucrative offer would be passed by using the naïve optimization approach). If your goal is to maximize market share, the naïve approach is for you. In Table 11-2, the customers from Table 11-1 are shown with the naïve campaign selection highlighted. The major advantage of the naïve approach is its simplicity. Each customer record needs to be examined only once per model, which allows for a quick selection process.

The second approach is the "average economic" selection method. Average economic optimization improves upon the naïve optimization by incorporating financial information about the value of each offer, so that instead of simply maximizing the number of offer responses, the total economic value can be maximized. In this scheme, each cross-sell offer has an economic value associated with it (and each offer's value can be different). This value is the average over the potential customers and is usually determined by looking at characteristics of existing customers in the historical dataset. For example, the value (to the company) for a new home mortgage might be, on average, $6000 per customer. Some customers might be worth more and some less, but on average they are worth $6000. On the other hand, a second mortgage might only contribute $5000 per customer, on average.

Table 11-3 shows the average economic scores for the customers listed in Table 11-1. Because the scores in Table 11-1 are the probabilities that a customer will respond to a particular offer, multiplying the economic values for each offer by the model scores, the matrix will generate the expected average economic value for each customer/offer combination. For each customer, the offer with the highest expected economic return is highlighted. For the sake of this

Table 11-1

Customer matrix

Customer ID	New Mortgage Score	Refinance Score	Second Mortgage Score
1391193	0.2422	0.4926	0.0872
1401936	0.8600	0.4465	0.0982
1491969	NULL	0.9700	0.4453
1623144	0.7854	NULL	NULL
1701338	0.5063	NULL	NULL
1810529	0.8210	0.5014	0.6386
1940842	NULL	0.5057	0.9177
1980368	0.2226	0.1352	0.0888
2039145	0.2928	0.1732	0.5244

Table 11-2

Naive campaign selections are highlighted

Customer ID	New Mortgage Score	Refinance Score	Second Mortgage Score
1391193	0.2422	**0.4926**	0.0872
1401936	**0.8600**	0.4465	0.0982
1491969	NULL	**0.9700**	0.4453.
1623144	**0.7854**	NULL	NULL
1701338	**0.5063**	NULL	NULL
1810529	**0.8210**	0.5014	0.6386
1940842	NULL	0.5057	**0.9177**
1980368	**0.2226**	0.1352	0.0888
2039145	0.2928	0.1732	**0.5244**

Table 11-3

Highest expected economic return is highlighted

Customer ID	New Mortgage Score	Refinance Score	Second Mortgage Score
1391193	**$1,452.94**	$985.28	$435.95
1401936	**$5,160.14**	$893.04	$490.80
1491969	NULL	$1,939.97	**$2,226.57**
1623144	**$4,712.41**	NULL	NULL
1701338	**$3,037.68**	NULL	NULL
1810529	**$4,925.71**	$1,002.75	$3,192.89
1940842	NULL	$1,011.48	$4,588.70
1980368	**$1,335.85**	$270.34	$443.90
2039145	**$1,757.01**	$346.34	$2,621.97

analysis, the average value of a new mortgage was $6000, a refinanced mortgage was $2000, and a second mortgage was valued at $5000.

Notice that the distribution of offers has changed from the naïve approach. In fact, none of these customers will be receiving the refinance offer under this scenario.

The third approach to optimizing the selection of an offer is to use unique financial information about each individual customer in order to calculate the expected return for a particular marketing offer. For example, it might make sense to use a customer's existing mortgage balance in order to estimate the value of a refinanced or second mortgage. The major difference between the "average economic" and "individual economic" optimization approaches is that the value associated with each customer/offer combination is now unique.

As with the average economic optimization, the economic values are multiplied by the model scores in order to estimate the predicted value. Table 11-4 shows the effect on customer selection when financial characteristics of individual customers are used to estimate the economic value of a particular offer.

In this example, the expected return from the customers shown is $24,339.21. In some cases, there is no choice to be made because there is only one viable option (for the customers who do not currently have a mortgage, meaning that they are not eligible for either a refinanced first mortgage or a second mortgage).

Table 11-4

The effect on customer selection when financial characteristics of individual customers are used to estimate the economic value of a particular offer

Customer ID	New Mortgage Score	Refinance Score	Second Mortgage Score
1391193	$1,060.76	**$1,432.80**	$120.20
1401936	**$4,511.21**	$132.04	$537.02
1491969	NULL	**$5,355.15**	$868.12
1623144	**$4,377.96**	NULL	NULL
1701338	**$1,444.20**	NULL	NULL
1810529	**$2,749.17**	$273.83	$864.60
1940842	NULL	$518.22	**$1,741.13**
1980368	$588.32	**$646.69**	$94.34
2039145	$856.38	$804.93	**$2,080.90**

These financial characteristics can get complicated, with numerous facts about each customer used to evaluate the value of a particular offer/customer combination. For example, you might want to compute the net present value (NPV) of a customer, evaluate their risk of filing bankruptcy, factor it into risk-adjusted NPV, and then combine this with the expected value for the mortgage offering. In the end, it might make sense to use data mining to explicitly model the (long-term) value of the individual offers, and then select the highest-value offers for each customer. This brings us back to naïve optimization in that we will now simply select the offer with the highest score. The only difference is that the score is now an expected financial value rather than a probability of response.

The final type of optimization is constraint optimization. It expands upon the other forms of cross-selling optimization by incorporating external constraints on the offer selection process. Constraint optimization will work with any kind of numerical score, such as a probability of response or economic value. Some possible constraints include the following:

- Maximum spending limit, regardless of the possible benefit of spending more. This might result in more inexpensive offers than would otherwise be made. Each offer will need to have a cost associated with it (e.g., at a minimum the cost could be the printing and postage cost associated with mailing an offer to a customer).

- Minimum and/or maximum numbers per offer type. For example, this might occur if there was a minimum number for a print run that was part of marketing campaign.

- Minimum and/or maximum numbers of offers per geographic region. You might want to make sure that your offers are distributed evenly across your sales territories.

- Minimum and/or maximum number of offers per segment of your customer base. Because of regulatory conditions, you might need to make sure that a particular segment (race, gender, etc.) of your customer base is not underrepresented in a marketing campaign.

Let's assume that you'll modify the previous example by requiring that each offer have at least three customers (and, because there are only nine customers in this example, this means that each offer should have exactly three customers selected). We will still use the "individual economic" matrix (Table 11-4). Table 11-5 shows the results when the process optimizes selection using the external constraints.

Although the changes are relatively minor (one customer who was originally selected to receive a new mortgage offer instead will receive a second mortgage offer), the campaign now meets the external optimization requirements. This results in a total value for the campaign of $22,454.64, which is approximately two thousand dollars less than the campaign that does not impose the external optimization criteria. It should be noted that when external constraints are included in the selection optimization, the total value will be less than or equal to the selection optimization without external constraints.

Sometimes, it is not possible to satisfy all of the external constraints that are specified. It might be that some constraints are

Table 11-5

The results when the process optimizes selection using the external constraints

Customer ID	New Mortgage Score	Refinance Score	Second Mortgage Score
1391193	$1,060.76	**$1,432.80**	$120.20
1401936	**$4,511.21**	$132.04	$537.02
1491969	NULL	**$5,355.15**	$868.12
1623144	**$4,377.96**	NULL	NULL
1701338	**$1,444.20**	NULL	NULL
1810529	$2,749.17	$273.83	**$864.60**
1940842	NULL	$518.22	**$1,741.13**
1980368	$588.32	**$646.69**	$94.34
2039145	$856.38	$804.93	**$2,080.90**

contradictory or simply that the characteristics of the customers do not allow for the constraints to be met. For example, one constraint might be that the customers selected for a particular offer be from each of the 50 United States and that each state have at least 1000 recipients of the offer. If there are only 500 customers from North Dakota in the pool, it will be impossible to select 1000 to receive the offer, regardless of the specified criteria.

In the event that all constraints cannot be met, the process can either "hard fail" or it can fail gracefully. In a hard fail, the process aborts when it is determined that all constraints cannot be met. The user is then informed of the problem, and they can reformulate the constraints and try again. In the case of a graceful failure, the optimization process attempts to meet as many of the constraints as possible, despite the fact that it is not possible to satisfy all of them. The constraints may be weighted so that the process takes into consideration their relative importance.

Constraint optimization of the offer selection isn't really a data mining exercise. Instead, it is a process that takes the results of individual data mining exercises and further optimizes them, based on additional user constraints. The actual optimization procedure can be performed by using standard techniques such as linear programming or simulated annealing.

Multiple Offers

In the previous examples, it was assumed that only one offer would be selected for each customer. The goal was to select the single best offer among a number of possibilities. An obvious extension to this process is to select and send multiple offers to customers. These offers could be packaged together (a selection of three coupons out of a set of ten choices) or they might be staggered in time.

The simplest approach to selecting multiple offers is to choose the ones with the highest individual scores, without regard to how these offers might interact. Optimization constraints such as "at most, three offers per person" can also be introduced to the process.

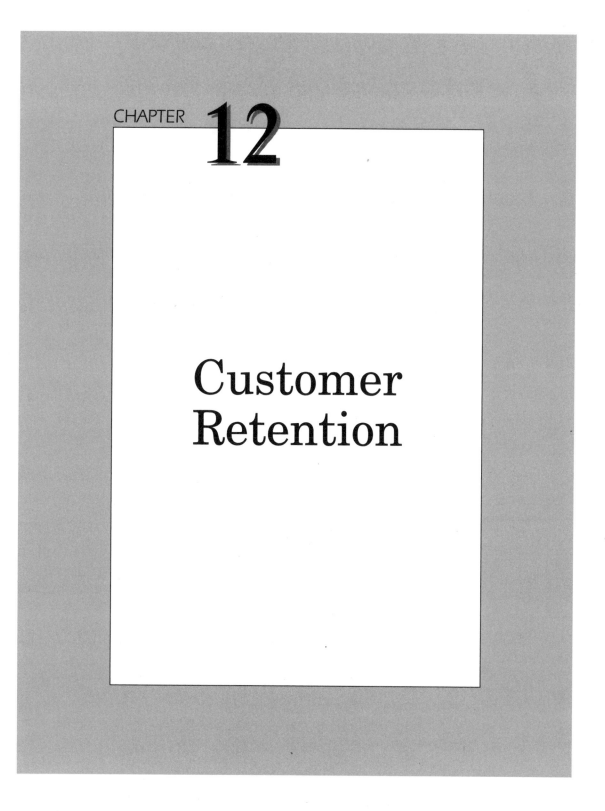

CHAPTER 12

Customer
Retention

Introduction

As industries become more competitive and as the cost of acquiring new customers increases, the value of retaining current customers also increases. For instance, in the cellular phone industry, it is estimated that the cost of attracting and signing up a new customer is $300 or more when the costs of discounted hardware and sales commissions are included. The cost of retaining a current customer, however, can be as low as the price of a phone call or the cost of updating their cellular phone to the latest technology offering. Although expensive, this is still significantly cheaper than signing up a wholly new customer. As you will see in this case study, the way that you use data mining to model the effect of different promotions or tactics designed to save your customer can have a significant impact on the overall effectiveness of your retention campaign.

The value of retaining customers rather than just acquiring new customers is not limited to the cellular phone industry. In their book, *Enterprise One to One*, Don Peppers and Martha Rogers show a simple example of magazine subscriptions. If annual subscription renewal (retention) can be increased by just 2%, the overall lifetime value of each customer, as measured by net present value, would increase by more than 25%. The reason for is that the longer that you can retain a customer, the longer you have to recoup your initial investment in that customer and in your acquisition costs overall. And this effect compounds year after year, as the cost of retaining the customer versus acquiring a new customer is enjoyed each year. In some industries, the acquisition costs may be low; but in many others (such as financial services, high tech retail, and telecom), they can be substantial.

In this chapter, we detail, in a case study, the effects of using data mining to predict which customers are at risk of churn in the cellular telephone industry. We discuss how those results can be incorporated and measured as part of an overall marketing campaign.

Churn in the Cellular Telephone Industry

Churn in the cellular telephone market is the number one problem today for the providers in the industry. Even worse news is that the industry is being opened up through new technologies to new competitors, so that although there used to be a maximum of two competitors per region, there can now be six or more.

Customer churn is the term used in the cellular telephone industry to denote the movement of cellular telephone customers from one provider to another. In many industries this is called customer attrition, but because of the highly volatile and growing market, and the somewhat limited competition, many customers churn from one provider to another frequently in search of better rates or for the perks of signing up with a new provider—such as receiving the latest and greatest cellular phone.

The problem is severe. Whereas other industries, such as the credit card industry, struggle with attrition rates hovering around 0.4% per month, the industry average for the cellular industry is 2.2% per month. In other words, about 27% of a given carrier's customers are lost each year when the contracts need to be renewed. Over a longer time period, it looks just as bleak. J. D. Power and Associates estimates that 90% of cellular users have churned at least once in the last five years.

Losing these customers can be very expensive because it costs from $300 to $600 to acquire a new customer in sales support, marketing, advertising, and commissions. Many of these new customers are less profitable than the ones that were lost. The average monthly bill has decreased from $84 in 1990 to just $52 in 1995. At these rates, it takes a cellular company nearly the full year of the initial contract just to recover its costs of acquisition.

Clearly, if a predictive model could be built for churn in the cellular industry, substantial money could be saved by targeting at-risk customers and by building an understanding of what the factors were that indicated high-risk customers. For instance, suppose that a moderate-sized cellular phone company of 500,000 customers had an annual churn rate of 25% (slightly lower than the industry average). Their acquisition costs were also better than the industry average at $300. They could still realize $7.5 million in savings if they could produce a predictive model that would help them reduce churn by 5%.

Because of these high costs of churn and the opportunity to prevent it, several companies have begun to provide targeted applications and consulting to build predictive models specifically for churn in the cellular phone industry. One such company is Lightbridge, Inc. of Burlington, Massachusetts, which uses the data mining technology of Classification and Regression Trees (CART) as part of its Churn Prophet application for building and deploying predictive models in the cellular industry.

Data Mining Using CART to Predict Churn

When deployed against a database from one of the largest cellular providers in New England, the predictive model produced by the CART algorithm from Lightbridge was able to identify a segment of the customer base that held 10% of the customers, but 50% of those customers who would churn. The segment is said to have a "lift" of 5 because 50% is five-fold the expected number of churners for a segment of that size (for 10% of the customers, you'd expect to also have 10% of the churners, all things being equal). This lift of 5 also means that you will see a five-fold increase in revenue from a marketing campaign using the data mining model, as opposed to utilizing a mass marketing approach. The entire lift chart is shown in Figure 12-1. A high-level view of the decision tree itself is shown in Figure 12-2.

Because CART was able to express the rules that were used in the model in a way that was understandable to the marketing managers responsible for reducing churn they also received some valuable insights into what caused their customers to be loyal or at risk of churning. For instance, some of these patterns included the following:

■ Subscribers who call Customer Service are more—not less— loyal to the carrier, and are less likely to churn.

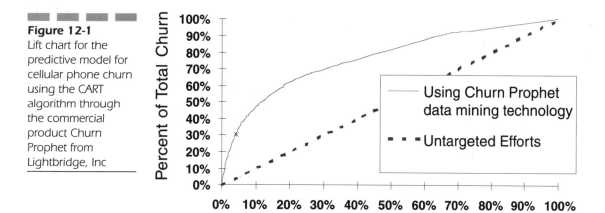

Figure 12-1
Lift chart for the predictive model for cellular phone churn using the CART algorithm through the commercial product Churn Prophet from Lightbridge, Inc

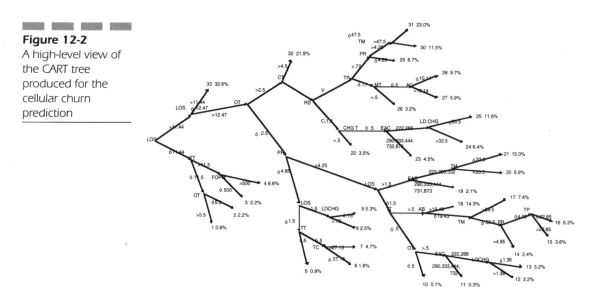

Figure 12-2
A high-level view of the CART tree produced for the cellular churn prediction

- Only the first-year anniversary appears to be a vulnerable time for customers. After the customer weathers the first anniversary without churn, the later anniversaries are relatively unpredictable.

- Several high-value customer segments were found to be at particularly high risk.

■ A geographic region of the northeast United States was discovered that had the beneficial findings of both high-value customers, as well as lower-than-average churn rates.

Data Mining Techniques to Use

In the previous example of a model and in the following case study, the models were made using the Classification and Regression Trees (CART) algorithm. One of the reasons that this data mining method was chosen was because the models that come from it can be interpreted by humans. As you'll see in the following case, the way the model is implemented as part of the overall marketing strategy and what "target" is set for the tool to predict can have a substantial impact on whether the implementation of the model is profitable. CART and other decision tree data mining techniques, such as CHAID (Chi Square Automatic Interaction Detector) and C4.5, are particularly good at being applied in real-world situations like this. Understanding the big picture and being able to communicate that to the way the data mining is applied can be critical.

Although other data mining techniques, such as neural networks, may provide excellent models, it is difficult to understand why. When the model is making its prediction it may not provide insights into why the churn is happening or give clues about what to do. Techniques such as segmentation and clustering might also be useful in such situations to provide such insights, although it is more difficult to use them to produce predictive models.

Case Study—Customer Retention for Mobile Phones

A particular wireless phone provider in the United Kingdom has a customer base of some 300,000 subscribers, each of whom have some ongoing cost of support as well as the initial costs of acquisition. Normally, there is some defined "economic life" of a consumer where the expected return will exceed the costs of acquisition and maintenance though that period.

As in the United States, the wireless phone industry is highly competitive and dynamic, and has experienced deregulation. Because of these changes in both the United States and the United Kingdom, the opportunities and pressures on customers to defect to the competition are only increasing.

The churn rate or annual percentage loss of customers at the carrier is over 40%, which is higher than the rate for the industry in general and higher than the rate that was planned for internally. This rate is unlikely to decrease because overall customer loyalty is decreasing as more providers penetrate further into existing customer and prospect pools. Additionally, barriers to defection, such as long contract periods, disconnection fees, and original cost of equipment purchases are less likely to be acceptable to new customers as other competing companies remove them from their offerings.

The Data

In this case study only non-corporate customers were considered in building a model for churn. This subscriber base thus consisted of some 260,000 mobile phone users. The data that was used included general demographic and customer data, as well as data obtained from the customer service center that captured inbound calls from the customers. (Dissatisfaction with service might show up as a consumer complaint before the customer cancelled their contract.)

Defining the Target to Be Predicted

Churn was defined as the connected or disconnected status of the customer at the end of April 1998, and the data used for the predictors in the model was from March 1998.

The Data Mining Implementation

The data was mined using the Churn Prophet tool from Lightbridge. Which is an implementation of the CART (Classification and Regression Trees) data mining algorithm. It differs little from the classical definition of CART, except that it mines the data directly within a relational database without requiring special preprocessing of the data. It also outputs the results of the model and its application in terms of segments that can be acted upon in marketing campaigns. These segments and their definition can also be added into existing OLAP tools for further analysis.

The Data Mining Model

When the model was run against the 260,000 customers, it produced a model with 29 segments (each segment corresponding to a leaf at the end of the decision tree produced by CART). Each segment was defined by certain customer characteristics, such as the type of contract the customer had and the length of service. Each segment was assigned a unique identifier number by the Churn Prophet tool, and in turn assigned a predicted churn rate. The top five segments with the highest predicted churn rates are shown in Table 12-1.

In the table, both the number of customers that matched the criteria for the segment when the model was created (the "create size") and the number of customers that fell into the segment when it was applied (the "apply size") are shown. It is interesting to note that even though the model was created on data in March and applied to data in April, there are often significant differences in the sizes of the segment. This can be an indication that the underlying customer data is changing rapidly and also may be an indication that the model may degrade quickly over time.

The first three segments may also be represented as a decision tree diagram, as shown in Figure 12-3. This is only a small part of the entire tree that was generated by the data mining software.

The 29 segments can be grouped for analysis and interpretation, as set out in Table 12-2. For each segment, the number of expected churners is calculated by taking the population in the segment and multi-

Table 12-1

This table shows the characteristics that defined the top five segments of consumers who were most at risk of churn

Segment Number	Create Size	Apply Size	Churn Rate	Description of the Customers in the Segment (Criteria defining the segment)
29	1161	403	84%	■ Contract type is equal to "N," which indicates "no contract"; these subscribers have connected without a contractual commitment.
				■ Length of service is less than 23.02 months; the mobile phone has been connected for less than 23.02 months.
				■ Length of service is greater than 9.22 months.
				■ One of 39 tariffs to which the mobile is connected.
28	900	360	65%	■ Contract type is equal to "N," which indicates "no contract."
				■ Length of service is greater than 23.02 months.
				■ One of 39 tariffs to which the mobile is connected.
24	2135	4249	61%	■ Contract type is equal to "D," which indicates a 12-month contract requiring three months notice to disconnect at the end of the first 12 months.
				■ Length of service is greater than 14.93 months.
				■ Length of service outstanding is less than 3.5 months. This is based on contract type and calculates the minimum contract term of the subscriber beyond the current date.
27	901	227	54%	■ Contract type equal to "N," which indicates "no contract."

Table 12-1
Continued

Segment Number	Create Size	Apply Size	Churn Rate	Description of the Customers in the Segment (Criteria defining the segment)
27	901	227	54%	■ Length of service is less than 9.22 months.
				■ One of 39 tariffs to which the mobile is connected.
18	902	7502	50%	■ Average other value is greater than −14.76, this indicates that miscellaneous credits applied to the account are not greater than £14.76 in value.
				■ Contract type is equal to "D"; a 12-month contract with three months notice is required.
				■ Customer type is equal to "R," indicating a consumer customer (Residential, not Business).
				■ Length of service is less than 20.54 months.
				■ Length of service is longer than 14.93 months.
				■ Length of service outstanding is less than 3.5 months.
				■ Tariff is one of 13 identified, which are a mix of current and obsolete tariffs.

plying it by the propensity to churn. The total churn volume expected in each segment is taken as a percentage of the total expected to churn across the total population (the total of all segments), and this is shown on a cumulative basis alongside the cumulative percentage of the base. The analysis shows the following:

- 5.2% of the base contains 27.7% of the expected total churn
- 10.5% of the base contains 41.5% of the expected total churn
- 19.7% of the base contains 55.8% of the expected total churn

Therefore, marketing campaigns targeted at 5.2% of the base 14,581 subscribers will address 7848 of the likely churners, a lift factor of 5.4. The lift factors across the entire base are represented in the lift chart, as shown in Figure 12-4.

The Business Implementation

By using this model for predicting churn, the top one-third of the customer base most likely to churn was selected to participate in a direct marketing campaign for June 1998. The total number of customers selected was 101,003, or 35.9% of the total customer base. Normally, such a large population would not be selected for the first

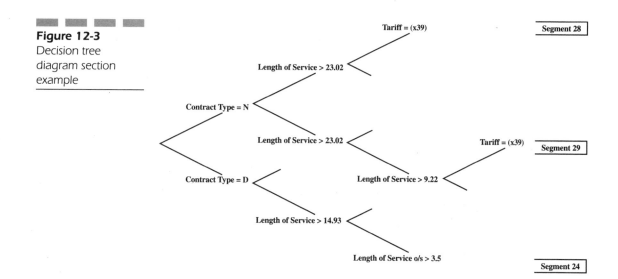

Figure 12-3
Decision tree diagram section example

Table 12-2 Segment Analysis—May 1998

Segment ID	Propensity to Churn	Segment Base	Churn Volume	Cumulative Base	Cumulative Churn	Cumulative % of Churn	Cumulative % of Base
29	83.72%	403	337	403	337	1.2%	0.1%
28	64.78%	360	233	763	571	2.0%	0.3%
24	60.66%	4249	2577	5012	3148	11.1%	1.8%
27	53.61%	227	122	5239	3270	11.6%	1.9%
18	50.22%	7502	3768	12741	7037	24.9%	4.5%
21	44.08%	1840	811	14581	7848	27.7%	5.2%
26	32.15%	649	209	15230	8057	28.5%	5.4%
23	28.54%	1705	487	16935	8544	30.2%	6.0%
17	27.08%	572	155	17507	8698	30.8%	6.2%
20	26.60%	1696	451	19203	9150	32.3%	6.8%
19	26.04%	5369	1398	24572	10548	37.3%	8.7%
9	25.56%	2955	755	27527	11303	40.0%	9.8%
8	21.11%	2125	449	29652	11752	41.5%	10.5%
25	20.36%	964	196	30616	11948	42.2%	10.9%
5	16.52%	7354	1215	37970	13163	46.5%	13.5%

22	15.62%	2400	375	40370	47.9%	135348	14.4%
15	15.12%	12550	1898	52920	54.6%	15435	18.8%
12	13.64%	2581	352	55501	55.8%	15787	19.7%
14	13.04%	41313	5387	96814	74.9%	21174	34.4%
7	12.71%	4189	532	101003	76.7%	21707	35.9%
16	12.20%	2167	264	103170	77.7%	21971	36.7%
13	8.68%	9513	826	112683	80.6%	22797	40.1%
6	7.55%	3911	295	116594	81.6%	23092	41.5%
4	6.91	13095	905	129689	84.8%	23997	46.1%
3	6.80%	32707	2224	162396	92.7%	26221	57.7%
11	6.00%	17140	1028	179536	96.3%	27250	63.8%
2	3.90%	21261	829	200797	99.3%	28079	71.4%
10	1.62%	3768	61	204565	99.5%	28140	72.7%
1	0.19%	76702	146	281267	100.0%	28286	100.0%

Figure 12-4
Cumulative lift chart
for May 1998 apply
phase

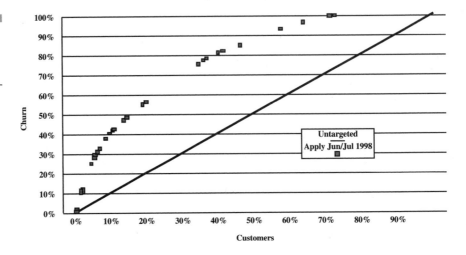

trial of a predictive model, but there were several business issues that drove this large selection:

- Rate changes had been recently implemented, and the provider had committed to notifying a specific proportion of the customer base within a short time period.
- Special funding was available to support the communication of these rates.
- There was a need to finally prove the effectiveness of predictive modeling for the long term.

All customers in the target population were offered three months of free line rental, in exchange for a contractual commitment for twelve months beyond the end of their existing contract. They could indicate acceptance of the offer through the return of a voucher in a reply-paid envelope, followed by subsequent mailing of a contract for signature.

Additionally, each customer received one of the following offers, depending on their current rate plan:

- For those customers on the wrong rate plan (either an obsolete plan or one not suited to their level of expenditure), a transfer to the correct plan was offered free of charge through direct mail.

Customers could indicate acceptance of the change in plans by returning a voucher in a prepaid envelope.

- For those customers on an appropriate rate plan, a customer service "healthcheck" letter was mailed, informing the customer that their rate plan and account had been checked, and that the carrier believed that the plan was the most appropriate for their needs.

Those customers who did not respond to these direct mail offers within one month were also contacted via telemarketing. Additionally, small control groups were set up for each segment from the predictive model, which would not participate in the promotion in any way.

The Results

The response rate to the offers differed according to the cellular telephone network that the customer was enrolled on. There were two different networks with quite different response rates to the offers:

- Network A: 1722 contracts received (14.9% response)
- Network B: 1496 contracts received (5.0% response)

The results across network and offer types were consistent for the first two months in reducing churn across the target group population, when compared to the control group. However, for the following months, churn is actually lower in the control group that did not receive the offer than in the group that was promoted. This can be seen for the customers on one of the network providers in Figure 12-5, in which the churn rates are lower for the promoted group than for the control group the first month after the promotion. The churn rates then were slightly higher for the promoted group than the control group, when measured after three and five months.

The reason for this difference is discussed later, but within the group that was promoted, it was found that after three months those who responded to the promotion had very low rates of churn (1.6%, as shown in Figure 12-5). Those who did not respond had very high rates

Figure 12-5
The number of disconnects was much higher among those who did not respond to the offers than those that did. The churn rate was nearly comparable, however, between those who received the offer (promoted) and those who did not (control).

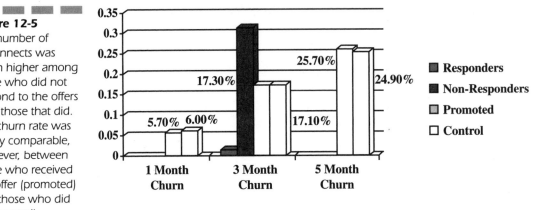

(30.1%)—in fact, much higher than the control group that represented what would have happened if there were no marketing program intervention at all.

When these churn rates are compared to the performance of the control groups, it can be seen that the campaigns dramatically accelerated churn in non-respondents, compared to them not being contacted at all.

The Performance of the Control Groups

One of the most important things to do in any application of data mining is to capture data that allows your system to improve over time by better understanding where the model is working well and where it is not working. This will also give the marketing group or other end users some sense of the reliability of the model and the data mining techniques. With this information in hand, they can make financial decisions about how much to change marketing programs, based on what the models predict. The first time data mining is performed during a campaign it should certainly be launched in a limited way, This will maximize learning about the system while minimizing risk, if the problem space proves difficult to predict or if the data processing systems do not have adequate quality controls.

The key step in the whole process of validation and measurement of the efficacy of the data mining initiative comes from the correct definition of control groups, keeping them uncontaminated and making sure that the results between control and test segments are compared. In this case, many control segments were defined. Although many were small enough to not provide statistically significant results, taken together, they showed that overall the predictions from the model were quite different from what was actually seen. These differences are shown in Figure 12-6.

Lessons Learned

This data mining application was well documented and proctored, and its results were measured by well-defined control groups. Because of the differences in the control group behavior versus what

Figure 12-6
Control Group Analysis shows that there is a wide discrepancy between the predicted churn rate for many segments and what was actually observed.

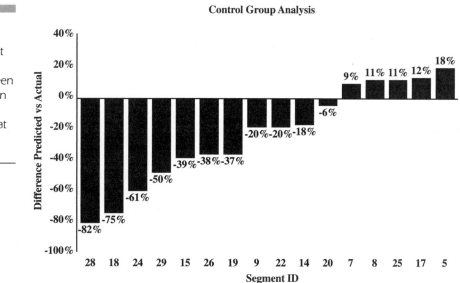

Control Group Analysis

was predicted by the model, it appears that the model itself should be improved. The distribution of the difference between predicted churn rates and actual churn rates in which those segments predicted to have high churn uniformly had lower churn than predicted. Those segments with predicted low churn had higher churn rates, indicating that the overall distribution of churn was less different than was predicted by the model (the model was overly aggressive in predicting high and low churn rates for the segments).

The greatest degree of error of the model occurred for those segments predicted to have the highest rates of churn. This indicates that the overall churn rate may have lessened from the time the data was collected to build the predictive model to the time when the model was actually deployed. This may have been due to overall changes in the market, or it may well have been due to some of the other marketing programs being pursued by the provider at the time.

These results point up the importance of designing rigorous experiments to test the model and its impact. Such experiments cannot be done in isolation, however, because contact through some other marketing program may well have impact on customer behavior. (For instance, it will be hard to define a control group as part of a direct-to-consumer marketing offer, if at the same time a massive broadcast campaign is launched through television, radio and print). This is, of course, a very difficult political problem to solve at most companies because marketing programs are still fragmented across product lines and sometimes even across different media for the same product.

Nonetheless, this provider concluded that the predictive models could accurately predict customer defection once the impact of overall marketing efforts was understood. The predictive model of May 1998 demonstrated that it was capable of highlighting the customers most at risk of defection, and that this risk could be derived from internal information. Achieving this level of success with a data mining program is important because it then allows for the improvement of the process and the data to support even better predictive models more seamlessly tied in with marketing initiatives in the future.

A Surprising Result

One surprising result from the project was the recognition that any marketing program that contacts the customer may by itself stimulate increased churn in customer segments that are not interested in the offer. Unfortunately, the increased churn caused by this effect can offset the benefits of the reduced churn achieved in the group of customers who do accept the offer made.

This result leads to the observation that the reason for defection may already exist with an individual subscriber, yet the motivation is not there to do anything. This is supported by the model, which uncovers far more customers in any given segment than actually do defect. Their circumstances (within the bounds of the information we hold) are equivalent, yet the motivation to defect is not there. Receipt of a mailing may provide that motive by drawing attention to the amount that the customer is paying each month or to the competitive offers available. It may even serve to simply remind the customer that they have a mobile phone and force a decision about renewal to be made.

Changing the Target of the Predictive Model

The marketing programs were successful when directed toward likely churners who accepted the offer, but were unsuccessful for customers at risk of churn but who were not interested in the offer. So, it was proposed that the data mining be performed in the future, to predict both the risk of churn as well as the likelihood of response to the offer. Thus, only those at-risk customers who would respond positively to the offer would actually be targeted. Those customers at risk of churn, but who would likely use any marketing offer only as a reminder to cancel their service, would be suppressed from any further marketing offers.

Other Data Sources May Be Helpful

To improve this modeling capability, it might also be helpful in the future to purchase and overlay commercially available customer data that could provide psychographic profiles. The value of individual lifestyle data needs further testing. In particular, testing needs to be done on lifestyle databases (such as LifeStyles UK, by CACI Ltd.) who claim to achieve a superior match rate by predicting unknown values for the entire United Kingdom population. They use a similar logic to that of Mosaic and RISC or PRIZM coding in the U.S.: that people who live in the same neighborhood are similar.

With such data, it was also recommended that data mining be used to define marketing groups within at-risk segments that might better match the particular needs and interests of that subsegment. For instance, it might be possible that for a segment of high-risk customers who are likely to churn if contacted, there may be smaller subsegments contained within the risk segment that have particular interest in co-marketing offers, or may even respond better to different marketing messages.

Considering Customer Value

There is a continuing debate about whether all customers are equal in value, therefore whether saving each customer is of different worth. The current external business environment makes it necessary that all customers (even unprofitable ones) be retained to enable volume targets to be achieved. As this environment changes, customer value should be used to segment and to target retention efforts.

Considering Save Teams and Other Marketing Efforts

Finally, it is recommended that the effect of save team operations be considered when developing the predictive model. The recording of the intention to disconnect should occur, and this data should be input to the predictive modeling so that a prediction can be made: which customers will have an intention to disconnect, and which customers will disconnect without expressing the intention in adequate time to be saved. The save team should then outbound call to prevent disconnection where it has been established that a customer group is receptive to proactive telephone contact.

Customer Retention in Other Industries

The cellular telephone (wireless communications) industry is not alone in having a problem with churn, although it may be labeled as attrition or defection, depending on the industry. This has long been a problem in retaining credit card customers over time, as well as for bank accounts. The airline and hospitality industries have been proactively implementing loyalty programs since the advent of frequent-flyer miles and discount hotel rooms.

Previously, some industries, such as retail, had little capability to capture customer purchase patterns. Thus, by definition, there was no customer attrition because the retailer never knew that they had a loyal customer in the first place. With the advent of retail purchases over the Internet, however, and some tracking of purchases through credit cards and loyalty cards, even retail stores are now able to track and improve customer retention and overall customer loyalty.

Even such industries as pharmaceuticals and health care, in which it is particularly hard to track customers because of privacy constraints, are finding ways to improve loyalty and reduce defection to competitors by using a summary descriptive level of the consumer in order to preserve patient confidentiality. And wherever there is data to track customer behavior, data mining can be used. Because of the consistent added expense of acquiring a customer rather than retaining one across all industries, data mining will be an effective method to target at-risk customers with the right marketing promotion and services to keep them loyal.

Special thanks to Robert Mansell for providing the detailed analysis and description in his dissertation for this case study.

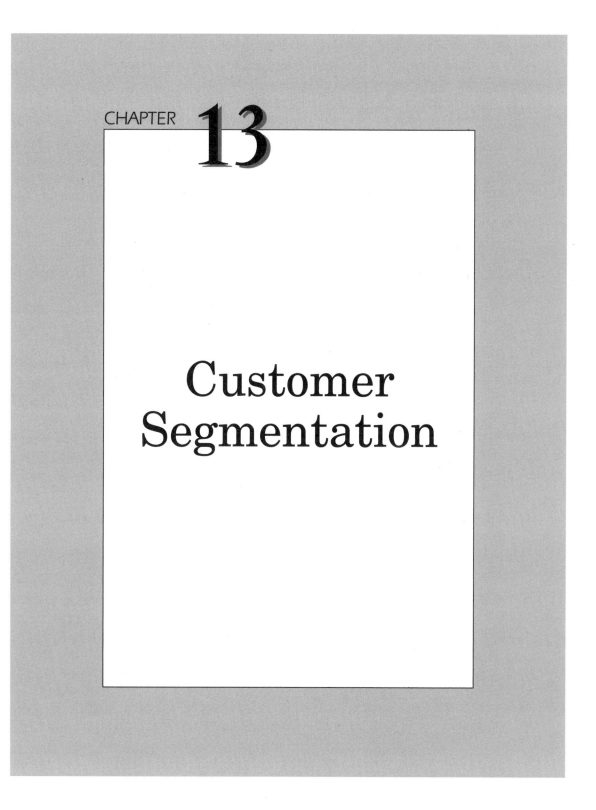

CHAPTER 13

Customer Segmentation

Introduction

Today, there is a lot of buzz about one-to-one marketing—knowing your customer and creating a long-term, lasting relationship with that customer. To some degree, these ideas are new; to some degree, these ideas are old. For instance, marketing has been tasked for many years with the understanding of the customer within an industry. Often, this has been done with older types of processes and methodologies, such as focus groups and outbound telephone interviews, and by looking at demographic data. Today, there is the opportunity to also understand the customer in much more detail. Companies such as Nielsen Marketing and Information Resources, Inc. (IRI) specialize in collecting data from consumer households in the United States and around the world in order to understand what types of consumers are buying which types of products—and why.

This data is available for a large number of consumers, although it is still mostly a small fraction of the total number of consumers. The difference today, though, is that the data is now often collected at a detail level, so that in general it is of much higher quality. For instance, you know exactly how much soap a particular household purchased, rather than how much soap you expect to be purchased for the average household within a particular region of the country.

What Is Segmentation?

Segmentation is the act of breaking down a large consumer population into segments in which those consumers within the segments are similar to each other, and those that are in different segments are different from each other. For example, even the simple act of organizing the customers in your database by the state they live in is an act of segmentation. Distinguishing between male and female customers is also is an act of segmentation.

The consumers within the segments may be similar to each other for a variety of different reasons. They may be similar in terms of where they live or their income, or they may be similar in the way that they think and behave. Or, they may be similar to each other based on some other factor that is important to someone else. For instance, people who like small economy cars versus those that like larger cars, or those who respond well to the postcards that a direct marketing firm mails versus those who will respond to telemarketing.

What Is the Value of Segmentation?

Segmentation is valuable because it allows the end user to look at the entire database from a much higher level—from a birds eye perspective. It also allows people to differentially treat consumers in different segments.

You can treat men and women differently—as long as you don't do so by price. If men are advertised to during football games, women are advertised to during sitcoms.

What is it worth to you if you know that only 20% of your customers are female? What would you do with that information? What is it worth to you to know that the 20% of your customers that did the most business last year have also contributed 60% of the revenue and 75% of the profits this year?

What is it worth to you to know that 10% of your customers last year came from urban areas, but that this year it was 23%?

How Is It Different from One-to-One Marketing?

One-to-one marketing is generally designed to give highly targeted offerings and personalization to each and every customer. Sometimes, one-to-one marketing is called marketing to a segment of one.

One-to-one marketing is the ideal marketing strategy, in which every marketing campaign or product is optimally targeted for each individual consumer. It is generally applicable in industries where a relationship can be formed with an individual customer: airline frequent flyer programs, hotel chains, or even at coffee shops. It can be used any time the product can be differentiated to better satisfy a particular customer.

Because of technology, mass customization can now be performed. For instance, men and women can now buy blue jeans that are custom tailored to their exact measurements. Such a product would not have been possible even a few years ago, but with the technology of the computer and the capability to program factories to create individual jeans, it is now possible.

In one-to-one marketing, this is not always possible. Uniquely understanding each and every customer's particular needs, and getting them right, can be a daunting task. Knowing what jeans to manufacture once the consumer has given the measurements is one thing; knowing which stocks a consumer will choose is quite another. In cases such as Amazon.com, though, the user can get relatively personalized service without a huge investment by the company in personnel to work with the consumer because the computer is powerful enough to do that by itself.

What Is Data-driven Segmentation?

In this chapter, we differentiate between segmentations that are created by human beings interviewing other human beings and those that are created solely by analysis of the consumer data. Some segmentation schemes are created by the use of the consumer information in the form of the results of focus group research or from the results of the data collected from telephone interviewing. Segmentations can be formed from these types of consumer data, but even stronger segmentations can be formed. These are formed not so much from what people say are their preferences, but by what they did. Did they buy more of the product when they received this promotion or did they buy less? If they live here, what was their average consumption? If they had an annual salary of under $30,000 per year, did they still buy the product at the same rate?

You'll see in the next few sections how several industries have begun to perform segmentations, both on what people said but also on what they did.

When you base the segmentation on what people actually did, such as the quantity of products they actually bought, it is called data-driven segmentation. There will always be room for segmentations to be expertly handcrafted by those few individuals who understand their products, the market, the competition, and their customers so well that they intuitively know what the important segments are, and what can and should be done with them.

There is also much use for segmentations that are done by collecting and organizing the information that comes from focus groups and telephone questionnaires. By their very nature, they can tell the marketer what the consumer or prospect is thinking. They can sometimes provide explanations that are impossible to glean from the promotional and transactional data alone.

How Is Data-Driven Segmentation Performed?

Data-driven segmentation is performed by using a variety of statistical and/or data mining techniques, most of which fall into two camps: predictive segmentations and clustering.

Data mining or statistics can be used to make predictions or projections about various pieces of missing data. (What will my stock price be at the close of market tomorrow? What is the average monthly phone bill for this person who is not my customer?) In building a model to predict these missing pieces of information, the data mining technique may sometimes be a segmentation of the database. Remember that to be a true segmentation, it must be the following:

- *Collectively exhaustive* Everyone in the database must fall into a segment (taken collectively, all the segments must be exhaustive in capturing every consumer in the database).

■ *Mutually exclusive*   Each consumer in the database must not fall into more than one segment (a given segment must exclude the members from any other segment).

Not all data mining models fulfill these criteria, so not all models create true segments. The ones that typically do are the decision tree methods and the clustering approaches. Within these techniques, there is one remaining important distinction: Is the segmentation being done through supervised learning or unsupervised learning?

Supervised learning, refers to techniques that create segments with some particular goal in mind (for example, creating segments of high and low value customers). What segmentation characteristics would distinguish between the anticipated value of a customer? The term gets its name from the analogy of a teacher who knows the right answer and teaches the student to learn how to come up with the correct answer. Sometimes, though, there is no right answer— the task is merely to organize the data in a more meaningful way. This is the task of unsupervised learning, where there is no supervisor or teacher; there is only data.

Examples of unsupervised learning that can be used to create segments are some of the clustering techniques that pull interesting commonalities from the data which help organize it. These segments represent not so much people who did the same thing (bought the product or turned in the rebate), but generally have similar characteristics.

Clustering and other unsupervised learning techniques in data mining can be very useful for helping to achieve a bird's-eye-view of all the customers and to make general statements about them. The PRIZM codes from the company Claritas are like this. The people that fall into one particular cluster do not necessarily buy your product at any higher or lower rate than those that fall into another PRIZM cluster. The clusters were predefined by Claritas; but not necessarily for your particular problem at the moment. This may seem like a problem, but in some ways it is quite helpful because you know the clusters' definitions, and they provide high-level data organization in a consistent way.

What Are the Different Uses of Segmentation?

There are several reasons to use segmentations in business. You can use it just to create a basic framework to define and communicate the fact that there are differences between the customers that could be captured at a very high level. Ideally, you'd like to know each customer individually, but the sad fact is that most companies are working with customer segmentation schemes that are many years out-of-date or completely nonexistent. The reality is that although you want to view each customer as an individual, which might mean that you effectively have 100,000 segments of one, if you had 100,000 customers, you would struggle to differentiate between profitable and unprofitable customers. Companies that can successfully manage and communicate 10 or more true customer segments are rare.

The segmentation schemes that do exist in companies are often in place for historical reasons. Either they are the remnants of some consulting project or they may have grown up over time and never been validated, either at a consumer-data level or by questionnaire via focus group or telephone interview. Most often, they are not the result of any serious validation of the segmentation via actual customer behavior.

They do serve the useful purpose of at least instilling in the company the ideas that not all customers are created equal and they do provide a means for communication. One marketer says to the other, "Did you see how the mailing to the Gold segment performed?" The other marketer then understands immediately what that means. The segmentation scheme that you use at the highest level of your company will take a long time to be accepted, but once it is accepted, it will provide a tremendous benefit within the company as a means of consistent and precise communications. It will also take a long time to displace if it is incorrect or becomes dated.

Understanding Your Business and Executing a Strategy

Company-wide communication for strategic planning reasons is just one reason why segmentation is used within corporations today. It allows for strategic planning and a way of focusing on the customer without having to worry about looking at all the customers at once. The CEO can now look at the different types of customers and see whether they are increasing or decreasing across time, or changing their buying habits from quarter to quarter or year to year. Knowing that the highest-profit customer segment is shrinking can be invaluable for knowing how to price your product to still be profitable with the other segments, or to change your product offering so that some new segment of highly profitable customers starts to grow.

Demographic Segmentation

Segmentation can be used to understand where your customers live, how wealthy they are, how well-educated they are, and so on. At the least, knowing where your customers live is critical to being able to contact them through a variety of marketing media.

Psychographic Segmentation

It can also be critical to be able to understand what your customers are thinking and why. This is what behavioral and psychographic segmentation can be used for. More importantly, understanding the psychographic and behavioral makeup of your customers can give important insights into what will change their behavior. This can include helping to decide which of seven postcards to send them to get them to try a product, or what the color and message should be on a new eighth postcard that your creative department is now designing.

Targeted Segmentation

Targeted segmentations are done when you have some target in mind (for instance, segmenting your population based on the target of high usage of your product). You can also segment the population based on the likelihood that you already use the competition's product. If you don't have perfect data, you can just target consumers who are likely to be current users of your product.

How Can Segmentation Be Performed?

Before you embark on creating and deploying a new and better segmentation scheme for your company, decide whether this segmentation scheme will be used for strategic and communication purposes, or whether it will just be used for the purpose of some particular targeting of a new promotion. Technically, there is not too much difference between them in their creation, but there is a large difference in their deployment.

If you intend for the new segmentation to be used at a strategic level within your company, be prepared to spend as much time training and communicating what the new segmentation means as you spend gathering the data, designing the segmentation, and validating it. Like the blind men and the elephant, what you think the thing is depends on which direction you approach it from. If the blind man approaches the elephant from the front and touches the trunk, he may assume that it is a snake-like creature. If another blind man touches the elephant's leg, he may assume that the elephant is more like a tree. Neither is right and neither is wrong. In much the same way, you will find that no segmentation will be a perfect description of the complete elephant that is your entire customer population.

What Are Some of the Questions to Ask of a Segmentation Methodology?

Before you get going, ask yourself the following questions about any segmentation strategy that you take on:

- Does the system leverage existing customer data? Or, does it only stand on its own without being modified to reflect the important differences inherent in your customers.

- Can the system reflect overall strategic corporate goals and plans? The segmentation will not be useful for strategic purposes if it is so complicated that no one can understand it, describe it, or converse about it with someone else.

- Can the segmentation methodology reliably be applied to your data? Does the segmentation make sense for your data? If your consumers are all children under the age of 10 and their parents, then it is unlikely that a segmentation scheme built to categorize the general US population is going to work particularly well.

- Does the segmentation methodology have reliable data or is it based on a small sample and then projected? How was the segmentation scheme built? Perhaps, it was created on the interviews with just a few hundred consumers and then projected onto a much larger database. This is not necessarily bad, but you should be aware of the limitations and variability that may be inherent.

How Is Data Mining Used for Segmentation?

Data mining is used for segmentation in a variety of ways. First, it can be used to define customer segments based on their predicted behavior. For instance, the leaf nodes of a decision tree can be viewed as individual segments. Each one is defined by certain customer characteristics and for all customers meeting those characteristics, there is some predicted behavior (for instance, the likelihood to respond to the free flashlight promotion).

If decision trees are used to create segments, then the data is guaranteed to be mutually exclusive and collectively exhaustive (no customer falls into more than one segment and every customer is guaranteed to be contained in one of the segments). Figure 13-1 shows how the leaves of a decision tree can form segments.

Not just decision trees, but any data mining technique that can perform classification can break up a customer database into segments. Each segment will consist of all of the customers that would be classified in the same category. For instance, all of the most profitable customers versus all of the least profitable customers would have their own segments.

Figure 13-1
The leaves of a decision tree can be viewed as creating mutually exclusive and collectively exhaustive segments.

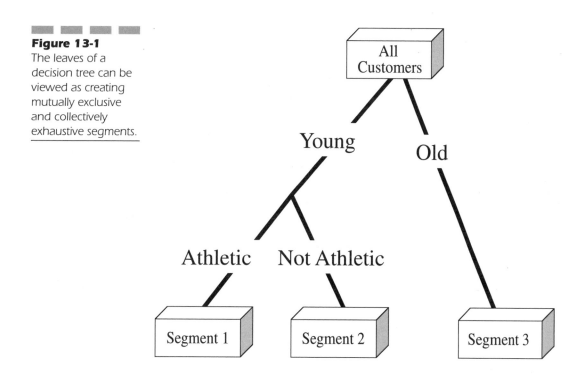

Segmentation can also be performed in a manner similar to clustering. In this case, there is no particular reason to group customers into segments—except that in general they are more like the others contained in the same cluster and less like those contained in other clusters. In general, this is done by giving equivalent weight to all of the characteristics of each customer.

There are also times when no sophisticated clustering or classification needs to be performed at all. All that is needed, at least as a first step, is that the data is organized in some simple way that helps to understand and manage the customer base. For example, you can use demographic clustering (grouping the rich urbanites separately from the poor rural consumers as the Lifestyle segments from Spectra do). Or, perhaps you just want to organize your customers into the most and least profitable, based solely on the revenue that they contribute to your bottom line.

Integrating Data-driven Segmentation

Sometimes, it is important to integrate new segmentation schemes that were developed directly from the data with other segmentation schemes that may already be in place. For instance, a segmentation of the customer base may have already been created by market research by using information gained from focus groups. In this case, small groups of current customers or prospective customers have come together to discuss your product or service. Often, these groups will reveal deep insights into their attitudes and what drives their behavior. This information can be very helpful for creating marketing promotions that match the needs and expectations of the consumer base. They may also be at odds with what appears to be happening to your customer base and its reaction to your product, based on the customer data that you have already collected. Another problem is that useful segmentation schemes can often be developed out of focus groups or even out of telephone interviews, but they are useful only for a conceptual understanding of the customer and how to communicate about that customer. These two things, by themselves, are very useful. But it will not be possible to convert the high-level segmentations of your customers into actionable segmentations based on your customer data because of the fact that the pool from which the data was gathered was necessarily a small one. The total of all people in focus groups is usually no more than a few hundred, and telemarketing may be a few thousand, but they generally represent just a small fraction of your total customer population.

Introducing and Removing Segmentation Schemes

A Segmentation Is a Common Corporate Language

One of the uses of segmentation is to give the direction to the company in terms of who its customers are—how they are different from each other and how they should be treated. In order to be effective, the segmentation must be communicated throughout the company. Once that is done, the entire company (from marketing to customer service to accounting) will know that there are differences between customers, and a different plan can be formed to treat each customer differently.

For instance, if the sales force knows that there are such things as gold-level customers and that they represent nearly twice the repeat business as do the other customer segments, the sales force can then craft programs that are targeted after these consumers. After knowing about the gold segment, the marketing department can craft marketing programs that support the sales initiatives, and customer support can create special phone lines and staff them at higher levels—specifically for those prospects that respond to gold level promotions.

If your organization can be compared to a large ship, then a good segmentation scheme can be compared to the rudder: just a small change and a little directional information given at the right point can move a massive organization in the right direction.

Getting It Right

To accomplish this change, the segmentation scheme does need to be well-thought out and be correct. It is of no help if faulty research is performed that leads to the understanding that there are only two important customer segments: (gold and silver) it in fact, there is another important segment that represents customers who are likely to transition from silver to gold status if they are given the right promotional message. This undiscovered segment represents a lost opportunity if it is not correctly treated, and it may also represent a segment that is highly susceptible to the offers from the competition.

Propagating and training the organization on a correct but incomplete segmentation scheme could do more harm than good. If the segmentation is just out-and-out wrong (your high-value customers and the small to mid-tier banks and not the behemoths), you could be sowing the seeds for putting yourself out of business.

Changing the Segmentation

In some ways, the segmentation that you choose and train your company on is like a virus. It starts small, but then slowly permeates throughout the organization. If it is a good virus, the organization succeeds. Over time, however, the segmentation becomes out-of-date—the market becomes saturated, new competition arrives, and a new market niche appears. It is important that whatever technique is used to create the market segmentation is regularly reused to update the segmentation. Otherwise, the segmentation that is being used by the company may not match the actual behavior of the customer.

Technically, changing the segmentation is much easier than changing it organizationally. To create a new segmentation, it is often exactly the same process that was used to create the segmentation in the first place: telephone interviews and the resulting data mining on those results and on any other customer information that is available. To change the segmentation organizationally requires an entirely new training initiative and some proactive effort to stomp out uses of the old segmentation. Do not underestimate the costs in either time or effort that it takes to re-educate the organization after a new segmentation has been created.

Case Study: The Pharmaceutical Industry

Industry Background

Many of the issues that face the pharmaceutical industry today are what we will talk about here. They include many issues related to consumer segmentation and overall understanding of their marketplace. It is a particularly fascinating industry these days because it is one of the most data-rich industries from a wide variety of sources. Like the financial services industry, it is undergoing a dramatic shift to include direct marketing efforts rather than the previous techniques of indirect marketing that were being used recently to market only to the middleman. In the case of pharmaceuticals, it was the physician who prescribed the drug; in the financial services, it was the broker who recommended particular stocks.

The capability to market directly to the consumer has arisen at least in part because of the relaxation of regulations in the pharmaceuticals industry. In the past, it was all but illegal to advertise or market in any way to the end user consumer. The belief was that they could be unfairly influenced into seeking a particular drug. Even today, there are strict requirements that the pharmaceutical companies can make no overt claims. If you have ever seen an advertisement on TV or in a magazine, you know that the ad space or TV time taken up by the disclaimer of side effects is almost as long as the ad itself.

Nonetheless, the capability to market directly to consumers who may be in need of the benefits that a particular drug could provide is a tremendous breakthrough in the industry. And it has created a huge new opportunity for the players in this space. Consider, for instance, that in the first three quarters of 1998, $896.7 million was spent by the pharmaceutical industry on *direct-to-consumer* (DTC) advertising across all media. This represents a 32.3% increase over the same period from the previous year. Over the 10 years from 1989 to 1999, the overall increase in DTC spending by the industry soared from $12 million to $1 billion. Companies such as Eli Lilly increased their spending on DTC by 437% from 1998 to 1999 (source: Competitive Media Reporting).

In general, these increases are only going to continue, and even more so as new prescription drugs come out of the laboratories of the pharmaceutical companies. With all of this effort in the consumer marketplace, it becomes even more important to understand how the consumers behave, how they think, and what motivates them to change their behavior. For example, there may be a segment of people in existence who don't fill all of their refills for a particular drug (usually to their own detriment because it is important to complete the course of treatment as it has been prescribed by the physician). This segment of consumers who do not comply with the physician's prescription represent a huge loss of revenue for the pharmaceutical companies, and it is important to understand who is in the segment and who is not. In general, though, this level of segmentation is not sufficient. Just knowing that there is a segment of noncompliance can show how many prescription dollars are left on the table, but it doesn't tell the pharmaceutical company how to change the behavior. In order to do that, they need more of a behavioral model of their customers.

Often, you can get a behavioral model by creating focus groups. Get a number of likely users of the drug in the same room and interview them to find out why they would or would not, or did or did not use the full prescription of the drug. You might find out, for instance, that there are two very strong beliefs within this noncompliance segment that keep the users from using the drug:

- Some users believe that they will build up resistance to the drug if they use it too much so that it will not work as well when they really need it. This is an idea that they may have gotten from drinking coffee and noticing that its effects were lessened as they drank it for consistent periods of time.
- Members of the other class of non-compliance users do not finish their prescriptions because they have an overall distrust

of the safety of the drug. They use just enough of the drug to relieve their symptoms, but then stop as soon as they feel better. For many drugs, which take some time to take effect, it may be that the drug's effectiveness is compromised if it is not used in a consistent manner.

Both of these segments display the same behavior of not complying with all of their prescriptions, but for very different reasons.

References

Smith, Mickey C. *Pharmaceutical Marketing Strategy and Cases*, Pharmaceutical Products Press, The Haworth Press, Inc., New York, 1991.

The Keys to Building the Solution

At this point the concepts of the technologies (Part II) and the business value and business application (Part III) have been introduced. All that is left is to show how to actually build these applications.

In this part we provide the blueprint for how to seamlessly merge the technologies with the business processes to create a complete CRM solution that is driven by Data Mining technology. Along the way we try to provide a roadmap that guides you around both technological and political hurdles that you will likely encounter in building your system.

The first step is to build the business case. Which is described in Chapter 14. In the following chapter we provide an overview of the end to end process of creating and deploying the Data Mining system for CRM. In chapters 16 and 17 the focus is on two of the most important and often neglected aspects of these systems: collecting and cleansing the data and actually using the data mining results to score and take action with your customers. In chapter 18 we show how such a system can be used to eventually not just manage, but optimize, your interactions with your customers. In chapter 19 and 20 we conclude by providing an evaluation of current data mining and CRM offerings and then providing a glimpse into the future of what these systems may be capable of within the next decade.

CHAPTER **14**

Building the Business Case

Introduction

From a survey of 63 companies, the Meta Group found that over a five to six year period, the average company had a negative ROI of $1.5 million on their enterprise resource planning installations (for example, SAP). Perhaps even more surprising, it took an average of 23 months to get the system up and running at an average cost of $10.6 million for the implementation and another $2.1 million to maintain the system for two years (*Information Week* 5/24/99).

The good news is that compared to ERP projects, data mining project life can be significantly shorter and the investment significantly smaller. As long as you don't do something wrong the ROI will be positive and substantial. The only difference is that usually with a data mining system you are creating a new business process that may well fall outside of existing budgets and business structure. ERP systems, however, are enticing to end users despite the high cost because they replace and, for the most part, improve existing processes. Thus existing budgets and organizational structure already exist to fund and deploy the ERP system. Interestingly, *Information Week* reported that the majority of the largest ERP projects were undertaken without a formal business case for the expected return on investment.

Data Mining Is Complex—If There Is Not a Business Case, Your Project May Stall

It is fair to say that it is easy to start a data mining project, but difficult to finish one. The reason that they are easy to start is that they use glamorous new technologies and focus on things that are important yet difficult to solve for the company. For instance, improving customer profitability is always the Holy Grail of any business. Because most data mining algorithms focus on improving customer profitability, chances are good that they will also help to improve it. The fact that data mining can create new wealth for the corporation is a good starting point at which to get noticed. Sometimes, the technology itself is complex enough that it becomes believable that these hard problems can be solved. That may be good enough to launch your project, but it may not be enough to keep it going when you need more computer resources or personnel. It's also difficult when you are trying to coax a DBA to give you a data extract that you need to mine for your project, when they are urgently trying to perform their own monthly database update. In order to garner the resources that you need and keep them available, you need to be able to make the business case for data mining. That will include not only being able to make a high-quality guess about new revenue from the data mining, but also about the costs. We'll show you how to make believable estimates on the revenue side, and what the factors are that determine the costs. You can plug in your own numbers as to how much your own resources will cost.

How Will You Know That You've Succeeded?

The project process that is described here consists of creating a working project timeline that allows you to demonstrate the value of the data mining project before you have implemented it. The thing that you want to do is to create a demonstration of the data mining system to show that if the modeling is successful, how it will perform, and how much new profit can be achieved. By doing so, you have set a stake in the ground. Now, all that is left for you to do is to prove it.

A Fundamental Shift in Business Strategy

As we mentioned before, ERP projects are started in order to improve existing business processes. Data mining applications, however, represent a fundamentally new way of doing business. This is especially true in the case of customer management, which for many organizations has not been data-driven and certainly not data mining driven.

In order to make such a shift successful, you will need a game plan, which is where a business plan will come in handy. In that plan, you will be outlining the creation of new business processes that will benefit from data mining. As we've said earlier, the areas where certain techniques benefit mainline enterprise processing (such as supply chain optimization and supplier management data mining) have shown the most promise in benefiting the relationships between you and your customers.

The reason for this is twofold. First, there is currently a lot of data about your customers from a wide variety of sources, whereas there might not be the same quantity or types of data available from some of your other business processes. Second, managing your customers is a much less precise process than is managing the number of products stocked on your store shelves or stored in your warehouse. For ERP-type applications, there is often a well-defined cost equation that does a reasonable job of defining in a precise way exactly what the behavior is of the system that is being improved. Given that customers are people, it is much harder to come up with these types of well-defined scientific equations in order to understand their behavior. Often, it is only through real historical experience that organizations can begin to understand, predict, and then direct the behavior of their customers. This is where data mining comes in.

Uncovering the Needs for Data Mining in Your Company

There may be many places within your company where data mining can be used. The first step in building a business case for data mining is to find an opportunity to use it. Here, we have given you several possible locations where you can start looking.

Poorly Executed CRM or Simple Campaign Management

If your company is currently executing direct mail, direct response television, television, or even directed e-mail campaigns, you may find that there is an opportunity to better target the campaigns. The business case here is pretty simple: look for some offer that is so expensive that a mass mailing does not make sense. For instance, if you are offering free samples of your product that cost $7 each time they are offered, then you will want to offer them only to consumers who are likely to continue to use the product after the offer has been received. Consumers that utilize the offer, but then move to the next product offer that you or someone else makes are not going to be long-term loyal customers who are worthy of your investment. Or the cost dynamics could be even simpler: You want to make marketing offers to consumers who either already have or will be purchasing a sports car. The offer itself costs $10 because of expensive creative, printing, and mailing costs.

Poorly Matched Customer Investment to Customer Value

If your organization is one of the enlightened few that does have some measures of customer value and customer profitability, then you may be able to find ways to better match customer value to customer investment. Look for opportunities to move customers from high-priced investment channels, such as the direct sales force, to lower-cost channels, such as direct mail or the Web. These kinds of opportunities for data mining include the need for understanding present and future customer value, and for building models that are capable of predicting sensitivity of consumers to changes in investment. For instance, some customers may never notice differences in service (if you suggest that they move to your Web site rather than calling your customer support personnel). Other customers may drop their contract and move to your competition. Data mining could be used here to determine which customer business would be lost and which would be retained.

Inability to Transition Customers to Higher Value States

Another place that data mining might be used within your organization is to find ways to move customers from their current level of value to higher levels of value. Are there existing offers that could be made to your customers to transition them so that they purchase more of your products and services? Or purchase more expensive options to the products and services that they currently have?

This is really a special case of the targeted marketing example. In this case, the outcome of the offer is what is most important and the overall effect on the consumer's purchasing behavior. This is a good place to start with data mining because it produces increased revenues, which is often an easier sell than reduced costs.

Defining the Business Value

The most important part of the equation in creating your business case will be the definition of business value that you use or how you will measure the value of the data mining project. There are many ways to measure the value besides a profit or return on investment. The data mining system that you put into place must deliver this value, but can also deliver less immediately measurable benefits such as long-term competitive advantage, increased leverage of existing assets (making the most from the data and data warehousing infrastructure that you have already created).

Increased Revenue

Perhaps the easiest concept to sell in the business case is the idea that by implementing a data mining system that you will provide increased revenue to your company. This can come from traditional means such as increasing the number of customers, increasing the dollar quantity purchased by each customer, or increasing the length of time that the customer stays a customer (customer loyalty).

Profit

Profit should be one of the strongest motivators in building the business case for data mining, but sometimes it is not. People are often wary of profit measures because they know that the numbers can sometimes be easily manipulated. Likewise, profit does not always imply business growth the way just plain increased revenues do.

Decreased Costs

Although saving a dollar you would otherwise have spent should be just as interesting as making a dollar you would otherwise not have made, measuring the value of the data mining system by focusing on cost reductions can be a difficult motivator. Part of this comes from the fact that when working with customer data, the data mining system will be mostly focused on working with data from sales and marketing channels. Both organizations are historically motivated by growth and are less interested in optimizing already existing processes. Part of this comes from the fact that in marketing, the bigger the ad budget the better; in sales, the revenue metric still holds strong.

Return on Investment (ROI)

Clearly, the best business measure of such a system is to measure by the return on investment (ROI) that the system provides. For every dollar invested in the data mining system, how many dollars did you make in return? Then, the question becomes simply this: Should you be investing in a data mining infrastructure or in hiring more sales people? Unfortunately, ROI metrics are often complex, and hard to explain and defend within the organization. They need to be made to senior management because that is the level at which decisions to allocated funds among the budgets of various departments can be made. For this reason, it can be a longer sell internally to motivate a project based on ROI metrics.

If possible, ROI estimates or profitability estimates should be displayed graphically to show the expected profit or ROI that is attainable with no data mining, minimal data mining, or fully optimized data mining. Some complete CRM systems have such optimization capabilities available internally, so that ROI and incremental profits due to the data mining model can be projected. In Figure 14-1, such a projection is shown using the Optas Direct tool.

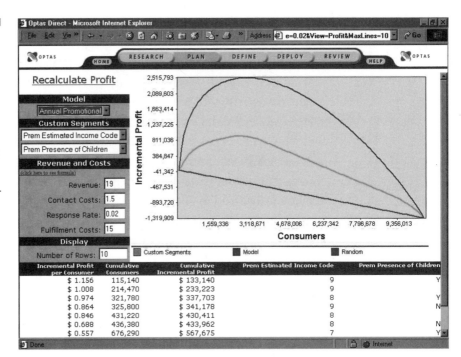

Figure 14-1
Interactive, Web-based Tools such as this one from Optas, Inc. can be used to easily show the increased profitability and expected ROI from the deployment of a data mining system

Competitive Advantage

One of the main additional business benefits of data mining is that it can provide competitive advantage to those companies that employ it. Typically, because data mining is used for problems involving customer data and customers are a relatively finite commodity, often the data mining systems are being used to optimize performance within a zero sum game. Those who win more business do so only at the expense of others who are less competitive. Thus, it may not be that data mining provides significant increases in revenue or profit, but it can be used to change the nature of the game being played so that those who employ data mining are the only ones left standing at the end.

Early Adopter

It may also be the case that one of the big benefits of data mining is that it imparts a significant advantage to the first few who deploy it within a given market. The early adopter may win new customers away from the incumbents, and then, by continuing to use data mining to improve loyalty, make it very difficult for the competition to regain their lost customers.

The Costs

From the business side, the value can be varied and can be measured in a variety of different ways—some of them quantitative and factual; others harder to measure and more strategic in nature. The cost side of the equation is more straightforward and its components less likely to change from implementation to implementation (although the magnitude of each component may change considerably).

The Data

One of the first costs of data mining comes from collecting, storing, processing, cleansing, and sometimes just plain paying for the data that will be mined. As you will see, the data typically comes in three main forms: consumer, transactional, and promotional. If you have just finished building your data warehouse and have focused on making sure that the data is cleansed, you are in good shape and can leverage that existing investment. If, on the other hand, your data is coming from a variety of different data sources where some of them have not been used before, then you may have a problem on your hands. Data mining is very good at finding errors and other problems in existing data sources. The general rule-of-thumb is that if the data has been collected but never used before for data analysis, then it is likely to be incorrect. It is similar to installing a home security system but never trying it out to see whether the alarm actually goes off at the right times. No matter how well the security system is installed or how well the data has been collected and documented, if it has not had to face the true test of being used, then there will almost certainly be unforeseen issues that will show up. Cleanliness of the data is one of the largest potential loopholes where many unexpected staff days and money can be spent.

The other costs of the data itself can come from the need to buy additional information about your consumers. For instance, you might want to "overlay" additional information about your consumers from other data sources such as census information and warranty card information. You can either enhance what you know about your customers and your prospects, or add new information that you would otherwise not have had. Typically, information that is overlaid includes more detailed information about personal interests (whether they like sailing or just watching a lot of TV, for example) or more detailed information at a household level: What is the household annual income? How much is their home worth? Do they have children living at home?

You may also sometimes purchase wholly new customer names and addresses from other lists.

Pricing the Infrastructure

In data mining, the most obvious infrastructure cost associated with your project will be the data mining software itself. It can be a time-consuming process to pick the right data mining software, but it can also be a great learning experience. The data mining software is not the only piece of software that you are likely to need.

You will also need some form of relational database to house the analytical data extracts that you create. Although some data mining systems, such as SAS, come with sophisticated database programs, many do not. They either rely on some other database to perform the decision process or ignore the problem altogether by assuming that there is no need for data management. They also assume that the data will be presented to the data mining system ready to be mined, and that the mining system itself will store the analytical data only as long as it is being mined without regard for backup or storage for later reference. Certainly, be wary of these kinds of systems because they do require the purchase of additional relational database management software, and they may not be well integrated with it.

Software costs may also include the need to purchase reporting and OLAP products to provide a reporting system for the results that the data mining tools present. When choosing these systems, look for reporting tools that are Web-based and make it easy to quickly make the data mining results available across the enterprise.

The hardware costs can vary significantly, based on the data mining product that is used. Some data mining software runs on low end PCs and some software is optimized for massively parallel computers. Generally, the more data the software can handle, the more expensive it will be.

Pricing the Personnel

As with most projects today, the most expensive part of the project will be the cost of personnel to build and maintain the data mining system. There are several key roles that should be filled in any well-run data mining project:

- *Data miner*.   This individual will have skills in analyzing data with data mining tools. Look for people who have an understanding of and a desire to understand the business problem that they are applying data mining to. You may find technically competent data miners who are unable to apply the technology to real-world problems, however.

- *Web interface designer*.   This individual can work with prospective consumers of the data mining models and information to produce a user interface that is easy to use. It should not mask the power of the underlying data mining model so that it becomes a "black box" that the user will not have confidence in. Many data mining projects do not include this position as a requirement, but as you will see, communicating your results effectively and getting the business users to make use of the value from data mining will be your biggest hurdle.

- *Data designer*.   This person will understand how to construct relational database tables and databases that will allow for optimal support of the data mining system as well as maintainability. It is important to again find someone who has a realistic sense of the trade-off between organizing data in a way that is optimal versus a way that is understandable and easily maintained as the data structures change.

- *Project manager*.   This person will be responsible for maintaining project design documents, and creating and enforcing schedules—including deliverables that may come from outside the data mining team (from marketing or IT, for example).

- *Marketing interface*.   This person will be part of the marketing organization, but will be responsible for communicating marketing's needs and in general interfacing with the data mining team.

- *Database interface*.   This person will be a part of the IT staff and be responsible for collecting and storing the data that will be used as the source data for the data mining system. They will be responsible for setting and enforcing deadlines for the cleaning and subsequent delivery of source data to the data mining team. They will also be the main contact point for explaining the meaning of the existing source data and providing the data dictionaries of that source data.

Costs to Sustain

The costs to sustain the data mining project will be dependent on how successful you are. Your team members may find themselves responsible for sustained support of providing a model or report once a month, or they may be responsible for the infrastructure for communicating customer information around the company. This is especially true if you have dedicated a Web interface designer to provide consumable information across the enterprise. In general, the costs to sustain will come from the following sources:

- Ongoing hardware and software maintenance costs
- Periodic updates of the source data (probably no less than monthly)
- Quality assurance and validation of the source data (if done correctly, this will be a significant task, especially as errors are found)
- Creation of new data mining models
- Deployment and application of data mining models
- Validation of data mining models

These tasks can generally be supported by your original team because as the development project comes to completion, the infrastructure will be in place to make the creation, validation, and deployment of data mining models more and more efficient.

Containing Costs: Leveraging Existing Investments

If you are trying to contain costs, especially on the initial project, look for the following opportunities:

- Work with a small sample of data so that an inexpensive data mining tool can be used, and smaller data storage and relational database systems can also be used.
- Leverage internal data mining experts. You may be surprised to find that within your organization there are already several experts at data mining who might be very interested in a project to build an infrastructure to make their efforts useful for solving real business problems, such as making customer relationships more profitable. Keep in mind that your goal should be to make data mining have an ROI impact at your organization. To that end, it is not a requirement that the data mining expertise reside explicitly on your team.

- Don't skimp on data quality or model validation. Your team will ultimately be responsible for the performance of the data mining system and it will be of little consolation to be able to blame IT for providing corrupted data or for a data mining model that was incorrectly built. The measurement and validation of the success of the data mining project should be wholly owned by your team.

- Although it may seem expensive, you may also consider outsourcing the production and application of the data mining itself. This will save on virtually all hardware and software costs. If done correctly, the deployment of the model can be performed within your existing CRM processes by your IT organization. Outsourcing will cost significantly less than performing the data mining within your team, but at the end of the day you will still not have made the investment in the hardware, software, or personnel to perform the data mining.

Build the Business Case

When you are looking to put together a business case for your company, you will have specific requirements that are dependent on the needs of your company and the industry in which it competes. The data will be different, the competition will be different, and the level of marketing and sales sophistication that is both possible and necessary will be quite different. The one thing that will not change is that if you can build a good business case for initiating a data mining driven CRM initiative, it will lead to more successful projects and more recognition and support for the initiative before, during, and after its initial launch.

15

Deploying Data Mining for CRM

Introduction

Assuming that you have successfully found a useful problem for a data mining application and that the myriad of political hurdles have been overcome, it is now time to actually execute the successful data mining application. This chapter provides a step-by-step recipe for the way that application can be launched and managed successfully. It avoids the common pitfalls of these projects, such as not having enough time spent in the beginning of the project to define the user, the problem, and the data. Another pitfall is not spending enough time at the end of the project to educate prospective users or to provide for continuation of the use for the data mining application after the initial launch.

10 Steps in Launching a Data Mining Application

We have defined ten important steps that you should follow when creating and launching your data mining application. They are as follows:

1. Define the problem
2. Define the user
3. Define the data
4. Now, really define the data (cleansing, organizing, data dictionaries)
5. Scope the project
6. Trial
7. Quality assurance
8. Education
9. Launch
10. Continuation

We will define these in more detail a little bit later. For now, just notice that none of the major 10 steps talks about actually mining the data. The reason for this is that the technical areas—such as creating the database to store the data for the application, and the installation and application of the data mining—are fairly routine tasks if these other 10 steps are followed. Users rarely get hung up on the execution of the data mining. They worry much more often about what the results of the data mining will be and how the data mining application will move from a one-off special project to part of the critical path for some important business process. For that reason, even technical steps such as quality assurance will focus here on how to perform and present the quality assurance so that it makes sense to the end user and they feel comfortable in using the results of the data mining application.

Define the Problem

The reason that the first step is to define the problem rather than to determine where to use data mining is that data mining can be used to either solve new problems or streamline manual analytical processes. The former use should always have an ROI number associated with it and a strong business case for increased profit. The second use usually has a decrease in cost associated with it or increased productivity for the same cost. The difficulty with the second use is that, for whatever reason, it is difficult to sell cost savings as part of data mining. Perhaps this is because it is a new technology and the people who are most likely to be interested in using it and building a project are also likely to be interested in new opportunities, not in restructuring old business processes. Thus, cost-saving is a less appealing opportunity to the types of in-house people who would be most interested in the data mining technology.

The second difficulty with using a data mining application to streamline an existing business process is that, more often than not, the people who would most need to help on such a project (the data analysts who understand the data and existing processes) are not motivated to help. This is because if the project is successful and data analysis is automated, they will either have to perform more analysis with the same resources or their jobs will be in jeopardy because fewer people can perform the same task that they currently perform. This is a difficult political hurdle because even if the data mining project is sold and motivated at the highest levels of the corporation, there is no possible way to detour the project around these data analysts. They are the only ones in the company who actually understand the data. It is always much easier to work with these data analysts on new important business problems than it is to try to implement systems that streamline and make their current work more efficient.

Find Something That Matters

Too often, with data mining projects the science quickly becomes more important than the business. Thus, often problems are picked because they are technically interesting or technically hard, even though they may have limited business value. For instance, people may choose neural networks to optimize a scheduling problem such as assigning consultants to client projects when a simpler existing system might do as well. Such an application may well be a technical success (it may even be superior to the current system), but it may cost more and may be more complex. Thus, users may resent it and not use it, and then fall back to the previous way of doing things.

Something that matters usually means something that is business-critical at the current time and is not being currently served. Examples might be finding and stemming fraud or customer attrition. As mentioned previously, it is almost an imperative that whatever problem is chosen that it have a believable and measurable return on investment measure (ROI) associated with it. With such a measure defined beforehand, the only debate will be a scientific one (did the data mining actually perform as well as it seemed to?) rather than a business issue (is it worth the money?). It won't be an issue because you should be able to show an ROI of four to five with a significant profit.

Define the Deliverables

After you have chosen a good problem to solve, it is equally important to define in a concrete way what the deliverables will be for both the project and the eventual data mining application implementation. The definition of the deliverables can come in a variety of different forms, including a design or project document, or even something as informal as a presentation. The important thing is not the medium; just that deliverables are defined at all. For instance, many implementations of data mining have no well-defined deliverables, so they default to just being an implementation of a data mining application. This is an easy goal to achieve, but a hard goal to sell or to gather continued support for.

An example of a better deliverable is to define, in some detail, the implementation of a data mining system that will reduce fraud by 5% in the next calendar year. This is a hard goal to deliver on, but an easy goal to rally support for. The goal is hard because its successful delivery involves much more that just data mining or the successful implementation. It means finding a way to incorporate those data mining results into the company's business processes so that real value is achieved. This will mean building a project (even if it is a prototype) that involves not just the data analytics. It also involves marketing, sales, finance, the data support organization, and the information technology group. This is a much harder problem, but it's one that ensures more long-term success. Figure 15-1 shows how the data mining application becomes a smaller part of the picture when the solution to the business problem rather than the technology is given priority.

Pick Something Well-Defined and Small

One of the biggest mistakes when picking a business problem is to pick a problem that is too large or too ill-defined. Pick something as small as possible that has real business value. The fewer different departments within the company that can be involved the better, but never sacrifice business value for size. Just be aware that the larger

the project gets, the longer it will take to complete. If it does turn out
to be a significant project, look to get an early win with some small
trial or prototype, and then define measurable milestones along the
way that show the continued business value as you proceed. These
will be important to make sure that you do not lose interest, and
then support for the funding as the project moves forward.

Understand the Existing CRM Process

Many times, data mining systems will be deployed to optimize existing CRM processes. In fact, a data mining system that does not hook
into a well-defined CRM process is likely to eventually fail because
it will rely too heavily on ad hoc approaches to servicing and supporting the customer. So if a CRM system and process does already
exist, it should be understood. The process and data flows (not nec-

essarily the particular features of the CRM product being used) also should be well-understood and documented.

If a CRM system is not already in place, at least the ad hoc and manual process and data flows should be understood and documented as much as possible. Figure 15-2 shows what a typical CRM process might look like and where data mining can be used to optimize it.

Define the User

After the problem is defined, it should be possible to define who will be using the system when it is completed. This may be more than one type of user, and they may be using it in a variety of different ways. These could include using the data mining application itself all the

Figure 15-2
Your data mining systems should fit seamlessly into your CRM process.

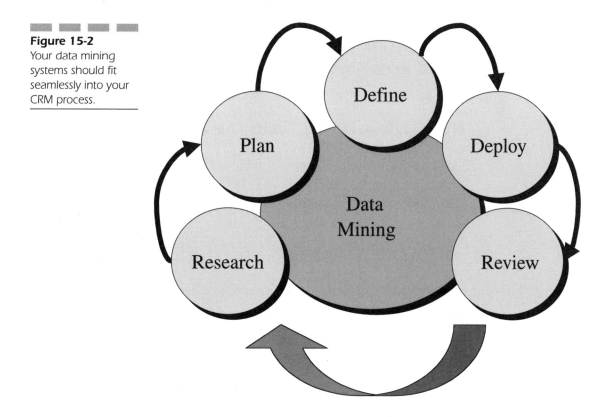

way to supplying, and then measuring the customer value metric and the computation of the ROI of the entire system. Defining the user and keeping a clear picture of who that person is in your head at all times during the project will help you to avoid the following mistakes:

- Delivering a system that is too complex for an unsophisticated user

- Delivering a system that is missing important functionality for a sophisticated user

Either mistake can result in a system that is unusable, but the first mistake (making an overly complex system) is the most costly. Not only is the system a mismatch for the user, but the user will become frustrated and won't use the system. It also implies that a lot of extra work has been done that didn't need to be done.

By knowing the end user will allow you to do the following:

- Provide a system at the right level of sophistication

- Optimally trade off between increased functionality and delays in project delivery

- Focus on the functionality that is most important

Build a Profile of Each User

The end game of knowing your user is to build a picture of who the prototypical users would be. You should know, for instance, at least the following information about these users.

- Their technical expertise (Can they use a Web browser? Can they create an Excel macro? Can they write SQL or an SAS procedure?)

- Their use of the system (every day, once a month, once a year)

- Their understanding of data mining (Do they understand the concept of statistical significance? Do they understand test and control sets for understanding the predictive power of a data mining model?)

- Their desire for details (Will they have confidence in the results of the system? Will they need to prove the validity for themselves?)

The answers to these questions will help you to build a profile of the users of the system and the answers will have significant impact on the way you present the results of your system to your end users. For instance, if the user does not understand statistical significance, it may be more important to provide a graphical view of the difference between test and control behavior over time than it is to provide a detailed statistical calculation—even though the latter is more accurate and should be done, regardless of whether it is provided to the user or not.

Use a QuickStart Program to Educate Your Future User and Elicit Needs and Desires

The way to get the answers to build the user profile is, of course, to ask the user, but often the user doesn't have any context to know what the data mining system could do or be without some background. For instance, the user may have an intuitive notion of what they want but no idea of what is possible. For this reason, it is often very beneficial to construct some form of what we'll call a "Quick-Start" program.

Such a program usually consists of two to four half- or full-day sessions between the data mining project leader and the prospective user community. These working sessions consist of the following parts:

- Education about data mining and how it has been used
- Discussion of the business problem and the construction of blue sky wish lists of how the user would interact with an ideal system
- Interactive sessions about how data mining applications could be deployed that would fulfill as many of the wishes as possible

By educating the group about data mining, you give them some background on what is possible and get them thinking about how to do it. You also build support for the project as more people become familiar with what data mining is and how it can benefit them. Once this educational process begins, you will find your users much more willing to work with you to solve problems, and much more understanding of why some elements of their wish lists are not possible deliverables.

At the same time, it is important during these sessions that you make a distinction between the wish list phase and the more pragmatic design phases because you don't want your users to be constraining themselves based on what they perceive is possible. It is possible to keep the scope of the features in the project under control by stating very plainly at the start of the wish list phase that not all feature requests will be possible deliverables. Figure 15-3 shows the broad outline of a typical QuickStart program.

Figure 15-3
QuickStart programs are used to initiate successful data mining projects by eliciting user feedback and beginning the process of user education.

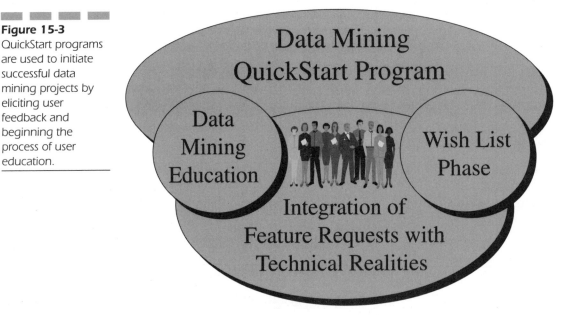

Define the Data

Data mining is driven by the data that is available, and the success of data mining is very much dependent on the quantity and quality of the data that is available. As in any computer program, no matter how sophisticated, the wrong information in the system will provide the wrong answers. In engineering, this is known as *Garbage In, Garbage Out* (GIGO). The short-term and long-term success of your data mining application very much depends on how successfully you track down, validate, and reliably move high-quality data into the system. The first step in this process is to locate and gain access to the data dictionaries that describe the contents of the databases that you will use.

Locate the Data Dictionary

The first step in building this reliable data infrastructure to support data mining is to locate the data dictionary or dictionaries that describe the data that will be used in your system. These dictionaries may be logical diagrams, relational database tables, spreadsheets, or text documents that contain information regarding the following:

■ The expected content of each column of data in the database

■ Some description of the origin of the data (how it was collected or calculated)

■ Expectations for the validity and usability of the data

In a perfect world, there would be an existing data warehouse with all necessary data nicely organized, defined, and easy to access. The reality is that even if a data warehouse exists, it will likely not contain all of the data that you will need to feed your data mining system to solve a business problem.

Although the reason for this is not entirely clear, one contributing factor is that because data warehouses are such massive engineering and IT projects, they necessarily move at a slow pace. You can't just go and add an extra column of data to a table in the data warehouse if the data warehouse contains 50 million customers and a terabyte of data. Instead, the change must be carefully considered and designed—all for very good reasons.

The problem, however, is that business is changing at a much faster rate. Because data mining is typically aimed squarely at today's business problems, especially with regard to customer relationship management, the data to support the business solutions is changing at a much more rapid rate than what can be reasonably accommodated by the data warehouse.

For instance, the data warehouse may be an excellent repository for customer demographic data. It may be ill-equipped, however, to supply Web site interaction data as the type of data that needs to be collected. Data is constantly changing, based on current marketing offers and the design and structure of the Web site itself. Nonetheless, Web site usage and traffic patterns may be critical input into the data mining system in order to provide the best and most predictive patterns of customer behavior. Figure 15-4 shows the continuum of the pace of change of data for different types of data systems.

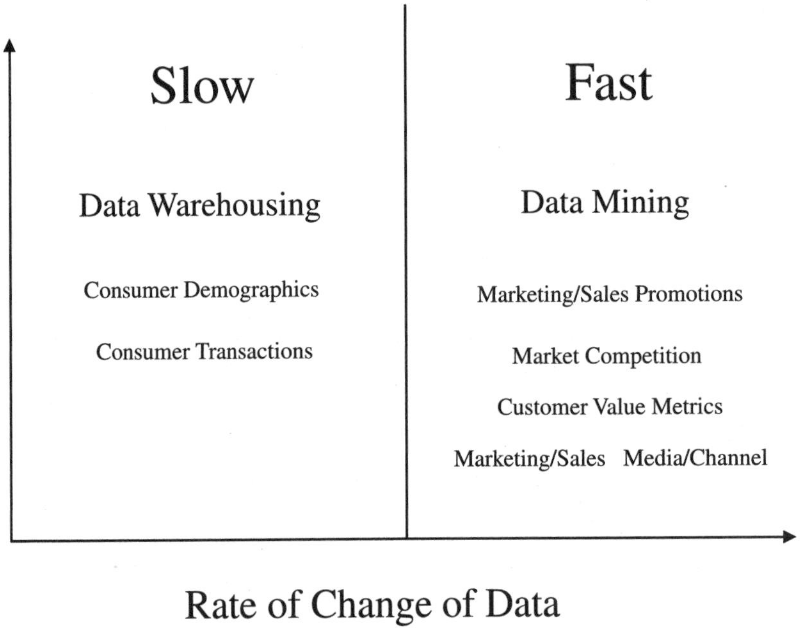

Figure 15-4
Because of their size, data warehouses necessarily take time to accommodate changes in data structures—data mining systems must react to changing data structures much more quickly.

Slow	Fast
Data Warehousing	Data Mining
Consumer Demographics	Marketing/Sales Promotions
Consumer Transactions	Market Competition
	Customer Value Metrics
	Marketing/Sales Media/Channel

Rate of Change of Data

This being said, if there is a data warehouse available, it is a good place to start. It is the most likely place for an up-to-date and accurate data dictionary to be found. Be prepared, however, to collect and merge multiple data sources and multiple data dictionaries in order to build the optimal data sources to feed your data mining application.

Locate the Data Librarians

After you have the data dictionary in hand, it is also important to locate the one or two people in the company who actually understand the data. These are the people we will call data librarians who understand the data well enough so they can tell you when the data dictionary is inaccurate. They can also give important information such as which data to avoid because it is rarely used and is unreliable. Here's a good rule-of-thumb: even if the data is being stored, updated, cleansed, and documented in the data dictionary but it is not currently being used for either reporting or business-critical operations, it is likely to be wrong. The reality is that if the data is being used, someone has gone before you to make sure that it is correct. If the data isn't being used, you are exploring new territory on your own.

Define the Metrics

Besides the data that you collect from existing sources, it is also necessary to define some of the metrics that you may be calculating from that source data. For instance, how will you define per-customer profit? Is it annual profit? Does it include a factor for fixed costs?

These types of calculations for data mining metrics, as well as the definitions of any source data or transformations of that source data, should be captured in a data dictionary that is specifically for the data mining application. Again, the dictionary doesn't have to be elaborate (for example, a Web-enabled view into an RDBMS metadata table); it just has to exist and be as current as possible. A text document kept in some central location is usually more than sufficient.

Now, Really Define the Data

The top three criteria in assessing the value of real estate are location, location, location; the top three criteria for a valuable data mining system are good data, good data, good data. You must emphasize allocating two major steps in your ten-step process to defining and understanding the data. Thus, even after you have acquired the data dictionaries and interviewed the data librarians, it will be important to spend even more time really understanding the data and double-checking what you have learned against the realities of the source data.

Assess Levels of Data Integrity

After you have begun to acquire some of the data, you should assess its integrity column by column. Specifically, look for the following problems:

- Percentage of missing values
- Mismatches in type between the data dictionary and the actual data
- Values not expected based on the data dictionary definition (for example, gender is supposed to be M or F, and the actual data also contains B and G)
- Values outside of expected bounds (for example, be suspicious of too many 150-year-old consumers in the database)
- Unexpected distributions of values (for example, your consumer population is equally distributed across the United States, but 90% of the consumers in the database are listed as living in Wyoming)

Validate Data Sources

Aside from validating each source database on its own, it is also beneficial to validate the data sources against each other. For instance, you may find that age may be provided by multiple data sources. It is an easy but invaluable exercise to measure the consistency of the age data as it is provided from different sources. Ideally, it should be identical for identical consumers, but often it is not.

Performing such validation steps can be laborious and time-consuming, but it is a necessary step for building a reliable data mining system.

Scope the Project

Another important aspect of a successful data mining project, like other development projects, is the capability to set and contain the scope of the project. Because of the business value of the data mining project, there will be many different constituencies of users and interested parties involved, and thus additional features can be requested from many different sources. Data mining projects have the opportunity to be much more contained than most data warehousing projects. Unfortunately, they also have the opportunity to become as large and complex as data warehousing projects unless they are scoped and contained in a responsible way. Doing a good job in defining the deliverables to the end user will go a long way toward keeping the project from getting out of hand.

Contain Scope Creep through a Launch Document

Every data mining application project should have a technical document associated with it that details the features to be released, a description of the business goals and the deliverables, and a timeline associated with it. This document is used to communicate and negotiate the scope of the project. With such a document, it is possible to come to agreement with the funding sponsors of the project on delivery dates and acceptable deliverables. Without such a document, there will be no vehicle for detailing the tradeoffs between scope and project time, and cost and there will be no record when decisions were made.

Scope Data Cleansing

To scope the costs of data cleansing consider the costs of the following:

- Name and address matching, and generalized re-duplication of the database
- Repair of missing or invalid data

These tasks are expensive in terms of both staff hours and software costs, and are generally best to avoid for the initial trial, if possible. That is to say, try to use only data sources that are clean and have good consistent consumer identification assigned. Data sources and data columns within those sources that require cleaning may be valuable input into the data mining system, but they are best left until after the initial trial.

Scope Data Movement, Modeling and Storage

As we have mentioned before, the data feeding the data mining system is likely to come from a variety of different sources and will need to be collected, loaded, and stored for the data mining system. For the initial launch of the trial, the data movement can be performed manually by tape or FTP transfer over secure intranet or extranet connections. Perform this manually at first, but always with an eye toward later automation. Also, be as selective as possible with the data sources to exclude unneeded data sources and columns. Anything that can be removed generates multiple savings further in the process, such as reducing storage costs and the complexity of the data storage model.

Scope Data Mining

Set the expectations for the delivery of data mining to one particular model. Companies that specialize in outsourced data mining services charge this way and it is a good way to measure whether the scope is creeping up on the requirements. If you set off to create a model of customer attrition and then find yourself also building models for the likelihood of customer value, retention, and response to marketing programs, you can clearly see that the scope has significantly increased.

The complexity and costs of building a data mining model vary greatly and depend on the difficulty of the problem. Considering the availability of good, reliable data and the ability to validate the model, data mining outsourcing companies usually allocate a minimum of four weeks of time to build and validate the model. But this is only time spent after the data has been collected, validated, and understood. It is not unusual to see three to four months taken up in the building of the models themselves if it is the first data mining that has been performed for this particular problem and with this particular data.

Scope Experimental Design and Measurement

After the model is built, it is also important to scope the way in which the performance of the data mining is measured. Your options are the following:

- Extend results from historical data to the future and apply rule-of-thumb assumptions about expected return on investment.

- Take action based on the data mining results and extrapolate early results to calculate overall ROI (for example, target a promotion and then wait just 30 days to measure the effect).

- Take action based on the data mining results, but wait until all results are available, and a full customer profitability measure and ROI of the promotion can be made. This may entail waiting a year or more to assess the effects of the promotion on customer retention or customer profitability rates.

Clearly, the third option is the best, but if you wait until all the results are in, you will have a project that is stalled, waiting for results with little else to do. Likewise, the first option is undesirable because your ROI results will be based on such rule-of-thumb assumptions without real execution that they will be unbelievable. Or, even if you can convince your audience scientifically, they will not be compelled at an intuitive (fundable) level.

The second option is the best compromise between getting actionable and measurable results, and keeping the project on a rapid pace of deployment. It is important, however, that agreement be reached and expectations be set via the launch document about how the efficacy of the data mining will be measured, long before the data mining is completed. Without such agreements made going into the project, the tendency will be to either deliver results prematurely or become ultra-conservative and wait forever for all results to be available.

Trial

One of the first visible signs of the success of your data mining application will be the trial. This trial represents a first application of the data mining models and results for a real-world business problem in an actionable and measurable way. It is, however, usually performed in a limited way. For instance, if a normal monthly mailing is sent out to existing customers with valuable offers aimed at retaining the customer, perhaps 5–10% of this customer population might now be targeted via the results of the data mining system rather than the way it was done in the past.

Don't Wait Too Long

One key to the trial is to not wait too long before you execute it and to always have it in your plans from the very beginning. Because it is part of the existing business processes, it will require a fair amount of planning and linking with other systems outside of the data mining project. Thus, these groups must be notified, and you must put the data mining trial on their schedules long before the data mining system is implemented or the first model is built.

Start Small, but Go End to End

The other key to the trial is to keep it small (for example, a small consumer population, just one marketing offer), but to make sure that it is real enough to go end to end—from the data collection and processing, to the data mining, to interfacing with existing marketing data structures such as mailing lists.

It will always be easier to perform a great job on the data mining, and then leave the details of execution for later. Resist the temptation. The purpose of the trial is not just to get the data mining system in place, but to work the bugs out of all of the data flows. By doing this in the trial on a very small data set, it is possible to quickly fix problems that will be very difficult to fix after the full customer database is flowing through the system.

It is also important to use the trial to debug your users. Because your users really don't know what a data mining system is before they see one, they really don't know what features they should be asking for when you first solicit user requirements. The trial system can also be used to help the users understand for themselves what they want to do with the system.

To this end, the trial system should have some working features for the end users, both in terms of manipulating data, performing the data mining, and then also executing the marketing campaigns based on the data mining. The system should also possess some forms of reporting the results. By putting these preliminary user interfaces in front of the users on a trial basis, you can gain valuable insights into what is useful and what is not useful to the user, and reprioritize your development efforts.

Quality Assurance

All throughout the launch process, quality assurance should be of the highest priority. Because, in order to have a successful system you are committed to working on a highly visible business problem with real and measurable profit (and loss) attached to its execution, you can ill afford to have any significant errors in the results. The data mining system is like the rudder and captain's control tower on a large ocean liner. They are only small parts of the overall structure, but they can have significant beneficial and detrimental consequences when used (steering into the harbor rather than into an iceberg).

Consider, for instance, the difference in quality requirements for different parts of the CRM process. Millions of dollars may be spent by ad agencies and marketing departments on customer focus groups and the production of a particular promotional mailing. If an error is made with the focus groups and the wrong color is chosen for the cover of the promotion mailing (if, for example, green is the best at eliciting response but blue is chosen), the results from the promotion will be degraded by some percentage amount (for example, from 5% response to 4.5% response). If, however, the data mining system is incorrectly implemented and the model incorrectly targets the least likely to respond rather than the most likely to respond, the decrease in response rate could be catastrophic (for example, from 5% response down to 0% response). In some ways, the very power of data mining in correctly directing ("steering") marketing processes also makes it more important than many other processes that the results are of the highest quality.

Make Quality Assurance a Process

One of the keys to assuring these high levels of quality is to make a plan for quality assurance to become a process, not just a one-time event. This will include devoting a significant portion of the launch document to the *Quality Assurance* (QA) process, and coming to agreement as to how QA will be done between different parties within the overall business system. A good first step is to specifically assign the QA role and only the QA role to one of the team members on the data mining project.

Validate and Communicate Model Results

This QA role will exist to not only validate the success of the data mining model, but also to double-check the work from other parties. Processes should be in place, for instance, to regularly validate the data flows coming in from the original data sources. They should also make sure that the targeting that was specified by the data mining system is what was actually executed by the marketing process. (For example, did the mail house mail the promotion to the right consumers?)

The other important part of this QA role will be to communicate the quality of the process that is in place. Even though most of the business end users of the data mining system will not understand the details of how the data mining or data process works, they will have a realistic intuitive feel for the risk of when such a complex system makes a mistake. Thus, they may not be able to express this fear, but it will be ever-present and will manifest itself in subtle ways, such as the lack of an enthusiastic commitment to actually take action based on the system. The only remedy is to aggressively and proactively demonstrate the quality and reliability of the system through reports, presentations, and interactive reporting tools (for example, Web-based OLAP systems).

Education

As a continuation of the QuickStart education programs, it is important that the usercommunity be regularly educated about the use and value of the new data mining system. This will include significant initial training, but also will require continually working with the users to educate them about what models and metrics are, and how they can access and visualize the results of the system.

The topics that require particular attention are the following:

- Description of the consumer base and the data that is available. This may seem perhaps too detailed, but without the end users having an understanding of the data, they will not have confidence in how the system is being used.

- How the data mining results are integrated into the customer relationship management system. This is important for the business users who will be most interested in viewing the data modeling as just another way to target customers, and will not be interested in how the data mining was performed or even in particular what the results were.

- The way the metrics are calculated for understanding the results of the data mining system. For instance, how is customer profit or customer response calculated?

After the initial training, it will be important to continuously update the users as the data is updated and the models change over time. This is best done with a seminar series of short focused presentations on the way the complete system is used to solve real business problems that the users are interested in.

Keep in mind that the reason for the importance of training for large CRM systems that deploy data mining is the peculiar juxtaposition of users who are responsible for high-level business processes relating to marketing and sales, but who must and can benefit from utilizing a very complex technology. Through training, the data mining system can be effectively utilized by those running the CRM systems, but they need constant attention initially. If training is performed well and consistently, the results will be users who reliably use the system without making errors and build confidence in the powerful results that are available from the data mining systems.

Launch

The launch of the first CRM programs that utilize data mining will be the most critical time for the long-term incorporation of data mining into your CRM processes. If it is done well, the data mining will be accepted and it will improve all facets of the CRM process. If the launch is not executed well, it will be difficult to recover, even more so than for other similar systems. The main reason for this is because the stakes are so high in terms of the amounts of money that are being invested into marketing and sales campaigns based on the results of the data mining system. For this reason, the system should be 100% error-free from the initial launch.

Select Your Initial Users

To execute a successful launch, you will want to select a core set of some three to five users, including the following:

- Market researcher
- Campaign planner
- Product manager or strategic director with overall financial responsibilities

These users will cover the aspects of the new features of the CRM system that the data mining provides by being able to trial the research, ROI and budget planning, and campaign execution. Note that there may be internal users who are data analysts, and they can participate in the trial, but they will be the most useful participants in helping to build and debug the QA processes for making the results of the data mining system actionable within the CRM system.

Keep Things under Wraps Until All Results Are In

After your core set of trial users is set, you should try to reproduce a recent CRM program—perhaps the last direct mail campaign that was performed. With your core set of users, you should be able to re-execute the program all the way up to the point of actually deploying the promotions to the customers. This time, however, you will be performing the targeting based on the results that come from the data mining system.

The results that you see should be kept under wraps until they can be formally validated. In the development of any predictive model for any program, there will be multiple times when the model is "over-performing" due to mistakes made in the data or the data mining process. This is to be expected, and such mistakes are eventually captured by the QA process and then corrected. What should be avoided is any announcement of the results of the model or even of the campaign until the full validation process has been performed. Overenthusiastic and premature reporting of exceptional results that later need to be retracted after QA is finished go a long way toward decreasing confidence in the system.

Help Your Users Interpret the Results

The last caveat in the launch is that even after the QA process has been completed successfully, the end users can misinterpret the results (for example, the results are correct but the conclusion drawn from them is not). For instance, a user could look at a revenue figure for new products sold in a cross-sell campaign subtract out the cost of the campaign and report the profit to senior management, without realizing that substantial portions of the revenue might have happened without any cross-sell campaign at all.

The best way to avoid this situation is to encourage your users to compare results with the data mining team and with each other before they report their findings. You will also get some mileage, as well as feedback, on the value of the system by sitting down and working with the end users to find and interpret the results.

Continuation

Adding data mining into your CRM process is not a one-time event. Like the training step, the data mining system must be an ongoing process overall. Much of this has to do with the updates to the data that are being used within the CRM system, as well as the predictive models that come from the data mining system.

As time goes on, it will be important for the data mining system to catalog and archive older models. This should be done so that they can be reused sometime in the future or to re-create the scoring to perform validation of the model over time. The performance of the model over time will be important because the major ROI-level impact of the data mining system may be felt at a cumulative level over the lifetime of the customer.

Conclusion—Making Data Mining Part of Your Business Process

The steps outlined in this chapter have been found to be very useful in successfully deploying data mining systems, especially as they are used to optimize existing CRM systems. The authors have tried to emphasize the steps (such as understanding the data and user education) that are less glamorous but present significant risks to the project if they are skipped or taken lightly. If the steps are followed, they will provide a path to a successfully launched data mining system—one that will continue to be used and improved over time.

CHAPTER 16

Collecting
Customer Data

Introduction

This chapter deals with some of the issues concerning customer data. In particular, it discusses how to classify the types of customer data, how to obtain it, and what to watch out for when it is obtained.

The Three Types of Customer Data

Alhough data about customers can come from a variety of sources, there are three main types of data (Figure 16-1) that are of interest to data mining systems that are being used for customer relationship management. This data does the following:

- Describes who the consumer is
- Describes what marketing or sales promotions were made to the customer
- Describes how the customer reacted to those promotions by transacting with the company

Figure 16-1
The three types of customer data.

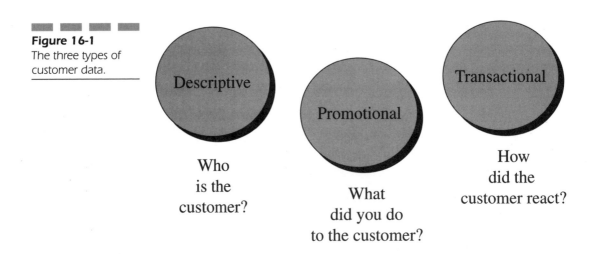

Descriptive

Who
is the
customer?

Promotional

What
did you do
to the customer?

Transactional

How
did the
customer react?

If you know these three things about the customer or even about an individual that is not yet a customer, you have enough data to begin to make predictions. You can perform pattern discovery with data mining or even begin to conduct experiments and optimize the marketing and sales interactions with these customers, Figure 16-2. Without any one of these three pieces of information about who the customers are, what was done to them, and how the consumers reacted, it is not possible to optimize or improve the system.

The reason for this is the following. In order to optimize and make as profitable as possible the interactions with your customers and optimize the performance of the CRM system, you must be able to differentiate between good and bad customers, and profitable and unprofitable customers. You must know who they are and how they differ.

Similarly, in order to know whether your investments in promotions and marketing are working, you must know and keep track of what you did to each customer. You are creating many small experiments with your customer base, and you must know what is

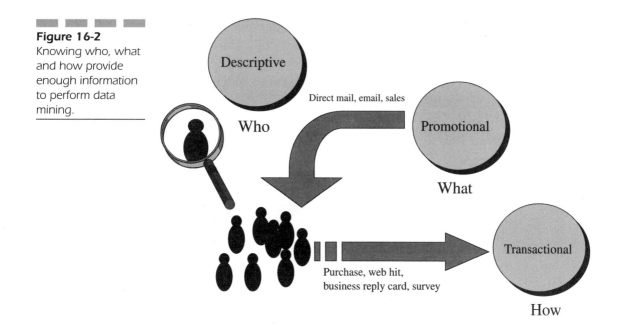

Figure 16-2
Knowing who, what and how provide enough information to perform data mining.

different in each experiment in order to judge best what is working and what is not working.

To judge the actual value of the system, you must be able to measure the results. If you don't know whether the result of the experiment was good or bad, then you really have not learned anything new that can be used to improve the system the next time around.

This grouping of data categories is also useful because it usually breaks down into different types of actual data stored in the relational database. It also is often a good delineation between the sources of the data. If you think about the data in these three broad categories, it will help you to make sure that your system is being fed with the types of data that it needs in order to successfully mine the data and produce an optimized CRM system.

Descriptive

Descriptive data is data about the customer or consumer. It is usually some form of summary data; in relational database terms, it can be stored as different columns in a single customer table. This type of data does not change very quickly because it is descriptive of the consumer. It includes information such as age, gender, location of home, number of children, household income, and individual income. This information can change, but generally at no faster than an annual pace (although information such as addresses and phone numbers need to be updated quarterly, or at least semi-annually, for the database).

Promotional

Promotional data includes information about what was done to each customer. The richness of this type of data usually depends on the sophistication of the CRM system. In its simplest form, it is a list of promotions of interventions that have been performed with the consumer (for instance, the mailing of catalogs, free samples, or coupons). Or it can include less-precise interventions with the customer, such as broadcast television or direct television advertisements (which also provide an 800 number or Web site), or radio, newspaper, and magazine advertisements. Or it could be very precise individualized information, such as outbound email and Web site hits from non-anonymous users.

The types of information that could be collected include the following:

- *Type of intervention.*   Sales, telemarketing, print advertising, broadcast advertising, Web advertising
- *Description of the intervention.*   Color of the postcard
- *Media.*   The markets that the ad ran in, the Web-site portals that carried the banners
- *Timing.*   The date and perhaps the time of day that the intervention took place
- *Description of intent.*   A brief description of who the intervention was meant for and why (why the color or the background music was selected)
- *Financial.*   The fixed and variable costs of the intervention

Transactional

Transactional data broadly defines all data that corresponds to an interaction with the consumer. This can include everything from a phone call, to the service desk, to the description of the products that the consumer purchased. This data, like promotional data, can change very rapidly over time. Thus, it is typically stored in data structures that provide for time-stamped transactional data to be stored that can be easily updated and changed. This is different from the descriptive consumer information, where even the types of data stored do not vary substantially over time. (For example, the types of information stored about each consumer are not radically different from the types of information that the U.S. Department of the Census stores about U.S. citizens.) The makeup of transactional data can vary dramatically within short periods of time (for example, new products are introduced that can be purchased, and older products can no longer be purchased).

Collecting Customer Data

Customer data can be collected from a variety of different sources. One nice thing about breaking up the data into descriptive, promotional, and transactional sources is that that this grouping also reflects where the data comes from to some degree. Descriptive data comes from information that either you have about the customer because they told you (for example, their interest in purchasing retirement plans or the number of grandchildren they have), or from purchased sources from some of the large data providers. It is possible to purchase large amounts of data from companies such as Acxiom and others. This data can include both demographic information that is similar to what the census provides, or preference data that has been compiled from many different sources (customer warranty cards and magazine subscriptions, for example).

Internal Sources

There are a variety of different internal sources that you can also use to find data. Because the CRM system will be mostly used by marketing, it will be easy to obtain promotional data. And because it is generated by the marketing department, it will often only be a matter of collecting it in some formal process or of requesting that it be collected from the mail house responsible for actually mailing the brochures or coupons.

Other internal sources include collecting the data from other existing processes, such as existing customer lists. This can sometimes be harder than it seems for two reasons:

- The data may be "owned" internally by one product group, which may not want to share the data with a CRM system that is beneficial to the entire enterprise. For instance, the savings bank division of a large bank may not want to share its current list of savings account customers with the brokerage arm of the bank because those responsible for the savings accounts recognize that each customer has only so much money that they can invest. Dollars invested in brokerage accounts usually means dollars lost from savings accounts. Unless there is an enterprise-wide vehicle to make it valuable to share consumer information across disparate divisions, it will probably not happen. Or, if it does, it will happen only sporadically under edict of senior management in a costly way.

■ The other reason that data is often not shared has to do with consumer privacy. If the company implementing the CRM system is large enough, it will likely have information about the same consumer available through different channels. Consumers generally don't mind if their information is kept within some bounds and not shared amongst large numbers of people. However, if they feel that information about themselves is being mishandled and not carefully monitored, they will feel uncomfortable. The problem is made worse by the power of data mining. Without data mining it would not be possible to find the patterns in customer data that could be transferred between different products or different markets. Because of the power of data mining, CRM systems can exploit limited knowledge about an individual in one market to provide limited information about a consumer in another market. This was not previously possible.

For instance, the consumer may not mind having new CDs or books recommended to them based on past purchases and interests. They, however, would not be particularly pleased if they learned that their preferences for music and literature was being used by a data mining system to determine their interest in magazine subscriptions. As you will see in the next sections, consumer privacy is a very important issue and it can become one of the most important issues, not only to the successful deployment of a data mining system, but for the whole CRM system and the overall health of the enterprise.

Web Data

Web-related data is becoming more and more important to data mining. This is happening because more promotional and transactional events are happening over the Web, and because the Web, as an entirely an electronic medium in which to conduct business, eliminates much of the issues in collecting and storing the information. Each and every user event—effectively everything the user does short of knowing where on the page they are looking at a given time —is captured in Web log files.

This produces a rich system of information in which every minute buying decision and influence can be measured. It is not yet clear how well this data can be used to perform data mining. For instance, will knowing exactly what path the consumer took through the Web site that lead to a sale and what path didn't really be significant? Or will they just be reflective of other motivations that can't be captured in just the Web data?

For instance, the consumer may be shopping for a book one day and already know what they want to purchase, and they are merely shopping for the best price. Their path through the Web site may or may not result in a sale (transaction event), but the path itself is irrelevant to the cause of the purchase event. There is only one number on one page that truly affects that event—that is the price. Luckily, there are many Web log-file analysis tools now on the market that are highly useful for combining this type of Web data with data mining to separate the true influencers of transaction events with those that are not.

Connecting Customer Data

Data Warehouses and Data Marts

Data warehouses are the Holy Grail for connecting customer information sources. They are supposed to provide a single localized database for all customer data that is relevant to making business decisions. They are generally monolithic large database servers that are fed by transactional systems. They are often defined technically by the way that the data is stored (star schema, snowflake schema, and simple denormalized flat file) and the hardware architecture to support them (which are critical issues, given the size of data that they are supporting). The bottom line advantage of data warehouses is that they provide support for making business decisions based on the transactional data, which yields a single version of the truth.

By this, we mean that one of the main realized benefits of a data warehouse is that it, often for the first time, defines who a customer is —in the simplest terms by providing a single unique identifier for each customer.

This is surprisingly a very difficult thing to do, given that customers are defined by interactions at many different touchpoints across the corporation, and that different customers may have been acquired for very different reasons—perhaps through mergers or corporate acquisitions.

The reality, however, is that data warehouses will be only one of many sources of data that support the data mining system for your customer relationship management system. The reason for this is that because the data warehouse is large and monolithic, it can change only very slowly. The transactional and promotional data, however, must change at the speed of the market and the competition. For this reason, the need for decision support and the data available within the data warehouse proper will always be out of sync. The needs of the data warehouse are ever-present, however, but it is perhaps better to think of data warehousing as a process to maintain a single version of the truth for each and every customer. As such, parts of the data warehouse will be static and some may be dynamic; they cannot all be stored within one monolithic structure and be consistently up to date.

Data Pumps and Connectors

An architecture that supports this view of the data warehouse as a process includes one with "connectors" or "data pumps." These are pieces of software that glue the entire system together, and regularly connect disparate data sources together so that they can feed the data mining system and the CRM system. These systems pieces provide a layer of abstraction between the way the data currently exists (which is never exactly perfect) and the way that the data is needed to support data mining for CRM. Providing this layer of abstraction allows the system tremendous flexibility to do the following:

- Accommodate new and changing data sources
- Rapidly change to accommodate new data and new data structures the way it is collected in existing data sources, rather than having to wait to change the way that it is stored at the source
- Perform a consistent way of moving and processing data that is repeatable and possible to validate
- Create an optimized data structure to support data mining and CRM without forcing these design constraints on other data sources within the enterprise

This means, for instance, that the design of the data warehouse can change dramatically and that the data structures for the CRM system can remain constant. Or, that the data structures supporting the CRM system can be highly optimized without having to accommodate the decision-support requirements of other parts of the enterprise.

These connectors can be as simple as SQL scripts that transform and move data between databases, or they can be complex separate products provided by third-party vendors. It is highly recommended for any CRM data mining system that some form of connector abstraction (Figure 16-3) be used to disconnect the changes in the source data from the changes in requirements of the CRM system.

Long-Distance Connections

Today's technology also provides for the capability to build and deploy these database connectors physically across long distances. You may, for instance, find it useful to connect not only to data sources within your own organization, but also to data sources

Figure 16-3
An abstract view of a
data mining system
with data
connectors.

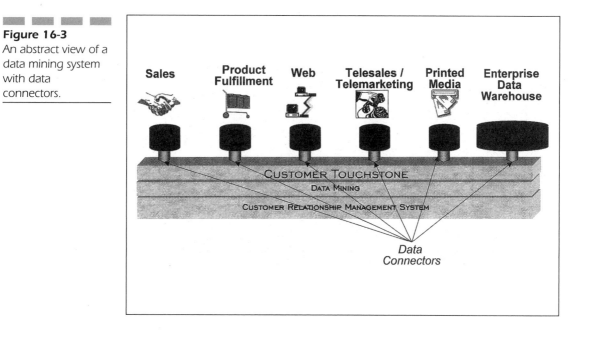

within the organizations of your vendors and partners. This can be done today by making use of secure Internet transfer technology without the need to create costly internal proprietary networks for data transfer, or costly and inefficient manual processes for moving and performing quality controls on your data. The technologies of virtual private networking (VPN) provide a secure virtual extension to your own internal computer network by using encryption technology and the Internet. These systems can run over high-bandwidth communications links such as T1 lines. For an increased feeling of security, you may also use a dedicated (though more expensive for the bandwidth) point-to-point solution such as Frame Relay. Whatever way you decide to go, the options are varied and the performance is much greater than even ten years ago, when shipping tapes overnight was an acceptable form of moving data. Today, that data can move seamlessly from database to database across states and corporations, and appear for all intents and purposes as if it resided directly within your own local database.

Using long-distance database connectors like this has several advantages:

- It provides the capability to connect to larger numbers of databases in a coordinated fashion.

- It allows a database-to-database transfer of data so that the errors that occur in dumping, loading, and transforming data from tape are eliminated.

- It accomodates rapid changes in data or data needs, which is common as marketing plans or targets change at the last minute for a particular promotion.

Customer Data and Privacy

No matter how you set up your internal data structures for customer data or how you obtain the data from outside sources, customer privacy will be important. Privacy is a loaded issue and only becomes more important as your CRM system becomes more powerful and begins to incorporate a data mining engine. In recent years, privacy concerns have taken on a more significant role in American society as merchants, insurance companies, and government agencies amass large data warehouses containing personal data. The concerns that people have over the collection of this data will naturally extend to any analytic capabilities applied to the data. Users of data mining need to think about how their use of this technology will be impacted by issues related to privacy.

In addition to privacy, as data mining begins to take hold in the business world, there will be a number of legal issues that are sure to receive attention. What happens if a characteristic such as race or gender finds its way into a model that is being used to make decisions about sending an offer for credit to your customers? What kind of liability will exist in such circumstances? Although we will not attempt to provide legal advice in this book, we want to make sure that you are aware that these issues will need to be dealt with if you use data mining to make decisions of a sensitive nature.

Privacy and Data Mining

In February 1998, an uproar broke out over CVS drug stores and their use of Elensys, a Massachusetts direct marketing company that sends reminders to customers who have not renewed their prescriptions. After receiving criticism over what was considered to be a violation of privacy of their customer's medical records, CVS terminated its agreement with Elensys. Although there was no direct mention of data mining during the controversy, Evan Hendricks, editor of *Privacy Times*, said that Senate hearings on medical privacy that were taking place around the time of the Elensys controversy included discussions of Elensys and the use of data mining for marketing activities. If and when this legislation is enacted, it could very well impose limitations on the use of data mining technology.

This is just the tip of the iceberg. Although the United States takes a much more laissez-faire approach to privacy when compared with the rest of the world, these policies are facing challenges. In October 1998, the European Union's Directive on Data Protection complicated the privacy landscape. Although the ultimate effect of the directive has not been felt as of the writing of this book, it is likely just the first in a series of events that will impact the technology of data mining.

According to the text of the directive, it will bar the movement of personal data to countries that do not have sufficient data-privacy laws in place. The European directive has a number of requirements for companies that deal with privacy-related data, including the capability for persons to access, challenge, and restrict the personal information held by a company.

American industry groups are arguing that voluntary controls currently in place in the United States are sufficient. Privacy advocates, on the other hand, argue that any controls must be backed by legislation. Whether or not voluntary measures will suffice is still an open question, but recent comments by EU officials have been critical of this voluntary approach.

Another critical evaluation of data mining and privacy was issued in 1998 in a report by Ontario Information and Privacy Commissioner, Ann Cavoukian. The report, "Data Mining: Staking a Claim on Your Privacy," said that data mining "may be the most fundamental challenge that privacy advocates will face in the next decade . . . "

The report looks at data mining and privacy in the context of the international "fair information practice" principles. These principles, established in 1980, dictate how personal data should be protected in terms of quality, purpose, use, security, openness, individual participation, and accountability. According to Commissioner Cavoukian, a number of these principles conflict with many current uses of data mining technology. For example, looking at the "purpose" principle, she writes:

> For example, if the primary purpose of the collection of transactional information is to permit a credit card payment, then using the information for other purposes, such as data mining, without having identified this purpose before or at the time of the collection, is in violation of the purpose and use limitation principles. The primary purpose of the collection must be clearly understood by the consumer and identified at the time of the collection. Data mining, however, is a secondary, future use. As such, it requires the explicit consent of the data subject or consumer.

Although broadly written use statements could be added to customer agreements to allow data mining, Cavoukian questions whether or not these waivers are truly meaningful to consumers. Because data mining is based on the extraction of unknown patterns from a database, "data mining does not know, cannot know, at the outset, what personal data will be of value or what relationships will emerge. Therefore, identifying a primary purpose at the beginning of the process, and then restricting one's use of the data to that purpose are the antithesis of a data mining exercise."

Cavoukian sees informed consumer consent as the key issue. Customers should be told how the data collected about them would be used, and whether or not it will be disclosed to third parties. The report recommends that customers be given three levels of "opt-out" choices for any data that has been collected:

- Do not allow any data mining of customer's data.
- Allow data mining only for internal use.
- Allow data mining for both internal and external uses.

Although Canada (except for Quebec) currently does not have laws limiting the use of personal information by private companies, Cavoukian calls for controls that are "codified through government enactment of data-protection legislation for private sector businesses."

These collisions between data mining and privacy are just the beginning. Over the next few years, we should expect to see an increased level of scrutiny of data mining in terms of its impact on privacy. The sheer amount of data that is collected about individuals, coupled with powerful new technologies such as data mining, will generate a great deal of concern by consumers. Unless this concern is effectively addressed, expect to see legal challenges to the use of data mining technology.

Guidelines for Privacy

Although it is not clear how restrictive or loose the laws will be in ten years regarding consumer privacy, there are some general guidelines for building your data mining system for CRM that, although not foolproof, can make you more likely to avoid difficulties later on. Note that these guidelines are based on current experience within the current law and limits of the technology. As we have seen with the example from Elensys, even if the laws are unclear and precaution is taken, irrecoverable harm can be done to your business if consumers perceive that your consumer privacy policies are inadequate.

Anonymity and Identity Information

In general, there is a distinction to be made between information that provides the identity of the consumer and information that does not. Obvious examples include full name or Social Security number. But even last name (if it is unique) or last name coupled with address will often be enough to uniquely identify an individual. You should try, if at all possible, to have your data mining system work with data that is anonymous and abstract the notion of an individual consumer into a unique, encrypted identifier (for example, a ten-digit number that only you can translate into an individual consumer's name and address.

Creation of this anonymous identifier is relatively easy. It need only be unique and, for promotional purposes, there should be some place where a table is stored that maps the identifier to the name and address. Clearly, the identifier should not be a simple permutation of the Social Security number, or some composite of address and other identifiable information. It should be randomly assigned and be completely independent of any descriptive, promotional, or transactional information that is available about that consumer.

Detailed versus Consolidated Data

Even if the consumer data that you are using is anonymous but is still at an individual "detailed" level, there is always the risk that someone could be identified—even without specific identifiers such as name, address, or Social Security number. For instance if you know the person's ZIP+4, age, and type of car, you can be well on your way to precisely knowing who that person is.

One way to ensure an even greater level of privacy for your customers is to work only with data at a consolidated or "rolled up" level. For instance, you might decide that you want to look at the performance of your marketing efforts and target based only on age and gender. So, the only data that you use for analysis is the response rate to the promotions and the dollars purchased for all combinations of age and gender—which should be about 240 different values (approximately 120 different ages and two genders). For a one-million consumer database, this means that, on average, the purchasing and buying behavior for more than 4,000 consumers will be combined together. The result is a segmentation that is still useful for performing data mining and marketing measurement and targeting, but the individual and his or her information is protected —for the most part.

The caveat for using consolidated data is that you still need to be cognizant of the fact that some rolled-up or consolidated data could just by its nature reflect a very few consumers or even a single consumer. For instance, in our age and gender example the 120-year old male segment might, if it contained anyone, contain only a single representative. Thus, some consumers cannot have their anonymity preserved, even within a million other people, if they are very old. The best way to prevent such underpopulated segments from occurring is to specifically review the sizes of each segment, and combine or cluster segments together that are similar but are underpopulated. These issues are also important for OLAP systems, in which consolidation is used, but often with segments that can be sliced and diced by a large variety of characteristics.

Information Used for Targeting or for Measurement

One other boundary that it will be important for you to decide whether you would like to cross is to determine whether you wish to use your consumer data for targeting or just for measurement. The distinction is that consumers are less worried about your knowing what they are doing and measuring how well they respond to a promotion than if they believe you are taking action based on what you know about them.

It can often be unsettling to receive promotions in the mail that are targeted to personal life events (for example, the birth of a child) or personal information (for example, the new medication targeted to the particular disease of the consumer).

The reality is that at some level, measurement is targeting in the sense that the only reason that someone would measure something would be to modify their actions based on what they learn. So, the distinction between measurement and targeting can be a slippery slope. For practical purposes, measurement is always a safer strategy.

Combined Sources

One other issue that contributes to concern over consumer privacy is the use of combined data sources. This issue was not always an issue because it was often difficult to collect data about a consumer other than within a limited context. Because of computer and database technology, it is now much easier to combine data about users from a variety of sources and build a more complete picture of the consumer. This often means knowing how your consumer is behaving for markets and for products outside of your own (for example, perhaps you purchased a list from a magazine or some other manufacturer).

The Anonymous Architecture

Although there is no possible solution to the issue of consumer privacy until the legal limits of the use of data about consumer behavior are better defined, there are general-purpose architectures for your data mining system that can specifically help. The configuration shown in Figure 16-4 provides a firewall between consumer

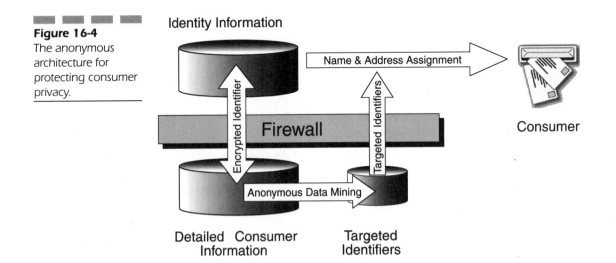

Figure 16-4
The anonymous architecture for protecting consumer privacy.

identity information and all other consumer information. Again, this in no way corrects all privacy issues, but it does allow for the data mining to be performed anonymously while still preserving the ability to target and measure at an individual level. Using an architecture such as this one, coupled with some vigilance of the state of maturity of privacy laws, will go a long way toward keeping you and your company off of the front pages of the local newspaper. You will also give your customers a sense of privacy and security about the way that you handle their data.

Legal Issues Associated with Data Mining

Almost every time a decision is made, there exists the possibility of legal repercussions. Deciding whom to grant credit to, which transactions might be fraudulent, or which customers deserve to receive a special mortgage offer are all sensitive issues. If the decision incorporates a characteristic that is not allowed by law, there might be problems. Over the past decade, a number of financial service companies have been fined because of improper selection techniques for the marketing of credit cards and other types of loans. Historically, the term "red lining" as been used to describe the process of excluding people who live in particular areas from receiving credit or other financial services. These exclusions often occurred because of the racial makeup of the excluded neighborhoods. Now that automatic processes are available in the form of data mining, care must be taken to make sure that prohibited exclusions do not make their way into patterns discovered by mining software.

In the case of data mining, the decisions are being made automatically, often hidden behind mathematical functions and complex selection criteria. If you will be using data mining technology as part of a sensitive decision (credit, for example), it is important to make sure that no legal problems arise due to the inclusion of the wrong variables in a data mining model.

The statistical and machine learning algorithms embedded into a data mining application do not know about race, gender, age, or any other characteristic that might be inappropriate to use when making a particular decision. From the point of view of the algorithms, a data field, is a data field. and it really doesn't matter what is behind the number. Statistical algorithms zoom in on correlations between a target variable and the input variables provided to the system.

One of the reasons that these issues are increasing in importance is that data mining allows for the rapid development of predictive models by analyzing large amounts of data (typically, all the data that you can find in your data warehouse). The fact that the number of predictive models has increased due to many more smaller sub-segments means that there is less time for up-front reviews of the data that is to be analyzed. The promise of data mining, that some of the analysis work can be automated, often means that less time is allowed for human involvement in the process.

Care should also be taken to make sure that variables that contain encoded information about other variables are also considered. For example, a variable in an insurance database that indicates pregnancy also encodes some information about gender. Another related issue involves variables with a strong correlation to data that should not be used. The classic example is the use of ZIP codes and the racial makeup of the specified neighborhood.

The key to minimizing problems is to perform a thorough review of the data before any analysis is done using a data mining system. Any questionable pieces of data should be evaluated to determine whether their inclusion in a model is both legal and desirable. Even if a particular piece of data is not forbidden, the fact that you can use a variable does not necessarily mean that you would want to use it. In our litigious society, it might be better to err on the side of caution.

It might also be prudent to do a post-mining analysis to determine whether any of the patterns found by the data mining system disproportionately affect a protected class. This would involve relatively simple statistical profiling of each protected class to evaluate whether the predictive model has excluded any (protected) groups.

Depending on the regulatory environment in your industry, you might want to do this analysis to determine whether there are any potential problems. In recent years, government regulators have required that some credit-granting organizations evaluate every decision point within their marketing campaigns to determine whether any implicit discrimination was taking place. As expected, this significantly increased the complexity of the marketing efforts.

In the end, competent legal counsel should review any concerns about the used of questionable data in a predictive model.

CHAPTER 17

Scoring Your Customers

Introduction

After a predictive model has been created by using data mining software, the model can then be used to make predictions for new data. The process of using the output of the data mining (the model) is separate from the process that creates the model. Typically, a model is used multiple times after it is created to score different databases. For example, consider a model that has been created to predict the probability that a customer will purchase something from a catalog if it is sent to them. The model would be built by using historical data from customers and prospects that were sent catalogs, as well as information about what they bought (if anything) from the catalogs. During the model-building process, the data mining application would use information about the existing customers to build and validate the model. In the end, the result is a model that would take details about the customer/prospects as inputs and generate a number between 0 and 1 as the output. This process is illustrated in Figure 17-1.

After a model has been created based on historical data, it can then be applied to new data in order to make predictions about unseen behavior. This is what data mining (and more generally, predictive modeling) is all about. The process of using a model to make predictions about behavior that has yet to happen is called "scoring." The output of the model, the prediction, is called a score. Scores can take just about any form, from numbers to strings to entire data

Figure 17-1

The data mining process

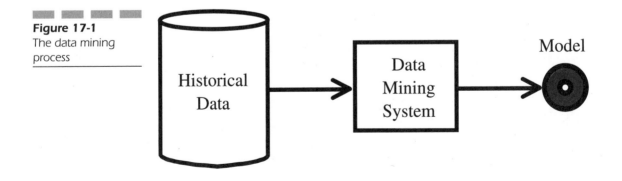

structures, but the most common scores are numbers (for example, the probability of responding to a particular promotional offer).

Scoring is the unglamorous workhorse of data mining. It doesn't have the sexiness of a neural network or a genetic algorithm, but without it, data mining is pretty useless. (There are some data mining applications that cannot score the models that they produce—this is akin to building a house and forgetting to put in any doors.) At the end of the day, when your data mining tools have given you a great predictive model, there's still a lot of work to be done. Scoring models against a database can be a time-consuming, error-prone activity, so the key is to make it part of a smoothly flowing process.

The Process

Scoring usually fits somewhere inside of a much larger process. In the case of one application of data mining, database marketing, it usually goes something like this:

1. The process begins with a database containing information about customers or prospects. This database might be part of a much larger data warehouse or it might be a smaller marketing data mart.

2. A marketing user identifies a segment of customers of interest in the customer database. A segment might be defined as "existing customers older than 65, with a balance greater than $1000 and no overdue payments in the last three months." The records representing this customer segment might be siphoned off into a separate database table or the records might be identified by a piece of SQL that represents the desired customers.

3. The selected group of customers is then scored by using a predictive model. The model might have been created several months ago (at the request of the marketing department) in order to predict the customer's likelihood of switching to a premium level of service. The score, a number between 0 and

1, represents the probability that the customer will indeed switch if they receive a brochure describing the new service in the mail. The scores are to be placed in a database table, with each record containing the customer ID and that customer's numerical score.

4. After the scoring is complete, the customers then need to be sorted by their score value. The top 25% will be chosen to receive the premium service offer. A separate database table that contains the records for the top 25% of the scoring customers will be created.

5. After the customers with the top 25% of the scores are identified, the information necessary to send them the brochure (name and address) will need to be pulled out of the data warehouse and a tape created containing all of this information.

6. Finally, the tape will be shipped to a company (sometimes referred to as a mail house) where the actual mailing will occur.

The marketing department typically determines when and where the marketing campaigns take place. In past years, this process might be scheduled to happen once every six months, with large numbers of customers being targeted every time the marketing campaign is executed. Current thinking is to move this process into a more continuous schedule, whereby small groups of customers are targeted on a weekly or even daily basis.

When marketing campaigns are infrequent, manual selection and scoring of the data is not a significant impediment to the process. There is usually significant lead time to allow for the various parties to do their work before the actual mailing will take place. When someone in marketing needs to have a segment of customers selected for the campaign, they simply call someone in IT. When the scores are needed, the statistician who created the model is asked to apply the model to the customers in the desired segment. Because the processing is performed manually, the possibility of an error being introduced into the system is considerable. To minimize errors,

- Make sure that the definition of the segmentation is correct and select the right customers for scoring. An error in this process is usually due to an incorrect translation from the marketing user's vocabulary to the syntax of an SQL statement executed by someone in IT.

- Make sure that the correct customers are scored. The correct database table needs to be scored. There is confusion sometimes regarding which table, among hundreds, is supposed to be scored. When the names of the tables are cryptic, as they often are (for example, JF432_IPG), the possibility of using the wrong data for scoring is possible.

- Make sure that the correct model is used to do the scoring. Assuming that the targeted selection of customers is a success, the number of models available could be quite large. In addition, multiple models might be similar (for example, one model predicts responses to a particular catalog for women aged 50–55, whereas another model predicts responses for men aged 50–55).

- Make sure that the scores are put in the right place. Just as confusion sometime exists with the data that is going to be scored, there can also be some confusion about the tables that contain the scores.

- Make sure that you understand how the scores are ordered. Are high values good or bad? If you want to select the best customers, you will need to know what score values represent those customers.

When the frequency of the marketing campaigns is increased so that they occur on a daily or weekly basis, there are two significant impacts on the campaign. First, the decreased time between mailings means that there is much less room for error when carrying out the individual steps in the process. If a mistake is found, there is less time to correct it compared to the less frequent campaigns. Second, the sheer number of scoring "events" will increase dramatically, due to both the increased frequency of the campaigns and an increase in the number of segments that need to be scored.

If the marketing campaigns that rely on the scores are run on a continuous (daily) basis, this means a lot of phone calls between marketing and IT, as well as between marketing and the modelers. The best approach to solving this problem is to use the campaign management software that is integrated with the scoring engine. If integrated software is not available, care will need to be taken so that difficulties are minimized.

Scoring Architectures and Configurations

The software systems that are used to carry out the scoring process are usually simpler than the applications used to build the models. This is because the statistical functions and optimization procedures that were used to create the model are no longer needed; all that is required is a piece of software that can evaluate mathematical functions on a set of data inputs.

Scoring involves invoking a software application (often called the scoring engine, Figure 17-2), which then takes a model and a dataset and produces a set of scores for the records in the dataset. There are three common approaches to scoring engines:

- A scoring engine software application that is separate from the model-building application.
- A scoring engine that is part of the model-building application.
- A scoring engine that is produced by compiling the model code (for example, C++ or Java) that is output by the data mining application. In this case, a model is itself the scoring application because it is an executable piece of software (once it is compiled).

The type of model generated will depend upon the data mining system that is used. Some data mining systems can produce multiple types of models, whereas others will generate only a single type.

In the first two cases, the scoring engine is a software application that needs to be run by the user. It might have a graphical user interface or it might be a command line program, in which the user specifies the input parameters by typing them onto a console interface

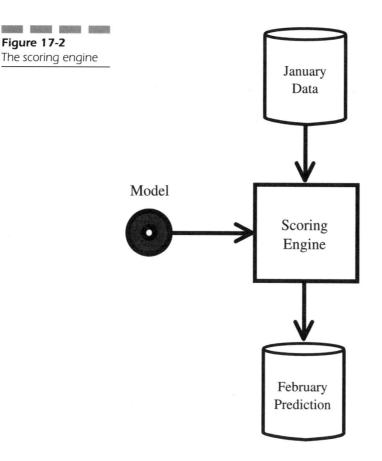

Figure 17-2
The scoring engine

when the program is run. There are usually three inputs to the scoring engine: the model that is to be run, the data that is to be scored, and the location where the output scores should be put.

In some cases, a data mining system might generate a model that can be executed by another software vendor's scoring engine. Although there are currently no standards for the specification of a predictive model, some data mining vendors have decided to use the modeling formats created by established statistical software vendors. As of the writing of this book, at least two data mining software vendors have optional model output formats that are compatible with the modeling language supported by the SAS Institute's software. Models that are written out in the SAS modeling format can then be executed by the SAS Institute's scoring engine (known as SAS/Base).

In the last type of scoring engine, the model acts as its own scoring engine. After the model is generated by the data mining software application, it will need to be compiled into an executable form. This step is usually done manually and often requires knowledge of system and programming level details (for example, linking ODBC database drivers). The primary reason to use a compiled model is to increase performance because a compiled model will usually run significantly faster than a model that requires a separate scoring engine.

There are obvious downsides to this approach, though. First is the fact that preparing a model for execution (compiling, linking, etc.) requires expertise that might not be available. Second, if the models change on a regular basis, they will need to be recompiled whenever they change. The use of compiled models can significantly increase the complexity of model management, especially if there are large numbers of models in use and/or the models change on a frequent basis.

Preparing the Data

Before you can score a model, you need to prepare the data on which the model is going to operate. Key to this process is the concept of consistency. The customers that are to be scored by the model should be consistent with the customer data that was used to build the model. For example, if a model was built using response data from low balance customers aged 40 to 50, it should not be used on customers aged 50 to 60.

A second type of consistency involves the type of interaction that will take place with the customer or prospect. The interaction needs to be consistent with the original data, or else the results might not be correct. The historical data that was used to build the model had a context that needs to be considered. The color of the envelope, the wording used in the offer, the type of offer, and other variables will affect the results of the interaction. If your model was built from historical response data for a mailing that used a blue envelope, the results that you will see if you send out a new offer in a green envelope could be different from what the model predicts. Care must be taken so that any assumptions, both from the marketing and modeling sides of the fence, are not lost when the implementation of a model takes place. A process (possibly part of a corporate knowledge base) should be maintained to describe customer segments, as well as the types of offers that are made to those customers/prospects.

After you are sure that the data is consistent with the historical customer data and interaction details, you need to map the individual columns (the variables) in your data set to the inputs of the model, Figure 17-3. The data that is to be scored using an existing predictive model needs to match the data that was used to build the model. Matching means that all of the data fields that were used as inputs to the model need to be made available for the model during the scoring process. It should be noted that not all fields that were

Figure 17-3
Mapping the data
to the model

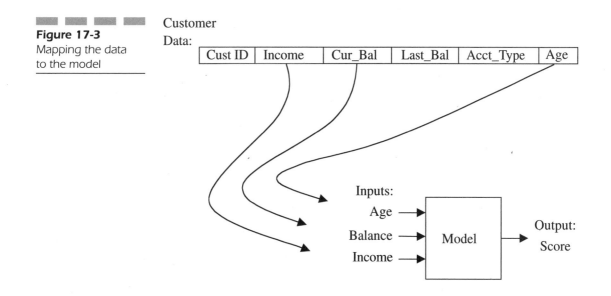

used to build the model are necessary when scoring the model. It is likely that many of the available fields were not used as inputs to the model because the data mining process determined that they did not provide any predictive information. Only the fields that were actually used in the in the model need to be included. This can usually improve performance because not all data needs to be passed to the scoring engine.

When mapping the data in the database to the inputs of the model, there are two types of mapping that can take place: direct and offset.

Direct Mapping

In a direct mapping approach, a variable that was used to build the predictive model and is included as an input is mapped to the same variable. For example, if the variable "Account Type" were an input to the model, it would simply map to the same variable. This approach is best used for input variables that are not part of a time series.

Offset Mapping

In offset mapping, the variables that were as inputs to the model are mapped to variables that are different from those used to build the model. This is often the case when input variables are part of a time series. For example, if a model was built using data from January, there might be inputs that are specific to that month (for example, "Outstanding_Balance_Jan"). When this model is applied to data after January, the inputs will need to be offset to match the time period for which the predictions are being made. When applied to February data, the input should be mapped to "Outstanding_ Balance_Feb." The easiest approach, if the data is in a database, is to use a database view to re-direct the inputs to the appropriate table and column. The view would be updated to whenever new monthly data was made available so that it pointed to the latest outstanding balance.

In the real world, the scoring process would probably use a combination of both direct and offset mappings.

The last step in preparing the data, if necessary, is to transform the input to conform to any requirements specific to the model. For example, an account type in the database that is represented as a string (i.e., "checking," "savings") might need to be transformed into numbers before it can be fed to the model. The form of the transformation is usually specific to the model type and should be specified by the person who created the model. Although this functionality should be incorporated into the model itself by the data mining system, some applications require the user to do any transformations manually.

Integrating Scoring with Other Applications

Scoring isn't something that takes place in a vacuum. After a model has been produced, other applications need to know that they exist and make use of the scores that they generate. Tight integration of data mining applications with other software systems is relatively new, but it is a trend that will continue for some time. Some of the software categories that are likely to embrace integration with data mining applications include *enterprise resource planning* (ERP), *Campaign Management*, and tools such as *Online Analytical Processing* (OLAP) and data visualization.

As an example, consider how a data mining system might be integrated with a marketing campaign management system. Marketing managers are interested in using the output of a data mining model in order to further refine the customer segments that they have specified. The simplest example might involve segregating a group of customers into separate yes/no categories. The customers that fall into the yes category will end up receiving a marketing offer, whereas the other group will not receive the offer. The marketing department will use a campaign management software system to manage the selection of the customers and the segments they fall into.

The closer that the data mining and campaign management software work together, the better are the business results. In the past, the use of a model within campaign management was often a manual, time-intensive process. When someone in marketing wanted to run a campaign that used model scores, he or she usually called someone in the modeling group to get a file containing the database scores. With the file in hand, the marketer would then solicit the help of someone in the information technology group to merge the scores with the marketing database.

Integration is crucial in two areas:

- First, the campaign management software must share the definition of the defined campaign segment with the data mining application to avoid modeling the entire database. For example, a marketer may define a campaign segment of high-income males, between the ages of 25 and 35, living in the Northeast. Through the integration of the two applications, the data mining application can automatically restrict its analysis to database records containing just those characteristics. This is important for the sake of data consistency between the data that was used to build the model and the data that will be scored by the model. By using the same definition, it will be more difficult to make a mistake and score records that are inconsistent with the records used to build the model.

- Second, selected scores from the resulting predictive model must flow seamlessly into the campaign segment in order to form targets with the highest profit potential. Any manual process involved with the movement of scores from the output of the model to a separate software complicates the overall process. Besides being a source of possible errors (for example, using the wrong score table), the delay associated with the manual processing could limit the frequency of marketing efforts.

Creating the Model

In the case of data mining for a marketing campaign, an analyst or user with a background in modeling creates a predictive model using the data mining application. This modeling is usually completely separate from the process of creating the marketing campaign. The complexity of the model creation typically depends on many factors, including database size, the number of variables known about each customer, the kind of data mining algorithms used, and the modeler's experience.

Interaction with the campaign management software begins when a model of sufficient quality has been found. At this point, the data mining user exports his or her model to a campaign management application, which can be as simple as dragging and dropping the data from one application to the other. This process of exporting a model tells the campaign management software that the model exists and is available for later use.

Dynamically Scoring the Data

Dynamic scoring is a type of software integration that allows the scoring process to be invoked by another software application that will use the scores for some other purpose. In our database marketing example, the campaign management system will interface with the scoring engine so that the scores are generated when the campaign manager needs the scores. Further, only the required records will be scored because the campaign management system determines when and what to score. Dynamic scoring avoids mundane, repetitive manual chores and eliminates the need to score an entire database. Instead, dynamic scoring marks only relevant record subsets, and only when needed. Scoring only the relevant customer subset and eliminating the manual process shrinks the overall processing time significantly. Moreover, scoring records segments only when needed assures fresh, up-to-date results.

After a model is in the campaign management system, a user (usually someone other than the person who created the model) can start to build marketing campaigns using the predictive models. Models are invoked by the campaign management system.

When a marketing campaign invokes a specific predictive model to perform dynamic scoring, the output is usually stored as a temporary score table. When the score table is available in the data warehouse, the data mining engine notifies the campaign management system, and the marketing campaign execution continues.

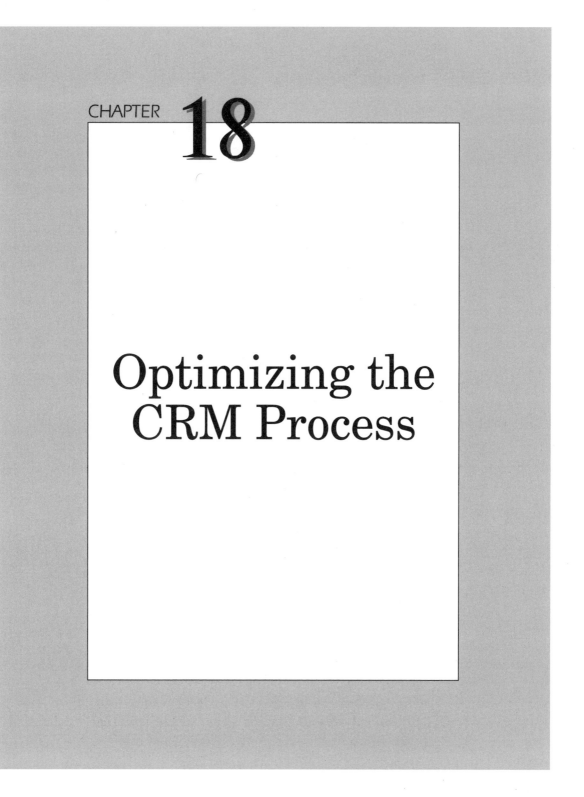

CHAPTER **18**

Optimizing the CRM Process

Introduction

All customers are not created equal. Some are profitable; some are unprofitable; some will become highly profitable; some will become unprofitable; and some will never be profitable throughout their entire customer lifecycle. Optimization is the science of "optimally" determining what can be done to make a customer as profitable as possible for as long as possible.

Despite the business opportunity, optimization techniques are not generally applied to customer relationship management, or sales and marketing. Optimization is thought to be too esoteric a science to be applied in situations in which intuition can be as important in making the right decision as cold hard facts about customer behavior. In fairness to the skeptics, it is harder to apply optimization to customer relationship management than it is to other areas of business. But, with advances in database technology, data mining, and the CRM systems themselves, optimization can be applied more often than not. When it is applied, it can be the single most important technique in your CRM system for increasing customer profitability.

Figure 18-1 shows an example of how a particular promotion as part of the CRM process could be optimized.

Improved Customer Profitability through Optimization

What Is Optimization?

Many people are familiar with the general idea of optimization, but may not know that there is a science of optimization that is available to businesses today. Typically, optimization is applied to problems where there is a well-defined measure of success. For instance, optimization is applied to airline scheduling (although it may be hard to believe that there is anything optimal about flight times). Constraints such as having the right plane ready at the right time

Figure 18-1

Profit of a particular promotion as part of an overall CRM process can be optimized by targeting the right consumers with the right promotion. In this case, $1.3 million can be achieved by targeting the top two million consumers from a data mining predictive model.

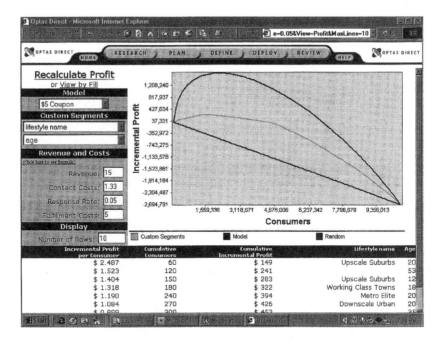

in the right airport to accommodate a given scheduled flight can be difficult because the cost of leaving an airplane idle for several hours when it could be in flight could mean critical dollars saved or lost. Sometimes, the constraints can be more complex when the difficulties of scheduling a well-rested crew is included. Sometimes, the constraints for optimization are difficult to accommodate, no matter what system you are using. For instance, in the early days of the airline industry, all stewardesses from India needed to be home to sleep in their home country each and every day. This constraint needed to be added in to all of the other constraints to provide an optimal schedule for the Indian airline.

It can be difficult to conserve fuel and optimally serve the customers. For example, hubs are convenient for airlines as places where they can congregate passengers in order to more efficiently have full flights. But the multiple hops they produce for travelers who mostly prefer direct flights can also have an effect on customer satisfaction and hence on customer profitability. Also, each schedule that is produced needs to also allow for some error. For instance, if the schedule is perfectly optimized, but a thunderstorm occurs in Boston that closes the airport for 45 minutes, the scheduling should be able to accommodate it without breaking down and causing massive delays throughout the system.

Although optimization is used in marketing today, it is used only within well-defined problems such as optimally conserving mailing costs for a direct-mail package while optimally mailing to only those people who are most likely to be interested in the offer. Determining what is optimal is performed by using data mining to build models to forecast what a customer will do in the future. In some ways, this is similar to other business-optimization problems such as airline scheduling. The behavior of the system cannot be so easily controlled, however—although an airline can mostly control when its flights are ready to take off, a direct marketer has limited control over whether a consumer will react positively to an intervention, and not all data is available for all consumers.

Optimization is used on small islands of applications within marketing, but the function of marketing is still viewed as more art than science. Customer relationship management is an attempt to bring some science to the marketing function. Overall marketing is still viewed as something that cannot be optimized, however, because there is so much that needs to be done by gut feel, by hunch, or by understanding larger global issues than are captured in the customer database.

The question about whether marketing is ready for optimization is really a question of whether marketing is "clean" enough so that the way that it is performed can be modified (hopefully improved) and the results then measured. The fundamental difficulty in marketing as it differs from scheduling airplanes is that with airplanes, success or failure can be measured in a much more real sense. The time airplanes spend idle on the runway, the fuel cost, and fuel consumption are all relatively easy to measure. With much of marketing, the game is harder to play because success or failure is harder to measure. The old adage, "I know I'm wasting half of my advertising budget, but I just don't now which half," is a good example of the promise and problems of applying the technique of optimization to customer relationship management.

If a thirty-second commercial during the Super Bowl costs $750,000, how do you know if that money is well spent? Even if you could collect all possible data, you would need to make some hard decisions about how to measure. For instance, if a person saw the commercial, did not buy within 30 days of having seen the commercial, but did buy a year later, how would you measure the impact of that $750,000 marketing investment? Is it based on the revenue that occurred one year later, or is that an independent event and the consumer would have made the purchase with or without investment in the Super Bowl commercial?

If optimization is going on within marketing, it is not necessarily performed where it is needed most. Instead, it is performed where the results can be most easily measured. It is similar to the old man on the darkened city street who was looking beneath a street lamp for the keys that had just dropped. When a passerby offered to help him look and asked if he had dropped his keys near the street lamp the man replied: "No, I dropped them over there, but there is no light over there. So, I am looking under the street lamp here where I can see."

Why Not Optimize Customer Relationships?

To many people, speaking of optimizing customer relationships or optimizing marketing processes doesn't make sense. How could you optimize something like a customer relationship or overall customer profitability? There are so many things that could go wrong. So many intangibles that can't be measured. So much of the win or lose is dependent on the creative nature of the marketing people, a good slogan, or a new color scheme. It would be like trying to predict and optimize next year's fashions based on a mathematical mode. Many believe that it is not possible. But why not? What makes it so hard?

As we have shown, optimization is already being used on certain small islands of functionality within the customer relationship process—mostly around the "lamp posts" (where the results can be seen and measured). These islands of optimization include the following:

■ Targeted marketing

■ Fraud detection

■ Attrition prediction

■ Cross-selling

■ Acquisition of new customers

To Optimize Something, You Must Have Control over It

One of the most important points in optimizing something is that you must be able to not only measure the effect of your changes, but also to affect the changes in the first place. This is true, for instance, in the optimization performed in nature. The genetic material (DNA) makes a change in the way an organism develops, and then the process of survival of the fittest measures the value of that change and determines whether the change is for better or for worse.

In classical marketing, this has been difficult because it has been difficult to measure. (How do you really measure all of the impact of a television commercial campaign?) It has also been difficult to test for different effects. For instance, in the past it would have been difficult to test out different looks and feels for a catalog or a magazine ad. The cost of design and printing for different variations of the same ad would be cost-prohibitive. Today, however, it is not uncommon for companies to try a variety of different possible messages and artwork for the mailing of a catalog. It is possible today to control and differentiate the type of the marketing intervention that is being provided across many different delivery channels.

Why Now?

Optimization of customer relationships is now a possibility, whereas before it was not possible. This has occurred for three primary reasons:

- New technology and its maturation
- Data, and its collection and storage
- Changes in business processes

There are, however, some trends that are now taking place that will allow the use of optimization within customer relationship management to expand. Because optimization requires measurement, any tools that allow for better and more consistent measurement can now be used to improve marketing. There was a good reason why marketing couldn't be optimized in the past—it wasn't that it wasn't a good idea back then, and now it is a good idea. It was always a good idea, but now with the changes in the way that marketing is conducted, it is possible to perform optimization. The time is right also because of the maturation of several new technologies:

- Data warehousing
- Data mining
- OLAP
- World Wide Web

We are also seeing today a dramatic increase in the quantity and types of data that are being collected. Some of this increase is due to the technologies that allow for its collection and its storage, but the data itself comes from a wide variety of sources. The time has come for optimization in the marketing function because of changes in business processes:

- Data-based marketing
- Enterprise resources planning (ERP)
- Electronic commerce
- Customer relationship management

These business processes are critical for the possibility of marketing optimization. Data-based marketing was historically limited to direct mail campaigns; the only "database" part about it was the fact that the name and address of the recipient was stored in the database. Partly because of the ease with which direct mail can now be generated, data-based marketing has become more important. It is no longer broadcast marketing where the same marketing message is sent to the entire consumer base.

The move toward enterprise resource planning has also had an impact on the possibility of performing the optimization of customer relationships. Previously, ERP systems laid the foundation for supply chain optimization in much the same way that database marketing has laid the foundation necessary to support electronic order capture and front office support for the sales force and for telemarketing. New data sources are also improving marketing performance because customer relationships can be managed better only when there is more information. Some of this data comes directly out of ERP systems, which are excellent sources of cleaned data pertinent to customer behavior. Likewise, data captured from electronic commerce systems is also valuable in that the data captured is fairly well structured because it was always in electronic form. There are not issues involved in the manipulation of the data or the original data entry.

Finally, the business process of customer relationship management is also a driving factor in the timing of the use of optimization. CRM is important because of the great disparity between the cost of acquiring a new customer and that of holding onto a current customer. For some industries such as wireless communications (cell phones), the ratio between the two can be ten to one. Also, the value of a current customer may be much greater than that of a new customer because in many industries it can take several years before a customer begins to purchase at their full potential.

These business processes both lay the foundation for optimization as well as build a business mind set (through CRM) for the importance of an optimal marketing function because of the importance of the customer relationship and keeping it profitable.

Optimized CRM

Today, there are a lot of ways that marketing is performed. For instance, we notice that the data that is coming in about our customers comes in from a variety of sources. But, also note that there are a large number of marketing organizations that are not measurement-based at all.

These organizations generate television and radio advertising, mailings, magazine advertising, and a significant Web presence, and yet have no way of collecting the information—either about their customers as they are or even about how they had promoted to them. Therefore, a catalyst is necessary. In scientific terms, a catalyst in a chemical reaction speeds up a process that might well have occurred so slowly without the catalyst or that would, for all intents and purposes, not have happened at all.

We believe, then, that this scientific term is valuable for capturing any and all interventions that a marketing organization might take with their customer prospects. For instance, one catalyst might be the sending out of coupons to likely users of the product. Another catalyst might be a television commercial (not a particularly measurable catalyst). Another catalyst might be a sales call that is made on the prospect by a sales person.

Fundamentally, marketing and sales are relatively simple. Consider, in the broadest view, that every person or corporate entity in existence is a possible prospect if only the right set of catalysts could be applied. The first question then is the following: What is the right catalyst or sequence of catalysts to apply? This then begs the real question, which is the following: What is the most profitable catalyst that can be applied?

When viewed in this way, the seemingly unconstrained and complicated world of marketing and sales starts to look more like a system that could be optimized. There is a collection of data, there is something that you can do to change the system, and there is a way to measure the impact of that change. If you can do this, then you are in a situation in which you can begin to optimize by recognizing what has worked in the past and trying subtle variations on those successes. Each time, try to become more and more effective in creating a profitable customer relationship.

If we look at things this way, then there are really two different aspects of the optimization problem. The first is to come up with a selection of possible useful catalysts from which to choose, and the second is to optimally assign a catalyst based on what you learned from the past use of the catalysts. The first step is creative and exploratory; the second is analytical.

The Complete Loop

As we have stated before, in order to optimize, one must first be able to measure. Then, one must have the ability to try different actions in order to compare and contrast which method is better. If you cannot measure, you cannot differentiate between good and bad outcomes; if that is the case, then you cannot improve. Likewise, if your system cannot incrementally improve based on past experience to better handle future cases, then that also does not allow for optimization. If the system can be measured and options can be proposed, but there is no accountable action taken to test out that improved strategy, then the cycle of improvement is broken.

Like a three-legged stool, there are three important steps to the optimization process, as follows:

1. *Measure.*   See what happened.
2. *Predict.*   Figure out something else to try based on what happened.
3. *Act.*   Try it out.

From a marketing perspective, this translates into being able to measure the outcome of whatever marketing intervention is performed (sounds simple, but it is the toughest step). Then based, on those measurements, you can make a prediction about what will happen next and what changes in the marketing intervention might give useful results that could be measured (note that both good and bad results are useful if they shed light on the efficacy of the marketing intervention).

As an example of a company going out of its way to measure the value and the marketing of its product, consider the video distributor who provided users with two bins in which to return the movie that they had just rented. One bin would be used if they liked the movie. The other bin would be used if they didn't like it. A little bit of extra effort in order to measure the customer satisfaction is well worth the effort in order to get the feedback from the users.

If, however, the video retailer does not make use of this information to improve its product, then marketing optimization, even at its most basic level, cannot be performed. It is very much like the three-legged stool, with one of the legs missing.

Optimal CRM Process: Measure, Predict, Act

Optimizing the CRM process requires a business best practice that consists of three main steps and an architecture for implementing and supporting those steps. The steps are formally named: "measure," "predict," and "act." They represent the steps in a cycle of customer relationship management that is continuously improving. The methodology is general enough that it is applicable to the vast majority of customer management functions such as the following:

- *Cross-selling.*   Selling a new product to an existing customer
- *Acquisition.*   Acquiring new valuable customers
- *Retention.*   Retaining existing valuable customers

To achieve these goals of better customer management, there are a variety of processes that are used over and over again by the marketing organization:

- *Targeted marketing*
- *Lifetime value prediction*
- *Channel management.*   Matching the channel to the customer in the most profitable way

In marketing, there typically exists a certain set of interventions that can be performed against the customer or prospect. Often, this is a fixed list that has been handed down from marketing personnel. Usually, these are new creative offers that have been created based on feedback from customers, either directly through phone interviews or focus groups, or just from the experience of particular marketing managers. These marketing products, campaigns or anything else represent the available arsenal with which to motivate the customer to do more business. If this arsenal of interventions already exists, then the remaining questions are relatively simple: "What do I do to whom, and when?" Assuming that there is some regularly scheduled launching of marketing programs (let's say, monthly), the question can become: "What should I do to whom?" Not doing anything should also be a viable intervention/catalyst, as well as anything else that might be used.

If you want to do a good job of answering the question: What should I do to whom? It pays to create a model of what the likely outcome would be if the variety of different interventions were to be applied. This is the predict step (based on past experience). This is what the technology of data mining is used for.

For a complete marketing optimization system, whatever is predicted must also be measured. For instance, it doesn't help to correctly predict customer attrition if you don't know what the value of a saved customer is. Also, it is important that the step of action is within the infrastructure of running the complete marketing optimization system. For instance, many of the classical decision support or business intelligence systems will leave off on the action step. These systems will often provide useful information about how to improve the marketing process to the customer, but the results are delivered in the forms of graphs or reports that a senior manager can look at and better understand their business. In some way, the CEO can act based on the report or the graph, but typically it happens outside of the systems that should be recording the purpose of the action and the deployment of the action. The CEO may be influenced by what they've seen in the results of the decision support system, but their action is "non-recordable" and non-measurable. For marketing optimization to realize the full potential, this action step must be recorded within the same system that provides the measurement and produces the predicted future behavior.

What Marketing Optimization Is Not

Marketing optimization is not data warehousing. Marketing optimization is an infrastructure in the same sense that data warehousing is an infrastructure, but along with that infrastructure comes a set of best practices that guide the use of that infrastructure specifically along the lines of business issues. Marketing optimization is top down in the sense that it starts with the overall marketing needs (which, in summary, is improved customer profitability), and defines the infrastructure and then the data, which is necessary to support those business problems. Data warehousing is most often created in a bottom-up fashion, starting with the infrastructure (mostly building an infrastructure to collect all available data) and then determining the business problems that could benefit from this infrastructure. For this reason, data warehousing projects are typically quite vast because they start with the attempt to collect all available data. Marketing-optimization systems can be much smaller and easier to manage, and more quickly provide a measurable return on investment because only the infrastructure necessary to support the best-practices methodology and the solution of the business problems is created.

Marketing optimization is not one-to-one marketing. Marketing optimization can be used to make one-to-one marketing more profitable per customer, but the emphasis of one-to-one marketing on individual consumers is somewhat at odds with the mentality of marketing optimization that operates often times at a higher level. It is typically at a level of segmentation rather than at individual customers. The main reason for this is that in order to measure customer behavior to a significant level, you need more than one customer as data input to measure. In another sense, one-to-one marketing also increases the number of possible interventions that can be placed on the customer. But many of the examples given for one-to-one marketing may be so limited in terms of the scope of customers receiving the intervention that measurement may not be valid. Or, as in many of the cases and as in the classical case of business intelligence and decision support, actions may be taken but they are not recordable or measurable. If what you did isn't recorded, then its effect can't be measured and it can't be changed because you don't know what you did in the first place.

Using Data Mining to Optimize Your CRMS

There are really two forms of optimization that are possible. One, in which there is a well-defined value that is being optimized—such as the total number of days that parts for a John Deere tractor sit at the factory after being purchased and shipped from the supplier before they are used to build a new tractor. Or the number of days that completed tractors sit in inventory before they are shipped for sale.

This measure of value can be calculated and optimized fairly accurately because the processes that control the time to build and to ship are fairly well understood, although complex. The other class of optimization problems is not only complex but also much less "causal" in that what affects and "causes" the increase or decrease in the important measure of value is not as direct or predictable. An example of this type of problem would be the typical class of problems in the CRM space. And this class of problems, in which it is difficult to optimize via techniques that make use of causal models, is often difficult because there are human beings in the loop who have very complex behavior. They can react in completely different ways, depending on small differences in the way that the system is constructed.

For example, as you have seen in the cellular telephone example, trying to "optimally" reduce churn by offering customers a lucrative offer of lower rates actually had the unforeseen consequence of increasing churn. Just the effect of sending the offer caused the customers to evaluate all of their options and, because there were competitive options, they moved to another carrier despite the better rates provided in the offer. Without a viable competitive offer, the outcome of the churn-reduction program could have been completely opposite. In a causal system, either these small changes result in small changes in the total value, or they can be controlled to the degree where they are effectively non-existent.

Often, companies are sending out multiple messages to their customers or prospects at the same time. These messages are used to overcome a variety of barriers that the consumer may be facing or feel that they are facing in making a buying decision for the company's product. Matching the right message to the right consumer can be as important as determining the message and the barriers in the first place.

Optimization Techniques

If you think simply about the training process in the data mining technique called neural networks, you could view it as a game of trying to find the best possible combination of link weights for a given network architecture (for example, the standard three-layer, fully connected between layers). The network is in fact fully defined by the numbers assigned to each link (for a network with five inputs, three hidden and two output nodes, there would be 21 links ($5 \times 3 + 3 \times 2$) and just 21 numbers that defined the full behavior of the neural network). The trick in training is to find those right numbers and this is what the back propagation algorithm accomplishes by changing the numbers each time to improve the accuracy of the network.

Back propagation is not the only way of determining these link weights, however. Genetic algorithms have also been deployed to try to find the best possible link weights. In Figure 18-2, a population of neural networks is being evolved. From one generation to the next, some networks do better and some do worse. Over time, however, the best solution in the population gets better and better.

Genetic algorithms simulate natural evolution on the computer. To do so, they simulate the DNA, which in nature describes how to

Figure 18-2
Optimization with
Genetic Algorithms.

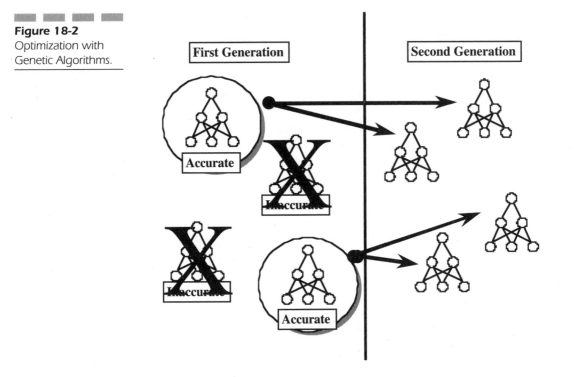

uniquely grow the animal or plant. The analogue to DNA in genetic algorithms is the list of numbers that represent the link weights in the neural network. In some ways, this list is like a chromosome, and each number is like a gene. Taken together, all of these simulated genes fully describe how to build the given neural network. In genetic algorithms, there are good lists of link weights that represent highly accurate neural networks and there are poor lists of link weights that represent neural networks that are no more predictive than random guessing. Genetic algorithms generate many different genetic guesses at the right link weights, and create a population of different neural networks. Survival-of-the-fittest techniques are then used to weed out the poorly performing networks and reward the more accurate ones.

If a network is particularly accurate, it will be rewarded by allowing it to "reproduce"—by making copies of itself with slight variations. These modifications to the link weights are made at random like genetic mutations, and sometimes result in improved performance. Those that improve continue to be modified until highly accurate link weights are evolved.

Genetic algorithms have proved to be an interesting way to determine link weights for neural networks but they have not, as of yet, shown themselves to generate better solutions or even comparable solutions in less time than back propagation does. They also have a problem of getting "stuck" on a suboptimal solution very early in the training, and can never find a better one.

Simulated Annealing and Neural Networks

We have used the analogy that back propagation is using a technique similar to what one does in climbing to the top of a hill. It is constantly trying to move in the direction that improves the network as much as possible, similar to the way one would walk in the direction that is most uphill if one were trying to get to the top of the hill. For neural networks, this means modifying the link weights the most, which will have the biggest impact on improving the performance of the network.

This art of hill climbing is an area that physicists have been interested in for years. In their case, they are looking at how metals cool and materials form crystals, but many of the same effects appear in all three areas. Because of the similarities between searching for the optimal solution and physics, several simulations have been tried in order to speed up the performance of neural network training. One technique is called simulated annealing.

Annealing is the process of cooling a metal or a glass at the right rates of speed, in order to minimize the number of defects that are formed in the structure of the material. Simulated annealing borrows the idea of heating and cooling a metal from the real world and applies it to removing the defects from a neural network. The idea is pretty simple: "Make large changes in the weights of the links early on in training; then slowly decrease the amount of change made to the network so that it can zero in on the best solution."

Allowing for these large changes in the link weights early on in the training process corresponds to a high temperature in a metal where the metal is just barely solid and is very malleable. Likewise, the neural network is "malleable" in the early part of the training, allowing for the trial of many very different values in the link weights. As time goes on, the changes in the link weights become smaller and smaller, and the removal of errors is done at a finer and finer level. The process is analogous to looking around the world for the highest mountain ranges before getting into the details of which particular outcropping of rock at the summit of Mount Everest or K2 is a foot higher than the other.

CHAPTER 19

Overview of Data Mining and CRM Tool Markets

Introduction

The data mining tools market is emerging from its infancy. Many of the tools described here are still in their first release, and several were in the beta stage at the time of this printing.

The situation is even more complicated in the CRM market, which is frequently considered to be a part and parcel of e-commerce and e-business, and thus moves at the Web speed. The CRM market, even more than the data mining tool market, is characterized by multiple vendors that are focusing on defining the market itself and their position in this market. This confusion is driven even further by the very dynamic nature of the market itself, which is undergoing a clearly visible activity of vendor consolidation, mergers, and acquisitions. Despite all these challenges, the market is maturing and the vendors are making significant progress in tool functionality, usability, and manageability.

The first part of this chapter deals with data mining packaged applications. These applications are based on several data mining techniques integrated inside better tools. Combined with best practices, well-defined methodologies and processes are finding their way into companies' production environments, in which data mining is becoming a part of an institutionalized process that includes organizational learning and growth.

Data Mining Marketplace

Let's consider the data mining marketplace from the point of view of a technology adoption curve. Here, the early adopters use leading edge technology to obtain a competitive advantage; as the technology matures, it is adopted by more companies and inserted into normal business processes, first as an add-on and then in a more integrated fashion. Also, the areas of applicability for data mining tools are growing larger and larger. For example, White Oak Technologies, Inc. (a Maryland-based data mining company) has been granted permission by the Federal Election Commission to sell its Campaign Miner system that discovers irregularities in federal political contributions. Nortel has developed a fraud-detection package, SuperSleuth Fraud Advisor, which employs neural network technologies.

The data mining tools industry, as opposed to the data mining techniques, is at the stage of immaturity and is trying to define the market and justify its existence. That's why we can see that the data mining tools market is being affected by the following:

- Continued tools integration by leveraging complementary technologies (e.g., OLAP)

- Emergence of vertical packaged applications and/or data mining components for application development

- Widely adopted strategies of partnership between data mining tools vendors and vendors of comprehensive solution providers (systems integrators; enterprise-scale vendors such as IBM, NCR, Oracle, Microsoft). For example, Oracle has selected several data mining partners as part of its Oracle Warehouse Initiative including Angoss, DataMind, DataSage, Information Discovery, SPSS, SRA International, and Thinking Machines

- Continued integration of data-visualization tools and techniques

Taxonomy of Data Mining Tools

We can divide the entire data mining tool market into the three major groups: general-purpose tools, integrated DSS/OLAP/data mining tools, and rapidly growing, application-specific tools.

The general-purpose tools occupy the larger and more mature segment of the market. They are by definition non-application-specific, and their scope is horizontal in nature. These tools include the following

- SAS Enterprise Miner
- IBM Intelligent Miner
- Unica PRW
- SPSS Clementine

- SGI MineSet
- Oracle Darwin
- Angoss KnowledgeSeeker

The integrated data mining tool segment addresses a very real and compelling business requirement of having a single multi-function, decision-support tool that can provide management reporting, online analytical processing, and data mining capabilities within a common framework. Examples of these integrated tools include Cognos Scenario and Business Objects.

The application-specific tools segment is rapidly gaining momentum, and the vendors in this space try to differentiate themselves by offering business solutions rather than a technology searching for a solution. The scope of these tools is by definition vertical in nature. Among these tools are the following

- KD1 (focuses on retail)
- Options & Choices (focuses on the insurance industry)
- HNC (focuses on fraud detection)
- Unica Model 1 (focused on marketing)

Tool Assessment: Attributes and Methodology

All these factors make it even more difficult to provide a unified description of the available data mining tools. Therefore, in general, the data mining tools can be characterized using the following attributes:

- *Product maturity and company strength.*   Due to the general immaturity of the commercial market for data mining tools, this category describes products that have been around for more than a year, as well as some products that were released within a few month of this writing.

- *Platforms and architecture.* Support for a wide variety of commercially available platforms; support for multi-tiered client/server model. The scaleability goal is to achieve near linear speedup and scaleup at run time as the amount of data (database size), number of variables, and the number of connected users grow.

- *Data interfaces.* Tool's capability to access relational databases, flat files, and other data formats.

- *Data mining capabilities including Techniques, algorithms and analytical applications.* The number of data mining techniques (ANN, CART, Rule induction, etc.) with a common user interface that the tool can support; an ability to create and compare multiple models; and an ability to support a number of different types of analysis including classification, prediction, and association detection.

- *Data manipulation.* Capability to transform and categorize continuous variables, create new variables, handle dates and time, handle missing values, etc.

- *Model (specification, interpretation, evaluation, deployment).* This category evaluates a tool on its capability to do the following:

  - Specify the model automatically or manually by a user
  - Explain the results and define measures of confidence (i.e., classification probabilities, confidence ranges, etc.)
  - Assess the model results by degree of fit
  - Report on the contribution of each variable to the model, on the lift, etc.
  - Deploy the model to score source databases
  - Extract rules from the model
  - Package extracted rules into a standard form (e.g., SQL code, procedural statements)

- Performance

  - *Accuracy*.   Prediction accuracy is based on the error rate of the prediction sample; the accuracy of the model can be measured by the lift

  - *Processing efficiency*.   Run-time optimized implementation of the algorithms

- *User interfaces*.   This category looks to see whether the tool supports a novice and/or an expert user; and provides support for the following:

  - *Business templates*.   Capability to provide pre-packaged, front-end templates to support specific business packages (e.g., target marketing, credit scoring, fraud detection)

  - *Metadata interface*.   Capability to support semantic mapping function; metadata access to code tables for categorical values; access to extraction, transformation, and migration rules; business view definition of the model's output

- Manageability

  - *Complexity control*.   This is one of the ways to improve model's generalization, and thus make the model more manageable. For example, using too many free parameters may lead to overfitting (discussed previously); this complexity can be controlled by weight decay. CART decision tree algorithms use a pruning phase to reduce the complexity of the tree model.

  - *Robustness*.   Tool's reliability and availability; capability to rapidly recover from the point of failure; instrumentation of key components in order to be integrated into a systems management framework (e.g., BMC Patrol, Tivoli TME10, etc.)

  - *Customization*.   Tools' capability to provide an open, flexible, and extensible architecture with published application programming interfaces and user exit points that allow the creation of user-specific, custom decision-support applications, as well as integration with other applications

Wherever possible, we'll discuss the tools using these categories. However, because the goal of this chapter is to provide a general overview of the leading data mining tools, the performance attributes that can be obtained only by doing an exhaustive product evaluation using real data will not be included in the discussion. (Unless the vendor provides a published benchmark or a user survey information about the tool's performance.)

Tool Evaluation

The tools discussed in some detail in this chapter include Clementine (SPSS), Cognos 4Thought, Cognos Scenario, Darwin (Oracle), Database Mining Workstation (HNC), Decision Series (NeoVista), Enterprise Miner (SAS), Intelligent Miner (IBM), KnowlegeSeeker and Knowledge Studio (Angoss), and Model 1 and PRW (Unica). Other tools are discussed very briefly. The level of detail available for some of these tools is limited due to the lack of product maturity. These tools are discussed in alphabetical order.

Clementine (SPSS)

Overview   Clementine is a data mining application tool from SPSS. This tool combines an intuitive graphical user interface with multiple types of analysis techniques, including neural networks, association rules, and rule-induction techniques. These analytical capabilities are offered in an easy-to-use visual programming environment.

The graphical metaphor used by Clementine is that of dragging, dropping, and connecting functional nodes on a screen. There are nodes for data access, data manipulation, data visualization, machine learning, and model analysis. The model development process consists of choosing the proper nodes from a pallet, placing them on the screen, and connecting the nodes.

Clementine has a rich set of data-access capabilities, including flat files and relational databases (via ODBC). What's more, Clementine has the capability to make the modeling results persistent by writing them back into an ODBC-compliant DBMS.

Input-data manipulations include match merges and the ability to derive new fields.

Clementine's data-visualization capabilities include scattergrams, line plots, and Web analysis.

Clementine is available on Intel Pentium systems running Windows NT, HP 9000 series running HPUX 10 and above, Silicon Graphics running IRIX, Sun SPARC running Solaris 2.x, and Digital ALPHA running Digital UNIX 3.x or VMS 6.x.

Data Access, Manipulation, and Preprocessing   Clementine can import delimited text files, comma-separated value files, and fixed record files (ASCII). Other data sources are available via a supported ODBC interface. Major relational database systems, including Oracle, Sybase, Informix, and CA-Ingres, are accessible via ODBC.

Clementine's data-manipulation capabilities include the following:

- Merging of records via record sequence
- Data balancing by increasing the proportion of records with certain characteristics
- User-defined aggregation
- Filtering of extraneous records
- New field derivation using user-defined formulas and logical operators
- Data-sampling capabilities, including first or last N records, 1 in N sampling, and random sampling

Data Mining Techniques, Algorithms, and Applications Clementine supports rule-induction algorithms, neural networks (including Kohonen networks), and association rules:

- Clementine's rule-induction algorithms are easy to understand: once trained, the algorithm creates a decision tree representing the rule. A frequent process that follows is to locate important variables at the top levels of the tree and then train a neural network with these variables.

- Clementine's neural networks are offered in a variety of topologies and training methods. A default one-hidden-layer network can be compared with a more complex two-hidden layer network for a performance assessment.

- Clementine offers Kohonen neural networks to solve clustering problems.*

- Association rules, as the name implies, associate a particular conclusion with a set of attributes. Associations can be found between any attributes, which proves to be very useful for applications like market basket analysis.

Clementine supports customer profiling, time series analysis, market basket analysis, and fraud detection.

Working with the Tool Model is specified in a visual programming environment using a connected nodes metaphor. There are dialog boxes with modeling nodes that help provide some control over the algorithms and training methods.

Clementine allows users to see what inputs are of predictive importance within the model, even though neural networks are inherently difficult to interpret. The decision tree algorithms support an interactive, easy-to-use rule browser.

Clementine offers a range of functions for model evaluation. These include an analysis node that reports the number of correct diagnoses made for the model input; confidence values ranging from 0 to 1; and matrix mode, in which a cross-tabulation among selected fields can be performed by the user.

---

*Kohonen neural networks are unsupervised learning networks that contain two layers of neurons: input layer and output layer. Every node in the input layer is connected to every node of the output layer. Although initially the weights of all connections are random, as the input is propagated through the network, the output nodes with the strongest response are considered the winners, and the weights are adjusted to reinforce the winning connection.

Clementine can export decision trees, neural networks, and Kohonen networks as a C code. After a model has been constructed in Clementine, it can be exported as a C code to be deployed in an outside environment. For example, if a neural network model has to be exported, Clementine will export three files: a header file, a function file, and a network definition file. Rules generated by a rules-induction algorithm can also be exported.

Clementine's visual programming environment is suitable for a novice. The modeling sequence is clearly presented, and various options enhance flexibility. An expert user who may want to manipulate Clementine's algorithms does not have that freedom. However, there are some options in the neural networks to adjust the learning rate and to control the pruning in the decision tree algorithms. Clementine does not offer business templates. Metadata interface was not available at the time of this writing.

Conclusion   Clementine is a strong product. In published customer benchmarks, it performs well both in terms of scaleability, predictive accuracy, and processing time. Overall, Clementine is positioned to be well-suited for both small-scale and large-scale analysis implementations.

4Thought and Scenario (Cognos)

Overview   Cognos has enhanced its position as one of the leaders in the OLAP marketplace by introducing two data mining tools to its portfolio: 4Thought and Scenario. These tools offer data-mining capabilities by exploiting neural networks and CHAID techniques. In general, these tools are supported on all Cognos platforms and are especially targeted for the Windows environment. Both tools can acquire data from spreadsheets, databases, and ASCII text files.

4Thought is built to handle a variety of business problems including price optimization, demand forecasting, and performance prediction and measurement. 4Thought uses *multilayer perceptron* (MLP) neural network technology, which is well-suited to analyze problems dealing with non-linear forms, noisy data, and small data sets. The two major analyses offered by 4Thought are time series analysis and customer profiling. Time series analysis looks for trends based on periodic behavior, whereas customer profiling deals with the demographic data to, for example, predict whether a customer will purchase a particular product.

Scenario is designed for classification and association problems; it can find relationships between variables in a data set. Scenario uses *Chi-squared Automatic Interaction Detection* (CHAID), and can produce multi-way splits for predictor variables. Scenario offers different analysis strategies, automatic sampling and tree generation. However, Scenario is not designed to deal with categorical target variables. Scenario is strong in data exploration and visualization.

Both Scenario's and the 4Thought's strength is their comprehensive and intuitive user interface, which is targeted mostly at a novice user. It uses graphing for a univariable analysis or a decision tree metaphor, and provides a good visual representation for data variations between segments, for trends analysis, and factor correlation. Scenario has a template to analyze profit information from competitive and seasonal data.

Cognos stated that it will integrate 4Thought and the Scenario with its PowerPlay (OLAP) and Impromptu (reporting) applications.

The Cognos products are supported on Wintel platforms running Microsoft Windows operating systems (Windows 95 or higher, and/or NT).

Data Access, Manipulation, and Preprocessing 4Thought can import data in the form of Excel spreadsheets, Lotus 1 2 3 files, SPSS files, delimited text files, comma-separated value files, fixed-width files. Additionally, access to relational databases is supported via ODBC driver from the Q&E database library.

Scenario can import data from flat files, Excel spreadsheets, and dBase tables. Also, Scenario can use Cognos Impromptu to import data from Borland Interbase, Centura SQLBase, Informix, Microsoft SQL Server, Oracle, Sybase SQL Server; and major database gateways including MDI DB2 Gateway, OmniSQL Gateway, Oracle Transparent Gateway, and Sybase Net Gateway.

Data-manipulation capabilities include the following:

- Sorting
- Missing value replacement (with a preceding value or using interpolation)
- Text string-to-numeric value converting
- Automatic blank-to-zero (and reverse) converting
- Filtering of extraneous and/or outlier records
- Limited data sampling capabilities (4Thought can support random sampling, but stratified sampling is not available)

Data Mining Techniques, Algorithms, and Applications
4Thought uses *multi-layer perceptron* (MLP) neural network technology, which generates input-to-output mapping based on computations of interconnected nodes. Each node's output is a non-linear function of the weighted sum of inputs from the nodes in preceding layers.

Scenario uses a decision tree algorithm based on CHAID. It produces rules that can be applied to unclassified data sets to predict which records will have a desired outcome. Scenario's decision tree algorithm is flexible enough to give the users an option of making a split on any variable, or a split based on a statistical significance.

Scenario supports classification and association problems and can be used in customer profiling and market segmentation. 4Thought is best-suited for time-series analysis, predictive modeling, and forecasting problems. Both tools allow graphical analysis of raw data through line, bar and scatter charts. Scenario offers graph view and tree view, both relying on the same general information. Scenario can handle binary, continuous, and categorical predictor variables; but it can only use numeric variable as targets.

Scenario offers three analysis strategies:

- *Certify mode.*   Requires at least 1000 records, half of which are held for testing, and it is aimed at producing results with high confidence.
- *Test mode.*   Requires fewer records, uses one-third of these for testing, and in general offers less-stringent criteria for grouping.

■ *Explore mode.* Doesn't have a minimum record requirement, and is designed for the initial data exploration.

Working with the Tool In Scenario, the model is specified in a visual programming environment by using a wizard. Scenario automatically chooses variable types, and allows the user to sample the data and partition the data into training and test samples. As was mentioned previously, Scenario offers three analysis strategies: Certify, Test, and Explore. Scenario can create a tree automatically, or let the user make every split in the tree. The user can bin continuous variables easily—Scenario produces a list of rank-ordered, statistically significant variables; and can split automatically on the highest ranking variable.

4Thought allows the user to specify the neural network model by first deciding whether it's for the time series analysis. The user decides on the nature of the time series (days, weeks, months, years, or user-defined). For both time series and predictive modeling analysis, the user creates the model via the Specify Model dialog box. The user has a flexibility of choosing a single or double layer network. 4Thought offers two modes of model testing to decide when to stop:

■ *Simple Test.* The tool partitions the data into training and test groups, and uses a test group throughout the training phase to determine the termination point.

■ *Full Test.* The tool constructs multiple models and tries to find an optimal stopping point.

4Thought provides the user with a graphical interpretation (a scattergram of the model versus actual data), as well as a dynamic listing of the critical variables. Scenario provides a graphical representation of the tree that is easy to interpret.

In Scenario, whether a graph or a tree view is used, the user can view summary statistics such as mean, median, standard deviation, etc. 4Thought offers a full statistical report, cross-section report, and Scenario report. The latter report allows the user to specify the values of all input variables to return the model's expected output response.

Scenario-built models are not yet exportable, but the follow-on versions are planned to have rules export capabilities. 4Thought can work in conjunction with Excel, Lotus 1 2 3, and SPSS; and can deploy a trained model as a mathematical function in any of these environments.

Conclusion   Both the 4Thought and Scenario expand Cognos' decision-support capabilities and provide some data mining functionality. In published customer benchmarks, Scenario shows good results and a user-friendly interface. 4Thought is reported to get reasonable ratings on performance and accuracy.

Darwin (Oracle)

Overview   Darwin, which was often considered to be one of the premier data mining tools, appears to justify its reputation. Recently, Oracle acquired Darwin from Thinking Machines, Inc. to enhance its product offering—especially in the CRM space, where data mining (as discussed previously) can play a critical role. The following discussion is based on Darwin features, as developed and marketed by Thinking Machines. (Oracle may decide to change any of the features, components, and the architecture of the tool.)

Darwin data mining tool set was designed as a complex product containing three data mining tools: neural networks, decision tree, and K-nearest neighbor. The *Darwin neural network tool* (Darwin-Net) provides a comprehensive set of functions for model building. It can handle both categorical and continuous predictor and target variables, and can be used for classification, prediction, and forecasting problems.

The decision tree tool (DarwinTree) uses CART algorithms, and can be used for classification problem-solving with categorical and continuous variables. K-nearest neighbor tool (DarwinMatch) can be used for classification problem-solving with categorical dependent variables, and categorical and continuous predictor variables.

Although each of the component tools has some deficiencies, Darwin includes a full set of functions for model evaluation. It produces summary statistics, confusion matrices, and lift tables for all types of models.

Darwin offers relatively strong user interfaces for novices and experts alike, although the interfaces appear to be better suited for an expert user.

Coming from a company that is known as one of the first makers of massively parallel computers, Darwin has a strong advantage in processing efficiency and scaleability. Its algorithms are optimized for parallel computations, and are flexible enough to run on parallel and serial architectures. This capability clearly didn't escape Oracle's attention, and it is positioned to help Oracle to become a premier vendor of database and application products that can scale to a large global enterprise.

Darwin is designed as a client/server system, with the server platform ranging from uniprocessors to SMPs, to massively parallel processors including Wintel systems running Windows NT; as well as UNIX-based products from Sun Microsystems, HP, IBM, NCR, and Compaq/Digital.

Data Access, Manipulation, and Preprocessing Darwin can import fixed length and delimited data from flat (ASCII) files and from relational databases via ODBC. Internally, data is stored in a proprietary format that can be effectively laid out in a multiprocessing system.

Darwin's data-manipulation capabilities include the following:

- Merging capability for separate datasets
- Dropping variables from a dataset
- Defining a variable type (e.g., categorical, ordered)
- Converting a serial dataset into a parallel dataset
- Data sampling and partitioning

Data Mining Techniques, Algorithms, and Applications The main algorithms supported at the press time are neural networks, decision tree, and K-nearest neighbor.

The neural network-training algorithms include back propagation, steepest descent, modified Newton, and several others. Transfer functions include sigmoid, hypertangent, and linear.

The decision tree uses CART algorithms that can automatically prune the tree by choosing the number of subtrees to be considered in the analysis.

The K-nearest neighbor algorithm is based on *memory-based reasoning* (MBR) technique. It predicts a dependent variable value, based on the responses of the K closest matching records in the training set, where the closeness of the neighbor is determined by minimizing the weighted Euclidean distance between the variables.

The Darwin neural network can be used for building predictive and forecasting models, and can handle categorical and continuous variables. The decision tree and K nearest neighbor tools can be used for the classification problems.

Working with the Tool   Darwin provides a rich set of options to specify the model. For the neural network, for example, Darwin allows to specify network architecture, topology, transfer functions, training algorithm, cost function, learning mode, and the maximum number of training iterations. These options are aimed at the expert user.

Even though neural networks are inherently difficult to interpret. Darwin offers a summary of the model architecture, topology, algorithms, and functions. The decision tree component describes the model as a set of simple if-then rules that can be examined by the user.

Darwin provides a comprehensive set of functions for model evaluation, including reports on error statistics, lists of misclassification errors, comparison reports of predicted and actual outcome, confusion matrix, and a lift table.

Conclusion   Darwin's advantage is in supporting multiple algorithms (with the plans to add genetic algorithms and fuzzy logic). It can run on several platforms in a client/server configuration, where the server can be a uni-processor, symmetric multiprocessor, or a massively-parallel processor. In the case of a multiprocessor server, Darwin can take advantage of the hardware scaleability features. In published customer benchmarks, Darwin demonstrated strong performance and scaleability. Overall, Darwin is positioned to be well suited for medium- and large-scale implementations. For example, recently Darwin was selected for large-scale customer relationship/loyalty applications by GTE and Credit Suisse.

Database Mining Workstation (HNC)

Overview   HNC is one of the most successful data mining companies. Its *Database Mining Workstation* (DMW) is a neural network tool that is widely-accepted for credit card fraud analysis applications. DMW consists of Windows-based software applications and a custom processing board. Other HNC products include Falcon and ProfitMax applications for financial services, and the *Advanced Telecommunications Abuse Control System* (ATACS) fraud-detection solution that HNC plans to deploy in the telecommunications industry.

DMW neural network supports back propagation neural network algorithm, and can operate in automatic and manual modes. Its model can be interpreted using comprehensive statistics and the functionality to compute correlations among predictor variables and their sensitivity relative to a dependent variable.

DMW offers a number of user-defined options that allow for a significant flexibility in algorithm modification, data preparation, and manipulation functions. DMW effectively handles categorical and continuous variables, and can be used for prediction, classification, and forecasting problems.

DMW offers interfaces for both novice and experienced users, including advanced tuning options and a scripting facility. DMW also offers a business template that is used for direct marketing campaigns.

DMW has earned a reputation of generating accurate and effective predictive model. Its processing performance and scaleability are sufficient to support major credit card-processing requirements.

Data Access, Manipulation, and Preprocessing DMW product directly supports fixed-length ASCII files. The product is shipped and integrated with DBMS/COPY utility (Conceptual Software, Inc.). This utility can convert major DBMS, statistical and spreadsheet formats into a fixed-length ASCII format suitable for DMW.

DMW data-manipulation capabilities include the following:

- Dropping variables from a dataset
- User-defined variable type
- User-defined number of categories
- User-defined data-normalization function
- Automatic transformation of categorical variables into binary
- Missing value substitution
- User-selected data sampling

DMW data-transformation module maintains metadata that describes configuration parameters, variables and data types, normalization functions, number of unique values, and values assigned to missing data.

Data Mining Techniques, Algorithms, and Applications DMW employs a back propagation neural network algorithm. A user can specify a transfer function (logistic, threshold, linear, Gaussian, inverse tangent, or hyperbolic tangent), learning mode, and several other parameters.

DMW creates predictive models for classification, prediction, and forecasting problems. Its main analytical application is fraud detection (classification) for the credit card industry.

Working with the Tool DMW offers a significant flexibility in specifying the model. Model can be specified manually or automatically, by defining major architecture and topological parameters. In the automatic mode, DMW can also select relevant predictor variables by performing a clustering analysis on the variable domain.

DMW offers two functions for model interpretation: sensitivity analysis, and the help function that explains individual predictions (e.g., this function can be used to explain why a loan application was rejected and how strong the rejection factors were).

For every model, DMW produces a log file and a history file that contain information on how many evaluations were performed, evaluation statistics, and tables of correct versus incorrect predictions. Evaluation results can be put into an Excel spreadsheet for further analysis.

Although DMW cannot score external databases directly, it offers an API called DeployNet for deploying models built with DMW.

Conclusion   DMW is a strong, mature product, and has been very successful in market acceptance. Its fraud detection/classification application is used in real time to analyze credit card transactions. This is a strong testimonial for the product's scaleability and performance.

Decision Series (NeoVista)

Overview   NeoVista Solution's Decision Series is a comprehensive data mining tool. The company evolved from a massively parallel hardware vendor MasPar Corporation. Similar to Darwin, this resulted in a strong understanding and solid implementation of scaleable, high-performing data mining solution.

Decision Series is a data mining and knowledge discovery environment that provides an integrated set of algorithms for descriptive and predictive analysis. The algorithms are effectively implemented with a variety of controls for additional customization by the users. The analytical capabilities include clustering, association rules, neural networks, and decision trees. The Decision Series seamlessly integrates these algorithms with the data access and data transformation engine. Given the company background, the tool is highly tuned for parallel operations on SMP systems, where the company claims to achieve near linear scaleability. The proof of the tool's scaleability may be found in the fact that in its deployment in the retail industry for the inventory management (e.g., WalMart), the Decision Series is used on a weekly basis to analyze point-of-sales data at the detail (SKU) level. This is the data that represents around 70 gigabytes (GB).

From the usability point of view, Decision Series is currently positioned as a tool for the technically sophisticated user. NeoVista is developing easy-to-use GUI interfaces, and offers an expert consulting service (the specialists are called *Knowledge Discovery Engineers*, or KDE). They are often working on-site as part of a prototype or a pilot project.

Decision Series runs on a variety of UNIX platforms, including Sun Solaris, HP-UX, and Digital UNIX.

The software architecture of the tool consists of several components and is object-oriented by design. The data mining engines— DecisionNet, DecisionTree, DecisionCluster, and DecisionAR—are built on top of the data access and data transformation layer, implemented as another engine called DecsionAccess. The data mining engines inherit DecisionAccess properties and therefore can be easily linked together.

Data Access, Manipulation, and Preprocessing   Decision Series imports any data source in the ASCII format, with the DBMS capabilities being developed and integrated into the DecisionAccess engine. Decision Series maintains metadata in the proprietary file structures. These files can be read by one engine and then passed to the next. Information can be added, modified, and saved for future use.

Decision Series data-manipulation capabilities include the following:

- Conditioning to remove outliers
- Format conversions (integer to float, etc.)
- *Pivoting.*   Converting multiple records into a single record with unique columns
- *Encoding.*   Converting numeric and character data to a specified records layout
- *Data sampling capabilities.*   Including first or last N records, 1 in N sampling, range value, and random sampling

Data Mining Techniques, Algorithms, and Applications   Decision Series supports neural networks, decision trees, clustering, and association rules:

- *Neural networks algorithm.* It is implemented in the DecisionNet engine. It utilizes a three-layer, feed-forward network with a single input node for each transformed input field. The algorithm uses a proprietary network-training technique, and it is unique in that it transforms all network inputs into a string of binary fields. This helps speed up the training phase. DecisionNet supports factor analysis that, similar to sensitivity analysis, can report on the level of influence that each input field has on the output prediction.

- *DecisionTree engine.* This engine uses C4.5 algorithm with some significant enhancements concerning tree training and rules generation. The latter can generate rules that are not mutually exclusive, which is a good technique to present a complex tree as a comprehensive set of business rules.

- *DecisionCluster.* This algorithm supports an unsupervised learning technique similar to the statistical clustering. It can handle categorical and numerical variables, and allows the user to specify one of two metrics (angle and Euclidean) to determine the distance between clusters and between observations.

- *DecisionAR.* The association rules engine, which is based on the unsupervised rule-induction algorithm that generates rules in the form {A implies B} and {A and B imply C}. Each generated rule has a confidence level and the support level.

The range of analytical applications supported by Decision Series covers classification modeling, rules generation, forecasting, and clustering applications for descriptive analysis (including market basket and sequential pattern analysis). These analyses can be done on large-size data sets, and the output from one algorithm can be used as an input into another (via DecisionAccess engine). In addition, NeoVista offers a business application (RDS-Profile), which is focused on the inventory management for the retail industry.

Working with the Tool Decision Series provides an extensive range of options for model specification. They include different architecture options for the neural network, limits on the depth and leafs in the decision tree, etc. Model can be specified via a GUI or using *Decision Access Script Language* (DASL).

For the decision trees, the model can be described as a set of relatively simple rules. Neural networks are inherently difficult to interpret, and Decision Series capabilities for this are no exception.

DecisionNet provides many statistics for model evaluation (residual mean squared error, mean, the confusion matrix, etc.). DecisionTree supports the confusion matrix, together with the confidence interval for the expected accuracy.

The models developed with DecisionNet, DecisionTree, and DecisionCluster can be run against other data sets using the forecast models as long as the data is read in and encoded by DecisionAccess.

Conclusion   Decision Series is a strong product, with well-thought through architecture and data mining algorithms. The tool is scaleable and can take advantage of parallel hardware architectures. In published customer benchmarks, it performs well in certain classes of problems (e.g., banking and retail applications), both in terms of scaleability, predictive accuracy, and processing time. Overall, Decision Series is positioned to be especially well suited for large-scale analysis implementations.

Enterprise Miner (SAS)

Overview   SAS Enterprise Miner is a formidable player in the data mining tools market. It leverages a significant power and influence of SAS statistical modules, and it enhances that suite by a number of data mining algorithms. SAS uses its *Sample, Explore, Modify, Model, Assess* (SEMMA) methodology to offer a data mining tool that can support a wide range of models including association, clustering, decision trees, neural networks, and statistical regression.

SAS Enterprise Miner is designed to be used both by novice and expert users. Its GUI interface is data-flow driven, and it's easy to understand and use. It allows an analyst to build a model by constructing a visual data flow diagram, which connects data nodes with the processing nodes using links. In addition, the interface allows for the insertion of the processing code directly into the data flow.

Because multiple models are supported, the Enterprise Miner allows a user to compare (assess) different models and select the best fit by utilizing the Assessment node. In addition, Enterprise Miner provides a scoring node that produces a scoring model that can be accessed by any SAS application.

SAS Enterprise Miner can run in client/server or in stand-alone configurations. Moreover, in a client/server mode, Enterprise Miner allows the server to be configured as a data server only, compute server, or a combination of the two. Enterprise Miner is designed to run on all platforms supported by SAS. The architecture supports a "fat" client configuration (requires full SAS license on the client), as well as a thin client (browser) version.

Data Access, Manipulation, and Preprocessing   The direct data interface is through the SAS data sets. However, data can also be accessed through standard SAS data procedures (e.g., SAS/ACCESS module for RDBMS and PC format data access). Oracle, Informix, Sybase, and DB2 RDBMS systems are supported via SAS/ACCESS.

Data-manipulation capabilities include all features available through the base SAS engine. Additionally, a variety of data sampling and data partitioning techniques are also supported via appropriate Enterprise Miner nodes.

Data Mining Techniques, Algorithms, and Applications   SAS Enterprise Miner supports association, clustering, decision trees, neural networks, and classical statistical regression techniques.

- *Associations.*   This algorithm allows both the association rules discovery (e.g., market basket analysis) and sequential pattern discovery

- *Clustering.*   Unsupervised learning technique used for initial knowledge discovery and data visualization.

- *Decision trees.*   Several decision tree techniques are supported: CHAID and Entropy Reduction (binary and categorical variables), and F-Test and Variance Reduction (for interval target variables).

- *Neural networks.* Several neural networks are supported, including *multi-layered perceptron* (MLP) and *radial-basis function* (RBF). A variety of transfer and error functions, as well as training methods are offered. These capabilities are designed to provide better predictive and runtime performance than standard back propagation

- *Regression.* Multiple regression techniques already implemented in standard SAS are supported by the Enterprise Miner.

Enterprise Miner supports market-basket analysis, classification, predictive modeling, customer profiling and a range of statistical analyses for econometric time series, operations research, and many others.

Working with the Tool   Enterprise Miner supports a number of options for building predictive models. The specification itself is a combination of drag-and-drop actions available through the visual programming environment. An extensive set of defaults makes it suitable for the novice user, as well.

Enterprise Miner offers log files and SAS source code for neural network interpretation.

Enterprise Miner supports two ways to evaluate the models: via the Model Manager or through Assessment nodes. The Model Manager is a good tool for analyzing the output results from a specific model. The Assessment node is useful for evaluating the generalization and robustness of a model. Both support lift charts, profit charts, ROI, and other indicators.

Models can be deployed directly by using the Score node, which saves the model in the SAS structures for subsequent application to data.

Expert users can take advantage of SAS Code nodes, which allow for inclusion of arbitrary complex code into the data flow. As far as metadata is concerned, Enterprise Miner uses the same metadata as the rest of the SAS system.

Conclusion SAS leveraged its considerable expertise in statistical analysis software to develop a full-function, easy-to-use, reliable, and manageable system. The wide range of modeling options and algorithms, well-designed user interface, capability to leverage existing data stores, and large market share in statistical analysis (allowing a company to acquire an incremental SAS component rather than a new tool), may all result in SAS taking a leading position in the data mining marketplace.

Due to its recent entry into the market, only a handful of published customer benchmarks were available at the time of this writing. These showed that Enterprise Miner performs well both in terms of scaleability, predictive accuracy, and processing time. Overall, the tool is positioned to be well-suited for the enterprise deployment in data mining and overall decision support applications of CRM.

Intelligent Miner (IBM)

Overview IBM Corporation was developing data mining solutions for a number of years by using its considerable resources of research laboratories from the United States (e.g., Watson Research, Almaden Research) and around the world (e.g., ECAM in France, Boblingen in Germany). The result of these efforts is a suite of sophisticated software solutions that encompass applied and fundamental research in the areas of artificial intelligence, machine learning, linguistics analysis, and knowledge discovery.

The product discussed here is marketed by the name of Intelligent Miner for Data (its sister product, Intelligent Miner for Text, is discussed in Chapter 20).

IBM's Intelligent Miner is vying for the leadership position in the data mining tools market because it offers the following:

- One of the most extensive sets of data mining techniques and algorithms

■ Very high scaleability in terms of data size and computational performance; in fact, the product is optimized to run on IBM SP massively parallel hardware system, the product runs on many IBM and non-IBM platforms.

■ Rich set of APIs that can be used to develop customized data mining applications; all data mining engines and data manipulation functions can be accessed through shared C++ libraries.

Intelligent Miner supports algorithms for classification, prediction, association rules generation, clustering, sequential pattern detection, and time series analysis. Intelligent Miner enhances its usability by employing sophisticated data visualization techniques and a robust Java-based user interface (targeted mostly at an experienced user). Intelligent Miner supports DB2 relational database management system, and integrates a number of sophisticated data-manipulation functions.

Intelligent Miner is a client/server system with the client controlling the user interface and data-visualization functions, whereas the data mining and data manipulation engines reside on a server. The server component is supported on the following platforms: IBM RS/6000 and IBM SP running AIX, IBM S/390 running MVS, and IBM AS/400. The client component runs on Windows 95 and Windows NT, IBM OS/2, and IBM RS/6000 running AIX.

Data Access, Manipulation, and Preprocessing   Intelligent Miner supports flat files and offers direct access to DB2. The latter allows users to develop discovery and predictive models directly from relational tables. DB2 server is used to deliver all data-manipulation and transformation capabilities to the product, and can act as a gateway to other relational data sources. If the flat files are used, the DB2 data manipulation functionality is not available, and additional utilities or development efforts are required to preprocess and transform data.

However, all model results are stored in flat files. Intelligent Miner uses a file structure called the Mining Base, which, in effect, is a metadata file that defines the formats of all files used by the product.

Intelligent Miner's data-manipulation capabilities that are based on DB2 capabilities include the following:

- User-defined aggregation and calculation
- Uppercase-to lowercase conversion
- Filtering of extraneous records and missing-value records
- Filtering fields
- Filtering records using a value set
- Grouping records and joining data sources
- Converting multiple category fields to a set of binary fields (pivoting)
- Encoding missing values
- Data sampling capability—random sample creation
- Running SQL

Data Mining Techniques, Algorithms, and Applications   Intelligent Miner supports neural networks, including Kohonen feature map, time series patterns, decision trees, clustering, association rules, sequential patterns, and radial basis function. Most algorithms are developed by IBM Research facilities, are unique IBM proprietary techniques, and are available only in Intelligent Miner.

- *Neural networks.*   Include two algorithms: a back-propagation network used for classification and a Kohonen feature map, which is an unsupervised learning technique used to partition records into similar clusters
- *Decision trees.*   This is a variation of the CART algorithm used to produce a classification model and can handle categorical and continuous data
- *Time series patterns.*   This algorithm was developed by IBM Almaden Research; it is used to find patterns in time series while filtering out the noise.
- *Clustering.*   Intelligent Miner offers the demographic clustering algorithm that clusters records based on their similarity score (similar to the KNN algorithm described previously).

- *Association / Sequential patterns rules.*   This algorithm was also developed by IBM Almaden Research. Its unique features are the capability to find association rules for items in a transaction file, and the capability to find all rules including compound and hierarchical rules. In a time-stamped transaction file, this algorithm can detect sequential patterns used to analyze customer-buying behavior and the market basket composition.
- *Radial basis function.*   This algorithm estimates the value of a dependent variable, based on its relationship to the values of the other fields in the record; this technique is used for a continuous value prediction.

Intelligent Miner utilizes a variety of algorithms to support a number of analyses, including discovery of associations and sequential patterns in transactions (market basket analysis) and time series (stock market analysis), customer classification/profiling, clustering, and predicting values.

Working with the Tool   Intelligent Miner offers a number of high-level parameters that users can specify for each data mining technique. Sample parameters include minimum support and confidence factors (associations and sequential patterns), desired accuracy rates (neural networks), and maximum and desired number of clusters (clustering).

The classification algorithms support training, test, and application modes; and offer a confusion matrix as an evaluation tool. Other evaluation methods are being developed.

The application mode can be used to deploy models to an external (not sample) data. Intelligent Miner offers an extensive programming library that helps users to build and apply models.

The richness of the algorithms and the variety of customization options make Intelligent Miner user interface more suitable to an expert user than to a novice.

Conclusion   Overall, Intelligent Miner (for Data) is one of the most scaleable and powerful tools in the market. Published customer survey benchmarks show that overall performance of the tool was good, with some algorithms performing better than others in different applications. IBM has committed significant resources to position the tool as a premier solution for the enterprise-scale data mining.

KnowledgeSEEKER and Knowledge Studio (Angoss)

Overview *KnowledgeSEEKER* (KS) from Angoss Software is a decision tree data mining tool. It uses a decision tree algorithm based on CART and CHAID to find relationships between the predictor and dependent variable in a dataset. As such, KS can be used for classification problems with categorical and continuous dependent variables.

The primary positioning of the tool is to provide data exploration capabilities. Its user interface offers a graphical representation of the decision tree model. The user can select every branch and specify the grouping of the predictor variable. An automatic mode in which all branches can be generated is also available. KS offers a number of tuning capabilities to an expert user, including a capability to modify the algorithm or limit the growth of the tree. KS includes an API to its statistical inference engine that enables external applications written in C to generate models and import their results.

KS is supported on Wintel platforms running MS Windows, and on several UNIX platforms including HP UX, Solaris, and AIX.

Data Access, Manipulation, and Preprocessing KS can import data from a number of file formats, including delimited and fixed-length ASCII files; Excel, Lotus, and Quattro Pro spreadsheets; SAS; SPSS; and S Plus. It can import data from a relational database using ODBC.

KS offers a data-manipulation function called *Edit View*. Using this function, KS users can do the following:

- Change a variable name
- Drop variables
- Redefine a grouping interval

- Specify a variable type
- Import records from an ODBC source based on an SQL query
- Specify missing values
- Partition data into training and test samples based on random distribution

Another function, *Map Data*, allows KS users to map existing values of a variable to new values.

Data Mining Techniques, Algorithms, and Applications   KS uses a decision tree algorithm based on CART and CHAID. This algorithm can be used in cluster or exhaustive modes. Although cluster mode is similar to CART for a continuous variable and CHAID for categorical variables, the exhaustive mode can consider more groupings than cluster, and identifies the most statistically significant variables.

KS can produce a list of rules that classify the data points into groups based on the difference in the distribution of the dependent variable. KS can classify binary, multi-valued and continuous data; and produces binary and multi-way splits for the predictor variable.

Working with the Tool   KS allows the user to specify every split in the tree, or to ask the tool to build the tree automatically. In the latter case, the user initiates the process at the root node. KS will identify the most statistically significant split from each node to build the tree. The already mentioned Edit View function allows the user to specify options affecting the model.

KS interprets the tree model and displays the resulting rules in a graphical fashion with comprehensive statistics for each node. These include classification probability, chi-squared value, degrees of freedom, and distribution of dependent and predictor values.

The rules of the model can be exported as a set of if-then statements, Prolog code, or an SQL script.

KS display a decision tree in a graphical fashion as a set of interconnected nodes. This interface allows a user to fully explore all the data under the analysis. For models that are too large to be displayed on a single screen, KS offers a function called *Tree Map* that can zoom out to show the entire tree in a small window.

Conclusion KnowledgeSEEKER is a mature product that established a sizable customer base in the area of target marketing. In published customer benchmarks, it produced reasonable performance and accuracy measures.

To continue the product momentum, Angoss expanded Knowledge-SEEKER into a larger analysis framework called Knowledge Studio in May, 1998. The focus for Knowledge Studio is to integrate data mining components from various vendors into the corporate environment. By providing decision trees, neural networks, Web interfaces, and Java portability, Angoss plans to position the Knowledge Studio as a key component for data warehousing development. Also, Knowledge Studio, which is primarily positioned to leverage Windows momentum, includes an SDK. The SDK is designed to help embed the product into vertical applications using ActiveX technology. Angoss has developed a number of high-visibility partnerships with several vendors, including Cognos, MCI/SHL, AT&T, and Tandem.

Model 1 and Pattern Recognition Workbench (Unica)

Overview At the latest DataQuest market survey, Unica accounted for the 9% market share behind IBM and Information Discovery. The reason for such a strong showing is the fact that Unica has acquired and counts Model 1 (originally from Group 1), together with its own *Pattern Recognition Workbench* (PRW).

■ PRW is a generic data mining tool, whereas Model 1 represents a vertical application for Unica, and is seen as the growth product line for the company. Model 1 is a highly automated data mining tool that supports a number of target marketing analytical capabilities.

■ Model 1 tool includes a Response Modeler module, Customer Segmenter module, Cross-Seller module, and a Customer Valuator module:

▪ Response Modeler identifies customers who are likely to respond to advertisement campaigns.

- Customer Segmenter module segments customers into groups with similar demographics and purchasing behavior.
- Cross-Seller module matches customers likely to purchase products.
- Customer Valuator module identifies potential high-value customers.

Although both PRW and Model 1 offer a number of sophisticated data mining techniques, including K nearest neighbor, K means, nearest cluster, radial-basis function (RBF), Gaussian algorithms for pattern recognition, CHAID decision trees, neural networks, genetic algorithms, regression and *Recency Frequency Monetary* algorithms (RFM), the tools have been designed for non-technical audiences. From a user interface point-of-view, PRW and Model 1 make an extensive use of wizards that lead the user through the series of sequential steps resulting in the final model. Unica tools automatically search through the various algorithms and parameter settings to select the best model. As models are constructed and evaluated, a visual lift chart is built automatically so that the user can easily identify the class of models that provide the best predictive accuracy and performance.

Both tools provide rich reporting capabilities that allow the user to review the models at various levels of detail. The reports rank the models and provide useful summary statistics on the models and the input data. The extensive use of wizards, marketing templates, and reports makes Model 1 especially well-suited for a novice user. However, an expert user has sufficient capabilities to manipulate many parameters for the tools' algorithms.

Overall, both tools represent some of the most automated data mining tools that are positioned to increase the effectiveness of broadly defined marketing applications.

To enhance its market applicability and increase market share, Unica has established a data mining consulting organization that it hopes can account for a significant portion of its revenue.

Both PRW and Model 1 are supported on all IBM-compatible Wintel platforms.

Data Access, Manipulation, and Preprocessing An import wizard can be used to define input files in ASCII formats, MS Excel, or binary files. DBMS/Copy utility is provided to translate files from other formats. Database files can be accessed via ODBC. Data manipulation capabilities include the following:

- Graphical view of raw input data
- Data cleansing, which allows users to replace invalid or missing input values
- User-defined file delimiters and end-of-record characters
- Handling of missing values
- Merging of several input files into a single input source
- New field derivation using user-defined formulas and logical operators

PRW supports several data partitioning options and offers simple random sampling.

Data Mining Techniques, Algorithms, and Applications. Unica employs the following algorithms in its Pattern Recognition Workbench and Model 1 modules:

- Radial basis functions (RBF) for supervised learning
- Unimodal Gaussian and Gaussian Mixture that compute the density function
- Fast, incremental, cross-validated, and step-wide linear regression
- Fast, incremental, step-wise, and cross-validated logistic regression
- Neural networks, including single back propagation model (Multi-layer Perceptron, or MLP), a set of these models (incremental mode), genetic search neural network (enhanced by a genetic algorithm), and several other network types
- CHAID decision trees

- K Nearest Neighbor (KNN), Nearest cluster (Nclus) and K
  Means (Kmeans)—a family of classification and clustering
  techniques

The PRW analyses support generic classification problems, whereas
Model 1 is targeted to broadly define marketing applications and
include customer response/campaign effectiveness prediction (using
the Response Modeler) and cross-selling analysis (using Cross-Seller
module).

Working with the Tool   Models are specified using the modeling
wizard, where the user is lead through a series of definition panels
that specify response variables, detail input, model architecture, and
mode (fast, incremental, etc.). An extensive set of options and defaults
is offered for all algorithms. Both PRW and Model 1 support an automated mode, in which the variables and/or parameters are selected
automatically, based on the optimization of the user-selected cost function (e.g., minimizing error) to generate the best model. After the
model is created, the user can employ the sensitivity analysis to see
the most significant variables; for a cross-selling analysis application,
a product cluster report can be generated. Similarly, lift charts and
model summary reports are available for model evaluation analysis.

Finally, Model 1 provides a targeted marketing template called
the Market Campaign Optimizer. It helps analyze potential campaigns and can even show the potential net profit by customer
ranking.

PRW models can be deployed as spreadsheet functions, or
deployed externally by generating C or Fortran code.

Conclusion   Unica's Model 1 and Pattern Recognition Workbench
(PRW) represent strong products that are especially well-suited to
marketing applications. Both tools provide an excellent ease of use
and good predictive accuracy.

Other Data Mining Tools

This section will very briefly look at several other data mining tools. Due to the very dynamic nature of the data mining tools market, the vendors of these tools are working on major enhancements of their products, as well as on new partnerships and alliances. Therefore, by the time this book is published, the market landscape could be quite different from the one depicted in this chapter.

IDIS (Information Discovery) *Information Discovery System* (IDIS) uses a proprietary algorithm for rule induction. The Predictive Modeler tool applies the rules generated by IDIS to make predictions. Both IDIS and Predictive Modeler can access relational databases, including parallel database environments running on SMP and MPP. Information Discovery also offers MAP/IDIS, which uses MapInfo technology to identify and display patterns as maps.

Knowledge Discovery Workbench (NCR) NCR's Knowledge Discovery Workbench is an integrated tool that combines data access to large database systems with several knowledge discovery algorithms. NCR plans to use third-party data mining tools as components in its Knowledge Discovery Workbench. For example, Clementine (discussed earlier in this chapter) is scheduled for inclusion into the tool. Overall, data mining algorithm offered by this tool include neural networks, rule induction, and decision tree. ODBC connectivity is a mechanism to gain access to Teradata databases.

MineSet (Silicon Graphics) Silicon Graphics is a leader in the area of interactive data visualization. Its MineSet data mining tool combines a number of data mining techniques with very robust and innovative, interactive, and highly intuitive 3-D data visualization. MineSet data visualization uses fly-though, drill-down, drill-up, and animation techniques. The tool includes comprehensive data transformation capabilities and the decision tree classifier algorithm that is linked to the data-visualization engine. Visualization is also used to perform hypothesis-driven analysis and exploration. Rule visualization engine interactively displays the strength and support for each rule.

NeuralWorks Predict (NeuralWare)   NeuralWare Predict is a comprehensive neural network-modeling tool that can be applied to a number of different business and scientific problems. Its primary metaphor is the Excel spreadsheet. The main distinguishing feature of Predict is its capability to automate many analytical tasks involved in building a network. The product is mature, very flexible, and thus is well-suited to an expert user.

Orchestrate (Torrent)   Torrent (formerly Applied Parallel Technologies) has developed its Orchestrate tool as a comprehensive framework for data management and data mining that can be deployed and take advantage of parallel computer architectures (SMP and MPP). Orchestrate is designed for scaleability, high performance, offers C++ based object-oriented interface, and offers a high-level shell environment for data management and data mining. The data mining suite provides a variety of techniques, including neural networks and decision trees. In addition, Torrent is looking to parallelize SAS Enterprise Miner.

CRM Tools

The current view of the *Customer Relationship Management* (CRM) is that it is the core activity of e-business. The technology area associated most often with CRM is personalization. Personalization focuses on tailoring the presentation of a Web site to individuals or classes of customers based on profile information, demographics, or prior transactions. The goal is to market and sell one-to-one and to enhance the user experience so the customer returns to the merchant's Web site.

Personalization Tools

Following is a representative list of personalization vendors and their products. This list is organized alphabetically, and the order of vendors should not imply their respective market share or the authors' preferences.

Art Technology Group *Art Technology Group's* (ATG) Dynamo suite utilizes artificial intelligence techniques to personalize the online relationship between the merchant and the consumer. The core of the application is the Java-based Dynamo Personalization Server. The Dynamo applications provide tools for storefront customization, transaction support, and targeted promotions.

ATG's Ad Station manages customer profiles, tracks customer behavior, and delivers targeted advertisements for large-scale sites and ad networks. It can track and report customer behavior in real time. The reports can be exported into spreadsheets for further analysis.

Brightware Brightware's Advice Agent for customer assistance is an example of case-based personalization software that is applied to interactive e-business events. Advice Agent provides assistance to customers by learning their needs, and showing them relevant information and solutions. It uses an automated Web dialog to provide the personalized advice and targeted content.

BroadVision This is one of the leading vendors in rules-based, e-business applications. Its One-to-One Command Center is integrated into BroadVision's One-to-One Enterprise and three vertical versions: Financial, Knowledge, and Commerce. It allows sellers to develop business rules that evaluate user information gathered during previous interactions and use it to target products and services during subsequent interactions.

Firefly Network, acquired by Microsoft in April 1998, provides personalization technology based on collaborative-filtering techniques. Additionally, Firefly allows users to see a log that indicates how their data has been used, to change profile information, and to request data not be used in the future on those sites that used Firefly personalization technology.

Net Perceptions   Net Perceptions' Realtime Recommendation Engine infers customer preferences from observed behavior and suggests items for purchase. For example, it can make inferences between the length of time one spends reading a news article and one's level of interest in that article. Other user actions that may indicate interest level in an item are bookmarking, printing, saving, scrolling, and making a purchase decision. The Realtime Recommendation Engine resides on a Web server, and interacts with other applications that create or use customer data through API calls. In addition to making complementary recommendations, the product also provides cross-sell table support.

Vignette   Vignette provides many Internet-based relationship management tools. Its enterprise products include *StoryServer*, which offers a capability to present content appropriate at each stage of the customer life cycle: from initial visitor to long-term customer. This capability is delivered through the component called Lifecycle Personalization. The software can use behavior data to infer visitors' interests and update navigation and content accordingly. It lets merchants recommend content based on the choices of visitors with similar interests. Vignette's *Decision Support* services component provides a business-level analysis of customer behavior to help determine the effectiveness of the content for attracting and retaining visitors.

Another CRM personalization application is the Vignette *Multi-Channel Server* that can coordinate all customer touch points, including e-mail, cellular phones, account managers, call centers, and Web sites; and provides each customer with personalized communication and service. The Vignette Multi-Channel Server allows customers to define what kind of information they want to receive as well as their preferred communication medium, such as telephone, pager, e-mail, or fax. Moreover, the Vignette Multi-Channel Server can combine all client preferences with customer profile information located in the enterprise data warehouse and/or customer data mart.

In a financial services application, for example, the Multi-Channel Server can automatically notify customers of important account transactions, such as incoming wires, lockbox receipts, controlled disbursement presentations, and transaction reports. Investment management events such as security maturations, trade confirmations, public offering filings, and stock price changes can be included as well. In addition, clients can choose to automatically receive market information such as morning notes, buy-sell recommendations, and rate sheets.

The *Vignette's Syndication Server* (VSS) helps establish distinct affiliate groups and build targeted packages for distribution across multiple affiliated Web sites. Vignette's Syndication Agent is a Java-based application that lets affiliates download these packages automatically and remotely, process the content of the packages, and remotely manage them over time. The Vignette Syndication Server is based on the emerging ICE protocol.

Vignette is working with more than 80 technology companies including Adobe, Microsoft, National Semiconductor, CNET, Net Perceptions, and Sun Microsystems. It is working with major content providers including News Internet Services, Preview Travel, Tribune Media Services, and Ziff-Davis. It is developing the XML-based ICE protocol that describes content syndication relationships between Web servers and provides for the automatic, controlled exchange and management of online assets between business partners.

A note on ICE Protocol　ICE, which stands for *Information and Content Exchange*, is an XML-based protocol that has as its goal the content syndication by providing the standard to build Internet trading networks, such as syndicated publishing networks, Web superstores, and online reseller channels. In this context, the syndication is defined as the controlled exchange and management of business-to-business assets.

ICE goes beyond being just an XML data format. ICE defines a complete server-to-server syndication protocol and processing model. The ICE protocol is built using XML for data formatting, and a variety of communication protocols. Specifically, ICE uses XML to describe syndication subscriptions, content packaging, scheduling information, business rules, and all other aspects of automated asset exchange. The ICE server-to-server protocol and processing model uses HTTP, FTP, and other standard technologies to provide a reliable and efficient method for automating the exchange of content, management information, and log data between syndicators and subscribers.

Campaign Management/Marketing Tools

Modern database marketing and campaign management solutions focus on three functions: campaign planning, analytical modeling, and reporting. Although most of the available tools today support all three, the tool vendors differentiate themselves by offering specific tool functionality and service and support.

In looking at the tool functionality, we prefer to assess the tool by the following criteria:

- *Data sources.*   Capability of the tool to integrate with a customer data warehouse or data mart, and related metadata repository

- *Modeling.*   Capability of the tool to integrate with a data mining engine (for example, SAS EM, IBM IM) in order to automate the process of creating and refining models for new campaigns

- *Scaleability.*   A tool should be able to support/manage a large number of marketing campaigns

- *Support for trigger events.*   A tool should be able to accept trigger events from operational systems, operational data store, and even from the analysis of data stored in a customer data warehouse; the events are business-defined, and may include a major purchase, relocation, life event (marriage, birth of a child), etc.

- *Reporting and analysis.*   A tool needs to provide for an automatic analysis of the campaign results, lifetime customer value, and proactive reporting

Among the marketing and campaign management tools, we'll briefly look at the following three tools and their vendors: VALEX from Exchange Applications, Prime Vantage from Prime Response, and One-by-One from Paragren.

- **Exchange Applications** (VALEX). Headquartered in Boston, the company is considered by many analysts to be among the leaders in campaign management software. VALEX suite is available in UNIX and Windows NT versions and is highly scaleable (it can run multiple continuous marketing streams against very large databases). VALEX uses a well-designed native Windows GUI interface, in which icons representing various activities are connected by the user to create campaign flows. VALEX's architecture is three-tiered client/server, with the client running the user interface, the middle-tier server running the campaign management software, and the data server that could be any standard relational DBMS. VALEX is closely integrated with SAS for the modeling support, and it supports trigger-based campaigns. VALEX can produce campaign-tracking reports, and integrates well with various OLAP tools for additional reporting and analysis capabilities.

- **Prime Response** (Prime Vantage) puts a lot of emphasis on features designed to support sophisticated trigger-based marketing. The product is based on a two-tiered client/server architecture with the bulk of the application running on the same database platform where the customer data store resides (Windows NT and UNIX are supported). The product supports managing scores, can regenerate scorecards, and can be integrated with SAS EM for the model management. Trigger events include event trees that can have many branches so that the next communication with the customers is determined by the history of previous communications and customer responses.

- **Paragren** (One-by-One), a Virginia-based subsidiary of Apac (a large telemarketer), is known for its strategy of enhancing its campaign-management tools with the data extraction and transformation aids for the modeler. The modeler can use One-by-One *Data Discoverer* module to define complex derived variables for the SAS EM, Darwin, or the One-by-One *Campaign Manager* module. The product is architected as a two-tier client/server application, with the server software co-located with the NT- or UNIX-base customer data warehouse (thus, using direct DBMS access instead of ODBC connections). One-by-One provides proprietary facilities for data manipulation after the data is extracted from SAS files instead of relying on SAS for these operations. The product supports trigger-based campaigns, and integrates with Oracle Express or Hyperion Essbase for complex reports.

Sales Automation and Customer Service Tools

E-business has created a market for software packages that assist organizations in implementing the customer relationship management function. These packages are designed to be used by customer service representatives and other employees who interact with customers. The customer interactions are not limited to the Web forms and e-mail channels. Web-based customer-service technologies have expanded to include Internet telephony and alternatives such as interactive text chats and call-back requests.

The use of IP telephony in Internet call centers allows customers to speak directly with call center agents while they are using their browser to access the organization's Web site. IP telephony is frequently integrated into pre-existing call centers. Also, for an individual consumer, using IP telephony is easy, inexpensive, and does not require extensive hardware and software knowledge (a multimedia PC or an IP phone set, and Internet phone software that is available for most operating environments).

Among better-known solutions aimed at customer interactions with the organizations are Siebel and Vantive.

Siebel   Siebel 99, a Web-based application suite, supports sales, marketing, and customer service. Its enterprise resource management solution includes the following applications:

- *Siebel Sales Enterprise* supports sales representatives who need to access data from remote locations by allowing data exchange between laptops, hand-held computers, and the corporate server.

- *Siebel Service Enterprise* features tools to support service request management, service environment profiling, and problem resolution using case analysis, product specifications, FAQ databases, and customer service solutions.

- *Siebel Field Service* supports field service operations such as maintenance schedules, repair requests, and parts exchanges and returns; and can provide detailed instructions regarding what materials are required for a given service order.

- *Siebel Call Center* integrates sales and customer-service functions by providing on-demand sales or service assistance to customers. Customer service representatives can access customers' histories and accounts, and then recommend up-sales products and services based on customers' historical purchases. The application supports *computer telephony integration* (CTI), *dialed number indexing service* (DNIS), *automated number identification* (ANI), and interactive voice response systems (IVR).

- *Siebel Marketing Enterprise* includes a pre-built data mart and an online analytical processing (OLAP) server for data analyses. It also includes market segmentation, campaign, call scripting, and workflow management tools.

- *Siebel InterActive* uses agent technology to gather personalized information automatically about potential customers, industries, and so on. Customized information is then delivered to the user's desktop.

- *Siebel Product Configurator* supports marketing, sales, and customer service operations. It manages product configurations to ensure that product and service pricing is accurate, and facilitates the creation of promotional product configurations that can be distributed to the appropriate sales and customer service channels.

Vantive   Vantive 8 is a suite of Web-enabled CRM applications that supports inventory, customer service, procurement, sales, field services, and marketing. Current version, Vantive 8, consists of five major applications:

- *Vantive Enterprise* is designed for use by employees who directly interact with customers. It can be integrated with the back office and legacy systems.

- *Vantive Sales* contains quote and proposal software as well as forecasting and enterprise-reporting software. The application has mobile capabilities.

- *Vantive FieldService* supports operations such as tracking and logging service requests, assigning service orders, tracking the time and materials spent on a given order, and managing inventory.

- *Vantive Support* is a CRM application that supports customer service operations via phone, fax, e-mail, and the Web.

- *Vantive HelpDesk* helps merchant sites establish a customized technical assistance system. It can route or respond to problem reports submitted over the Web or a corporate intranet.

In addition to Siebel, Vantive, and many others, major telecommunications providers have become players in the Web-based customer service. For example, MCI's Click'nConnect service places a button on corporate Web sites that will launch an IP telephony call via an Internet gateway that is routed to a call center agent's telephone. AT&T's InteractiveAnswers, Sprint's Give Me A Call service, and Ericsson's IPT solution (an Internet-based application package that allows phone-to-phone, fax-to-fax, PC-to-phone, or PC-to-PC connections over IP networks) are other examples of similar service offerings.

CHAPTER 20

Conclusion: Next Generation of Information Mining and Knowledge Discovery for Effective Customer Relationship Management

This chapter briefly looks at a broader scope of information discovery processes, and emphasizes the need to be able to understand not only the traditional data types (numbers and characters), but also the complex data types such as text. Indeed, the volume of information contained in the myriad of corporate documents alone (e.g., word processing files, presentation files) is thought to exceed the information contained in traditional alphanumeric data stores by a factor of three to five. Add to this all the Web documents, and this number becomes really big. Thus, the capability to analyze and understand that huge ocean of complex data is rapidly becoming a business imperative. The area of information technology focused on analyzing textual information is known as *text mining* (as opposed to *data mining*, which implies numerical data), and it is discussed in this chapter.

Additionally, this increase in the information volume relates not only to the pure number of bits and bytes that need to be processed by a mining algorithm, but also to the number of significant variables—facts that affect the predictive outcome. As the number of variables grows, our ability to analyze all of them at the same time has to be enhanced in a radical fashion. Thus, the second topic covered in this chapter is a discussion of new approaches to utilize the power of the human brain to help understand the otherwise difficult-to-handle multidimensional, multivariable space. Among the approaches that this chapter briefly touches on is what has become known as *semantic computing*.

Business Intelligence and Information Mining

In their day-to-day operations, all businesses collect large quantities of data: data about orders, inventory, accounts payable, point-of-sale transactions, and customers. In addition, businesses often acquire data, such as demographics and mailing lists, from outside sources. The capability to consolidate and analyze this data for better business decisions can often lead to competitive advantages, and learning to uncover and leverage those advantages is the focus of the *strategic* business intelligence.

In the current and emerging competitive and highly dynamic business environment, only the most competitive companies will achieve *sustained* market success. In order to capitalize on business opportunities, these organizations will distinguish themselves by the capability to leverage information about their marketplace, customers, and operations. A central part of this strategy for long-term sustainable success will be an active information repository—an advanced data warehouse, in which information from various applications or parts of the business is coalesced and understood.

The shortest path from complex data to knowledge discovery is information mining. Note that we call it information mining, not just data mining, to reflect the rich variety of forms that the information required for business intelligence can take. Information mining implies using powerful and sophisticated tools to do the following:

- Uncover associations, patterns, and trends
- Detect deviations
- Group and classify information
- Develop predictive models

As was discussed in the previous chapters of this book, information mining in the form of data mining has brought significant competitive advantage to many organizations, in industries such as finance, health, insurance, retail, and telecommunications. New information mining techniques can uncover knowledge that would be difficult to obtain through other approaches, thereby delivering real competitive advantages.

From a technical perspective, the real keys to successful information mining are its algorithms: complex mathematical processes that compare and correlate data. Algorithms enable an information mining application to determine who the best customers for the business are or what they like to buy. They can also determine at what time of day, in what combinations, or how an organization can optimize inventory, pricing, and merchandising in order to retain these customers and cause them to buy more, at increased profit margins.

A number of the preceding chapters discussed algorithms and techniques used in data mining in detail. However, an extremely large volume of information is stored in a non-numeric form: documents, image and video files. The next section deals with the process of mining textual information that can be found in the myriad of documents, memos, letters, contracts, patents, transcripts of speeches, e-mail messages, and similar sources.

Text Mining and Knowledge Management

Text mining is a subset of information mining technology that, in turn, is a component of a more general category of *Knowledge Management* (KM). Knowledge, in this case, refers to the collective expertise, experiences, know-how, and wisdom of an organization. Knowledge is more than simple data or information; it includes context, alternatives and facts that help in the decision-making process. In a business world, knowledge is represented not only by the structured data found in traditional databases, but in a wide variety of unstructured sources such as word documents, memos and letters, e-mail messages, news feeds, Web pages, and so forth.

Information Week describes knowledge management as "the process of capturing a company's collective expertise wherever it resides—in databases, on paper, or in people's heads—and distributing it to wherever it can help produce the biggest payoff." Contemporary knowledge management tools work with existing textual objects and can encourage collaborative work in order to share the unwritten texts in individuals' heads. The tools and products in the knowledge management market include, but are not limited to, search engines, document management systems, and groupware products.

Text mining as a key technology that enables knowledge management is analogous to data mining in that it uncovers relationships in information. Although it is analogous to data mining, it is different. Indeed, data mining is the application of statistical and machine learning algorithms to a set of data to uncover previously unidentified connections and correlations. To date, data mining has provided valuable insights to organizations looking to interpret customer behavior and build predictive models. However, data mining works mostly with structured data that is often numerical in nature, which is stored in a cleansed, rationalized, static database that is typically at the heart of the data warehouse or data mart (see Chapter 2 for more details).

Unlike data mining, text mining works with information stored in an unstructured collection of text documents. Specifically, *online text mining* refers to the process of searching through unstructured data on the Internet and deriving some meaning from it. Text mining goes beyond applying statistical models to data files: in fact, text mining uncovers relationships in a text collection, and leverages the creativity of the knowledge worker to explore these relationships and discover new knowledge. Many text mining algorithms help in the discovery of new knowledge by complementing the ideas and logic that exist within the knowledge worker's head.

Text mining is particularly relevant today because of the enormous amount of knowledge that resides in text documents that are stored either within the organization or outside of it. The advent of the Web and online publishing has drastically increased the amount of information stored in textual form. Organizations that rely on ongoing research and on information available from internal and external sources have to overcome significant challenges in working with this overwhelming volume of text. The entire collection of textual information available to a given organization is simply too large to read and analyze easily. Furthermore, it changes constantly (especially Web-based information), and requires ongoing review and analysis if one is to stay current. Text mining addresses these problems by defining tools and techniques designed to analyze and understand this kind of dynamic information.

Benefits of Text Mining

Possible benefits from using a text mining solution include the following:

- *Increased value of corporate information.* By deploying text mining, organizations can increase the value of corporate investments in existing information systems. Text mining allows companies to more effectively gather and use the corporate knowledge hidden in large collections of unstructured text, and thus eliminates the need for costly reintegration or replacement of older data repositories.

■ *Lower integration costs versus other text-processing technologies.* Many existing text-processing technologies (e.g., document management) require a tremendous amount of system integration and expert consulting before they can be deployed. Many traditional search products require corporations to spend significant resources building topic trees or indexes by hand. The advanced text mining products reviewed in this chapter integrate with popular collaborative workflow solutions, requiring very little upfront integration. They process text automatically, thus eliminating costly setup and configuration.

■ *Increased productivity of knowledge workers.*   Text mining solutions make it easier for knowledge workers to find information within large corporate repositories of text; these solutions allow users to navigate the information they need by following the key semantical concepts that are important to them.

■ *Improved competitiveness.*   Similar to the claim of data mining, text mining can facilitate better and faster decision-making.

Text Mining Technologies

In general, there are two key technologies that make online text mining possible. One is Internet searching capability, and the other is text analysis methodology. Few products combine both.

Internet Searching

Internet *searching* has been around for only a few years. With the explosion of World Wide Web sites in the past few years, numerous search engines designed to help users find content appeared practically overnight. Yahoo, AltaVista, and Excite are three of the earliest. Search engines (and directory services) operate by indexing the content in a particular Web site and allowing users to search the indexes. Although useful, first generations of these tools often were wrong because they did not correctly index the content they retrieved. Advances in text mining applied to the Internet searching resulted in *online text mining,* representing the new generation of Internet search tools. With these products, users can gain more relevant information by processing smaller amount of links, pages, and indexes.

Text Analysis

Text analysis as a field has been around longer than Internet searching. Indeed, scientists have been trying to make computers understand natural languages for decades; text analysis is an integral part of those efforts. Although many leading researchers have attacked the problem of deriving and representing meaning from natural language documents, a variety of standards and technical approaches to text mining still exist today, which results in the absence of an undisputed winner.

The automatic analysis of text information can be used for several different general purposes:

- To provide an overview of the contents of a large document collection; for example, finding significant clusters of documents in a customer feedback collection could indicate where a company's products or services need improvement

- To identify hidden structures between groups of objects; this may help to organize an intranet site so that related documents are all connected by hyperlinks

- To increase the efficiency and effectiveness of a search process to find similar or related information; for example, to search articles from a news service and discover all unique documents that contain hints on possible new trends or technologies that have so far not been mentioned in other articles

- To detect duplicate documents in an archive

In summary, text mining can be used anywhere where there is a large amount of text that needs to be analyzed. Although automatic processing does not allow the depth of analysis of human reading, it can be used to extract key points, categorize documents, and generate summaries. Here are some of the real-life examples of where text mining using automated text analysis can be deployed successfully:

- *E-mail management.*   A popular use of text analysis is for message routing, in which the computer "reads" the message to decide who should deal with it. Another application of text mining is for statistical analysis of the nature of messages.

- *Document management.*   Text mining has helped some companies to get a handle on the thousands of documents they have in storage. By mining the different documents for meaning as they are put into a document repository (or retroactively, if necessary), a company can establish a detailed index that allows the location of relevant documents at any time.

- *Automated help desk.*   Some companies use text mining to respond to customer inquiries. Customers' letters and e-mails are processed by a text mining application. If the application can figure out what the customer wants with a reasonable degree of confidence, it automatically sends the appropriate information to him or her.

- *Market research.*   A market researcher can use online text mining to gather statistics on the occurrence of certain words, phrases, concepts, or themes on the World Wide Web. This information can be useful for estimating market demographics and demand curves.

- *Business intelligence gathering.*   This is the most advanced use of text mining. Currently, many companies are gathering information about their markets, competitors, and business environments by means of automated intelligent Web crawlers, which represent some of the most advanced forms of online text mining. Companies such as Infonautics offer products that watch the Internet for news relating to pre-specified subjects and give a summarized report.

Semantic Networks and Other Techniques

A key element of building an advanced system for textual information analysis, summarization, and search is the development of a *semantic network* for the investigated text. A semantic network is a set of the most significant concepts—words and word combinations—derived from the analyzed texts, along with the semantic relationships between these concepts in the text. A semantic network provides a concise and very accurate summary of the analyzed text. Analogous to the Artificial Neural Networks, each element of the semantic network—a concept—is characterized by its weight and a set of relationships to other elements of the network—a *context node*. Each relationship between elements of the network is assigned a weight as well.

The entire spectrum of text-analysis tasks can be executed as soon as an accurate set of semantic networks for the investigated texts is constructed. In fact, a properly constructed (discovered) semantic network enables applications that can support an automatic execution of many tasks. These tasks include text abstracting; creation of an easy-to-navigate, personal knowledge base; clustering a corpus of documents; classification of incoming messages; "smart" semantic search for information in a set of texts or on the Internet; a user-friendly navigating mechanism for an electronic book; and many others.

To emphasize, the first step of an effective text analysis is the development of a semantic network of this text. Of course, the effectiveness of a text analysis system depends critically on the effectiveness of the algorithms utilized for building a semantic network. In the majority of existing approaches, a semantic network is developed on the basis of some predefined rules and concepts. However, a much stronger algorithm can create a semantic network completely automatically, on the basis of an investigated text alone, without any prior background knowledge about the subject. In this case, the relative importance of a text concept is defined only by its connections to other concepts present in the network.

This is an idea behind a few products. One of them, called Text-Analyst system (Megaputer Systems, Russia), builds a semantic network automatically on the basis of an advanced homogeneous text processing. The user does not need to specify any rules or provide seeds for developing a network. A created semantic network depends only on the structure, vocabulary, and volume of the analyzed text. In fact, TextAnalyst implements algorithms similar to those used for text analysis in the human brain.

Other Techniques   Of course, different vendors compete with each other on several fronts, including text mining techniques.

Specifically, Cambio uses absolute positioning, pattern recognition, fixed and floating tags.

SemioMap applies computational semiotics, the formal study of signs carried by patterned communications. The SemioMap software extracts all relevant phrases from the text collection. It builds a lexical network of co-occurrences by grouping related phrases and enhancing the most salient features of these groupings. In short, Semio looks at the proximities of phrases in combination in the text. The underlying technologies combine lexical processing, information clustering, and graphical display.

Autonomy's Agentware architecture combines high-performance, pattern-matching algorithms with contextual analysis and concept extraction to automate the categorization and cross-referencing of information, improve the efficiency of information retrieval, and enable the dynamic personalization of digital content.

These text mining products are discussed in the next section of this chapter.

Text Mining Products

There are a number of text mining products in the market today (see Table 20-1). Some of the products that are briefly discussed in this section include the following:

Agentware (Automony)   Autonomy offers three kinds of products relating to online text mining (these make up its "Agentware" family of products):

- *Knowledge Server.*   Provides users with a fully automated and

Table 20-1

Text Mining
Products

Company	Headquarters	Product
Aptex Software, Inc.	San Diego, California	SelectResponse
Autonomy	Cambridge, England	Agentware
Data Junction	Austin, Texas	Cambio
Excalibur Technologies Corp.	Vienna, Virginia	RetrievalWare
Fulcrum Technologies, Inc.	Ottawa, Canada	DOCSFulcrum, SearchServer
IBM Corporation	White Plains, New York	Intelligent Miner for Text
InsightSoft-M	Moscow, Russia	Cross-Reader
Intercon System, Ltd	Jerusalem, Israel	DataSet
Megaputer, Inc.	Moscow, Russia	TextAnalyst
Semio Corporation	San Mateo, California	SemioMap
Sovereign Hill Software, Inc.	Hadley, Massachusetts	InQuery
Verity, Inc.	Sunnyvale, California	KeyView, Intranet Spider

precise means of categorizing, cross-referencing, and presenting information.

■ *Knowledge Update.* Monitors specified Internet and intranet sites, news feeds, and internal repositories of documents; and creates a personalized report on their contents.

■ *Knowledge Builder.* A toolkit that allows companies to integrate Agentware capabilities into their own systems. Agentware is interfaced with the documents on the Internet rather than after they have been gathered. It also has some semantic analysis capability.

Agentware's product architecture combines innovative high-performance pattern-matching algorithms with sophisticated contextual analysis and concept extraction to automate the categorization and cross-referencing of information, improve the efficiency of information retrieval, and enable the dynamic personalization of digital content.

Autonomy's strength lies in its high-performance, pattern-matching algorithms. These algorithms are enhanced by Shannon's principles of information theory, Bayesian probabilities, and the latest research in neural networks. Agentware's Adaptive Probabilistic Concept Modeling (APCM) technique can analyze a text and identify the key concepts within the document because it understands how the frequency and relationships of terms correlate with meaning. Agentware employs advanced pattern-matching technology (non-linear, adaptive digital signal processing) to extract a document's digital essence and determine the characteristics that give the text meaning. After Autonomy's APCM technology has identified and encoded the unique "signature" of the key concepts, APCM creates a Concept Agent to seek out similar ideas in Web sites, news feeds, e-mail archives, and other documents. Because it does not rely on key words, it can work with any language.

The Dynamic Reasoning Engine (DRE) is at the heart of Autonomy's Agentware system. The DRE is based on advanced pattern-matching technology that exploits high-performance, neural network techniques originally developed by Autonomy's parent company, Neurodynamics. The DRE applies APCM to perform four main functions: concept matching, agent creation, agent retraining, and standard text search. The DRE accepts a Boolean term or natural language query and returns a list of documents containing the terms ordered by relevance to the query.

Cambio (Data Junction, Inc.)   Cambio is a product that examines documents and extracts meaningful data to a database file. It is an offline tool, but can easily work in conjunction with a collection of documents gathered by a Web crawler. Cambio uses absolute positioning, pattern recognition, fixed and floating tags, and other methods to mark the data elements in a text file. Cambio does not have the semantic-analysis functions of the other products. It, together with a Webcrawler that gathers documents, represents the "entry-level" online text mining system.

Intelligent Miner for Text (IBM)   Intelligent Miner for Text (IMT) is a software development toolkit. Applications developed with IMT can harvest information from text sources such as letters, Web pages, and online news services. IMT offers the capability to extract patterns from text, organize documents by subject, and search for documents that match a given topic. IMT has text-analysis tools and an advanced search engine, enhanced with mining functionality and capabilities to visualize results. These Web tools provide all the elements to develop text mining solutions. IMT also comes with some sample applications that can be modified to the users' needs. This product represents the high end of the online text mining market, with both the comprehensive Web-searching capabilities and advanced semantic analysis.

The IMT *Language Identification* tool uses clues in the document's contents to identify the languages, based on a set of training documents in the languages.

The IMT *Feature Extractor* can operate in two possible modes. In the first, it analyzes that document alone. In the preferred mode, it locates vocabulary of words in the document that occurs in a dictionary, which it previously built automatically from a collection of similar documents. When using a collection of documents, the feature extractor is able to aggregate the evidence from many documents to find the optimal vocabulary. It can then assign a statistical significance measure to each vocabulary item.

Using fast and robust heuristics, the name extraction module locates occurrences of names in text and determines what type of entity the name refers to: person, place, organization, or "other" (such as a publication, award, war, etc.). The *name extraction module* does not require a pre-existing database of names. Rather, it discovers names in the text, based on linguistically motivated heuristics that exploit typography and other regularities of language. It operates at high speed because it does not need to perform full syntactic parsing of the text.

The IMT *Term Extraction* module uses a set of simple heuristics to identify multi-word technical terms in a document. Those heuristics, which are based on a dictionary containing part-of-speech information for English words, involve doing simple pattern matching in order to find expressions having the noun phrase structures characteristic of technical terms. This process is much faster than alternative approaches.

Clustering is a fully automatic process that divides a collection of documents into groups. The documents in each group are similar to each other in some way. When the content of documents is used as the basis of the clustering, the different groups correspond to different topics or themes that are discussed in the collection. Thus, clustering is a way to find out what the collection contains. To help to identify the topic of a group, the clustering tool identifies a list of terms or words that are common in the documents in the group. Clustering can also be done with respect to combinations of the properties of documents, such as their length, cost, date, etc. The clustering tools in the data mining version of the tool (Intelligent Miner for Data) would also be applicable to that kind of problem.

The IMT *Categorizers* in the toolkit work by extracting characteristic features from the documents being categorized, then comparing these features to a set of features for each category, which was extracted from the example documents during the training phase. This approach ensures a compact index and rapid processing.

The text search engine of IMT offers a number of advanced features, making it one of the most advanced products of its kind on the market today. It implements a number of different search paradigms inside the same search engine. The heart of the search engine is an index structure that supports Boolean, free text, and hybrid queries. Phonetic searches are possible on the same index structure. A special-purpose index supports fuzzy searches and the double-byte character set-based languages: Japanese, Chinese and Korean.

IMT *Examples: FinanceWise*, a search engine developed by Risk Publications and IBM Securities and Capital Markets, enables users to search for comprehensive financial market information on the Internet. An application called *Technology Watch* uses IMT text mining algorithms to analyze patent applications in order to discover major trends in worldwide research in certain industries, research investment concentration, and research content within certain demographics.

IBM *Technology Watch* is an IMT application that uses the technique of relational data analysis perfected by the IBM European Centre for Applied Mathematics in Paris (ECAM). It analyzes the selected patents or text documents, and automatically classifies them by content into a number of groups. IBM Technology Watch ensures that the patents or documents within each group are as similar as possible, and that the different groups are as distinct as possible from each other. In summary, IBM Technology Watch provides a visual summary of the analysis, in the form of a map showing the different groups, of the number of patents in each group and the keywords characterizing each group. A visual indication of the relationships between groups is given by the colored lines joining them. (The colors indicate the strength of the relationship.) Projections on nodes (typology, size, descriptors) or projections on links are also available.

SemioMap (Semio Corporation) SemioMap is a text mining product that scans large bodies of text and builds searchable concept maps of the information. You can then explore the concepts in a large collection of text documents without having to scan through all the files. Semio requires all the documents to be gathered using a Web crawler. After Semio has all the documents to analyze, it works through them one by one and interprets their meaning. It does perform automatic semantic analysis, but it is designed to be used with user interaction throughout, rather than in batch mode.

SemioMap uses proprietary text mining technology (SEMIOLEXTM), which was developed by Semio founder Claude Vogel. It applies computational semiotics, the formal study of signs carried by patterned communications.

The SemioMap software extracts all relevant phrases from the text collection. It builds a lexical network of co-occurrences by grouping related phrases and enhancing the most salient features of these groupings. The patterns built by SemioMap reveal the conceptual backbone of the text collection. The conceptual backbone is the key concept that attracts and concentrates meaningful relationships, the core zones of intricate groupings, and the transitive rods of topics that spin the whole semiotic network of knowledge nuggets. The underlying technologies combine lexical processing, information clustering, and graphical display.

TextAnalyst (Megaputer, Inc.) TextAnalyst is an intelligent text mining and semantic information search system that implements a unique neural network technology for the structural processing of texts written in natural language. Its functionality is similar to that of Semio. It is intended mostly for interactive operation, with collections of documents that have already been gathered. TextAnalyst can be used to create knowledge bases, semantically search for information, and abstract texts automatically.

This text mining software builds a semantic network in three steps. Text is pushed through a variable-length window one symbol at a time. Symbols can be letters, punctuation, or blank spaces. The window can be set from two to 20 symbols wide. As a stream of text is passed through the window, snapshots are made that are used to create a representation of words, word roots, and word groupings in the text.

The next step is to identify how often these concepts are encountered together in some semantic piece of the text, such as a sentence.

After this step, the system has a preliminary semantic network developed, in which every word has a weight and every concept found has a corresponding weight, based on a frequency analysis. The relationships between terms also are weighted, based on how often they occur together.

The third step in the process involves the use of a neural network similar to the Hopfield networks, which are one-dimensional neural networks in which all neurons are connected.

The initial semantic network is used as an input to the neural network. The result is a refined semantic network. Through reweighting of relationships, the network is renormalized, producing a final semantic network.

The creation of the semantic network is the most important underlying element. TextAnalyst applications include building knowledge bases, analyzing the contents of arbitrary texts, abstracting texts, classifying texts into specified subjects, and performing semantic searches of information.

Using the Power of the Human Brain

Over the last 25 years, organizations in all sectors of industry have accumulated massive volumes of data. They developed or purchased numerous kinds of data processing tools and technologies to organize, administer, and provide access to it. The increasing amount of data, in conjunction with increased competition and organizational restructuring, have forced enterprises to start using data mining techniques and processes in order to search for and discover the non-trivial nuggets of information buried in their databases.

However, these data stores and the knowledge buried in them are human artifacts. An argument can be made that because communication between computer and user has always been and always will be within the semantic context of human understanding, a new class of tools—called *semantic computing* tools—may be required to take full advantage of this fact.

One company has offered an approach to data mining that is "as different from data mining tools as archaeology is different from mining." The company is called ASOC (which stands for the Associative Computing), and it is developing *semantic* computing tools. The following section has been adapted from ASOC publications and is included in this book to accurately describe the semantic computing paradigm.

"The advent of the information age changes the environment in which companies struggle for survival. Developing "mining" tools is a useful, but narrow view to respond to that challenge. Although the analogy with mining is a widely used metaphor, the situation is more aptly compared with the evolutionary pressure that led to the development of sensors, nervous systems and brains to provide organisms with rapid and highly useful access to the rich information in their natural environments and, thereby, to give them the edge of rapid reactions that privilege animals over plants.

It seems that organizations must undergo an analogous evolutionary step to participate in an ever-richer data environment. This will necessitate the development of technology to design and create artificial *perception systems* for organizations. These will enable them to "feel" and "see" objects, regularities, opportunities, and dangers in those high-dimensional data spaces that are important for their survival."

As a first step toward this goal, we will have to build extensions of our natural senses into artificial data domains for which they were not originally evolved. Although this may still appear to be a very ambitious approach, there is at least one company that has already completed its first commercial prototype of a data vision system based on that philosophy. The company is called ASOC (which stands for Associative Computing), and its product is *sphinxVision*.

The company states that its tool draws heavily on a class of adaptive algorithms that are now believed to describe much of the processes that underlie the self-organized formation of sensory feature maps in the brain. These same algorithms have already proven highly successful in many applications. ASOC has developed and extended this approach during the last years, and has combined it with a high-performance graphical user interface that can bring the user almost directly "in touch" with data spaces of very diverse kinds.

Although most other approaches are toolboxes with an often diversed collection of different methods (ranging from neural networks and genetic algorithms to various statistical algorithms), the ASOC product follows a different strategy. One of the amazing abilities of human senses is that they allow us to identify objects, opportunities, and dangers in a direct and almost effortless manner, without having to consult a user manual or follow any sophisticated sequence of evaluations. It seems obvious that we should "require a similar quality for a system that extends our natural perception into artificial data spaces," the company developers say. Although this is more easily said than done, the current version of *sphinxVision* already goes a remarkably long way toward this ambitious goal.

The key is a concept that the company calls *semantic computing*. For the user, semantic computing means that he or she can work largely isolated from the level of particular algorithms, and can instead focus on the semantic concepts that are of immediate concern for his or her domain.

A Note about Semantic Concept   Let us consider the representation of human knowledge, which is communicated between individuals by means of language. Language consists of a series of single words, each of which is associated with a certain meaning. The combination of multiple words in a sentence (conforming to a given grammatical structure) yields a higher degree of meaning by embedding the words in a context. The composition of this context is governed by certain semantic rules for combining words into meaningful sentences. Knowledge is expressed and communicated in a world of meanings ruled by semantic contexts. The semantic concepts exist within the universe of semantic contexts.

If the user already knows which semantic concepts are appropriate, *sphinxVision* allows the user to directly investigate dependencies and irregularities among the concepts. It does so by offering holistic, dimension-reduced *data landscapes* that can be rendered in various ways to exploit the highly developed pattern-recognition abilities of our brain to make even subtle relationships in a high-dimensional space detectable at a glance. After such patterns have been identified, *sphinxVision* offers various ways to apply established traditional methods to aid further analysis.

However, the company stresses that the concept of semantic computing goes significantly farther than this. In many cases, the proper semantic concepts for an analysis are not clear from the outset, but must instead be found as part of the analysis itself. This cannot be fully automated. It always requires leveraging the domain expertise of the user. Much of ASOC's pioneering work on semantic computing is directed toward offering an intuitive, yet highly controlled link between the domain knowledge of the user and the database under investigation. An important prerequisite for this is the capability to generate landscapes of data objects laid out interactively before the user's eyes.

For example, consider a typical application in financial services—an application designed to identify "risk customers." The desired result of this application is to identify a category of "risk customers" by using a process of extracting appropriate records from a real-world customer database, which contains customer records with fields such as "income" and "age," among others. Here, the entire population of customers can be represented as a collection of different size and color objects (size, color, and other attributes can be arbitrary assigned based on the value combinations of the customer record attributes).

This graphical representation of a data landscape clearly and quickly depicts, among other things, where your good credit customers are located. And it does it in a multidimensional, flexible, 3-D animation that enables you to see more than just a couple of variables, as you currently do with pie and bar charts (see Figure 20-1).

In semantic computing, a user can now identify subsets of objects whose color combinations indicate that they should represent the concept of "risk customers." This tentatively formed semantic concept can then be evaluated in various ways. For example, it can be used to make customer risk-assessment predictions within a particular acceptance policy. It can also be introduced as an additional user-defined concept, whose dependencies with the already existing concepts can be investigated. Based on such evaluations, it can be interactively refined by changing its boundaries in the current data landscape. Of course, at each step it is also possible to extract conventional numerical descriptions, such as average values, or one- and two-dimensional dependency plots.

Figure 20-1
ASOC visualization of the data landscape.

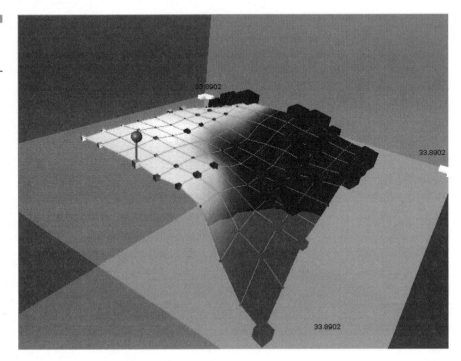

Finally, when the refinement of a user-crafted concept is complete, it can be saved as a *reusable semantic model* for later applications or evaluations. This makes it possible for a user to create a library of different variants of the "same" semantic concept. For example, a bank could develop several "risk customer" concepts over time, each of which may be specifically tailored to a different type of financial service. In this way, semantic computing can be very flexible, can support the modularization of an important part of the experiential knowledge inside an organization, and can make this knowledge also available at a distant site.

Through an innovative, interactive, 3-D graphical user interface, users can drive the presentation to formulate new hypotheses and be guided to use their intuition, with or without asking any questions about your analyses of data. *SphinxVision* provides a dashboard to help users navigate this complex data landscape (see Figure 20-2).

Figure 20-2
SphinxVision control panel.

ASOC uses a unique patent-pending semantic computing technology that is based on the different interdependent knowledge objects called *Data Agents*, *Scenarios,* and *Semantic Models*. Agents and Scenarios are always combined into an Agent-Scenario pair, Figure 20-3. Agent-Scenario pairs are used to extract contexts from a high-dimensional data space; they form the computerized equivalent of semantics. The Data Agents linked together according to *their* context are grouped together in the Scenario.

Conclusion

Although the data mining *tools* market is relatively small at the same time the data mining *application solution* market is growing exponentially.

At least a part of this growth is attributed to the widespread adoption of the Internet and the inevitable ascendance of all forms of e-business.

So, although it is difficult to predict the future, let's look at some prevailing trends in the marketplace—the trends that rely on or otherwise take advantage of the data warehousing and data mining technologies.

Figure 20-3
Visualization of an
Agent-Scenario pair.

Knowledge Management

Knowledge Management is a discipline that promotes an integrated approach to fostering the creation, retention, accessing, sharing, and leveraging of an enterprise's intangible assets for business gain.

A knowledge warehouse is a well-ordered, hierarchically structured compound of knowledge-based services that allows for the solution of a wide spectrum of data maintenance and analysis problems, ranging from housekeeping trivia to the creation of sophisticated forecast models. Examples include the projection of future product sales based on current customer data collected from daily business, or an early-warning system for the detection of likely churns for a telecommunication company.

From the end-user perspective, a knowledge warehouse appears as a collection of services.

Customer Relationship Management in the e-Business World

The stated goal of CRM is the capability to handle customer interactions consistently across channels and functions. This capability is critical to building loyal, profitable customer relationships. As companies make massive investments in data marts, middleware, and new applications, they expect the CRM applications to be able to support their strategies.

As e-business continues to mature and affect radical changes throughout all aspects of the business, the focus of new e-business-enabled application software will shift away from narrowly defined commerce platforms toward a broader vision of managing customer relationships. Moreover, the marketing will continue to evolve into an outbound, personalized closed-loop activity as evidenced by increased targeted e-mail marketing, personalized Web sites, and more sophisticated tracking and trend analysis.

The majority of today's CRM products have strong capabilities in tracking phone-based or in-person client interactions that employees log in the applications. However, other customer data (such as transactions or credit history) are accessible only through specialized APIs. As a result, CRM applications can't provide a single view of the whole relationship—a view that can be used in future interactions.

Moreover, many CRM applications are task-based and provide a robust recordkeeping. These are good qualities that by themselves don't help companies to form personalized, cross-functional relationships with customers on the Web. Often, successful commerce sites use separate, Web-native applications with commerce-specific customer data and business rules. As customers shift to the online channel, the authors believe that new CRM products and suites will be significantly enhanced to become the focal point of the multi-channel, multi-function relationship management.

The future CRM suite will synchronize multiple customer-facing systems into a cohesive, relationship-building engine by doing the following:

- Building a complete, real-time understanding of the customer

- Giving customers and suppliers more control over aspects of the relationship (e.g., the type of service they prefer or the information they are willing to share)

- Building Web-enabled products from the ground up to change the economics of customer support via great self-service, and gain access to the massive amounts of customer data available on the Web

To summarize, companies must change how they manage relationships. A new model that Forrester Research calls eRelationship management (eRM) is defined as follows:

"A Web-centric approach to synchronizing customer relationships across communication channels, business functions, and audiences."

To implement this new e-business CRM model, companies should do the following:

- Create a *dynamic customer context* that can address every customer interaction that is different from a view of the customer constructed from data contained in the applications. This can be achieved by collecting and organizing historical customer data, calculating high-level metrics for each customer (i.e., customer profitability, satisfaction, and churn potential), and assembling and delivering dynamic context to customer touch points.

- Generate *consistent, custom responses* by delivering a consolidated rules engine for routing, workflow, personalization, smart navigation, and consistent treatment of customers.

- Build and maintain a *Content Directory* to point to company, product, and business partner content; and give to employees, business partners, and customers.

Clearly, all these activities require a mature and robust decision-engine technology that is based on the data mining techniques and applications discussed throughout this book. Many companies will embark on the road to "CRM dominance." We will most likely see many traditional CRM players, as well as major ERP vendors, engage in focused development and/or acquisition to solidify their position in this growing market.

Application Services Providers

The previous section attempted to look at the near- and long-term trends for Customer Relationship Management. Another interesting development in the area of CRM is related to the fact that CRM is one of the key application areas for the Application Service Providers (ASPs).

The Gartner Group defines four models for ASP services:

- *ASP Consortium Model.* The ASP sits between end users and the software vendor, providing services and software

- *ASP Partner Model.* Both the software vendor and the ASP deal directly with the enterprise

- *ASP Escalating Support Model.* The ASP is the front-end contact for the enterprise and uses the software vendor for support

- *ASP Joint Support Model.* Both the ASP and software vendor work with the enterprise through a business partner, usually a system integrator

In the majority of ASP-related deals, these service and technology providers are responsible for the installation, limited customization, maintenance, and support of CRM software. Even though these services can be implemented for client/server applications, many newer deals have focused on Web access to applications. For example, one of the fastest-growing CRM ASP services is for Internet service providers, which provides CRM Web site-hosting services. Another similarly fast growing ASP service is the decision engine service. The latter is designed to provide application-hosting services for applications such as fraud detection (i.e., the HNC Falcon application service used by all major credit card issuers), cross-sales and up-sales recommendations, and market segmentation.

Clearly, these application services are direct implementation of data mining applications, and in the opinion of the authors, this area represents another significant growth opportunity for data mining applications.

The new data mining ASP products and services would have to be flexible, adaptable, and secure—to name just a few requirements for this class of applications. Additionally, data mining ASP services should answer questions about licensing and technical architecture with a special focus on the way existing applications can be "retrofitted" into an ASP environment and how an ASP application can be integrated with legacy applications maintained in-house.

Organizations that do not have significant capital to invest in CRM initiatives or do not anticipate a high rate of change in their customer relationships are probably the best candidates to take advantage of the ASP CRM services.

These implementations of your CRM system via application service provider do not preclude your having control over your data mining system. On the contrary, data mining systems can be integrated with CRM systems provided over the Internet by having the data mining functionality hosted by the ASP as well as by having the data mining system resident locally and integrating with the CRM ASP system via secure extranet.

This second approach allows maximum freedom in model development and choice of data mining tools, while leveraging the existing data pumps and data connectors that connected your local data stores to the outsourced CRM system. These two approaches can be seen graphically in Figures 20-4 and 20-5.

In conclusion, we see that the new millennium has introduced not only Y2K-related concerns, but also brought with it an information revolution and transformed the way we live and do business. This

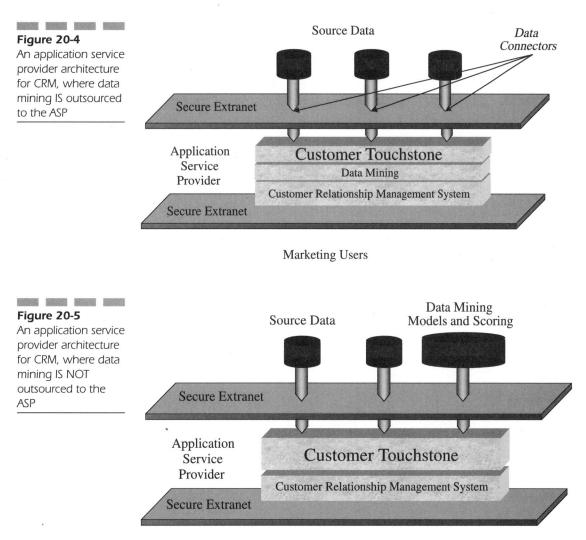

Figure 20-4
An application service provider architecture for CRM, where data mining IS outsourced to the ASP

Figure 20-5
An application service provider architecture for CRM, where data mining IS NOT outsourced to the ASP

age of e-business is moving at the Web speed and often brings with it many surprises, not all of them welcome. Those who miss opportunities will be left behind. But those who manage to survive the day and to leverage capabilities offered by data mining and similar powerful technologies can discover valuable trends in their data, build and strengthen relationships with customers, partners, and suppliers, and will find themselves in an enviable position of sustained competitive advantage. Indeed, the future for data mining and CRM is closely linked with the enormous potential of e-business and therefore looks extremely bright. It will clearly allow companies to compete and win on entirely different levels from those of today.

GLOSSARY

Accuracy   A measure of a predictive model that reflects the proportionate number of times that the model is correct when applied to data.

Application Programming Interface (API)   The formally defined programming language interface between a program (system control program, licensed program) and its user.

Artificial Intelligence   The scientific field concerned with the creation of intelligent behavior in a machine.

Artificial Neural Network (ANN)   See Neural Network.

Association Rule.   A rule in the form of "if this then that" that associates events in a database. For example the association between purchased items at a supermarket.

Back Propagation   One of the most common learning algorithms for training neural networks.

Binning   The process of breaking up continuous values into bins. Usually done as a preprocessing step for some data mining algorithms. For example breaking up age into bins for every ten years.

Brute Force Algorithm   A computer technique that exhaustively uses the repetition of very simple steps repeated in order to find an optimal solution. They stand in contrast to complex techniques that are less wasteful in moving toward and optimal solution but are harder to construct and are more computationally expensive to execute.

Cardinality   The number of different values a categorical predictor or OLAP dimension can have. High cardinality predictors and dimensions have large numbers of different values (e.g. zip codes), low cardinality fields have few different values (e.g. eye color).

CART   Classification and Regression Trees. A type of decision tree algorithm that automates the pruning process through cross validation and other techniques.

CHAID   Chi-Square Automatic Interaction Detector. A decision tree that uses contingency tables and the chi-square test to create the tree.

Classification   The process of learning to distinguish and discriminate between different input patterns using a supervised training algorithm. Classification is the process of determining that a record belongs to a group.

Clustering   The technique of grouping records together based on their locality and connectivity within the n-dimensional space. This is an unsupervised learning technique.

Collinearity   The property of two predictors showing significant correlation without a causal relationship between them.

Clustering   The process of grouping similar input patterns together using an unsupervised training algorithm.

Conditional Probability   The probability of an event happening given that some event has already occurred. For example the chance of a person committing fraud is much greater given that the person had previously committed fraud.

Coverage   A number that represents either the number of times that a rule can be applied or the percentage of times that it can be applied.

CRM See Customer Relationship Management.

Cross Validation and Test Set Validation The process of holding aside some training data which is not used to build a predictive model and to later use that data to estimate the accuracy of the model on unseen data simulating the real world deployment of the model.

Customer Relationship Management The process by which companies manage their interactions with customers.

Data mining The process of efficient discovery of nonobvious valuable patterns from a large collection of data.

Database Management System (DBMS) A software system that controls and manages the data to eliminate data redundancy and to ensure data integrity, consistency and availability, among other features.

Decision Trees A class of data mining and statistical methods that form tree like predictive models.

Embedded Data Mining An implementation of data mining where the data mining algorithms are embedded into existing data stores and information delivery processes rather than requiring data extraction and new data stores.

Entropy A measure often used in data mining algorithms that measures the disorder of a set of data.

Error Rate A number that reflects the rate of errors made by a predictive model. It is one minus the accuracy.

Expert system A data processing system comprising a knowledge base (rules), an inference (rules) engine, and a working memory.

Exploratory Data Analysis   The processes and techniques for general exploration of data for patterns in preparation for more directed analysis of the data.

Factor Analysis   A statistical technique which seeks to reduce the number of total predictors from a large number to only a few "factors" that have the majority of the impact on the predicted outcome.

Field   The structural component of a database that is common to all records in the database. Fields have values. Also called features, attributes, variables, table columns, dimensions.

Front Office   The part of a company's computer system that is responsible for keeping track of relationships with customers.

Fuzzy logic   A system of logic based on the fuzzy set theory.

Fuzzy set. A set of items whose degree of membership in the set may range from 0 to 1.

Fuzzy system   A set of rules using fuzzy linguistic variables described by fuzzy sets and processed using fuzzy logic operations.

Genetic algorithm   A method of solving optimization problems using parallel search, based on Darwin's biological model of natural selection and survival of the fittest.

Genetic operator   An operation on the population member strings in a genetic algorithm which are used to produce new strings.

Gini Metric   A measure of the disorder reduction caused by the splitting of data in a decision tree algorithm. Gini and the entropy metric are the most popular ways of selected predictors in the CART decision tree algorithm.

Hebbian Learning   One of the simplest and oldest forms of training a neural network. It is loosely based on observations of the human brain. The neural net link weights are strengthened between any nodes that are active at the same time.

Hill Climbing Search   A simple optimization technique that modifies a proposed solution by a small amount and then accepts it if it is better than the previous solution. The technique can be slow and suffers from being caught in local optima.

Hypothesis Testing   The statistical process of proposing a hypothesis to explain the existing data and then testing to see the likelihood of that hypothesis being the explanation.

ID3   One of the earliest decision tree algorithms.

Independence (statistical)   The property of two events displaying no causality or relationship of any kind. This can be quantitatively defined as occurring when the product of the probabilities of each event is equal to the probability of the both events occurring.

Intelligent agent   A software application which assists a system or a user by automating a task. Intelligent agents must recognize events and use domain knowledge to take appropriate actions based on those events.

Kohonen Networks   A type of neural network where locality of the nodes learn as local neighborhoods and locality of the nodes is important in the training process. They are often used for clustering.

Knowledge Discovery   A term often used interchangeably with data mining.

Lift   A number representing the increase in responses from a targeted marketing application using a predictive model over the response rate achieved when no model is used.

Machine Learning   A field of science and technology concerned with building machines that learn. In general it differs from Artificial Intelligence in that learning is considered to be just one of a number of ways of creating an artificial intelligence.

Memory-based reasoning   A technique for classifying records in a database by comparing them with similar records that are already classified. A variant of nearest neighbor classification.

Minimum Description Length Principle   The idea that the least complex predictive model (with acceptable accuracy) will be the one that best reflects the true underlying model and performs most accurately on new data.

Model   A description that adequately explains and predicts relevant data but is generally much smaller than the data itself.

Nearest Neighbor   A data mining technique that performs prediction by finding the prediction value of records (near neighbors) similar to the record to be predicted.

Neural network   A computing model based on the architecture of the brain. A neural network consists of multiple simple processing units connected by adaptive weights.

Nominal Categorical Predictor   A predictor that is categorical (finite cardinality) but where the values of the predictor have no particular order. For example, red, green, blue as values for the predictor "eye color".

Occam's Razor   A rule of thumb used by many scientists that advocates favoring the simplest theory that adequately explains (or predicts) an event. This is more formally captured for machine learning and data mining as the minimum description length principle.

On-Line Analytical Processing (OLAP)   Computer-based techniques used to analyze trends and perform business analysis using multidimensional views of business data.

Ordinal Categorical Predictor   A categorical predictor (i.e. has finite number of values) where the values have order but do not convey meaningful intervals or distances between them. For example the values high, middle and low for the income predictor.

Outlier Analysis   A type of data analysis that seeks to determine and report on records in the database that are significantly different from expectations. The technique is used for data cleansing, spotting emerging trends and recognizing unusually good or bad performers.

Overfitting (overtraining)   The effect in data analysis, data mining and biological learning of training too closely on limited available data and building models that do not generalize well to new unseen data. At the limit, overfitting is synonymous with rote memorization where no generalized model of future situations is built.

Predictor   The column or field in a database that could be used to build a predictive model to predict the values in another field or column. Also called variable, independent variable, dimension, or feature.

Prediction. 1   Then or field in a database that currently has unknown value that will be assigned when a predictive model is run over other predictor values in the record. Also called dependent variable, target, classification. **2.** The process of applying a predictive model to a record. Generally prediction implies the generation of unknown values within time series though in this book prediction is used to mean any process for assigning values to previously unassigned fields including classification and regression.

Predictive Model   A model created or used to perform prediction. In contrast to models created solely for pattern detection, exploration or general organization of the data.

Principle Components Analysis   A data analysis technique that seeks to weight the importance of a variety of predictors so that they optimally discriminate between various possible predicted outcomes.

Prior Probability   The probability of an event occurring without dependence on (conditional to) some other event. In contrast to conditional probability.

Radial Basis Function Networks   Neural networks that combine some of the advantages of neural networks with those of nearest neighbor techniques. In radial basis functions the hidden layer is made up of nodes that represent prototypes or clusters of records.

Record   The fundamental data structure used for performing data analysis. Also called a table row or example. A typical record would be the structure that contains all relevant information pertinent to one particular customer or account.

Regression   A data analysis technique classically used in statistics for building predictive models for continuous prediction fields. The technique automatically determines a mathematical equation that minimizes some measure of the error between the prediction from the regression model and the actual data.

Reinforcement learning A training model where an intelligence engine (e.g. neural network) is presented with a sequence of input data followed by a reinforcement signal.

Relational Database (RDB) A database built to conform to the relational data model; includes the catalog and all the data described therein.

Response [em]A binary prediction field that indicates response or non response to a variety of marketing interventions. The term is generally used when referring to models that predict response or to the response field itself.

Sampling The process by which only a fraction of all available data is used to build a model or perform exploratory analysis. Sampling can provide relatively good models at much less computational expense than using the entire database.

Segmentation The process or result of the process that creates mutually exclusive collections of records that share similar attributes either in unsupervised learning (such as clustering) or in supervised learning for a particular prediction field.

Sensitivity Analysis. [em]The process which determines the sensitivity of a predictive model to small fluctuations in predictor value. Through this technique end users can gauge the effects of noise and environmental change on the accuracy of the model.

Simulated Annealing An optimization algorithm loosely based on the physical process of annealing metals through controlled heating and cooling.

Structured Query Language (SQL) A standard for the non-navigational data access and definition language used in relational databases.

Supervised learning   A class of data mining and machine learning applications and techniques where the system builds a model based on the prediction of a well defined prediction field. This is in contrast to unsupervised learning where there is no particular goal aside from pattern detection.

Support   The relative frequency or number of times a rule produced by a rule induction system occurs within the database. The higher the support the better the chance of the rule capturing a statistically significant pattern.

Targeted Marketing   The marketing of products to select groups of consumers that are more likely than average to be interested in the offer.

Time-series forecasting   The process of using a data mining tool (e.g., neural networks) to learn to predict temporal sequences of patterns, so that, given a set of patterns, it can predict a future value.

Unsupervised learning   A data analysis technique whereby a model is built without a well defined goal or prediction field. The systems are used for exploration and general data organization. Clustering is an example of an unsupervised learning system.

Visualization   Graphical display of data and models which helps the user in understanding the structure and meaning of the information contained in them.

REFERENCES

Data Mining
Pieter Adriaans and Dolf Zantinge/1996

Data Mining With Neural Networks: Solving Business Problems
from Application Development to Decision Support
Joseph P. Bigus/1996

Data Mining Techniques: For Marketing, Sales, and Customer Support
Michael J. A. Berry, Gordon Linoff/1997

Data Warehousing, Data Mining, and OLAP
Alex Berson and Stephen Smith/1997

Neural Networks for Pattern Recognition
Christopher Bishop/1995

Classification and Regression Trees.
L. Breiman, J. Friedman, R. Olshen, and C. Stone/1993

Discovering Data Mining: From Concept to Implementation
Peter Cabena (editor)/1997

Nearest Neighbor (NN) Norms: NN Pattern Classification
Techniques
B. Dasrathy/1990

Seven Methods for Transforming Corporate Data into Business
Intelligence
Vasant Dhar and Roger Stein/1997

Introduction to Data Mining and Knowledge Discovery
Herbert A. Edelstein/1998

Advances in Knowledge Discovery and Data Mining
Usama M. Fayyad (Editor), et al./1996

The Nature of Mathematical Modeling
Neil Gershenfeld/1998

Data Mining: A Hands-On Approach for Business Professionals
Robert Groth/1997

Solving Data Mining Problems Through Pattern Recognition
Ruby L. Kennedy, Yuchun Lee, Benjamin Van Roy, Christopher D.
Reed/1997

Data Mining Your Website
Jesus Mena/1999

Data Preparation for Data Mining
Dorian Pyle/1999

Exploratory Data Analysis
John W. Tukey/1977

Predictive Data Mining: A Practical Guide
Sholom Weiss/1997

Data Mining Solutions: Methods and Tools for Solving Real-World
Problems
Christopher Westphal, Teresa Blaxton, and Chris Westphal/1998

Data Visualization and Information Design

Visualizing Data
William Cleveland/1993

The Elements of Graphing Data
William Cleveland/1994

Visual Function: An Introduction to Information Design
Paul Mijksenaar/1997

Envisioning Information
Edward Tufte/1990

Visual Explanations: Images and Quantities, Evidence and Narrative
Edward Tufte/1997

The Visual Display of Quantitative Information
Edward Tufte/1983

Visual Revelations
Howard Wainer/1997

Information Graphics
Peter Wildbur and Michael Burke/1998

Information Architects
Richard Saul Wurman/1997

CRM and Database Marketing

The Marketing Information Revolution
Robert Blattberg, Rashi Glazer and John Little/1994

Enterprise One to One
Don Peppers and Martha Rogers/1997

The One to One Future
Don Peppers and Martha Rogers/1997

The One to One Fieldbook
Don Peppers, Martha Rogers, and Bob Dorf/1998

The Loyalty Effect: The Hidden Force Behind Growth, Profits, and
Lasting Value
Frederick Reichheld/1996

The New Direct Marketing
David Shepard Associates/1994

Data Warehousing

Data Warehousing in the Real World
Sam Anahory and Dennis Murran/1997

Building, Using, and Managing the Warehouse
Ramon Barquin and Herb Edelstein/1997

Database Management: Principles and Products
Charles Bontempo and Cynthia Saracco/1996

Data Warehouse: From Architecture to Implementation
Barry Devlin, Barry/1997

Data Warehousing for Dummies
IDG Books/1997

Building the Data Warehouse
Bill Inmon/1996

The Data Warehouse Toolkit
Ralph Kimball/1996

Database: Principles, Programming, Performance
Patrick O' Neil/1994

OLAP Solutions: Building Multidimensional Information Systems
Erik Thomsen/1997

INDEX

T

ABOUT THE AUTHORS

Alex Berson is a Chief Technology Officer of enCommerce, Inc., a leading global provider of authentication, authorization and secure Internet portal management software, and has over 20 years of experience in information technologies. Mr. Berson holds a Ph.D. in Computer Science and a M.S. in Applied Mathematics, and is an internationally recognized expert, author, educator and practitioner who has over 20 years of experience in information technologies including e-business, data management, data warehousing and data mining, and enterprise application integration. Berson is an active member of IEEE Computer Society, ACM, XML International Digital Enterprise Alliance, and many other organizations. He is an advisory editor for the McGraw-Hill Professional Books division. He has published numerous technical articles in trade magazines, and is a best-selling author and co-author of many professional books including *Data Warehousing, Data Mining and OLAP, Client/Server Architecture, SYBASE and Client/Server Computing*, and *APPC: Introduction to LU6.2*. These books are published internationally, and have been translated into many languages including Chinese and Korean.

Stephen Smith is President and CEO of Optas, Inc., the leading provider of web-based Customer Relationship Management tools for the pharmaceutical and healthcare industries. Mr. Smith holds a BSEE from the Massachusetts Institute of Technology and an MS from Harvard University. He has been working toward the application of Data Mining and Data Warehousing technologies to CRM for the past 15 years. His initial work included research into new data mining techniques and optimized database sorting for massively parallel supercomputers. His recent work has included applying these technologies to real world business problems in managing customer databases, including directing the teams that were responsible for the creation of the data mining tools: Darwin (at Thinking Machines, now Oracle) and Discovery Server (at Dun & Bradstreet). Mr. Smith has also co-authored *Data Warehousing, Data Mining and OLAP* from McGraw-Hill publishers. He can be contacted for questions or comments via email at ssmithdm@optas.com.

Kurt Thearling is Senior Director of Software Development at Wheelhouse, a leading eMarketing and CRM services company, where he is responsible for managing all software development efforts. He has spent much of the last decade evaluating, designing, and building decision support and customer relationship management (CRM) applications. Most recently he was Director of Analytics at CRM software vendor Xchange Inc., where he was responsible for integrating data mining, reporting, and optimization into a suite of marketing automation applications. Prior to Xchange, he held senior technology positions at Dun & Bradstreet, Pilot Software, and Thinking Machines Corporation. Dr. Thearling received his Ph.D. in Electrical Engineering from the University of Illinois and has multiple undergraduate engineering degrees from the University of Michigan. He is a regular speaker at industry events and has written numerous articles on the topics of decision support and CRM technology. His extensive data mining and CRM web site can be found at www.thearling.com.